Adobe Acrobat 5: The Professional User's Guide

DONNA L. BAKER

Adobe Acrobat 5: The Professional User's Guide

Copyright © 2002 by Donna L. Baker

ISBN (pbk): 1-59059-023-6

Printed and bound in the United States of America 12345678910

Editorial Directors: Dan Appleman, Peter Blackburn, Gary Cornell, Jason Gilmore, Karen Watterson, John Zukowski

Technical Reviewers: Susan Glinert, Carl Orthlieb

Managing Editor: Grace Wong

Copy Editor: Nicole LeClerc

Production Editor: Kari Brooks

Compositor: Susan Glinert

Indexer: Ron Strauss

Cover Designer: Tom Debolski

Marketing Manager: Stephanie Rodriguez

Distributed to the book trade in the United States by Springer-Verlag New York, Inc.,175 Fifth Avenue, New York, NY, 10010 and outside the United States by Springer-Verlag GmbH & Co. KG, Tiergartenstr. 17, 69112 Heidelberg, Germany.

In the United States, phone 1-800-SPRINGER, email orders@springer-ny.com, or visit http://www.springer-ny.com.

Outside the United States, fax +49 6221 345229, email orders@springer.de, or visit http://www.springer.de.

For information on translations, please contact Apress directly at 2560 Ninth Street, Suite 219, Berkeley, CA 94710.

Phone 510-549-5930, fax: 510-549-5939, email info@apress.com, or visit http://www.apress.com.

This book is dedicated to my parents, Grace and Ernie.

Contents at a Glance

Contents

About the Author

Donna L. Baker has worked as an information-development consultant for many years. She has expertise in online and Web training, Web design, and interactive knowledge products including databases. She has been involved with a number of industries, notably education and health, and she has been a software and business applications trainer and educator, either full-time or freelance, since the early 1990s. She also worked for a software company as a technical writer.

Her interest in graphic design started in the mid-1980s when she bought her first computer. Her skill and passion increased as software and hardware developed.

Donna has worked as a freelance graphic designer since 1995. She writes 11 magazine articles each year on graphics and Web applications; you can find her monthly articles in the online magazine *WindoWatch* (http://www.windowatch.com/), for which she writes as the Fairy Software Princess. Her articles have also been featured on the StudyWeb and CreativePro Web sites. In addition, Donna is the author of *CourseBuilder for Dreamweaver f/x and Design* (The Coriolis Group, 2001).

Donna lives in the heart of the Canadian prairies with her husband, Terry; her daughter, Erin; two dogs; and a cat.

Donna can be reached by e-mail at dbaker@skyweb.ca.

Acknowledgments

This book is dedicated to my dad. A pretty cool guy. Years ago, when I started design school, he used to tease me about coloring inside the lines. I suppose he wondered where I thought I would go with that kind of education. Guess this is it. This book is also dedicated to my mother. She never questioned what I was doing in school, only if I was maintaining my honor roll standing and whether I would ever finish. Not likely.

This book was fun to write. Not that it wasn't demanding, deadline-laden, hard work—but it was still fun. The experience of diving into a piece of software and staying there until you capture every nuance of its innards is like little else in this world. So thank you to Adobe for building such a sweet product. A very special thanks to Carl Orthlieb for his masterful (and masterfully intense) technical review of my Acrobat JavaScript chapter.

I would like to thank the people and organizations who provided real-life materials for inclusion in this book. Thanks to Wildflower Farm, Society for Manitobans with Disabilities, Kathleen Kotchon, and Terry Dyck.

It's the people in your life who make it interesting. To my husband Terry—thanks big guy. The same goes for Brad. And a most special thank you to my precious daughter, Erin, who has it all worked out. The more books I write, the more traveling she can do with me. Sounds like a plan.

A heartfelt thanks to the people at Apress, especially to Gary Cornell for taking on this project. Thanks to Grace Wong, managing editor, for her words of wisdom and guidance, not to mention her efforts to keep this project on schedule. Thanks to Nicole LeClerc, copy editor, for her masterful work with my words. A special thanks to Susan Glinert, technical reviewer and compositor, for her technical editing expertise and her page composition skills. And thanks to Stephanie Rodriguez, marketing and public relations manager, for her marketing wizardry.

Thanks again to my wonderful and dear friends Margaret Werdermann and Lois Laulicht. Without both of you, there wouldn't be as much of me.

Thanks again to Rave and Abby. Big dumb dogs, and smarter than I am. At five o'clock in the morning, they are the ones gracefully reclining on the couch—I am the one at the computer.

Finally, a special thanks to the musical masters who joined me on this journey, especially Tom Waits, BB King, and Tom Wilson.

Introduction

I am a designer, and designers design; I am a writer, and writers write; I am in the business of writing and design, and businesspeople do business.

Now, aside from stating the obvious, what do we have here? Complex needs for the right tools and for the right means of communicating with clients and audiences. Wouldn't it be nice if there were one piece of software that would allow all these divergent needs to come together in a unified way to communicate? I am happy to report that there is such a piece of software, and that is what this book is about: Adobe Acrobat.

Who This Book Is For

This book was written for both designers and businesspeople. Acrobat has numerous functions that are applicable to both designers and businesspeople at large. Securing, sharing, and network processes come immediately to mind.

This book is *not* written for the novice, which is why the title includes the word "professional." My working assumption was that anyone reading this book has a design background sufficient to understand what I am referring to. I do not discuss simple design ideas in this book. Instead, I make the assumption throughout that you, the reader, understand what the design terms and processes mean. That doesn't mean I don't provide theoretical information. I certainly do! I also do not assume that everyone reading this book has advanced knowledge in all areas such as print or Web delivery. As we all know, print output and Web output, for example, are as different as night and day. Therefore, for you print wizards, some of the information in the print chapter may seem elementary. And the same applies to the Web wizards.

Regardless of your area of expertise, I have included a feature that I think you will find very useful. Sprinkled liberally throughout the chapters are Workflow Tips. I wanted to make the information and ideas in this book immediately useful to you, and the Workflow Tips are designed for that purpose. When you read through a chapter, you will find that they describe ways to use a particular feature, how to choose settings, when to use one process over another, and the like. My purpose was to answer the question you often ask when reading a book: "So what can this do for *my* work?"

What about the businesspeople I referred to? Are they expected to know how to be designers? Absolutely not. Many parts of Acrobat have strong business applications, and they are addressed from that perspective. Such things as network publishing, for example, can't be differentiated on the basis of the user. My goal in addressing business needs flow from the capabilities of the program itself.

How This Book Is Organized

The chapters follow a logical process. I cover all of the common processes you can perform with Acrobat, as well as numerous specialty functions. In general, to create a specific form of output will require using specialized features. I coordinated the chapters' content to follow this model. The first three chapters deal with new features in Acrobat 5, discuss the interface, and describe processes used to create PDF files. Chapter 4 introduces security, signature profiles, and certificates. Chapter 5 discusses editing and commenting, two powerful functions of Acrobat.

The next group of chapters discusses specific forms of output. Chapter 6 looks at document structure and bookmarking. Chapter 7 deals with streamlining output, including Web output. Chapter 8 explores accessibility issues and how to make a file accessible by using tagged PDF formats. Indexing and cataloging are the subjects of Chapter 9.

Chapter 10 is the first chapter that introduces forms; it discusses the fundamentals of PDF forms. Chapter 11 turns to print and Acrobat Distiller. It includes watched folders, color, and fonts. Chapter 12 is a collage of advanced activities, including video and date stamping. Chapter 13 is devoted to e-books—their creation, structure, security, and distribution. Chapter 14 covers networking issues. Chapter 15 is a comprehensive-project chapter. Through a series of projects and discussions, I describe how to build components for a company that will streamline that company's workflow. That, after all, is the name of the game.

The final chapter, Chapter 16, covers Acrobat JavaScript. This chapter is purposely the last in the book. Throughout other chapters I discussed Acrobat JavaScript in relation to specific functions or types of output. This chapter is designed to give you an overall understanding of how Acrobat JavaScript works. It is very powerful, and it can be used to extend your Acrobat PDF projects, but it isn't for everyone.

This book also has three appendixes. Appendix A lists the URLs referred to in the book, as well as other sources for information, reference, and interest. At the time of this book's writing, all URLs were correct. Given the nature of the Internet, most will still be valid when you use this book but you might find one or two that don't work.

Appendix B discusses the plug-ins shipped with Acrobat. This appendix describes what they are, who provided them, and how they integrate into the product as a whole.

Appendix C describes the components of the A.C.E. (Adobe Certified Expert) exam for Acrobat 5. It also lists the chapters where you may find information relating to the exam domain.

I included both tutorials and projects throughout the book. I use tutorials to explain how a particular process or procedure works, whereas a project is a step-by-step description of how to complete a series of tasks.

About the CD

This book is accompanied by a CD, on which you will find all the materials needed to complete the chapters' projects. I have also included materials used to create the tutorials, in case you want to follow along with them as well. The projects' files come in two forms: raw and complete. The raw files are those that I start a project with; the complete ones are the finished output. You can use these completed projects in a number of ways. For example, you can use them for reference, to see how Acrobat works. Use them instead of working through a project to see how the project is developed. And you can also use them for troubleshooting if you run into difficulties trying the projects yourself.

Enjoy the book. I know you will enjoy Acrobat.

Chapter 1

Welcome to Acrobat 5

*Everyone knows what a PDF file is: a file
you read in a special reader. But where do
the PDF files come from, and what else
does Acrobat do? You'll be surprised!
Think of everything from forms to e-books
to screen readers, and Acrobat 5 can take
you there. This introductory chapter will
introduce you to both Acrobat 5 and the
structure of this book.*

Welcome

Computers have been around for a long time. So have I. In my two-decade relationship with these amazing machines, I have learned a few truths. First, they aren't scary, and nothing will explode if you hit the wrong button. Second, they truly are machines. That is, I do actually know more than my computer, even if we don't always speak the same language. (I have to repeat that to myself on occasion, but it is still true, nevertheless.) And third, once I reach the point where I work less and the machine works more, I have reached a state of silicon nirvana.

And this last point, ladies and gentlemen, is the reason I am writing this book. We now have very sophisticated software available to us. Sadly, most people use only a small portion of what a program is capable of doing. So, on the average machine, if you consider the number of high-tech programs installed, that is a whole lot of functionality just being wasted. And what a waste. Every time you have to physically redo a piece of work already completed because it won't import into another program, for example, you are doing your computer's work. If you have spent good money for computer equipment and software—and we all have—wasting that kind of functionality doesn't make sense.

One of my activities (maybe even a hobby) over the last few years has been figuring out how to integrate and combine information created in one program with that of another. Some of the results have been pleasing, some not so, but it has certainly been a learning experience. I tend to work in two separate realms: as a power user of both office-type applications (word processing, spreadsheets, databases) and graphics programs (Web design, interactivity, illustration, image editing). I have happily seen the edges blur between the different program types. But there are still edges.

And then this one super-program comes along. Welcome to Acrobat 5.

What's New in Acrobat 5

I am very excited about this program. As I mentioned earlier, making things work together is one of my avocations. I have long used some of the functionality of Acrobat, but I never found a reason to move into it in great depth. Until this version. Acrobat 5, as we will explore throughout this book, is certainly new and improved.

Subsets of the population have been using the program for some time, however, and this use is growing. In April 2001, Sean Conley, a senior product manager at Adobe Systems, pointed out (at a presentation at Seybold Seminars in Boston) some advantages of the program:

- More than 200 worldwide government agencies have adopted Adobe PDF.

- Millions of PDF documents are posted on government Web sites worldwide.

- Adobe PDF is the de facto standard for value documents on the Web.

- Adobe PDF is the de facto standard for electronic documents in the publishing industry.

Adobe's technical and marketing approach with the release of Acrobat 5 is to move publishing to an advanced level—that is, progressively from desktop publishing to Web publishing to network publishing. I'll discuss these concepts a bit further in this chapter.

New functionality within Acrobat 5 deals with such things as workgroup collaboration over networks. Research from Datamonitor, Ovum, Lyra, IDC, and Adobe Market Research done in 2000 estimated that by 2003

- Wireless Internet users will increase to 350 million.

- Home users of broadband will increase to 40 million.

- There will be 16 billion Web pages, and 90 percent of all Web sites will be personalized.

Note
I will consider network publishing in Chapter 13.

New Features in Version 5

This version includes a number of upgraded and new features, which have resulted in some interesting new types of functionality.

A major change to the program came about as a result of the new version of the PDF file format. This format allows for tagged files. Tagged files let you easily repurpose content for different types of media or output devices. For example, you might use the same material for an on-screen presentation, an e-book, a Web page, or with a screen reader.

Tagged Adobe PDF

The new tagged Adobe PDF format is a magical thing. This enhancement allows PDF files to contain a logical document structure. Why is this such a good idea? Tagging a document's structure into components, such as the title page, chapters, sections, and subsections, allows the document's content to be easily repurposed. Tagged PDF documents can be reflowed to fit small-screen devices. A tagged format also allows the documents to be more readily accessible to the visually impaired. For demonstration purposes, I converted this chapter's original file into a PDF file, and a partial list of the chapter's tags are shown in Figure 1-1.

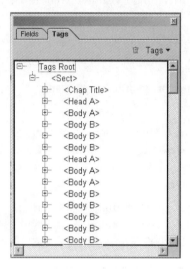

Figure 1-1
A partial list of tags for this chapter after it was converted to a PDF file

How does it work? If a document's structure is tagged, it doesn't matter whether the screen is 15 inches across or 5 inches across. Instead, any component defined as a section, for instance, will follow in sequential order under a component defined as a chapter. For folks using screen-reader software, for example, this will allow them to navigate a document in the proper reading order.

Note

Several chapters (including Chapters 6, 7, 8, and 9) discuss how to use tagged Adobe PDF files for a variety of purposes.

To facilitate tagging and using tagged information, this version of Acrobat includes a Tags palette (its uses depend on the desired output, of course).

Greater Graphics Support

You'll find some good improvements in the area of graphics support. Remember when you would convert a file into a PDF and some of your images would translate well, while others looked, at best, mediocre? That is in the past. This version of Acrobat displays transparency objects from both Illustrator version 9 and Photoshop version 6 in Adobe PDF. It includes enhanced printing controls for customizing output, as well as an option for tiling page sections for output. In addition, you can now preview overprint settings on screen and in print, and more Acrobat Distiller options are available (more about that later).

Note

Chapter 11 covers printing features and issues.

And the icing on the cake? Color management. Acrobat 5 supports the Adobe Color Engine (ACE), also used with Illustrator 9 and Photoshop 6.

Converting Documents

Acrobat 5 now provides an automatic conversion process from Microsoft Office applications—Word, Excel, and PowerPoint. When you install Acrobat, it automatically installs menus into these programs that convert documents, spreadsheets, and slides with a single click. I use Acrobat on the Windows 2000 Professional platform, using Office 2000 Professional versions of the software. Office XP programs are supported with the Acrobat 5.0.5 upgrade.

Converting any of these file types to a PDF file is a single-click process. As shown in Figure 1-2, I converted an early version of this chapter into a PDF file. This is the first page of the file, with my layout preserved. A second feature is also installed, which converts a file and then e-mails it to a recipient.

Note

In Chapter 3, we will dive into document conversion.

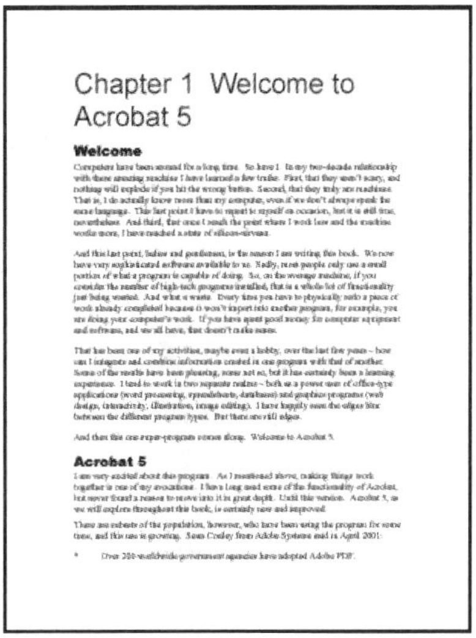
Chapter 1 Welcome to Acrobat 5

Welcome

Acrobat 5

Figure 1-2
One-step conversion of a file from a Microsoft Word document to a PDF file

Creating Instant Documents from Web Sites

Just add hot water and stir! Kidding. But it is that simple. It is now possible to create a PDF file from a Web site instantly. Enter the URL for the Web site, and Acrobat downloads the desired files. Along with simple download, the formatting and layouts of the pages are preserved, as are the links within a page.

These options can be customized, of course. When converting a Web site to a PDF file, you can specify the number of page levels, up to and including an entire site.

Note

In Chapters 3 and 6, we will look at the process of converting a Web site to a PDF file and its options.

Document Distilling

For documents from programs other than the Microsoft ones I listed earlier, it is also easy to create PDF versions. This is done using Acrobat Distiller. Distiller is part of the main Acrobat installation. Acrobat Distiller is basically a virtual printer. Once installed, it is accessible through the Windows Printers folder or in the Chooser on the Mac. If Distiller is selected as the printer, when you execute the Print command, you create a PDF file. You can then save this file and export it for use as you would any other PDF file.

Note

Chapter 11 provides a great deal of information on Acrobat Distiller issues and uses.

Distiller may also be used to create complex documents where the components are processed each according to their needs and then combined into a finished product. For example, text, line art, and photography may all be handled as subdocuments in Distiller and then recombined in Acrobat.

Recycling Content

Although you can recycle PDF document contents and extract or modify different components of a document, Acrobat is not a word processor. If a document's text needs changing or updating, save the file in Rich Text Format (RTF). This format is accessible by any word processing program. Acrobat is also not an image editor or illustration program. However, images may be extracted from a PDF document and used in another document. Available formats for extraction include JPEG, PNG, and TIFF files.

Note

See Chapter 6 for ways to recycle and repurpose content.

Another useful feature with regard to graphic content is the ability to access other Adobe products from within a PDF document. For example, you can modify a Photoshop image in a document in Photoshop by double-clicking the image on the page. The same applies for Illustrator files in a PDF document.

New Security Features

The enhanced security features are terrific. Content creators have a great deal of control over the use of a document. The 128-bit encryption technology in this version of Acrobat is sophisticated enough to provide varying levels of control over access to the document's components. A document can be locked completely, and only someone with a password is allowed to see it. Alternatively, you can specify that a document be viewed but not printed, printed, printed at low resolution, copied to the clipboard, or not copied, extracted, and so on. For other recipients who are viewing a document in Acrobat rather than in Acrobat Reader, additional protections exist. For example, drawings, tables, charts, and the like can be "locked" so that only those with a password can modify these components. This prevents any unauthorized changes.

The final big security feature is the use of digital signatures. Through a system of signature authentication between a creator and users, a recipient of a file can verify the authenticity of a document. This process also identifies any alterations made to the document. A recipient who checks a document that has been altered after it was initially signed won't allow for signature verification. Authoring information can also be added to a document for reference. The initial dialog box for creating a self-sign security profile is shown in Figure 1-3.

Figure 1-3
Signing a document requires that you first create a profile.

Enhanced Collaboration

Collaboration is one area where Acrobat leaves the rest of the pack in the dust, so to speak. A palette of tools gives a great deal of collaborative freedom to users collaborating on a project. Unlike programs that allow only comments to be attached, in Acrobat that is just one small way to make your opinions known. Available options include everything from electronic sticky notes (similar to comments) to e-signatures.

The analogy is a printed document. Suppose you are creating something. Imagine that! Anyway, suppose you are creating a piece of work in conjunction with several other associates. What usually happens is that the primary author makes copies of the work and distributes those copies for comments among the group. Group members add notes, cross out text, suggest moving parts of the work, and so forth. This all then returns to the primary author for revision, and one hopes that none of the important revisions are missed. And what happens if there is a conflict of opinion among the participants? Well, the usual solution is to circulate the document again. When everyone is happy, and everyone has duly signed off on the project, depending on the workflow, the job is finally finished.

Now imagine that you can do the same thing digitally. You can. In addition to the ubiquitous sticky note, you can use a host of other communication tools. Some can be quite amusing, as shown in Figure 1-4.

For example, you can create your own custom stamps that can be applied to a document to express your pleasure (or displeasure!) creatively.

Figure 1-4
Adding comments and sharing information with others doesn't always have to be serious.

Note

See Chapter 5 for discussions on collaboration and document editing. I explain how to use comments in the next chapter.

You can add bookmarks to make navigating throughout a large document simpler for a team. A PDF in progress can have attached sticky notes, highlighted text, and crossed-out text. The approval process can be accomplished with e-signatures. Text can be highlighted, crossed out, and spellchecked for errors. Finally, for those among us who simply must draw all those big arrows and slashes across parts of pages, there is even a pencil tool.

Network Publishing

Network publishing is a new functionality. This version of Acrobat supports collaboration over networks. In order to accomplish this, Acrobat 5 supports a number of network and database protocols that allow for storing and sharing information online simultaneously. This is a different way of working with Acrobat. Network publishing options run the gamut from setting up "watched" folders using Acrobat Distiller to sharing comments to storing linked media files and indexing databases. More about this later in the chapter.

Indexing

Creating an index for a PDF document is not new. But look at what you can do now—because Acrobat 5 supports Open Database Connectivity (ODBC), the indexes can be incorporated into a searchable database. This is so cool. Imagine indexing a set of documents in Acrobat, and then using the Acrobat Catalog command to create a full-text index of your PDF documents and document collections. This full-text index is a searchable database of all the text in a document or set of documents. Pushes that old filing cabinet one step further back into time, doesn't it? Finally.

Creating Forms

Forms are a pervasive part of our lives. We use them for everything from ordering online to entering contests to filling out government documents of all types. Consider the usual way we complete many documents. A form is filled in on paper, and it is then given to the appropriate body for processing. This means a clerical person will take the information we have added to the form by hand and enter it into a digital format for processing. What if this could be processed electronically from start to finish? It can.

The forms capabilities of Acrobat 5 are highly developed—so much so that Adobe has coined a term for them: *e-forms.* Acrobat 5 provides a means to create electronic forms based on both PDF and Extensible Markup Language (XML). This impacts the way organizations collect and use data on two separate levels. First, a recipient can use a form by accessing a printed copy of a PDF file. This approach helps a company or organization maintain layout and structures for its forms.

We can now go one step further by using XML and JavaScript capabilities available in this version. Forms may be used online that will collect data and transmit it to a server for processing. The forms are also capable of calculation. Having these options enables organizations to acquire information much more quickly. Maybe one day those messages telling us to "please allow 6 to 8 weeks for delivery" will be a thing of the past!

Note

We will discuss form creation and customization in Chapter 10, and we'll look at enhancing a form's function using JavaScript in Chapter 12. Chapter 16 is devoted to JavaScript and covers more form functions.

Accessibility Features

I mentioned the tagged PDF format earlier. Along with providing output for a variety of devices, these features are an important step in making documents more accessible to individuals with disabilities. Support for accessible documents for both visually and physically impaired users is new to Acrobat 5. The basis for this functionality lies in the tagged PDF file format.

In Chapter 8 we will look at making changes to the basic PDF document to make it accessible, as well as the other components required for a totally accessible document. We will also look at how to test a document for accessibility and how to add or modify other features, such as using alternative text for images.

The tagged PDF format allows users to zoom in and reflow text on the screen. Other usability improvements include enhanced keyboard shortcuts and support for high-contrast viewing. Acrobat 5 supports the Microsoft Active Accessibility Application Programming Interface (API) for the Windows platform. This allows for integration with assistive technology products, including screen readers from a number of vendors.

To evaluate a document for accessibility, Acrobat includes an Accessibility Checker tool. This tool evaluates a document and produces a report you can use to make your work more accessible. The report summary for the PDF file for this document is shown in Figure 1-5.

Figure 1-5
The Accessibility Checker report for the PDF version of this chapter. As you can see, I would have lots of work to do to make this document accessible.

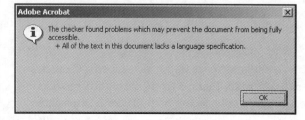

E-Books

The e-book format is big news. I have been using e-books since the time of the Glassbook reader (was that only a couple of years ago?). Anyway, the key to repurposing a document for use as an e-book is the tagged PDF format. When text has been tagged, repurposing it for an e-book format is not difficult. Add to this features such as interactive forms and security measures, and you're looking at a potentially powerful medium.

Handheld Devices

Handheld devices are another big news item. Seems everyone is getting on the handheld bandwagon. And why not? Small, portable devices that allow you to communicate and access information—visually rich information—are the next wave. Because the technology exists to interface with larger systems such as networks and the Internet, it is only logical that software should be able to create information that can be readily displayed on these tiny screens.

Again, the key to designing content for these devices is the tagged PDF format. The ability to reflow text is critical. One of these days I am sure we will finally see wristwatch-sized devices come to market.

You Can't Use Acrobat Without PDF

The PDF file format is integral to the functionality of Acrobat. I daresay that most people know what a PDF file is: a file that has to be read in a

Note

Chapter 8 discusses accessibility issues and processes in depth.

Note

Chapter 13 explores creating e-book output.

Note

I have included handheld devices in output discussions in Chapter 7.

special viewer and that shows images and page layouts as well as text. But what actually is PDF, and where did it come from?

The short answer: PDF stands for Portable Document Format. It was created by Adobe Systems; version 1 was released in 1992. PDF is built on another technology also created by Adobe, a language called PostScript. PostScript is used to describe documents. It runs on both Windows and Macintosh platforms. Acrobat 5 uses version 1.4 of the PDF file format.

How PDF Files Work

As I mentioned, you can't use Acrobat without PDF. The file format is based on how the PostScript language works. Different components of the language interpret different parts of a file. Together, they make up the PDF documents we use. PDF version 1.4 describes a document's structure and metadata. I have shown some of the "behind-the-scenes" information from the PDF file I made from this chapter's file in Figure 1-6.

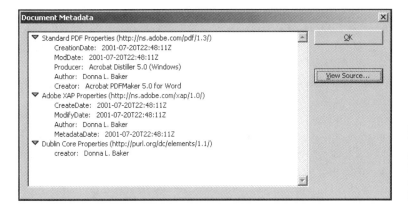

Figure 1-6
The metadata components of this chapter's PDF file. Metadata is just one component of the information for this file type.

Here is a brief rundown of the basic components that make up PDF files:

- Text and graphics are converted to a page description.

- A cross-reference table is used to locate and access pages. This process is almost independent of the total number of pages in a document.

- PDF files store font name and characteristics. When a document is viewed, the font used in the document will appear if it resides on the viewing computer or if it is embedded in the file. If neither of these applies, PDF uses a Multiple Master font to simulate the missing fonts (for Type 1 and TrueType font formats).

- PDF uses both binary and ASCII data. Because of this, the PDF output is portable across many different environments.

- This version can describe transparent objects created from Illustrator 9, Illustrator 10, and Photoshop 6.

- PDF can use a number of industry-standard compression filters, including JPEG, ZIP, and LZW.

- PDF is designed to be extensible. Plug-ins can extend the file format.

What Can Acrobat 5 Do?

The Adobe PDF file format used by Acrobat is becoming the workflow standard in many industries, ranging from publishing to financial services to government. This has happened because users need to use information more intelligently and they need to be able to share that information more effectively.

Let's Pretend . . .

Consider this common scenario:

I spend the better part of a week working on a layout for an important document for a client, complete with text, graphics, spreadsheets, charts, and tables. I send draft copies to the client, who complains about a range of issues, none of which I can control. He doesn't have the application I used to create the document, so I rebuild the thing in a program he has. Then he says he doesn't have the fonts I used, and the layout is skewed. So I send him the fonts, or reset the thing again using fonts he is sure to have (after all, every computer *must* have Times New Roman and Arial installed!). So now he can open the document. But when he prints it, it doesn't look the same at all due to printer differences. So I reset the thing again. Now the client can print it, but my original design is so hacked up by now, it could have been written in Notepad for all the style that is left (a slight exaggeration, but you know how it feels).

The next day the client calls again and says he would like to have this document available on his company's Web site. So I start all over again, this time in a Web layout program. And, by the way, he would also like to be able to use it in other programs for some of his recipients who don't use the same program for viewing and printing that his company does, so he requests another version. Oh yeah, and one of the board members uses a screen reader, so can I configure a copy that can be used with a reader? And could I make a couple of changes to all the versions I've created so far?

Chilling, isn't it? By now, if this were a real scenario, I would be gnashing my teeth and spewing dire threats to anyone who dares to encroach upon my space. My family would have left home for a few days, the dogs would be hiding, and I would be seriously considering a new career as a grocery bagger.

Consider the same scenario if I were using Acrobat. First, I would be able to create the document in one or several different programs and then combine the whole works into a single PDF file. Shipping a draft to a client for review and approval would be no problem. The client could open the file using Acrobat Reader software, which is free.

Once the file were opened, all my lovely formatting, fonts, and graphics would be displayed exactly as I created them. The client wants a printed copy? No problem. It would print on any printing device. Repurposing content? Well, that might or might not cost extra, depending on the desired output. Transferring some of the document's information to a Web page would be a simple matter. Transferring some of the content to a handheld device would require tagging the document, as would making the document work with a screen reader. Finally, moving the document from one program to another for others to work on? Easy. I could export the document into Rich Text Format, and many programs could then import and use the information.

As for making changes, it would still require some effort on my part, but at least it would be consistent types of changes. If the client had access to a full version of Acrobat, he would be able to add comments, request changes, and the like before the draft got to the finished stage. And I could lock the document to prevent others from making changes to it until it was finally ready for delivery.

What a difference a piece of software can make! Along with stream-lining many of the work processes and saving time, I can preserve both my masterpiece and my marriage.

You may have the sense that Acrobat's scope is extensive. Not all of its features will be used by everyone all the time. The "problem" is that the program can do so much. How do you sort out what you want to do, or could do, from those things that will never apply to your work? Some-times it depends on context. Before we get into using Acrobat for specific purposes, let's look at it in the greater scheme of things.

Context Is Key

Time for another slice of life. You have just moved into a new home or apartment. Doesn't matter if you have moved across the hall or across the country. You are standing in your new living room, surrounded by stacks and stacks of open boxes, each containing little bits of your life and your personality. What do you do? First of all, let's go out on a limb and make the assumption that you will actually unpack these boxes. I know that many of us are guilty of packing and moving the same stuff time after time without actually using any of it, and the boxes are shoved into closets or used as bases for makeshift tables and the like. But humor me. We shall unpack these boxes. How is it done?

Well, depending on the individual, there are a number of ways to approach this problem. Some folks stand in the middle of a room for a very long time planning the locations of all their treasured items and then systematically (sometimes even alphabetically!) unpack each item that belongs to a specific location, whether those items are in one box or several. Others may start from the boxes, unpacking and placing items as they come to them. And still others prefer to dump out all the boxes into great piles and then sort things out from there. I think I most closely resemble the latter group.

Once the stuff is unpacked, where does it belong, and what will it be used for? Consider the lowly lamp. There is absolutely no design reason why a lamp may not see service in a number of rooms. How do you know where to put it? Well, it will depend on your needs in the given circumstances.

I am sure by now you must be wondering where this discussion is heading; with a bit of imagination and a leap of faith, this is the point of this book. Information is just so much stuff, all of it packed into little compartments conforming to the particular requirements of the stuff, whether that be a long skinny box to pack a floor lamp or a heavy rein-forced carton to hold books.

So how do you unpack information? As I described earlier, it may be a systematic process of building a specific document for a specific project (this doodad belongs on the second shelf of the display cabinet and nowhere else); a more general document that may be modified as required (the cookbooks that were in my old kitchen will now be on a shelf in the new living room); or a multipurpose, multifunctional document that can be used in a variety of projects in a variety of formats (this table may either end up as a breakfast area in the bedroom or a side table in the living room, or it may hold more boxes of stuff in the basement).

We are all of us standing knee-deep in information, with an ever-increasing need to use that information for more and more purposes at faster and faster speeds. And, just as unpacking your belongings requires a system, so does unpacking information in order for it to be used. Quite a concept. Speaking of which, let's have a look at the whole concept of publishing information.

Publishing—What a Concept

Publishing, as we all know, has been around since the time of Mr. Gutenberg. In a more modern sense of the word, and to frame what we can do since the arrival of Acrobat 5, I have presented the progression in publishing sophistication as a continuum. This is shown in Figure 1-7.

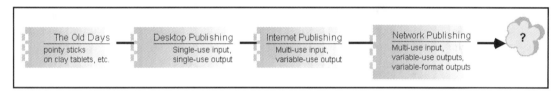

Figure 1-7
Advances in publishing from prehistory to the future

Let's jump right over "the old days" and start with the revolution that was desktop publishing.

Desktop Publishing

Some time ago, *desktop publishing* was hailed as the best of the best. I had my first PC in the early 1980s, and sometime soon thereafter I found something called a desktop publishing program. This was, of course, revolutionary. Rather than being forced to use a professional printer to set a formatted page and its elements, I now had the freedom to do it myself. Granted, the output was less than stellar, but the idea of being able to do the design and layout myself was wonderful. If it was something really important, I could copy it on to a floppy—a real floppy—and bring it to a production house.

Some years later, with the advent of laser printers and color printers (or more correctly, when these printers became economically practical), the revolution was mainstream.

This approach has one big problem (which certainly still exists): Somebody always had to print this stuff. Setting up a document would usually require several draft prints as the masterpiece was being designed and went through its approval process. The more sophisticated the work, the more revisions were required. When it was finally complete, I would store one of these compositions on a disk or on the hard drive as space became more available. I would also likely have a printed copy stored in a folder someplace. Filing has never been my forte, so I seriously mean someplace.

Then there was distribution. Mail worked, and of course I would also have to send a letter stating what stuff I was mailing someone. Later this could be done by fax, but the early faxes used strange and smelly paper rolls, and they weren't always reliable, so I'd also mail a paper copy. More paper. And now the person receiving the stuff would have to file it someplace.

Now suppose that several months later I wanted to reuse some portion of that earlier work. I would have to find the floppy, open it, copy and paste what I wanted from it, and then complete the design and start the approval/draft processes all over again. For the finale, of course, the same printing and distribution processes.

This idea can be summarized best by considering the relationships involved. Basically, we are describing a one-to-one relationship. For each effort I make, a single medium is being used to produce a single message. The message is then distributed to a single recipient.

Things started to change with the advent of the Internet.

Internet Publishing

The Internet, the World Wide Web, and e-mail. Extremely powerful forces in the last decade. From a publishing perspective, these forces heralded change. Now my work could be freely distributed for the entire world to marvel over—whether or not it should. And with or without my knowledge, of course.

Remember the days when a browser was black text on a gray background? I remember the days before that, when the only way to access information was using UNIX, on a black screen with yellow lettering. Advances in both technology and design software have yielded some amazing works, which will continue to improve.

It is now possible to integrate a variety of materials from numerous sources into a Web page. The outputs, however, are still limited and depend on the designer's input. For example, a page of wonderful information might or might not be available in a printer-friendly format. Barring that, it's the old copy-and-paste activity, or saving the entire page—ads, multiple tables, and all. More and more downloads are becoming available as PDF-formatted files. Finally, the recipient will have more control in terms of layout, as well as security.

The freedom of the Internet has also resulted in the freedom to copy and download anything you can find. How do I know if my work is being copied and used by others ostensibly as their own? No way to tell unless I come across something by chance, which isn't likely to happen. I can attach a digital signature to an image, but that still doesn't guarantee security.

Acrobat has been around since the mid 1990s. Using this program has progressively given me both more security and more freedom. I can finally preserve the integrity of my work and create works that stand on their own as I created them.

From a relationship perspective, Internet publishing is akin to a one-to-many relationship. As I described previously, the outputs are controlled by the designer. Whether or not there are different outputs depends on what decisions are made and the work done by the designer. However, production of a single type of output might be used by numerous recipients (many). Offering recipients an option to download information of various types from a site has been a commonplace activity for the past several years.

But what if we could finally compose something from a number of inputs, manipulate the same material in a variety of ways, and distribute it to many users? Well, we can do that now. Introducing network publishing.

Network Publishing

Acrobat 5, in conjunction with several other forces, is ushering in yet another new era. We have entered the realm of *network publishing*. We now can publish to an extensive and ever-growing array of outputs. In addition to using monitors and printers, we can now output information to handheld devices and e-books. These outputs are used in conjunction with the Internet, intranets, and extranets.

The whole idea of network publishing is just so doggone cool. Imagine this: Using a variety of inputs, information can be shared (in numerous ways, including online) as it is being developed. The *same* information can then be modified and formatted for output on some incredibly interesting devices and formats. And, not only can the same information be reformatted depending on output requirements, but the entire pool of information held within an enterprise can be indexed, cataloged, and archived. Such a wonderful idea for a paper file–phobic person like me.

Influences

I suppose this continuing evolution is inevitable. Things that were unknown half a decade ago are now becoming mainstream. It seems everyone has an Internet connection, and bandwidth is becoming more accessible. Many of us now have broadband satellite connections at home; I hadn't even thought this possible three years ago. E-commerce has become commonplace. Server and network software is more friendly, widespread, and compatible with an ever-growing number of devices. Most of my circle of friends have networks in their homes. And, no, we are not all geeks. (Actually, I guess it depends on your definition of the word, but none of us wears a propeller beanie!)

What is the outcome? Demand for content. The content must be personalized, available on a variety of devices, and available anytime. Acrobat 5 rises to this challenge admirably. As I will introduce in the next section, you can choose among a number of ways to reuse content and deliver it via different outputs.

Functioning as a workgroup team member has become commonplace, and network publishing expands the functionality of workgroups. Rather than simply routing e-mails and comments among workgroup members, Acrobat 5 takes this process one step further through its support of Web Distributed Authoring and Versioning (WebDAV), ODBC, and Microsoft Office Server Extensions. Workgroup members, regardless of location, can simultaneously review and add comments in a browser and then upload comments to a shared Web or network server for simultaneous viewing. In conjunction with various security settings, digital and electronic signatures for online approval and processing completes the document-cycle process.

So now we have seen that what we do has changed, and it will continue to change. How does that help in understanding how to use this book? Well, I wanted to give you some context for approaching the new and enhanced functionality in the program. For example, without the short description on network publishing, you wouldn't understand the purpose of Chapter 14. Also, by knowing some of the advancements and changes that are occurring around us on a daily basis, you will gain a better understanding of how to use Acrobat in your work.

Now you have a context with which to approach the information in this book. Using that context, I now want to describe how I have divided up the information into a series of processes.

From the Inbox to the Outbox and Beyond

I may have mentioned a time or two that this is complex software. With the exception of these early chapters—which use somewhat of a show-and-tell format to describe how the program physically works—I have taken a processes approach to Acrobat 5. Why? To help you make sense of it all.

I have summarized my approach into the set of interrelated operations shown in Figure 1-8. I have broken down the uses of the program into three major components: document creation (input), document management (processes), and document distribution (output).

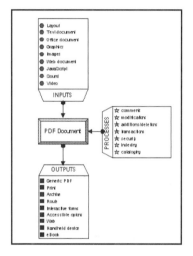

Figure 1-8
An overview of Acrobat 5's functionality

At the core of the matter is the PDF document. A whole range of inputs can be used to create the document. Once the document has been built, it can be modified, shared, stored, and made secure. Finally, the document can be distributed in a range of different forms of output. Let's explore these processes a bit further.

Document Creation

In Figure 1-8, the central element is a PDF document. The document is created from a collection of different inputs that range from text to images to JavaScript. The more rudimentary inputs are likely familiar to anyone who has ever used Acrobat. Lay out a document, and save it as a PDF file. As you can see in Figure 1-9, the list is quite a bit more extensive than that.

Figure 1-9
Inputs for
document creation

We will consider how the basic PDF document is created. We will also spend a considerable amount of time looking at some of the specialized types of input. Some are used for fairly generic effects, such as sound clips. Others, such as JavaScript, can be used in conjunction with XML to create interactive forms that can streamline many data input processes.

Document Management

There are two subsets of the document-management process; the process as a whole is shown in Figure 1-10.

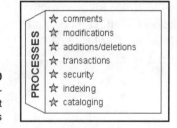

Figure 1-10
The document-
management
process

Some of these management processes refer to an individual document, while others are used for managing a number of documents. We will look at the particulars of each of these functions, both from the technical aspects of performing the function as well as the use and place of each in managing your workflow. As with the inputs, some of these processes are fairly generic; others are more specialized.

Document Distribution

Finally, we will consider distribution of PDF documents, or outputs. As you can see in Figure 1-11, a substantial number of differing outputs are available.

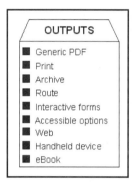

Figure 1-11
Document-distribution options

I have organized this list in a specific way. First is the generic PDF we are all familiar with, which is most often printed. Next is archiving and routing outputs, which follow along from the indexing and cataloging processes referred to earlier. Then I have listed a number of specialized outputs. Remember that these specialized outputs all start from the generic PDF file. However, each of these areas is sufficiently complex and requires enough intelligent decision-making to warrant thorough discussion.

So let's review. So far, I have described both new functionality and major processes available in Acrobat 5; I established some context for using the program; and I discussed processes for creating, managing, and distributing PDF documents.

One more question remains. For whom are the users creating, managing, and distributing these documents? Read on.

Who Should Read This Book

I would like to say that this book is for everyone, but that is not really the case. Certain parts of the book can be used by large portions of the population, but other areas are specific to particular industries. I think, though, that there is something here for everyone who is in any kind of business that requires management and use of information—which is an awful lot of people!

Before I describe specific audiences I have written this book for, here is a high-level list of what can be done using Acrobat 5. Do you do any of these things on a regular basis?

- Import documents and export documents in a variety of formats

- Repurpose content for different forms of output, including e-books

- Attach security features to a document

- Share and collaborate on documents

- Attach different forms of communications to documents

- Create forms

- Repurpose content for Web deployment

- Plan work more efficiently and effectively

If you recognize any of your work activities in this list, this book has something for you. As you can see in this quote from the April 2001 edition of *US Business Reporter*, available online at http://www.activemedia-guide.com/pkg_adobe.htm, is there really anyone in the world who wouldn't be a member of the audience?

> *"Adobe is uniquely positioned to make a further dramatic impact not only on how society creates visually rich information, but also on how it distributes and accesses that information electronically. Adobe software helps people use the computer to express, share, and manage their ideas in imaginative and meaningful new ways, whether the choice of media is static or dynamic, paper or electronic. Adobe products enable people to create, send, view, print, and manage high-impact information, thereby helping them and their ideas stand out. Adobe's strategy is to address the needs of professional publishers, business publishers, consumers, and companies who need to solve document and printing problems."*

All marketing and PR information aside, there are several groups of people who stand to gain the most from using this book.

But Seriously, Who Is This Book For?

This is a design book. It is written for graphic designers from many disciplines—basically any designers looking to enhance their workflow and work smarter. As such, I have written it with essentially four groups in mind:

- General graphic designers working in a variety of media, especially print, Web, and interactive media

- Web designers responsible for management of information across a variety of platforms (intranet, extranet, Internet, network)

- Publishers and document-management enterprises, particularly those who are responsible for knowledge-management activities

- Business professionals (regardless of the size of the enterprise), given the collaborative nature of this version of Acrobat, as well as its ability to repurpose information

This book will not teach fundamental design skills. I am assuming that designers using this book will be at least at an intermediate level. The focus will be on helping you apply your skills to working more efficiently and securely. The last two groups in the preceding list may find some portions of the book unsuitable for their purposes—for example, print output. Collaboration and workflow are key concepts in this book. As such, these topics are applicable to all groups.

Regardless of whether you are the person who is responsible for understanding how and why to tag a document or you are the person who says, "Make this thing work," there is something for you in these pages. Enjoy!

Up Next

If you are one of that rare breed who reads a book from cover to cover, you must be wondering when I am actually going to get down to business. That time is now.

In this chapter we looked at the new functionality added to Acrobat 5, and I've provided context for using the program. Up next, we will jump into Acrobat 5 and see how to make it work. Chapter 2 looks at how Acrobat functions. We'll check out the interface and complete our first projects. Let's go.

Chapter 2

How Acrobat Works

*Before we start our adventures in
creating wild and wonderful products
in Acrobat, let's have a look at the
components of the program
and learn how to use them.*

What's in the Cupboards?

In Chapter 1, I said that people generally take advantage of only a very small portion of a program's capabilities. Since you are reading this, I am assuming that you don't want to be one of those people. Good for you.

The simplest way to start to learn how a program works, and what its capabilities are, is to go through the menu items and toolbars. Open everything, read what it says, look around. Go through dialog boxes, see where they lead you. Remember, you really can't break it.

I would advise, however, that you perform these exploratory functions without an important document loaded into the program—just to be on the safe side!

In this chapter, I want to open all the drawers and cupboards and have a good look around. We are also going to do two projects using some of the commenting and editing tools.

A Look at the Interface

First things first: the interface. Figure 2-1 shows an entire Acrobat window as it appears with a document open. In this case, I have shown the Adobe Acrobat 5 Help files. Let's have a brief look at the components.

<div class="sidebar">

Workflow Tip

Why Did I Pick This Page As an Example?

Shooting an image of the introductory page to the program's Help files was not accidental. Most of what you need to do your work efficiently and intelligently is in these pages. And using Help files is just like any other skill—the more you use it, the more adept you become.

</div>

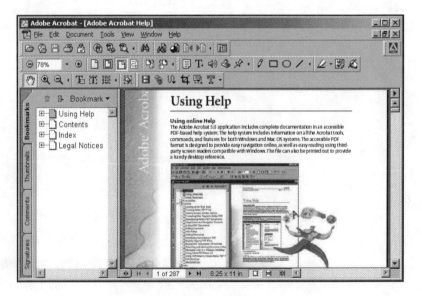

Figure 2-1
The Acrobat 5 interface

Menus

Acrobat 5 offers seven drop-down menus, and their layout is common to most programs. The sequence starts with File and Edit options, and then moves to specific program functionality options and to Window and Help menus. Above the menu bar is the title bar, showing both the program's name and the name of the file in brackets. We will look at the menu options later in this chapter.

Toolbars

Below the menu bar in Figure 2-1 you'll see most of the toolbars. Acrobat 5 includes a set of eight toolbars. You can rearrange and combine them at will, and toolbars may be docked or floating. Toolbars displaying a small arrow indicate that you can expand and collapse the contents, as shown in Figure 2-2. We will look at the toolbars again in the next section.

Figure 2-2
The Viewing toolbar options. The left image shows the expanded toolbar; the right image shows the collapsed toolbar. You can see that the direction of the arrow has changed.

Document Pane

The document pane houses—go figure—the document itself. Several menu and toolbar items control how the document is displayed. At the top right of the document pane's scrollbar is a triangle. Clicking this triangle will open a small selection of command options, as shown in Figure 2-3.

Figure 2-3
Commands accessible from the document pane

Status Bar

At the bottom of the program's interface, under the document pane, is the status bar. The status bar shows the number of the current page, and it contains some simple navigation controls and page-scrolling options. When you apply security settings, a small gold key will appear to the right of the page-scrolling options. The status bar configurations are shown in Figure 2-4.

Figure 2-4
The status bar components.
As you can see, the
document displayed is page
1 of 9, and the pages will
scroll continuously.

Navigation Pane

Borrowing from a standard Web page layout, Adobe has placed a navigation pane to the left of the document pane. This pane consists of a series of tabs used to control movement throughout a document based on function. The default set of navigation tabs are shown in Figure 2-5. In a newly created document, the four tabs shown—Bookmarks, Thumbnails, Comments, and Signatures—are displayed by default. As you can see in the figure, there is an overlay on page 1. This box indicates that this portion of this page is being displayed in the document pane.

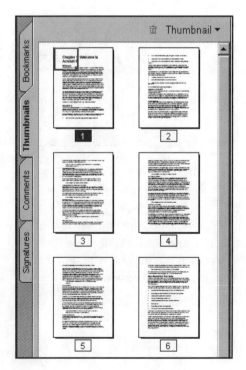

Figure 2-5
The default
navigation pane with
the Thumbnails
tab displayed

You can also see a drop-down arrow to the right of the Thumbnail title at the top of the palette. Clicking this drop-down arrow will open a set of options for using the Thumbnail palette, as shown in Figure 2-6.

Figure 2-6
The Thumbnail drop-down menu options

I've Read the Help Files, I've Looked at the Menu Items, and I Still Can't Find What I Want to Do!

This has to be one of the most annoying dilemmas known to humans in this computer-centric era. The more sophisticated the program, the more pervasive the problem. Here are a few more tips for finding what you want, courtesy of the program's design.

- In addition to labeling the tools, Adobe Acrobat labels the entire toolbar. If you hover your mouse over the bar, as shown in the following image, the actual name of the tool collection will appear.

Both toolbars and tools are labeled.

- Not sure if you have selected the right tool? Try the context menu options. With a tool selected, click the page and then right-click (Windows) or Control-click (Mac OS). Functions available for the tool you have selected will be displayed, as shown in the following image. Don't forget that you will have to actually select something on the page in order to make the context menu appear.

Context-sensitive options for the TouchUp Object tool, part of the Editing toolbar

- Don't have each and every toolbar open and expanded. This has always been one of the most interesting things I have observed over the years teaching software to students. Many are of the opinion that if a toolbar exists it should be open, regardless of whether there is even the most remote possibility that it will be used. Removing some of the visual clutter may help you find what you are looking for more readily.

- If you are working along with this book, check the index.

- Still can't find what you want? Save your work and go for a walk. Amazing what a bit of distance and time can do.

Note

This is not an exhaustive examination of these program segments and their contents, but rather an additional orientation and background for working through this book. As I recommended earlier, please use the Help functions within the program for detailed information. I have also listed a number of URLs in Appendix A, including links to discussion groups, mailing lists, and Web sites that you can visit to access more information on using Acrobat 5.

Menus and Palettes and Toolbars, Oh My!

As you might have guessed from this section's title, we'll now focus on menus, toolbars, and palettes.

The Major Menu Items

As I mentioned earlier, Acrobat 5 offers seven major menus. Rather than mindlessly listing the content of each item (which would be sleep-inducing), I simply want to point out some of the functionality available to you. First, let's have a look at the menu setup, shown in Figure 2-7.

Figure 2-7
The Acrobat 5 menu bar

File Options

Many of the File menu options will be familiar to you. Here you will find such functions as the Import command, which is used for importing comments and form data as well as scans. As you'd expect, the Export command exports comments and form data, and also is used for extracting and exporting images.

Document Properties now lists Data Objects and Metadata, in addition to the regular properties, such as fonts, trapping keys, and indexes. You can access the Document Security dialog box from this menu as well. Finally, as shown in Figure 2-8, the Batch Processing command submenu offers many options. We will look at these options in Chapter 14.

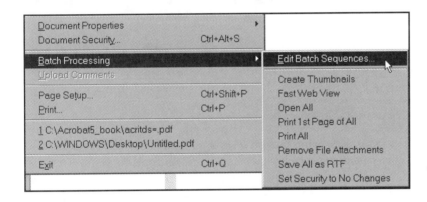

Figure 2-8
The Batch Processing commands

Edit Options

The Edit menu commands are fairly straightforward; the usual functional editing and searching options remain. However, there are two new components I'd like to mention. The first is an expanded Search command, which includes Query searches, as shown in Figure 2-9. These expanded command options enable you to perform full-text searches against an indexed database.

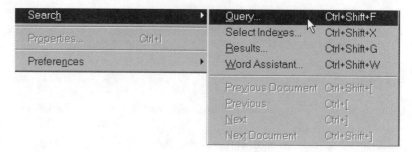

Figure 2-9
The expanded
Search commands

The second item of note is under the Preferences submenu. As shown in Figure 2-10, Preferences include security (via the docBox plug-in). You'll also find options for Web Capture and Internet Settings. Clicking the latter option opens the Internet Settings dialog box in your default browser.

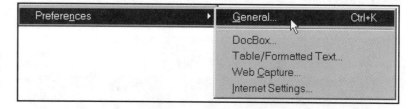

Figure 2-10
The Preferences
submenu options on
the Edit menu

Document Options

The Document menu options let you navigate through a document, move between views and documents, and manipulate pages. There is one command I want to mention here: the Set Page Action command. When you select this command, you'll see the Page Actions dialog box shown in Figure 2-11.

This dialog box is used to increase interactivity in a document. As you can see in Figure 2-12, clicking the Add button reveals numerous integrated actions that you can use in your document. We will be using the Set Page Action command many times throughout this book.

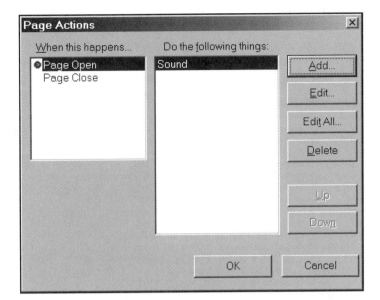

Figure 2-11
The Page Actions
dialog box

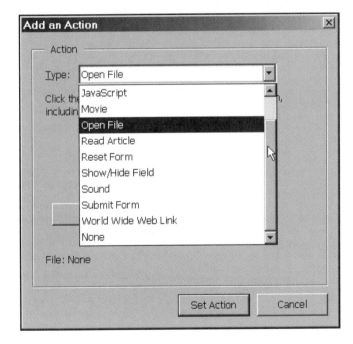

Figure 2-12
The page actions available
within Acrobat 5

Tools Options

Note

A number of online tools are also available that I didn't include in Table 2-1.

What is software without tools? And do we have tools! Rather than walking through each Tools menu item individually, I have compiled most of them into Table 2-1 for easy reference.

Table 2-1 Major Tools in Acrobat 5 and Their Primary Purposes

Tool	Function
Comments	This tool lets you manage comments in a document, including filtering and summarizing.
Compare	This tool allows you to compare two documents or two versions of a signed document.
Digital Signatures	This tools lets you manage and verify signatures and sign documents.
Self-Sign Security	Use this tool to manage your signature and its uses.
Spelling	This tool lets you spellcheck forms and comments.
Web Capture	This tool contains options for capturing and using Web pages.
Accessibility Checker	This tool allows you to assess a document for accessibility requirements. You set the parameters in the appropriate dialog boxes.
Catalog	Use this tool to create a full-text index search of documents or collections of documents.
Distiller	One of the big guns, this tool serves as a simulated printer for creating PDF files.
docBox	A powerful plug-in, this tool is used for digital publishing and secure distribution of rights-to-use documents.
Forms	Use this tool to manage field alignments, templates, and tabbing order.
JavaScript	This tool launches the JavaScript console and is used to manage JavaScript elements in a document. You can also access the Page Actions dialog box from here.
Locate Web Addresses	Use this tool to manage URLs in a document.
PDF Consultant	Basically, this tool does as its name implies. It will analyze a document, it can be used to remove such items as comments, it audits space used by different elements, and it can optimize a document.
TouchUp Text	This tool lets you modify text in a number of ways and deal with some of those weird things that can happen when you're doing an OCR import.

View Options

The View menu commands are the old standbys: zooming, rotating, and scrolling. Under the View menu you will also find the proofing and overprint options, as well as the grid options.

Window Options

Again, the content of the Window menu is much as you would expect. You will find the list of toolbars in this menu (more about them later), and you will find the list of palettes. As shown in Figure 2-13, the palettes behave like other Adobe products in that they can be reconfigured, moved, and rearranged. For illustration purposes, I have the whole works open in the same collection. You can access functions for each palette by clicking the arrow to the right of the palette's name.

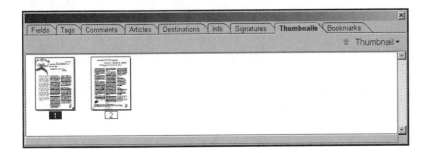

Figure 2-13
The collection of palettes assembled into one group (not a very practical arrangement from a working standpoint)

Help Options

Several useful features are available within the Help menu. As I have mentioned, the program Help files are here, as are Web-based help and information sources. Two additional components of note: a JavaScript reference and a plug-ins reference.

The Acrobat JavaScript Guide is a comprehensive, 295-page guide to using JavaScript in Acrobat 5. This version supports extensive JavaScript binding, which means you can use the program to customize forms and documents by expanding their utility and interactivity. We will look at using JavaScript in several chapters, and Chapter 16 is devoted to JavaScript.

The other reference of note is the description of the plug-ins integrated into Acrobat. In Figure 2-14, I've selected the Web2PDF item to view a description of the plug-in and a list of its dependencies.

Now for the toolbars. And then we will finally get down to business and do some projects using this newfound knowledge.

Note

Please refer to Appendix B for the lowdown on all the integrated plug-ins.

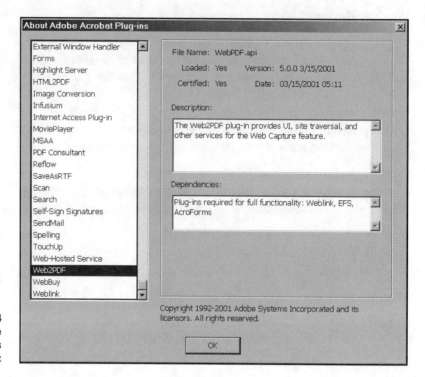

Figure 2-14
The About Adobe
Acrobat Plug-ins
dialog box

Toolbars

Again, I am not going to cover each and every element of each and every toolbar. Instead, I will show images of the different toolbars (there are eight in all) and include a description in table form. As you can see in Table 2-2, I have expanded all the toolbars.

Table 2-2   Acrobat 5 Toolbars and Their Functions

Toolbar	Name	Function and Purpose
	Adobe Online	This links Acrobat to Adobe.com. It provides for automatic notification of updates and upgrades, other product information and technical support, and listings of plug-ins and patches.
	Basic Tools	This toolbar contains hand and zoom tools common to Adobe applications. The lower four icons are used for specific selections: type, columns, tables, and graphics.

Table 2-2 Acrobat 5 Toolbars and Their Functions (Continued)

Toolbar	Name	Function and Purpose
	Commenting	This toolbar offers a palette of tools analogous to adding different elements to written documents, from notes and text to stamps; to shapes and lines; to specific markup devices such as highlighting. (We will use this toolbar in this chapter's projects.)
	Editing	Editing in Acrobat refers to object types that can be added to a document (e.g., movies or forms) or used to modify the document (e.g., cropping). The icons in the second block are used for touch-ups.
	File	The icons in the first block contain standard file functions. The icons in the second block allow you to connect to various online PDF services. Find and search functions are next, and then icons for navigating through a document using highlights. The last icon enables you to close the navigation pane.
	Navigation	A simple directional palette, this toolbar contains the same icons you'll find on the status bar at the bottom of the interface's window.
	View History	This toolbar contains useful features for moving between two views, such as full-page to a magnified section.
	Viewing	This toolbar offers a basic set of tools, such as generic zoom tools, as well as page-size and page-rotation options.

Well, I think at this point we have all had quite enough of this show-and-tell process. Coming up next are discussions and projects on two functional uses of the power of Acrobat: comments and markups. First, commenting functions.

Adding Comments to a Document

Finally, some real action! Remember, comments are not just comments but can take a variety of forms, depending on a number of factors:

- Your mood

- The toolbars you have open

- Your method of working and communicating

- Any corporate policies or procedures you may be bound to

In addition to attaching notes or comments to a document, you can include images or sound files. One interesting feature we will be looking at in a project coming up is the capability to import and export comments. As we will see, this is a handy, space- and timesaving feature.

Using the Commenting Tools

As listed in Table 2-2, Acrobat provides three sets of commenting tools: comments, graphic markup, and text markup.

Adding a Note

In Figure 2-15, I have added a simple text comment to a page. The color bar and the icon for the note are yellow. Adding a comment is like inserting any type of object: Select the note tool and click the document to place it.

To deselect the note tool, click the hand tool (on the basic toolbar), or select another tool or function.

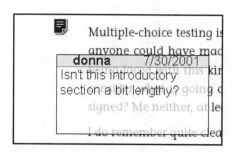

Figure 2-15
A simple text comment on a page. Note that the text box is semitransparent.

While the comment is still selected, you can modify its properties if desired. Suppose you're in a lavender mood. Right-click the text comment icon (the dark overlay on the icon indicates it is selected), and select Properties from the context menu. The Note Properties dialog box shown in Figure 2-16 will open. Simply change the color as desired. I chose a lovely shade of lavender, which you will see here as a paler shade of gray.

Figure 2-16
The Note Properties dialog box

In Figure 2-17, you can see the customizations I have added to the note. I added my last name in the properties. Back on the page, I resized the display.

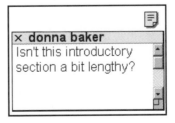

Figure 2-17
The revised text note

Let's have a look at the other types of commenting that can be added. I am not going to go into a lengthy discussion of how to create and modify each of the types; the discussion on notes can be applied to most of the other types as well, with a couple of exceptions that I will explain. Remember that you can access any customizations through the right-click context menu.

Adding a Free Text Comment

Free text comments are similar to notes, with one exception. Like a note, a text comment can be added anywhere and moved as required. The difference is that this comment type is always visible, as you can see in Figure 2-18.

Attaching Sound Comments

You can add sound clips as a comment just as you can the other types. You have the option to add prerecorded sound as a comment or record your own audio comments. As you can see in Figure 2-19, I have embedded a sound file from an external source. Also, to give credit where credit is due, I changed the authors' names in the Sound Properties dialog box.

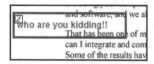

Figure 2-18
A free text comment. This type of comment remains visible.

Figure 2-19
An attached sound comment

Attaching an External File

The file attachment tool enables you to embed a file at a specific location in a document. An attached file is managed as part of the main document. For example, if you are creating a general business document, you can attach spreadsheets in areas of the document referencing specific data. If you then e-mail the main document, the embedded files will be attached to it. As you can see in Figure 2-20, optional icons are available that represent the type of file attached.

Workflow Tip
Using External File Icons

When developing a communication system within a workgroup, you may want to use the icons on a regular basis for specific types of attachments. Just as comment colors may be assigned, so may the attached file icons. For example, my comments and attached files may be colored red, and other members of my group can use other colors.

Figure 2-20
The File Attachment Properties dialog box, which enables you to attach an external file. The document name serves as a description for the comment.

"Return to Sender"

Remember the old days when nearly everyone had a stamp or two to use for various purposes? Some people had so many stamps, they had racks to hold them. Well, those days are back, in a digital way.

Stamps are added like other comments. They come in quite an assortment, as you can see in Figure 2-21. Also, you can create custom stamps, which we will do in Project 2-1.

To add a stamp, click the stamp tool, and then click the page location where you want it placed. The stamp will have a bounding box for resizing. Change to another stamp by right-clicking the stamp and selecting

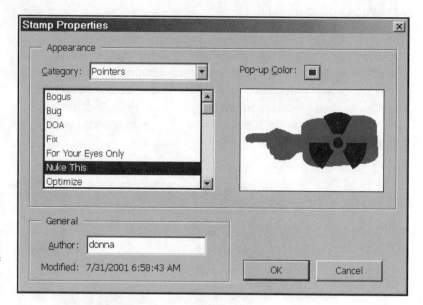

Figure 2-21
The stamp tool
assortment. One of
the pointer options
is shown.

Properties from the context menu. Once a stamp is selected, it will be used for all subsequent stamps until you change its appearance again.

The final group of commenting tools are used for marking up documents.

Marking Up Documents

Markups come in two flavors: graphic and text.

Adding Graphic Markups

Some people simply can't communicate with words. For them, the order of the day is lines and squiggles. Acrobat 5 has something for everyone—even this group. You can use the graphic tools to add visual notations to a document, and those visual notations can be accompanied by text notes (maybe to explain the scribbles!). The four tools available are the pencil, square, circle, and line tools. Each works as a basic drawing tool. A sample "writing" effort is shown in Figure 2-22.

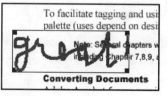

Figure 2-22
Using the pencil tool—
but not very well!

Marking Up Text

These tools are similar to those found in word processing programs. You can highlight, underline, or strike through text. All these effects are applied using a click-and-drag process. Use Ctrl-drag (Windows) or Alt-drag (Mac OS) to mark up a rectangle. Figure 2-23 shows highlighted text and an attached note.

Note

You can add a note to any of the markup tools. Double-click the comment and type the text in the note window that pops up.

Figure 2-23
Highlighted text comment with a note attached. The note also contains the text that was highlighted in the document.

Creating Custom Stamps

As I mentioned earlier, Acrobat maintains a library of stamps. You can add custom stamps to the library to use for corporate functions, personal expression, or other any other purpose. Once you've created a stamp, you can add it to the stamp library. Here are the basic rules:

- A stamp can only be stored in PDF format.

- You must store the file in the correct location.

- The stamp must be categorized and named correctly.

Let's look at how these rules are satisfied:

1. Create the element you want to use as a stamp in any format and convert it to a PDF file.

2. Store the files in the Acrobat Plug-ins subfolder Stamps (within the Annotations folder). This is the only location Acrobat will look for stamps. The four sets of stamps shipped with Acrobat are stored in four PDF documents. Each stamp is on its own page of a document.

3. Speaking of pages, this is where the naming conventions comes in. The files should be saved with the filename or title as the category name. Name your files using this format:

   <CategoryName><StampName>=<Label>

As an example, let's look at one of the stamp sets. Perhaps the simplest thing is to show the finished product, which I've done in Figure 2-24. In this image, I have shown the page template structure for the file called Words.pdf. (You access the template files for the current document by selecting Tools ➤ Forms ➤ Page Templates.)

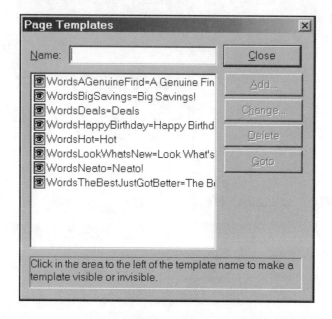

Figure 2-24
The contents of the Words.pdf stamp file. The stamps use the naming convention described earlier.

In order to best illustrate how this works, let's create a custom stamp.

Project Project 2-1. Customizing Stamps to Create a Personal Monogram

Time to have a little fun (although this could certainly be a serious endeavor). Let's make a monogram to use for personalizing documents.

What You Need

Well, nothing actually. All you need is imagination and basic tools—both of which, I think I am safe in assuming, anyone reading this book already possesses.

Note

A finished copy of my file is on the CD in the Chapter 2 Projects folder; the file is named custom.pdf.

Build the Basic File

In the interest of simplicity, I have started with a Microsoft Word file.

1. Construct your monogram in whatever source program you prefer. I created the image shown in Figure 2-25 in Microsoft Word and then exported it as a PDF file by clicking the Convert To Adobe PDF button (which self-installs with the Acrobat installation).

Figure 2-25
My personal monogram

2. Open the file in Acrobat.

3. Choose File ➤ Document Properties ➤ Summary.

4. Type **custom** in the Title text box to name a new category.

5. Click OK. Save the file.

Let's assume that this category will be used for other custom stamps in the future.

Store the File As a Template

We have to name the page as well, and then add the stamp as a template for the file. To do so, follow these steps:

1. Make sure the file is still open. Select Tools ➤ Forms ➤ Page Templates.

2. Name the stamp page using the format I described earlier. Figure 2-26 shows the template page with the name I chose: CustomMonogram=Monogram.

3. Click Add, and then click Yes. Save the file.

Workflow Tip

How Did We Get from Stamps to Templates, and Why Are Templates Listed Under Forms?

Once you've created a template, you can reuse it at will. Anything can be formatted as a template—in this case, our stamps. The difference between a pasted copy of an object and a template is the formatting and structure that come along with the form of a template, regardless of its use.

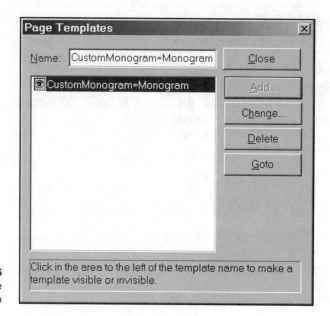

Figure 2-26
The completed template
for this stamp

Saving the File for Reuse

Before we finish this project, we'll save the file so we can reuse it. Remember I said earlier that the files must be stored in a specific location on the hard drive in order for Acrobat to access stamps? Here's how to do that: Select File ➤ Save As. Navigate to the Stamps subfolder, and save the file into that folder. Figure 2-27 shows the location on my computer where my stamp is stored.

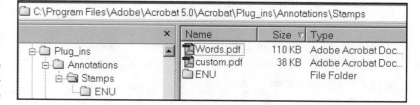

Figure 2-27
The final resting place for
my custom stamps file

Need proof that your plan worked? Open any document and add a stamp to a page. Just right-click the stamp and select Properties from the context menu. As you can see in Figure 2-28, the new custom category has now been added to the Stamps Properties dialog box.

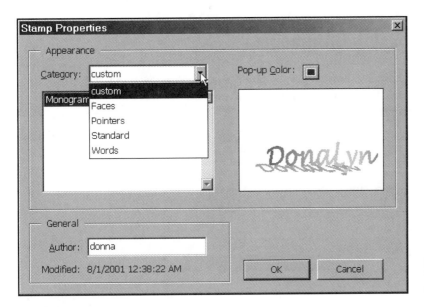

Figure 2-28
The custom stamp is now available for use.

As we have seen, comments come in many shapes and formats. This allows users to work with the program in ways they find most comfortable. You can manage a group of comments. Let's have a look at how this works.

Managing Comments

Regardless of type, all comments behave in the same way. Acrobat recognizes each as a variation of the same type of functionality. As a group, comments can be

- Used for navigating through a document

- Filtered and sorted

- Searched

- Summarized

- Imported and exported

All that! Let's have a look at how these things work.

Workflow Tip
Get Rid of What You Don't Need

Just as you can add stamp categories, you can also delete them. If you are using only a handful of stamps on a regular basis, add them to a custom set and delete the other files (or move them out of the stamps folder). In the event you might need the other stamps again, move their files back or replace them from the installation CD.

Navigating Through a Document Using Comments

Earlier I showed you the palettes in the Window menu. Obviously, we will be using the Comments palette. You can sort the comments by type, author, page number, or creation date. Click the Comments title to open the drop-down list and select a sort option. The default option is by page number, as you can see in Figure 2-29.

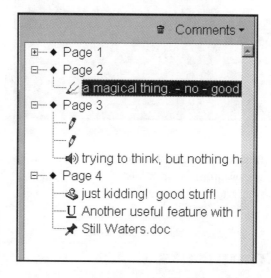

Figure 2-29
The default comment display listing comments by page number

Text associated with a comment also appears. For graphic and text markup comments, text under the comment is displayed as a place-holder for the comment's location in the document. You can also see that the file comment shows the name of the file I attached earlier.

Here's how comments behave:

- Click a comment in the list. The page on which the selected comment is located appears in the document pane, and the highlighted comment scrolls into view.

- Navigate between comments by clicking another one in the navigation pane.

- Click a sound comment. It will play to the end and stop automatically.

- Launch attached files by double-clicking the file attachment; the method for closing the file depends on the file format and program used to create the file.

Using Filters and Sorting Comments

These functions are great for large or complex documents. To open the Filter Comments dialog box shown in Figure 2-30, select Tools ➤ Comments ➤ Filter.

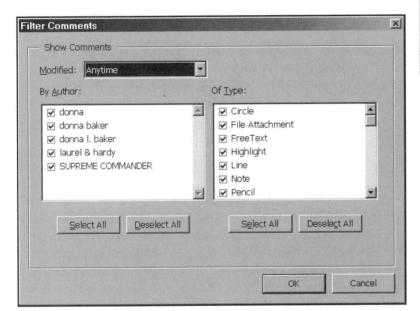

Figure 2-30
The Filter Comments dialog box

Choose your filtering options:

- Select an option from the Modified drop-down menu. This will serve as a time basis for your filter (anything from 24 hours to 30 minutes).

- Deselect author or type options as desired. By default, all author names and types are selected.

- Click Select All or Deselect All beneath the comments types list or author list to display or hide comments.

Searching Your Comments

Acrobat has a comment search feature that enables you to find specific comments based on their text. It functions in the same way as a general text search function. Select Tools ➤ Comments ➤ Find (or click the Comments drop-down menu on the tab and click Find). Enter your search text and select a search option. When you click Find, the document pane will display the page containing the comment, and the comment will be selected.

Importing and Exporting Comments

Comments can be saved as a Form Data Format (FDF) document, which can then be imported into and exported from documents. When comments are imported into a document, they will automatically place themselves in the correct location, and they will not affect other comments in the document.

You can export either all the comments or a filtered set of comments. Exported comments are placed in their original positions in a new empty FDF document. The FDF document is much smaller than the original because it contains only comments. The smaller file size makes it more convenient to distribute by e-mail or other means.

That has been a lot of information to absorb. I think it is time to put it into action. In the final project of this chapter, we will first add comments to a document, and then we'll look at two management functions using those comments: creating a summary document and importing/exporting comments.

Workflow Tip
What Will an FDF File Do for Me?

Actually, quite a bit. Consider this scenario: You are the author of a document. You are also on a tight deadline. The document must be reviewed by three other people. In the "old days," you would have had to route the document to each of the three people, or send them all paper copies, and then collect their comments and try to make sense of it all. Instead, send them each a copy of the file to review. Have each reviewer send back only the FDF document, which is much smaller than the original document and can be easily e-mailed. Import their FDF files into your document. All their comments will be collated into your document. Organize their comments as required. And get to work—deadline, remember!

Project Project 2-2. Adding and Managing Comments in a Document

To start this project, open the file called project2.pdf, which is on the CD in the Chapter 2 Projects folder. In the same folder, you will also find a copy of the finished document, project2_finished.pdf.

Adding Comments

Try out the different comment options. Make sure you use at least two authors.

1. Add an assortment of comments to the document. The comments I added are shown in Table 2-3.

Table 2-3   Description of Comments to Add to Your Source Document

Page	Type	Location	Author	Note
1	Highlight	First sentence, paragraph 1	donna	"define location"
1	Strikethrough	Last phrase, sentence 2, paragraph 1	george	"'or any other purpose' Remove this phrase"
1	Rectangle	After numbered list	george	"Add a subheader here - Page Templates"
1	Rectangle	Around Page Templates image	donna	"resize this smaller. Wrap text to the right."
1	Highlight	Description of Figure 2-24, second sentence	donna	"list the code snippet again"
1	"AS IS" stamp	Description of Figure 2-24, second sentence	george	"leave this as is. code snippet two paragraphs above."
2	Line	"Workflow Tip"	george	"change this from tip to first paragraph of Page Template subheading."

2. Save the file with a different name (I used project2_finished).

3. You may also want to color-code the authors, which I have done. All comments by donna are green; those added by george are blue.

Generating Comment Summaries

Now we will use the information from the comments you just added. First you will generate a comment summary, which is a separate PDF document that lists all the information about the comments in a document. One of the information blocks from the summary you will generate is shown in Figure 2-31.

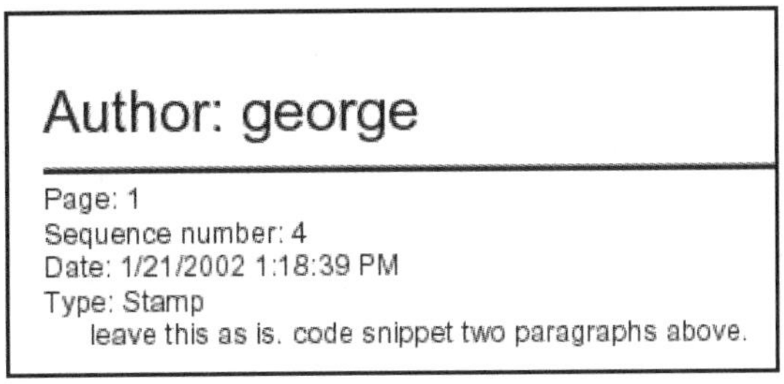

Author: george

Page: 1
Sequence number: 4
Date: 1/21/2002 1:18:39 PM
Type: Stamp
    leave this as is. code snippet two paragraphs above.

Figure 2-31
Information generated by a comment summary

Note

You can also sort or filter the comment summary file. Select a sort option—author, date, or page. You can filter the comments by clicking Filter. The Filter Comments dialog box discussed earlier will open.

Here's how to create a summary:

1. Open the project2_finished.pdf file.

2. Select Tools ➤ Comments ➤ Summarize.

3. Click OK.

4. Acrobat creates the new file. Save the file as comments.pdf.

Moving and Sharing Your Comments

Now let's look at how to export and import your comments. Again, make sure you have the project2_finished.pdf file open.

Exporting Comments

We will start with exporting. Follow these steps:

1. Choose File ➤ Export ➤ Comments.

2. Browse to the location you want the file stored, and name the file. I named my file comments.fdf.

3. Click Save.

Importing Comments

At the risk of creating a very circular process, now I want you to import the comments back into a "commentless" copy of the file—in this case, the original file you started with! In order for an import to work correctly, the copies of the file exported from and imported to must match.

1. Open your original document, project2.pdf. Choose File ➤ Import ➤ Comments (or select Import from the Comments palette drop-down menu).

2. Browse to the comments.fdf file, and click Select to open the file.

3. Acrobat will add the comments to your document.

This brings our discussion of commenting tools and functions to an end—except for one aspect, which we'll look at the next section.

Note

Want to test this process for accuracy? Open both the original file with the imported comments and the project2_finished.pdf files. You will see that both have the same comments applied in the same locations.

Setting Preferences
for Comments

I've described changing attributes on a comment-by-comment basis.
But what if you want to change the default settings for your comments?
Read on.

1. Select Edit ➤ Preferences ➤ General, and then select Comments
   from the list. The window shown in Figure 2-32 will open.

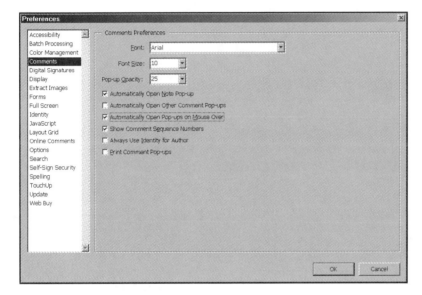

Figure 2-32
The Preferences settings
for Comments

2. Select the desired Font and Font Size options.

3. Set the opacity value for the comment pop-up windows.

4. Select other options for viewing notes as desired.

5. Select Show Comment Sequence Numbers to have the comments
   numbered according to when they were created.

6. If you are the only person using your machine, you may want to
   select the Always Use Identity For Author option to set the author
   name from the Identity preference consistently.

7. To have the text notes associated with a printed comment, select
   the Print Comment Pop-ups option.

8. Click OK to close the window and save your settings.

Up Next

So there we have it: an introduction to the interface and component elements of Acrobat 5. As I have said several times, Acrobat 5 is complex software because it can do so much. I hope the orientation I provided in this chapter makes everything more understandable.

In this chapter, we looked at adding comments to a document, and we created a custom monogram to use as a stamp. In addition, I discussed managing comments in a document. Which brings up a question: Where do the documents come from in the first place? The answer is the subject of the next chapter.

Chapter 3

Creating PDF Files

In the previous chapter, I supplied a PDF document for you to use in our projects. But how does a file become a PDF file, and what kinds of files can be used? Inquiring minds, read on.

Where Do the Files Come From?

I recall the first time I opened Acrobat, which I think was version 3. By that time, I had been working with software for years and thought this was just one more weapon to add to my digital arsenal. Well. Didn't work out so smoothly right from the start. I nonchalantly opened the File drop-down menu and moved my mouse over to click New. Which wasn't there. Tried my usual shortcut keys. Nothing.

After looking through all the menu options and cursing the gods for creating such a devilish piece of software, I decided to track this strange mystery to its source. The Help files. Whereupon I learned that I couldn't create a new blank file in Acrobat, but I could convert and import all kinds of things. The moral of this tale? You still can't create a new blank file in Acrobat, but you can do a whole lot of fancy stuff with files from darn near anywhere else.

The fascinating thing about using this technology is the versatility. Remember how Forrest Gump said his momma told him life was like a box of chocolates? So is Acrobat. In this box, you have an assortment of little packages that all look the same. They are composed of different elements cooked up in a number of ways, wrapped in the same sweet stuff, and taste (or work) equally well. But enough of the "Death by Chocolate" references. The point is that you can use several methods to create PDF files using material from different sources, which is the focus of this chapter.

Some of the options are truly one-click easy. Some applications, such as Adobe's FrameMaker, PageMaker, InDesign, and Photoshop, have a Save As PDF option. In other instances, you will have to use a two-phase approach. The options are as follows:

- Exporting a file as a PostScript file and converting it with Acrobat Distiller

- Printing to Acrobat Distiller

- Using the PDFWriter (Windows only)

- Using the Adobe PDFMaker 5 macro

Creating PostScript Files

What happens if the application you are working in doesn't let you create a PDF file? Fear not. If you can create a PostScript file, you can create a PDF file from it with Distiller. PostScript files require an AdobePS driver and an Acrobat Distiller PostScript printer description (PPD), both of which are autoinstalled when you install Acrobat.

Creating PostScript files is different in Windows than in Mac OS systems. I'll outline the process for each.

Creating a PostScript File in Windows

First, let's look at how to create a file from a Windows application. In some applications, it might take a bit of configuring.

1. Make sure the document is open in the application it was created in.

2. Select File ➤ Print. The Print dialog box will open.

3. From the list of printers, select Acrobat Distiller, which is generally the default PostScript printer. (Depending on the program, you may have to open the Setup dialog box to select the printer from the list.)

4. Click either Print To File or Save To File.

5. In the Save As dialog box, name the file and storage location. Use the .ps file extension (PostScript).

6. Click Print or OK.

Now let's have a look at the same process on a Mac.

Creating a PostScript File in Mac OS

As I mentioned, the process is a bit different on a Mac. Here's how to do it:

1. You must have a default PostScript printer set up with the AdobePS printer driver. If you don't, select Chooser ➤ AdobePS Printer Driver ➤ PostScript Printer. Click Setup, click Select PPD, and then choose Acrobat Distiller from the list. Click Select, and then click OK. Close the Chooser.

2. With the document open in its original application, select File ➤ Page Setup. Select the PostScript printer from the Format For menu and click OK.

3. Select File ➤ Print and select Save As File.

4. From the Format menu, select PostScript Job. Click Save.

5. In the Save As dialog box, name the file and storage location. Use the .ps file extension (PostScript).

Workflow Tip

I Can't Print to File. What's the Deal?

If you are printing to Acrobat Distiller, you must send the fonts to Distiller. Click Properties in the Print Setup dialog box for the Acrobat Distiller printer. Then, verify that the option Do Not Send Fonts To Distiller is deselected on the Adobe PDF Settings tab of the Acrobat Distiller Properties dialog box.

Creating Adobe PDF Files from PostScript Files

Once your file has been converted to a PostScript file, the second stage is to run it through Distiller. Here's what you do:

1. Launch Acrobat Distiller.

2. Select File ➤ Open, and browse to the location of the file to be converted.

3. Click Open, and enter a name and location for the file.

4. Click Save. If you hold down the Shift key (or Option on the Mac) and click Save, the PDF file output will have the same name as the PostScript file and will be stored in the same folder.

Creating PDF Files Using PDFWriter

In Windows, Acrobat can create PDF files using either PDFWriter or Distiller. PDFWriter, which is a printer driver, converts files directly to PDF from within another application. Use PDFWriter when

- Your machine is RAM-challenged.

- You are time-challenged (PDFWriter is faster than Distiller).

- The document being converted is simple and doesn't have any EPS (Encapsulated PostScript) graphics.

Follow these steps:

1. With the document open, select File ➤ Print.

2. Select Acrobat PDFWriter from the Printer Name menu.

3. Choose any of the usual options: page range, number of copies, and so forth.

4. Click OK. The Save As dialog box will open.

5. Add the name and location for the PDF file.

6. Edit information about the document by clicking the Edit Document Info button. The dialog box shown in Figure 3-1 will open.

7. Click Save.

Note

Clicking the View PDF File option in the dialog box will automatically open the file in Acrobat when it has been processed.

Workflow Tip

Why Bother to Edit Optional Information?

Because it can save you a lot of time. Suppose you have a series of files all with similar names. If you take a few seconds when saving the file originally to add a subject, this information is displayed when you are browsing for the file. I show a section of my Windows Explorer layout in Figure 3-2. Because I added a subject to the document information, by hovering the mouse over the file name, I can access the information I need and don't have to open all the files to find the one I need.

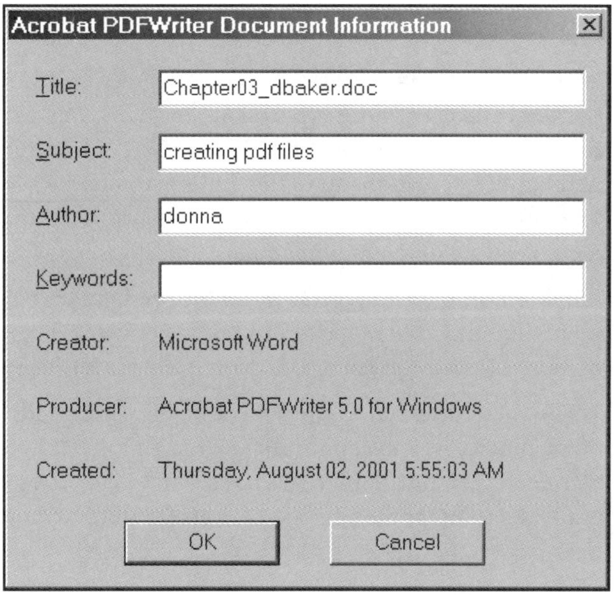

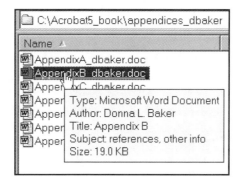

Figure 3-1
The Document Information
dialog box. Use it.

Once the file has been saved, including optional information, you can access it in the usual fashion using Windows Explorer, but you'll now be able to see the information you added, as shown in Figure 3-2.

Figure 3-2
Information displayed for a file in Windows Explorer

Converting Microsoft Office Files

For the ultimate in luxurious file conversion, try the custom macro, Adobe PDFMaker 5. (If this gig doesn't work out, maybe I can write ad copy for a cruise line!) Seriously, though, this is one slick little option. I am currently using it in both Windows 2000 ME and Windows 2000 Professional systems, and with alternate versions of the Microsoft Office applications as well. From both experience and testing, I have found that the processes invariably work.

When Acrobat is installed in Windows, a macro is autoinstalled into the standard Microsoft Office applications, including Microsoft Word 97/2000, Excel 97/2000, and PowerPoint 97/2000. The autoinstall feature adds an Acrobat drop-down menu to the main menu bar, as well as two icons. The icons, shown in Figure 3-3, are used for converting a file to PDF, and for converting and e-mailing a file, respectively.

Figure 3-3
The PDFMaker
toolbar options

I find that in the regular scheme of things, I use this macro function more than any other type of document-conversion method—probably because I have been using Office programs extensively for a while.

The Acrobat menu in Figure 3-4 shows the commands installed as part of the macro. As you can see, the menu contains the commands for the two conversion functions, as well as an option to view the file in Acrobat, and a selection for the Change Conversion Settings dialog box.

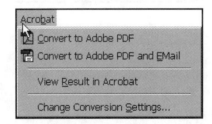

Figure 3-4
The PDFMaker
menu options

Using the Conversion Settings Dialog Box

If you select Acrobat ➤ Change Conversion Settings, a dialog box will open. Let's look at the available options.

The Settings Tab

The dialog box opens with the Settings tab, which is shown in Figure 3-5. On this tab, you can select a general set of conversion settings from the drop-down menu. You can also create and save your own custom settings (which I've done, as you can see in the figure; "version5" is a custom setting. I'll discuss custom settings a bit later). The other feature I want to point out is the Restore Defaults button. If you have made changes to any of the settings and want to restore the default settings, simply click the Restore Defaults button.

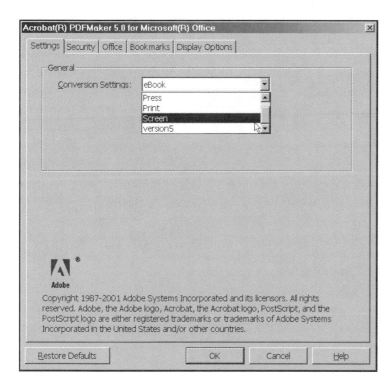

Figure 3-5
The Settings tab. Note
my custom settings.

The Security Tab

Next is the Security tab. Figure 3-6 shows the contents of this tab. Use
this tab to set passwords and permissions. One feature of note is the
level of encryption. As you can see in the figure, you are limited to a
40-bit encryption level. If you are converting a document that requires a
higher level of protection, you will have to use custom settings.

The Office Tab

The third tab lists a number of options, both general and specific to the
application you are accessing the macro from. As shown in Figure 3-7,
the first section lists a number of general options, and the next section is
specific to the program. For example, five Microsoft Word features are
listed; Microsoft PowerPoint has only one feature listed.

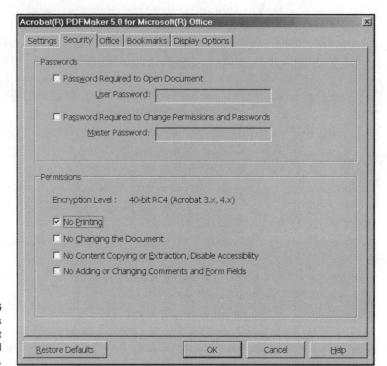

Figure 3-6
Security tab settings in PDFMaker. Set both passwords and permissions here.

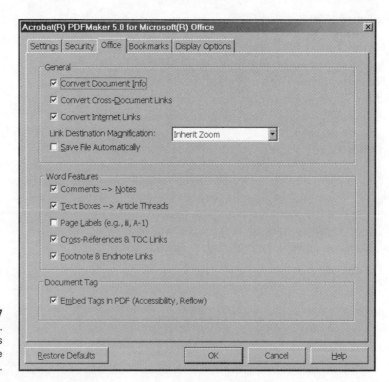

Figure 3-7
Office tab options. The content is specific to the host program.

The Bookmarks Tab

The fourth tab is specific to Microsoft Word. As shown in Figure 3-8, it is used to set Bookmark options. Optional settings include using either headings or styles as bookmarks. This will allow you to readily convert a document and maintain all the advanced settings you have created. Figure 3-8 shows the default settings for this tab.

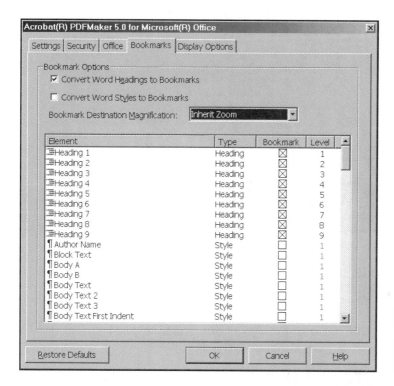

Figure 3-8
The Bookmarks tab options. This tab is exclusive to Microsoft Word.

The Display Options Tab

The last tab is the Display Options tab, shown in Figure 3-9. This tab allows you to control how objects will appear in Acrobat once they are converted and exported from Microsoft Word. Again, the default settings are shown.

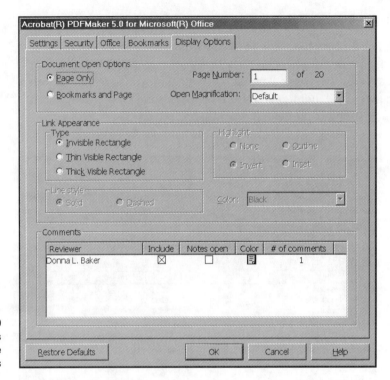

Figure 3-9
The Display Options
tab, with the
default settings

Customizing the PDFMaker Conversion Process

Once you have made your changes in the dialog box, click OK to process and convert your file.

You might be wondering where my custom settings appeared from and how I created them. Earlier I showed you the Settings tab, with my custom settings displayed in the drop-down menu. What you couldn't see in that figure was a button named Edit Conversion Settings hidden behind the drop-down menu. If you click that button, a whole new dialog box pops up, complete with its own set of five tabs to customize the job options.

Rather than go through each tab and discuss its contents, I have condensed the information into Table 3-1.

Table 3-1 Custom Job Options

Tab	Settings
General	This tab lets you set file options, such as using thumbnails, and view Acrobat version compatibility. You can also select page ranges and set page size.
Compression	This tab contains options for color, grayscale, and monochrome images. You can select the downsampling type here, as well as the type and amount of compression.
Fonts	Use these settings to control output file size by setting font embedding commands. Options include embedding all fonts, embedding subsets of fonts (which depends on the percentage of characters used), and listing fonts that you would like to either always or never embed.
Color	This tab contains many settings. You can select from a number of Adobe Color Settings options and color-management policies. You can also define working spaces for Gray, RGB, and CMYK, and make device-dependent data settings, such as overprint and color-removal settings.
Advanced	This tab contains options such as PostScript type and gradient conversion. It also contains several Document Structuring Convention options.

In Table 3-1, I mention that the Fonts tab of the Job Options dialog box is used to control embedding. I have shown a portion of this tab in Figure 3-10 to illustrate an important point (and present a segue into the next Workflow Tip). As you can see in the figure, some of the fonts cannot be embedded, due to licensing restrictions. Take some time when planning your work to review any font restrictions. What's the point of designing beautiful work if the font you have your heart set on isn't commonly available or can't be embedded?

That was a lot of information to read and digest. Let's put some of it to work with our first project.

Workflow Tip
To Embed or Not to Embed . . .

Why embed a font? Quest for perfection, of course. When fonts are embedded, anyone accessing the file can see and print your work as you intended it. If you are using Distiller to convert a file containing PostScript fonts, the fonts can always be embedded. The same can't be said of other types of fonts. What happens if fonts are not embedded? Acrobat has substitute sets of Multiple Master serif or sans serif typefaces. Depending on how the PDF file is defined, the master fonts can be reconfigured to fit and will maintain your line and page breaks. The whole plan can break down with decorative or script fonts, however.

What's the solution? Previewing and good decision making. You can readily preview a file to determine your course of action. With the file in question open, select View ➤ Use Local Fonts. You can then preview and print your document using substitute fonts. Any font that can't be substituted will display bullets and an error message. Try again after embedding the missing fonts.

Remember, it will always be a tradeoff between visual perfection and file size.

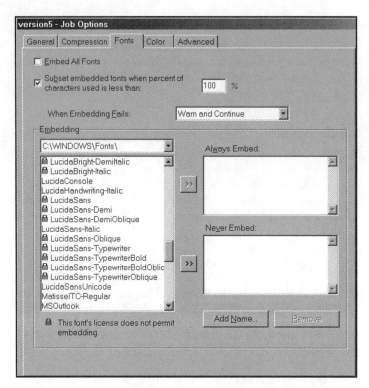

Figure 3-10
The Fonts tab of the
Custom Conversion
Settings dialog box
showing locked fonts

![Project] **Project 3-1. Applying Stage
Makeup: Converting and
Combining Microsoft Office
Files to Create a Manual**

Note

The manual (copyright
© 2001 by Kathleen
Kotchon) was written and
illustrated as a course
project by a colleague
and friend of mine,
Kathleen Kotchon. She e-
mailed me the manual for
my opinion and input, and
she has graciously
allowed me to use it as
the source material for
this chapter's projects.
By the way, Kathleen is a
wonderful actress, as
well as being a great
technical writer.

The projects in this chapter use a manual created in Microsoft Word as
source material. However, there is no Microsoft Word file in the project
for you to work with, for one very specific reason. Look at Figure 3-11.
This image shows a listing in my Windows Explorer. As you can see, the
manual.doc file weighs in at a whopping 20MB. It is not, therefore, on
the CD. What you will find on the CD in the Chapter 3 Projects folder is
manual.pdf, which is a dainty 1MB. You will also need the PowerPoint
file cover.ppt.

Name ▲	Size	Type
🅿️ cover.pdf	56 KB	Adobe Acrobat Document
cover.ppt	531 KB	Microsoft PowerPoint Presentation
manual.doc	20,163 KB	Microsoft Word Document
🅿️ manual.pdf	1,052 KB	Adobe Acrobat Document

Figure 3-11
File sizes for the same document in both their native and PDF formats

Getting Started

Let's first convert the covers, which were created in Microsoft PowerPoint.

1. Open the cover.ppt file, which is located on the CD in the Chapter 3 Projects folder.

2. In PowerPoint, click Convert To Adobe PDF to convert the file.

3. Select a location to store the file and leave the default name, which will be cover.pdf after conversion.

4. Click OK to save the file and start the conversion process. Then, close PowerPoint.

Adding the Manual's Covers

Now we will add the covers to the manual. Along the way, I'll point out some features and conversion issues that we'll deal with later in the book.

1. Open manual.pdf in Acrobat. Look at these features:

   • Note that the Table of Contents is active. This is because it was built correctly in Microsoft Word. That is, it was created using fields, which are converted to active links in Acrobat.

   • Open the Bookmarks tab. Expand the sections. You will notice that in some instances the bookmarks are blank. This is a conversion issue related to the style settings applied in Microsoft Word and the TOC levels attached. A portion of the Bookmarks window is shown in Figure 3-12. This is easily corrected, and we will do that in Chapter 6.

2. Select Document ➤ Insert Pages. Browse to the cover.pdf file's location and select it.

3. Still in the Insert Pages dialog box, select either Before Page 1 or First, and then click OK. Both cover pages will be inserted before the manual's Table of Contents page. The two Thumbnails windows are shown in Figure 3-13.

Note
You may need to alter some conversion settings. Click Edit Conversion Settings to open the dialog box. Make sure that the Embed Fonts option is selected on the Fonts tab and that Convert Gradients To Smooth Shades is selected on the Advanced tab (the cover uses some gradients).

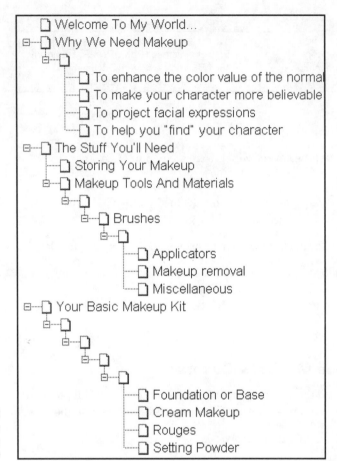

Figure 3-12
Some of the
bookmarks from
the converted file

Figure 3-13
The cover images

4. Move the back cover to the end using the Thumbnails window. Click the back cover thumbnail and drag it to its location at the end of the file.

5. Save the file.

We're also going to add a Web page to this file. But first I'll discuss how HTML file conversion works with Acrobat.

Note

If you do not have Microsoft PowerPoint, a copy of cover.pdf is on the CD in the Chapter 3 Projects folder.

Converting HTML Files

As you saw earlier, there are a number of ways to convert text-based and image files into PDF documents, in some cases maintaining the structure and characteristics of the source file. The same thing can be done with HTML files.

Any file displayed in a browser, whether from the Web or a local intranet, can be converted to a PDF file. After conversion, the file will still maintain its links, and page links can be converted to bookmarks. In this way, the integrity and navigation of the file is maintained. This can all be done in one streamlined process using the Web Capture tool. Before you can capture HTML files, however, Acrobat has to know how to communicate with your browser and the Internet.

Configuring Internet and Proxy Settings

Before you use Web Capture, ensure that you can access the Web by following these steps:

1. Select Edit ➤ Preferences ➤ Internet Settings.

2. In Windows, click the Connection tab in the Internet Properties dialog box and enter the required information. If Microsoft Internet Explorer has been installed on your system, the Internet Properties dialog box is the same as that used to configure Internet Explorer.

3. In Mac OS, select Use An HTTP Proxy Server. Enter the proxy URL and port number in the text boxes.

4. Click Apply to apply the settings and close the Preferences dialog box.

Now let's go get some files.

Downloading Web Pages in Acrobat

It is simple to get Web pages into Acrobat. In fact, there are a number of ways to incorporate files, depending on circumstances. As we look at the Web Capture tool, I'll show you the different options and explain how I downloaded HTML files I have stored locally.

When a Web page is downloaded, many elements are incorporated, including

- HTML pages

- JPEG and GIF files (for an animated GIF, the last frame is downloaded)

- Elements such as tables, links, frames, background colors, text colors, and forms

- Cascading Style Sheets (CSS) information

- Some JavaScript

Let's start from nothing.

1. Open Acrobat. Select Tools ➤ Web Capture (or File ➤ Open Web Page). The Open Web Page dialog box, displaying the default URL shown in Figure 3-14, will open. Enter the URL you want to capture, select a previous URL from the drop-down list, or click Browse to locate a file locally.

Note

Adjust the settings as required. The Levels setting refers to the site hierarchy. The default setting for Levels is 1. But beware! If you enable the Get Entire Site radio button, you may end up with literally hundreds of pages.

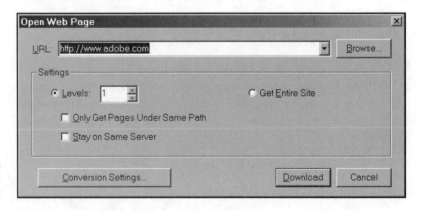

Figure 3-14
The initial Web Capture settings

2. Click Conversion Settings to open the dialog box shown in Figure 3-15. As you can see in this figure, the Conversion Settings dialog box includes both general and page layout options. Most of these items are self-explanatory. Make any setting changes and click OK to close the dialog box.

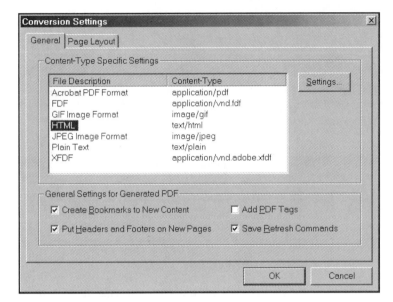

Figure 3-15
The Conversion Settings dialog box for customizing Web Capture settings

3. Back in the Open Web Page dialog box, click Download to start the conversion process. As the file is being downloaded and converted, Acrobat will display a Download Status window indicating the progress of the conversion, as shown in Figure 3-16. You can stop the download process at any time by clicking Stop.

4. When the download is complete, the Download Status dialog box will close and the file will be loaded into Acrobat. Select File ➤ Save to save the file.

A sample of the file I downloaded and converted is shown in Figure 3-17.

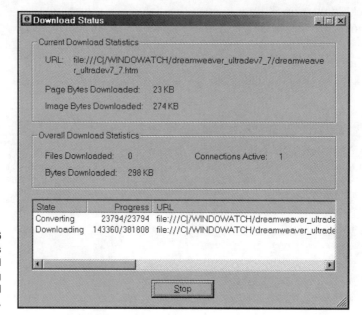

Figure 3-16
The Download Status window. Note the local URL of the file being downloaded and converted to PDF.

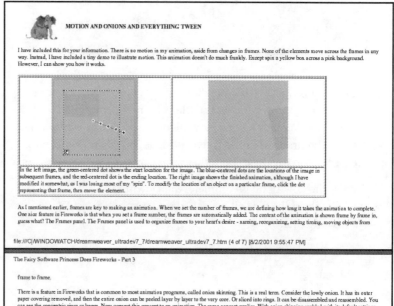

Figure 3-17
Portions of two pages of the converted HTML document

I want to point out some features of the converted file:

- Although you are looking at a grayscale image, the color converted perfectly.

- I set custom page margins to make the page layout more appropriate for printing.

- The table is correctly sized with the right border thickness and color.

- The fonts translated well (as you would expect using a default HTML font).

- The default settings include a header and footer. The header is the page's title, and the footer includes the file's location, as well as the date and time downloaded.

- I added page numbers, which are included in the footer in a "page x of y" format.

- The little elephant image is the final frame of an animation—his trunk is not actually cut off.

Once a file is open in Acrobat, either from the Web Capture process or elsewhere, the remaining commands become active on the Web Capture submenu, which is shown in Figure 3-18.

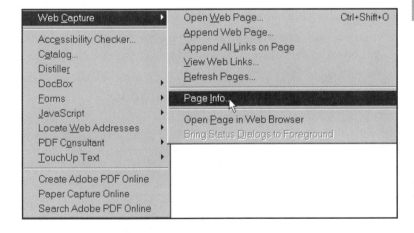

Figure 3-18
The Web Capture tool options

I want to discuss two other areas of Web Capture tool function: appending pages and Web links.

Workflow Tip

If the Preferences Are Self-Explanatory, Then Why Show the Dialog Box?

Well, I am glad I asked. You see that Reset Conversion Settings To Defaults button at the bottom of the box? If you are doing a fair number of HTML file conversions, you will likely find the default settings are usually fine. On those occasions where you have to modify the settings, however, it is much simpler to open this one dialog box and click this one button than to open all the conversion settings boxes and restore the settings one by one—only to find out later that you forgot something!

Note

You can also open a link's Web pages in a new PDF document. Right-click the Web link (Control-click on a Mac) and select Open Web Link As New Document from the context menu.

Appending Pages to a PDF Document

You can add a Web page to any open PDF document. When a site is appended to a file, only the top-level page is downloaded. It will be broken into multiple pages depending on page length.

Appending another level to a site previously downloaded and converted to PDF will not download levels already present, but only additional levels. A special group of appending commands deals with links in pages.

Converting a Link's Web Pages

Earlier, I mentioned that links are downloaded along with the other information in an HTML file. Acrobat refers to these as Web links. The Web Capture tool provides two options. You can either download and append the links directly or view the links first. Once the files are downloaded, links in the original PDF file are changed from Web links to internal hyperlinks.

There are several methods of appending a link's page to your current document. The one I use most often is the simplest. Move the pointer over a Web link, right-click the link (or Control-click on a Mac), and select Append To Document from the context menu. This is perhaps the simplest way to move through a series of links in a document and screen out what you want to attach from what you don't.

Alternatively, you can select Tools ➤ Web Capture ➤ View Web Links to open a list. Select the links you want to download and click Download.

What if you want the whole works? Still simple. Select Tools ➤ Web Capture ➤ Append All Links On Page.

Setting Web Capture Preferences

As with other functions, you can set Web Capture preferences. You access the preferences by selecting Edit ➤ Preferences ➤ Web Capture. The dialog box shown in Figure 3-19 will open. The preferences are self-explanatory.

We have looked at how to download and convert files and configure the process to meet work requirements. Time to put some of that into practice.

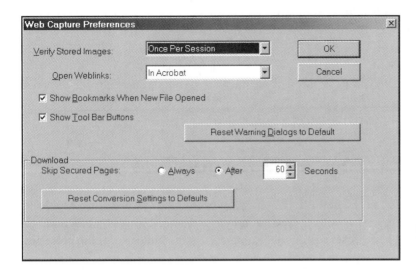

Figure 3-19
The Web Capture
Preferences dialog box

Project   Project 3-2. Converting HTML Files to PDF Documents

This project picks up where Project 3-1 left off. You will need the finished output from that project. If you chose not to do that project, no matter. Start with the manual.pdf file on the CD in the Chapter 3 Projects folder. The file doesn't have the covers attached, but it will work for this project just as well. I have included a copy of the finished project on the CD in the Chapter 3 Projects folder; it is named manualB.pdf.

1. Open the manual.pdf file you saved earlier, or open the copy on the CD.

2. Move to the Bibliography page. We will attach the first level of the Web site referenced in the Bibliography.

3. Using the Text Select tool on the Basic Tools toolbar, click and drag to select the URL. Copy it.

4. Select Tools ➤ Web Capture ➤ Append Web Page.

5. Paste the URL you copied into the URL line at the top of the dialog box.

6. Click Download. The Download Status window will appear. When the download is complete, it will close.

7. The downloaded page will now be listed in your Thumbnails window as the last page (appended files are always at the end).

Note

You can test the link on the page. Clicking a link will activate the Download Status window and bring in more pages. These pages will be appended to your document. Delete them after testing.

8. In the Thumbnails window, click the Web page and drag it into the location before the back cover.

9. Save the file.

This chapter's phase of the makeup manual project is complete. So far we have converted the files, combined files, and added a Web page. Up next: scanning files into Acrobat.

Importing Scanned Files

In the last of this three-part journey into discovering sources for PDF files, we now turn to scanning processes—first words and then images. I will discuss scanning documents, but the image-scanning processes also apply to digital camera images.

Scanning Paper Documents

The key to scanning is a driver—specifically, a TWAIN scanner driver. Nearly all scanners are now TWAIN-compliant. You scan into Acrobat using a plug-in, appropriately called Acrobat Scan. Here's how to add a scanned paper document:

1. In Acrobat, choose File ➤ Import ➤ Scan. The dialog box shown in Figure 3-20 will open.

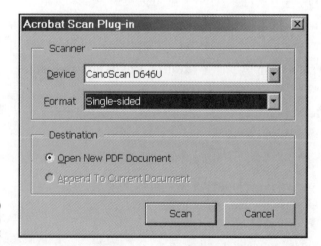

Figure 3-20
The Acrobat Scan
Plug-in dialog box

2. Choose the scanner device and page format from the drop-down lists.

3. Select a destination. You may either add the scanned pages to the end of an open PDF document or open a new file. As you can see in Figure 3-20, since I had no open file, I don't have the second destination available.

4. Click OK.

5. When your scanner's interface launches, set the options you require.

6. Follow the process for your scanner to complete the scan.

7. Click Done (this button will appear in the dialog box after the first page is scanned). Save your PDF file.

Let's look at a couple of outcomes from scanning a document into Acrobat. Figure 3-21 shows a page from this very chapter that I printed and scanned into Acrobat. Aside from the fact that it is crooked and muddy, it is also useless in this format. What has been scanned in is an image—a bitmap, to be specific. Wonderful for an image, but not if I want to do anything with the information.

Note

Even if you install a TWAIN driver after installing Acrobat, the new driver will appear in the menu. To install an Acquire plug-in, add the plug-in to the Plug-ins folder in your Acrobat Scan folder.

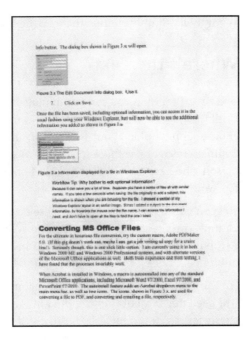

Figure 3-21
The scanned page

Need proof that it is an image? First of all, none of the text-manipulation tools are active. Second, I extracted the image(s) from the file. The results are shown in Figure 3-22. And no, this isn't just a copy of the earlier image! This is a bona fide extracted JPEG file.

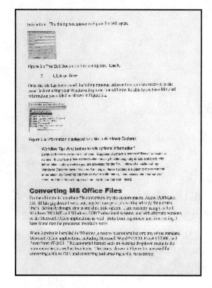

Figure 3-22
The image extracted from the scanned page. What's the deal? It's all image.

What to do? Simply change the way the document is captured.

Where's the Text?

Text isn't text unless you can manipulate it, tag it, index it, change it.... Until then, it is just an *image* of text. To make text *text*, you have two choices: Either upload your scanned document to the Create Adobe PDF Online service or use the Adobe Capture plug-in. Being the kind of person who likes to do things myself, I opted for the plug-in. But first, a few words about the online service.

You can access the online service by selecting Tools ➤ Create Adobe PDF Online. The Create Adobe PDF Online Web site will launch in your Acrobat window. Follow the on-screen instructions. Remember, this is not a free service.

For those who prefer to do the conversion "at home" so to speak, you will need the Acrobat Capture plug-in. The plug-in is used for optical character recognition (OCR). Basically, it translates images of text and tries to substitute words and characters. The plug-in is available at http://www.adobe.com/products/acrobat/pluginreg.html. Make sure you have a good Internet connection—the plug-in is 14.3MB.

Note
I found the Acrobat Capture download and installation process very simple and sleek. And error-free. I have installed it in two different operating systems, and I have not experienced any difficulties using it.

Once the plug-in is downloaded and installed, it will appear in the Tools menu as the option Paper Capture. You will also find information about it in by selecting Help ➤ About Adobe Acrobat Plug-ins. By the way, a Help file on the plug-in is also available in PDF format.

Now let's go back to the original page.

Capturing Pages

Even the functions sound different. Scanning is passive. Capturing is very active. Here's how to do it. I started with my same crooked page open in Acrobat.

1. Select Tools ➤ Paper Capture. The dialog box shown in Figure 3-23 will open. Select the desired Pages options (I have only one page). The plug-in has a 50-page capture limit.

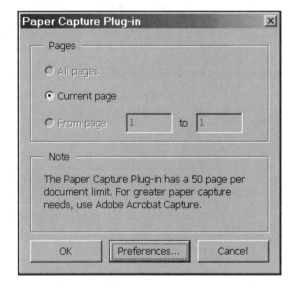

Figure 3-23
The Paper Capture Plug-in dialog box

2. Click the Preferences button to modify any of the capture settings. The preferences are shown in Figure 3-24.

3. Click OK in the Preferences dialog box to close it and return to the Paper Capture Plug-in dialog box. Click OK to start the capture process.

4. The plug-in will rasterize the page and then perform a number of page recognition and structure processes. Be patient!

5. When the process is complete, the dialog box will close, and Acrobat will redraw the page. Save the file.

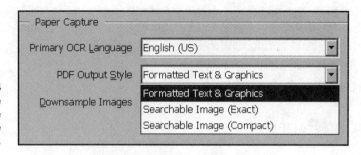

Figure 3-24
The Paper Capture
preferences. The
PDF Output Style
options are shown.

Not the Usual Suspects

You will still have to contend with a number of issues before the page is ready for final output. Primarily, you may have to make corrections. Remember, the plug-in "reads" bitmaps of text and tries to substitute words and characters for the bitmaps. Acrobat will mark any words as suspect when it isn't sure of the translation. Here's how this process works:

1. Select Tools ➤ TouchUp Text ➤ Show Capture Suspects. Any words flagged as suspect will be outlined by a red box.

2. Select Tools ➤ TouchUp Text ➤ Find First Suspect. The first suspect word is highlighted on the page, and its original bitmap image appears in the Suspect Image window. Figure 3-25 shows a block of text from my demo.

Figure 3-25
Text on the captured page
showing suspect text

3. Click Accept to accept the change, or click Next to skip to the next suspect. To change the spelling, select the TouchUp Text tool and edit the word on the page. Then click Next to move forward.

4. Close the Suspect Image window when you have finished by clicking the X in the upper-right corner of the window.

I want to conclude the discussion for this chapter with a bit more information on the TouchUp Text tool.

More on the TouchUp Text Tool

As you could see in my example, once the page had been captured more work had to be done. Although it generally translated well, there may be times when the work begins *after* you run through the suspect list. Here are a few hints for using the TouchUp Text tool:

- The TouchUp Text tool makes changes line by line only.

- Text attributes can be modified (except for the Font and Embedding attributes).

- If a font is installed on your system and is not embedded, you can change characters.

- You can unembed an embedded font.

- You can set text appearance, including font, size, fill and outline colors, scale, baseline shift, tracking, and spacing.

Up Next

The mystery is solved! In this chapter, I discussed PostScript files and the various PDF printer options. We have looked at importing files from different sources, including Microsoft Office applications. I also described how to capture Web pages as well as scanned pages.

Once a file is safely into Acrobat, you can apply many functions, and it can be converted to numerous types of output. The problem is, once you have imported, modified, converted, and exported, what happens to all your hard work? Well, nothing, if the document is secure. And that, coincidentally, is the subject of the next chapter: security.

Workflow Tip
When You Suspect There Are Too Many Suspects

Let's face it. In this example, there was a lot of work to be done. Where possible, get a PDF version of the original document. Not only will it have all its tags attached, but also the suspect correction process will be moot. In those circumstances where you cannot get the original document, however, it can sure beat re-creating it from scratch!

Workflow Tip
Line by Line Can Be a Drag

The TouchUp Text tool is used to edit text. This is true. It is also true that it only works one line at a time. Editing large amounts of text is not an efficient use of your time. Instead, edit the document in the program where it was created originally, then re-create the PDF file, or part of the file. If a segment of the PDF file you created initially is fine, just regenerate the corrected pages and insert them as required.

Chapter 4

Making Your Documents Secure

A lot of effort goes into creating the complex documents we work with every day—images, text, drawings, information of all types. It's important to protect a document's integrity, and it's equally important to control access to a document. Let's look at how to make your documents secure on all fronts.

Protecting Your Work

If you have been reading along since the beginning of this book, you may recall that in Chapter 1, I waxed enthusiastic about the enhanced security features available in Acrobat 5. In this chapter, I will examine all the security features at your disposal and show you how they work. We will encrypt files, lock documents, build and share signatures, and create and share certificates. Sounds like a lot, and it is.

We will deal primarily with the security features installed with Acrobat 5. Because a number of security systems integrate with Acrobat, I'll mention those at the end of the chapter as well. You will find much more information on the third-party security systems on the Acrobat 5 installation CD.

Basically, I will cover four separate processes:

- Protecting a document using passwords

- Protecting content and manipulating aspects of a document

- Adding signatures to a document to identify creation or modification operations

- Sharing documents with others using certificates

The first process attaches password protection to a file. The second deals with granting the recipient different levels of permission to modify a document. The third process deals with signing documents to verify the content and status of a document. Finally, the sharing process entails distributing signature information to specific recipients so they can verify that you are who you say you are.

Acrobat 5 uses 128-bit RCA encryption technology, which is a format created by RSA Data Security, Inc. This is a good thing because you can provide varying levels of control over access to the document's components. On the other hand, if you are sharing documents and want recipients not using Acrobat 5 to have rights to a document's content, that can be a bad thing. Fear not. In circumstances where this might be a factor, you can optionally choose to encrypt a document with 40-bit RC4 encryption, which is compatible with Acrobat 3.*x* and 4.*x*.

The final security dimension is the use of digital signatures. Through a system of signature authentication between a creator and users, document authenticity can be monitored. This applies to the original document as well as versions. In addition to enhancing overall document security, you can view different versions of a document based on signature. Information about your digital signature can be shared with a select list of people who can, in turn, read the protected files you send them.

We will delve into each of these areas. But first, a few explanations on security concepts in general.

What Does a "Secure Document" Really Mean?

Security in a digital world is akin to home security. Just as you lock your doors or have passwords for your alarm system, so too do you lock a file or encrypt it. Acrobat 5 can protect documents by using two levels of passwords. Depending on which version of the software you are using, you have access to different levels of protection. Let's have a look at them.

The earlier versions of Acrobat used 40-bit RCA encryption. Using a few different methods we will look at later, you can protect a document at this level (just as you would lock your door). Table 4-1 lists the options for 40-bit RCA encryption.

Table 4-1   40-Bit RCA Encryption Settings in Acrobat 3.*x* and 4.*x*

Encryption Setting	Prevents the User From . . .
No Printing	Printing the file
No Changing The Document	Making changes, including form field creation
No Content Copying Or Extraction, Disable Accessibility	Copying text and graphics or using the accessibility interface
No Adding Or Changing Comments Or Form Fields	Adding or changing these areas

Acrobat 5 uses a more powerful 128-bit RCA encryption algorithm. As you can see in Table 4-2, the rights given to a recipient can be defined more precisely.

Table 4-2   128-Bit RCA Encryption Settings in Acrobat 5

Encryption Setting	Functions Allowed
Full Access	Allows access to any component of the document, printing, copying, extraction, full access to content.
Enable Content Access For The Visually Impaired	Allows document contents to be copied (required to support the Accessibility feature).
Allow Content Copying And Extraction	Allows selecting and copying of contents.
Changes Allowed - None	Locks down the file so that users cannot do anything with it.

Table 4-2   128-Bit RCA Encryption Settings in Acrobat 5 (Continued)

Encryption Setting	Functions Allowed
Changes Allowed - Document Assembly Only	Allows users to manipulate pages (insert, delete, rotate), as well as create bookmarks and thumbnails.
Changes Allowed - Only Form Field Fill-in Or Signing	Allows users to sign and fill in forms.
Changes Allowed - Comment Authoring, Only Form Field Fill-in Or Signing	Allows users to do everything in the previous two options, plus add comments.
Changes Allowed - General Editing, Comment And Form Field Authoring	Users can access the document for any purpose except content extraction or printing.
Printing Not Allowed	Allows no printing rights.
Printing Low Resolution	Allows users to print each page as a bitmapped image.
High Resolution or Fully Allowed	Allows users to print as desired.

We will spend a considerable amount of time in this chapter discussing signatures: how to make them, how to use them, and how to share them. Before we plunge into the world of Acrobat security settings, I think a couple of definitions are in order, just to round out the background for this chapter.

First, passwords. As everyone knows, a password is a secret word or phrase that allows a user access to a program, system, or file.

Next, encryption. Encryption is translation of data into a secret code. In order to have access to the file and be able to read it, you must first have access to a key or password that will decrypt it. Encryption is done using mathematical algorithms.

Finally, public-key encryption. This is not so much a separate definition as a subset of encryption in general. Acrobat uses the RC4 algorithm, developed by RSA Data Security, Inc. This encryption device is based on the fact that there is no simple way to factor very large numbers. As a result, deducing an RSA key is extremely time-consuming and uses a lot of processing power. The RSA algorithm is the de facto standard for encryption, especially for data transmitted by Internet methods.

Public-key encryption, as we will see later, requires two keys: a *public* key and a *private* key. If I want to send you a secure message, I use your public key to encrypt the message. When you want to decrypt the message, you use your private key. With the public-key system, only a public key can be used for encryption, and only a corresponding private key can be used for decryption.

Now let's see how to actually do some of these things in Acrobat.

Security Settings

Passwords can be set at "user" and/or "master" levels. They can be added to a file through either Distiller or Acrobat. Coming up, we'll look at the processes.

First, a few rules on passwords:

- Passwords can be added at any time—either at file creation or whenever you save the file in Acrobat.

- A PDF file with both user and master passwords can be opened by using either password.

- Opening a file with a user password will temporarily disable any security restrictions set in the file.

- Passwords can use any characters, but they are case-sensitive.

Let's look at an example of how these rules work, and then I'll show you how to add passwords.

Adding Security to a PDF File

I mentioned that security can be set in Distiller or in Acrobat. Here's how:

1. Open the Security dialog box.

   - From Distiller: Open Distiller, then select Settings ➤ Security. The dialog box shown in Figure 4-1 will open.

   - From Acrobat: Select File ➤ Document Security. The dialog box shown in Figure 4-2 will open. Select Acrobat Standard Security from the Security Options drop-down list. The dialog box shown in Figure 4-1 will open.

2. Enter your passwords in the User Password and Master Password boxes. Click the check box next to the option to activate the option.

3. Choose the security settings desired based on encryption level. The options were listed earlier in Tables 4-1 and 4-2.

4. Click OK to close the dialog box and then save the file. If you have added security to a document that was previously unsecured, the dialog box shown in Figure 4-3 will open.

5. Retype your password. If you have set both levels of password protection, the dialog box will be displayed twice. Click OK.

Workflow Tip
Protecting Your Work

If you are like me, and I am willing to bet there are lots of designers reading this who are, you become quite protective of your work. It's not that we don't want people to *see* it; we just don't want anyone *wrecking* it. Right? The solution is to use two levels of password protection. When you are sharing a file with team members, give them the user password so they can access your file. Set the security restrictions on the content, and add a master password. Your master password is yours. Your client or team member can admire your work without changing it.

Note
Acrobat Standard Security is installed with the typical installation of Acrobat. It is the program's default security handler. We will look at the Self-Sign Security functions later in the chapter.

Note
User and Master passwords must be different.

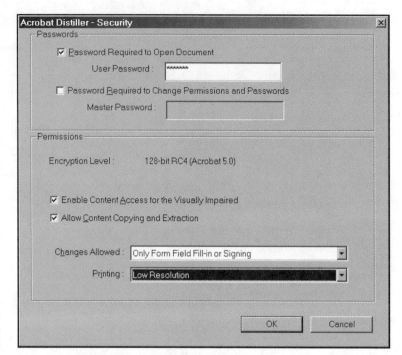

Figure 4-1
The Acrobat Distiller
Security dialog box

Figure 4-2
The Acrobat Document
Security dialog box. The
Security Options drop-
down list is shown.

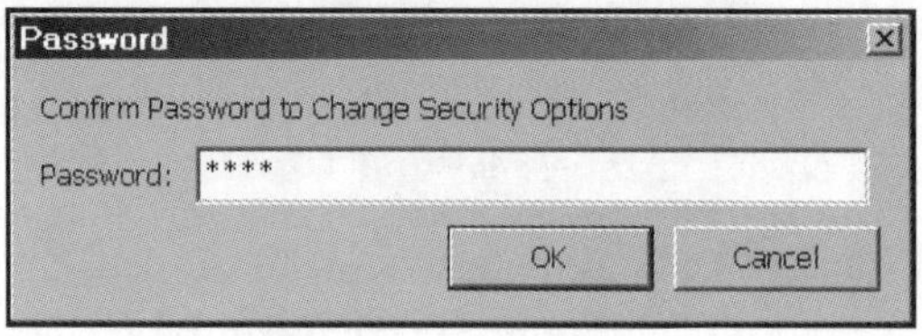

Figure 4-3
You must confirm
all passwords.

Checking Your Settings

Not sure if you set the right permissions on the file? Select File ➤ Document Security to open the Document Security dialog box. Click Display Settings (hidden by the menu in Figure 4-2). The summary window shown in Figure 4-4 will open.

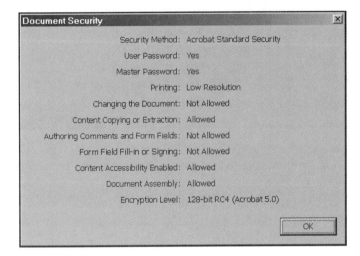

Figure 4-4
Use the Document Security summary to review the settings attached to a file.

This is perhaps more a demonstration of how to actually use the password and security functions and their effects than a project. I think it is important, though, because next we are moving into encryption—which is a whole new ball game.

You will need the file called project1.pdf, which is on the CD in the Chapter 4 Projects folder. If you want to convert the file yourself, I have also included project1.doc and the title file, title.jpg.

Start with the Basic File

Let's start with the unprotected file.

1. Open project1.pdf in Acrobat.

2. Open the Document Security dialog box by selecting File ➤ Document Security. Click Display Settings. As you can see in Figure 4-5, this document is free for the taking, so to speak.

Note

Have a look at the Bookmarks palette. You can see that it lists the column headings. This is because I set these elements as heading styles in Microsoft Word. Acrobat translated these features as bookmarks. The main title is an image, and you would have to set a bookmark for it manually.

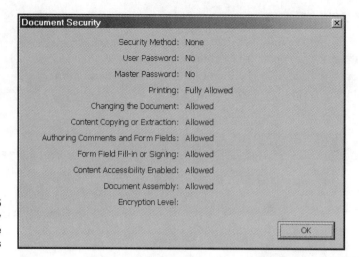

Figure 4-5
The Document Security
summary before we
add restrictions

3. Test some of the features to see how an unrestricted file works.

   • Using the Touchup Text tool on the Editing toolbar, select a line
     of text (as shown in Figure 4-6).

Figure 4-6
The file actions
are functional—
for example, selecting
text for alteration.

Encryption Setting	Prevents the user from...
No printing	printing the file

   • Extract the title image by selecting File ➤ Export ➤ Extract
     Images As ➤ JPEG/PNG/TIFF (select one). An Export dialog box
     will open. Close the dialog box.

   • Test-print the file. Because this is a completely unrestricted doc-
     ument, it should print clearly.

Add the Settings

Now add the security settings to the file.

1. Select File ➤ Document Security. When the Document Security
   dialog box opens, select Acrobat Standard Security from the Security
   Options drop-down list.

2. In the Standard Security dialog box, click the User Password check
   box and type **User**. Repeat in the Master Password box (enter
   Master as the password).

3. In the Permissions section, the default Encryption Level is 40-bit RC4. Click the drop-down arrow and select 128-bit RC4. You will see that the dialog box now has different selections. Make the following choices:

- Click both the Enable Content Access For The Visually Impaired and Allow Content Copying And Extraction options.

- Click the drop-down arrow for Changes Allowed and select Only Form Field Fill-in Or Signing.

- Click the drop-down arrow for Printing and select Low Resolution.

4. Click OK. A password confirmation will appear. Enter the password(s) again, and click OK again. Click the Close button.

5. To apply the security changes, save the file.

Test the Document

Finally, let's test out the password settings.

1. Close the file, and then reopen it. You will be prompted for your password. Enter the user password (in our case, **User**).

2. Test the same functions as listed earlier. You will note that there are no options for exporting images, the editing palette is non-functional, and print output is typically low resolution.

3. Attempt to change the document's security settings. Select File ➤ Document Security. When the dialog box opens, click Change Settings. A password entry box will appear. Try entering the user password again. The message shown in Figure 4-7 will appear.

4. Try again with the master password (in our case, **Master**). Acrobat will accept the password and display the Standard Security window. The settings are now active.

5. Close the dialog box without making changes.

Note

When the file opens, you will now see a small gold security key in the status bar at the bottom of the window. This indicates that security settings have been attached to the file. You can also access security dialog boxes by clicking the key. If you right-click the key, a pop-up label for the applied settings will be displayed.

Figure 4-7
You'll see this password error message. It's not a Caps Lock issue; the wrong password was entered.

The aim of this project was to show you how the different security settings function, as well as how the passwords work. Remember that a file can be opened using either password. Unless you log into a file using the master password, however, the security settings are disabled.

And that brings to an end our discussion of "simple" password protections for a PDF file. Now it's on to signatures.

Acrobat Self-Sign Security

Self-Sign Security is a signature handler plug-in for Acrobat that is installed with a typical install of the software. This plug-in is used for signing documents. Signing documents is a process, not a singular event. When you sign a check or other official document, you add your signature to validate it. In a similar way, a digital signature identifies you as the person signing a document. Digital signatures store additional information about both the signer and the state of the document when it was signed (almost like a snapshot).

Acrobat Self-Sign Security uses a private/public key (PPK) system that verifies both the authenticity of a signature and the integrity of a signed document version.

Once you create a signature, it is associated with a profile. Each profile contains two keys. You use the private key to sign a document. When you attach a signature, the public key is embedded in the signature and is later used to verify your signature. How? An encrypted checksum is stored when you sign, and a public key decrypts the checksum when a signature is verified.

You do not verify your own document. You already know who you are and the state of a document when you signed it. Verification is done by others. In order for other users to do this, you must provide them with your public key, contained in a certificate.

The process sounds complicated, and it is complex. But once I go through the different aspects of the process, you should have a good understanding of the whole concept. Here we go. We will start with how Acrobat uses signatures.

Using Signatures

Along with allowing you to sign a document to indicate completion of some process, Acrobat uses the signature process in a number of other ways. These include

- *Version control:* Once you have signed a document, changes you have made are preserved. You can also return to a different signed version.

- *Verification:* It is often important to know who has done what when you're working in a workgroup. You can verify signatures to ensure the authenticity of what you have received.

- *Management:* By using the Signatures palette in Acrobat, you can locate any version of a document that has been signed. You can also compare two versions of a signed document.

- *Encryption:* You can encrypt a PDF document to distribute securely to specific recipients.

Let's look at the first part of this process (well, after the software has been installed!). The first thing to be done is to create a profile.

Creating Your Signature Profile

A signature handler profile stores a number of items. Each profile consists of several elements, stored in different ways. They are

- Your private key, which is encrypted

- Your public key, which is wrapped in a certificate

- A list of Trusted Certificates, which are certificates others share with you

- A timeout value, which is a time set to determine when you must enter a password before signing

Starting the Process

The first thing to do is start a new user profile. This can be done at any time, whether or not you have an open document.

1. Select Tools ➤ Self-Sign Security ➤ Log In.

2. The Self-Sign Security Log In dialog box will open, as shown in Figure 4-8.

Note

If you have more than one signature handler installed in Acrobat, a preliminary dialog box will open that lets you select the handler. You can optionally set a default signature handler in the selection dialog box.

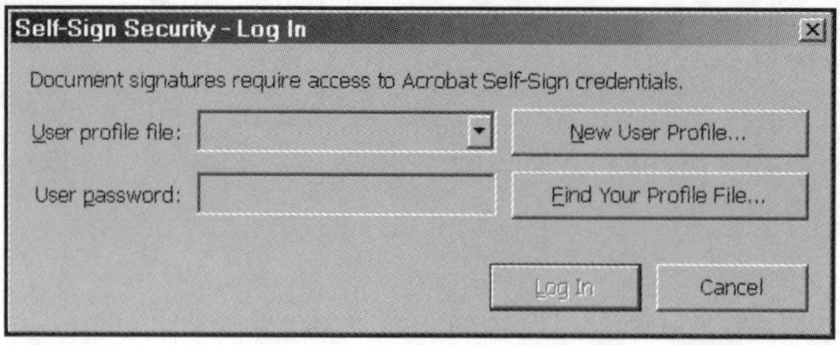

Figure 4-8
The Self-Sign Security–
Log In dialog box

3. Click New User Profile to open the Create New User dialog box, shown in Figure 4-9. Add information as shown in the figure. Only the name and password information are required.

Workflow Tip

Back Up Your Profiles

No automatic backup file is created with new profiles. Once you are logged into your profile, select Tools ➤ Self-Sign Security ➤ User Settings. In the User Settings dialog box, select User Information. Click the Backup For Profile File option. Browse to the location to store the file, and click OK (Backup on a Mac).

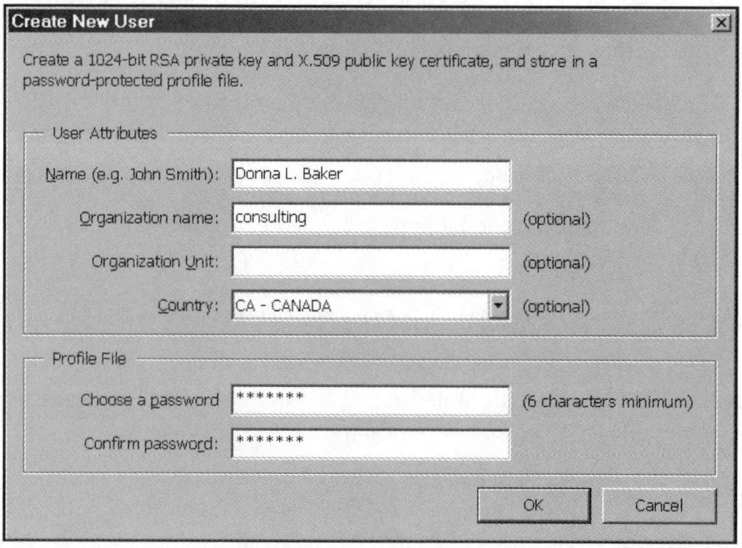

Figure 4-9
Information required to
create a new user profile

4. Click OK, and save the new profile.

Logging In and Out of Profiles

You have to log into a profile to use it. Log out of a profile to change to another profile, or to work on an unprotected document.

1. Select Tools ➤ Self-Sign Security ➤ Log In.

   • If you are already logged in and want to change to another profile, use this command as well. The command changes to Log In As Different User.

   • If you are already logged in and want to log out, use this path as well, and click Log Out<profile name>.

2. Select a profile from the drop-down list, or click Find Your Profile File and browse to find a profile.

3. Enter your password, and then click Log In.

Up next is a look at user settings.

User Settings

Once a profile has been created, you can change the settings. The User Settings dialog box, shown in Figure 4-10, has a number of options. We will look at two of them now. You access these settings by selecting Tools ➤ Self-Sign Security ➤ User Settings.

Note

The User Information panel will display the information entered when you initially created the profile.

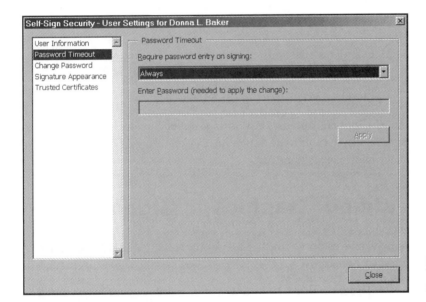

Figure 4-10
The user settings for my default signature

Changing Password Options

You can change a password's options without changing your signature once you are logged in. Here's how:

1. Click Change Password in the left pane.

2. Enter your current password in the Old Password text box, and then enter your new password in both the New Password and Confirm Password text boxes.

3. Click Apply. Click OK to dismiss the alert about your new password.

4. Click Close. You have a new password.

By default, profiles are set to prompt for a password every time you sign a document. That can be changed.

Changing Password Timeout Options

Once you are logged in to a profile, you can select from a number of password prompt timeframes, ranging from specific periods of time to never.

1. Open the User Settings window. Click Password Timeout in the left pane.

2. Choose a time value from the drop-down menu.

3. Enter your password in the text box. Click Apply. Click OK to dismiss the alert about your new password timeout.

4. Click Close. The timeout period has been reset.

Another option from the User Settings dialog box deals with signatures, specifically changing the appearance of signatures. Let's have a look at this option. This can be fun.

Adding Graphics to Signatures

Why would you use a picture or graphics and text in a signature? A number of reasons:

- To personalize a signature with a replica of your handwritten signature

- To add a company logo

- To meet legal requirements (a number of types of information can be displayed)

- To use for different purposes

I have three different signatures to use for different purposes, as you can see in Figure 4-11. I use a generic one for simple documents, one with my signature for more formal documents, and one with a specific look when I want to sign documents as the Fairy Software Princess (no kidding—she even has her own e-mail address).

Figure 4-11
Create a number
of signatures for
different purposes.

Whether you add a graphic or a picture to a signature, the process is the same. Because Project 4-2 deals with creating a custom signature (similar to the middle one in Figure 4-11), I will just give you a few general pointers on using images in signatures:

- You must create the image in PDF format.

- You are not required to size an image to any particular dimensions. Acrobat Self-Sign Security will copy only the picture out of the page, and it will crop or scale the image to fit in the signature field.

- You can give a title to a picture, which becomes the name for the signature.

- You can use Palm Organizer files (this option is grayed out if no Palm files are available).

- You may add or change text that appears with the signature.

- You can change your signature as you would any other user settings.

Enough talk. Time for some action.

Project Project 4-2. Creating a Personalized Signature with a Graphic

Perhaps this project title is a bit of a misnomer. After all, every signature is just that—personalized. In this project, we will use a scanned signature and a graphic to create a custom signature file. There are no CD files for this project.

Sign Here

First you need a signature. I created the PDF file from within Photoshop. Follow the same steps to use Illustrator.

1. Write your signature on a piece of paper.

> **Note**
> You could create the signature block in any program capable of performing the functions, then export it or print it to Distiller. However, I like the automatic features available in Photoshop and Illustrator. The only restriction is that the file ends up as a PDF file, with the image centered on the page.

2. Open Photoshop or Illustrator. Select File ➤ Import ➤ Scan x (depending on your hardware).

3. Follow your scanner's import method.

4. Crop the image as necessary. If you want, add a graphical element on another layer, as I have done in Figure 4-12.

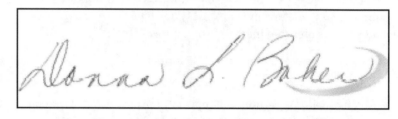

Figure 4-12
My completed
signature block

5. Save the file as a Photoshop (or Illustrator) PDF file, and close the program.

Create the Custom Signature

Now we have a signature block to be imported into Acrobat for a custom signature block. Let's set up the signature appearance.

1. Open Acrobat.

2. Log into Acrobat Self-Sign Security by selecting Tools ➤ Self-Sign Security ➤ User Settings.

3. Select Signature Appearance in the left pane of the User Settings dialog box, and click New.

4. When the Configure Signature Appearance dialog box opens, enter a title for the new signature, click Show Imported Graphic, and click Import Graphic From PDF File.

5. Browse to the location where the image file is stored and select it. It will appear in a sample window.

6. Click OK to select the image and return to the Configure Signature Appearance dialog box, shown in Figure 4-13.

7. In the Configure Text panel at the bottom of the dialog box, select text items you want to appear with your picture. By default, and in my example, I have left the entire list selected.

8. Click OK to close the dialog box. Leave the User Settings dialog box open.

Note

If you are not using a secondary graphic, you can scan the signature image directly into Acrobat. Select File ➤ Import ➤ Scan. Once the scan is complete, save the file and continue with the next section.

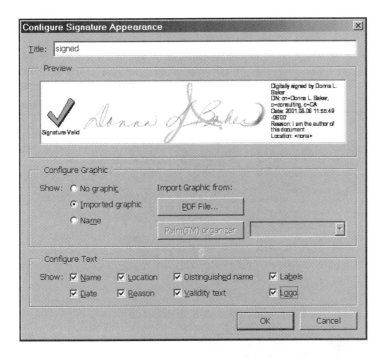

Figure 4-13
The completed custom signature.

One last item, and then this project is finished. You should also create a certificate for your signature (more on that coming up soon). For now, follow these steps:

1. Click the User Information option in the left pane of the dialog box. The user information you entered earlier is listed.

2. Click Export to File. An Explorer window with the default location for storing certificates will be displayed. The file will also have "CertExchange" added to the beginning of the name. Click Save to store the file.

3. An Export Certificate information dialog box will be displayed. Click OK to close the dialog box. Click Close to close the User Settings dialog box. Your custom signature as well as a certificate to share with others is now saved and ready for use.

Note

You can edit or delete pictures, change the graphic, or change text items from the User Settings window. Click Select Signature Appearance in the left pane, and then click Edit. Click Delete to remove a custom signature completely.

Did This Happen to You?

I want to draw your attention to something that might happen when you're using PDF files created in another Adobe program. As I mentioned, I created my signature block in Photoshop. When I browsed for the graphic to insert in the custom signature, one of two different options opened (depending on which trial I was engaged in). Look at the following two figures.

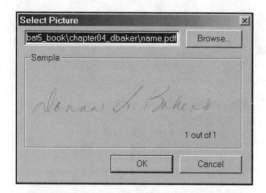

Two versions of the same image. What's the difference?

The difference between the two images is based on transparency. The image on the top was a correct save in Photoshop; that is, once the image was manipulated, I saved it as a Photoshop PDF file. The version on the bottom resulted from opening the Photoshop PDF file, reconfiguring my little rainbow swirl, and then closing it again. When I did this, I neglected to check the image's transparency. In terms of the final output, it will have no effect unless I want to use the Acrobat logo. The logo is placed on the background layer with the signature overlaying it, which covered most of the logo. Make changes to your source document and resave the PDF versions to preserve transparency.

We have created these lovely signatures. Alternatively, we also have the option to use a generic signature. Which begs the question, what do you do with a signature? Read on.

Using Signatures, Custom or Otherwise

Using signatures in Acrobat is the same as routing a document around an office. Each person who receives a document can add comments and sign the document. So too with digital signing. The good thing about a digital signature is that changes can be attributed directly to the person making them, which removes guesswork. Another nice feature of digitally signing a document is that you can look at different versions of the same document sorted by who signed the document and when.

You use signatures in a number of ways and for a number of purposes. In this section, we will look at

- Signing a document

- Signing a document in a browser

- Deleting signatures

- Verifying a signature

- Viewing versions

All this with just one object.

Document Signing Alternatives

Documents may be signed either in Acrobat or in a browser. Here's how to do both. We'll start with basic signing. (I'll assume that you are already logged into your signature profile.)

Adding a Signature

To add one more level of complexity, Acrobat allows a signature to be either visible or invisible. The only difference is that an invisible signature does not appear in a block on the document's page. It is, however, visible in the Signatures palette.

Note

Don't delete a signed page. This will also delete the signature.

1. Select Tools ➤ Digital Signatures ➤ Sign Document. Click OK.

2. When the cursor changes to crosshairs, click and drag to place the signature on the page.

3. The Sign Document dialog box will open, as shown in Figure 4-14.

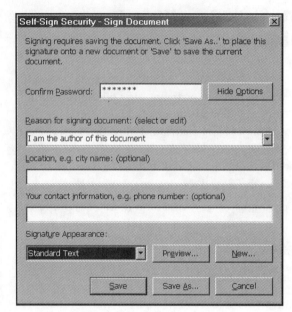

Figure 4-14
Add information and
select the signature
appearance from the Sign
Document window.

4. Re-enter your password. Select the options for the signature from the selections in the dialog box.

5. Click Save. Use Save As to save the file with a different name.

If you want to save a file with an invisible signature, select Tools ➤ Digital Signatures ➤ Invisibly Sign Document. Continue with steps 3 through 5 (you don't have to specify a page location for something that is invisible—logically).

Signing a Document in a Browser

Signing a document in a browser uses a bit different process. A document signed in a browser saves only changes made to the file.

Figure 4-15
Use this signature
tool icon to digitally
sign a document
in a browser.

1. Open the file in your browser. Click the digital signature tool icon on the Acrobat toolbar displayed within your browser (you have no Acrobat menu access). The tool is shown in Figure 4-15.

2. Click and drag to draw a rectangle.

3. You will be prompted to log in. If you have already logged in, the window shown in Figure 4-14 will open.

4. Enter your password for confirmation, and then choose any options you desire for the signature.

> **Note**
>
> If you are already logged into the signature profile, you will not see the password entry window.

5. Click Sign.

6. To save the entire file, click the Save icon on the Acrobat toolbar, and save the file.

Removing Signatures

Sometimes you have to take signatures out. You have two options: Either remove a signature completely or remove the contents from a signature field. Both can be handled in basically the same way:

- *Remove one signature or clear a field:* Click the signature to select it. Right-click the signature and select Delete Signature or Clear Signature Field. (You can also access the same command by selecting Tools ➤ Digital Signatures.)

- *Remove all the signature fields in a document:* Select Tools ➤ Digital Signatures ➤ Clear All Signature Fields.

So these are the options for actually getting a signature into or out of a document. In the next section you'll learn how to prove that you are who you say you are—better known as *signature verification*.

Verifying Signatures

You can verify signatures in one of two ways. Look at Figure 4-16, which shows a portion of the Signature window of a document. Notice that one of the signatures has a green check mark next to it, while the other two have question marks. This indicates that the first signature is valid and the other two are unknown.

Signature ▾
⊞ ✔ Donna L. Baker, 2001.08.07, Valid
⊞ ? Donna L. Baker, 2001.08.07, Validity Unknown (Invisible Signature)
⊞ ? Donna L. Baker, 2001.08.07, Validity Unknown

Figure 4-16
Signature verification display

All three signatures use my profile. I added the signatures to the file, and then saved and closed it. When I reopened the file, what I saw were three question marks. This is how I validated the first signature:

1. I logged into my profile, and then I right-clicked the first signature in the Signature window and chose Verify Signature from the context menu. The same right-click method applies if you select a signature field in the document pane. (Use Control-click on a Mac.)

Workflow Tip

Why Are There Signature Removal Options?

It depends on what you want to do with a signature. If you have added a signature, and then see it was added too hastily, for example, you can delete it completely. If you want to add a number of signatures to a document to coordinate with different functions, you may want to add a number of signature fields that correspond with the different processes. That way, when the signature fields are full, your work is done.

Note

If you do not log into your profile first, you will be prompted when you right-click a signature.

Workflow Tip

Watch Out for Those Signatures

Do not use the Save As command in the regular course of working with a document. If you use it at any time except when attaching a new signature, all other signatures attached to the file will be deleted. If you have to change the name of a file at another time, do it from outside Acrobat in Windows Explorer (or Find on the Mac).

2. Once the program checked the document and signature to make sure nothing had been changed since the document was signed, the check mark replaced the question mark.

The signature has been verified. But what if the signature comes from someone else? This is the second validation method, and it requires user certificates. The next section covers certificates and verifying them.

Viewing Signature Information

All the signatures attached to a file are displayed in the Signatures palette. Their status and the order in which they were added are also shown. For any signature, you can click the plus sign (+) to expand the signature and see other information entered when the signature was added. Figure 4-17 shows expanded information for a signature.

Figure 4-17
Signatures expanded to show data added when they were created

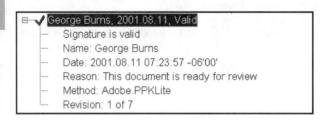

More information is available on signatures, just there for the viewing. Click a signature to select it. Click the Signatures palette drop-down menu and choose Properties. The window shown in Figure 4-18 will open.

Note

You can get information on a specific signature on a page using context menu options. Right-click a signature (Control-click on a Mac), and select Properties from the context menu.

From this window, you can verify signatures and view different versions of the document (more about that coming up). You will also see the text information entered when the signature was created. Click Show Certificate to display the signer's user certificate. Click Verify Identity to open another window showing more information, including the fingerprints for the user identification.

Note

None of this information can be changed in these windows. You can copy and paste it to alternate locations if desired.

Viewing Alternate Document Versions

I noted previously that Figure 4-18 includes an option to view versions of a document. In this last topic about signatures (and hasn't it been l-o-n-g?), I want to explain how to view different versions of a document. I mentioned that signatures are used to create a "snapshot" of a document at the time it is added—or more correctly, an appended version. This ensures that each version is unique and unalterable.

To view the version corresponding to a particular signature, select View Signed Version from either the Signatures palette or the context menu. Acrobat will open the selected version in a new file.

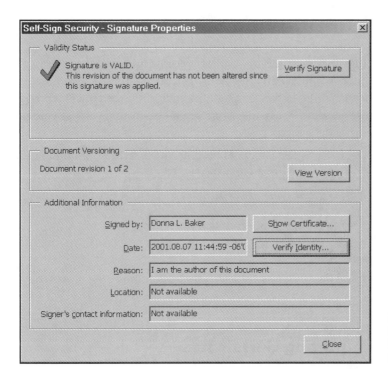

Figure 4-18
Signatures information.
Everything you could
possibly want to know!

Finally, if you want to see a written summary of changes made to a document between versions, select a signature by clicking it. Then select Compare Signed Version To Current Document. A summary window similar to that shown in Figure 4-19 will be displayed in a new file.

Figure 4-19
A summary of changes
made to a document

And that, in a nutshell, is how signatures work in Acrobat. Okay, maybe a giant clam shell.

Sharing Is a Good Thing

This final section is about sharing certificates and the key (no pun intended) to making the public/private key (PPK) encryption process work. Earlier in this chapter I introduced the idea of PPK encryption. I use your public key to encrypt the message, and you use your private key to decrypt it.

We will look at a number of events and activities surrounding sharing and encryption, including

- Importing Trusted Certificates and creating a list of recipients

- Managing your recipient list

- Sharing your certificate with others

- Importing a certificate from a signature on a document.

First up is importing certificates, and then building a recipient list.

Importing Certificates

You cannot add someone to a list unless that person's certificate resides on your computer and is available to the signature handler. Otherwise, as shown in Figure 4-20, it is like hosting a party and not sending out the invitations.

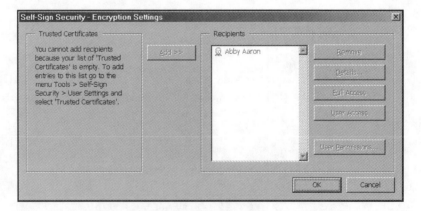

Figure 4-20
You have to add
certificates to your
system to build a list.

But where do the Trusted Certificates come from? Like most things digital, a certificate is nothing more than a specific type of file. This file can be e-mailed to you, or you can access it through a network file process (which Chapter 14 covers). You can even walk a copy on a floppy over to someone—how archaic.

Certificates are stored on your hard drive. When you receive a file, which is saved with an .apf (Adobe Profile File) extension, store it with your other files. On my computer, the files are stored in My Documents\Adobe\Acrobat.

Adding a new certificate is a one-window process. Select Tools ➤ Self-Sign Security ➤ User Settings. The dialog box shown in Figure 4-21 will open. Click Trusted Certificates to open a list of current certificates stored in your system.

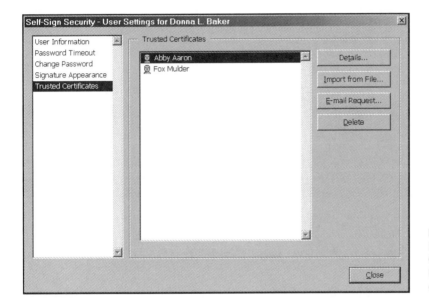

Figure 4-21
My list of Trusted Certificates—at this point, I have loaded two certificates.

To add files, click Import From File (which opens a window that lets you browse for the file), or click E-mail Request (which opens a form that allows you to e-mail someone you want a certificate from).

Building a Recipient List

Now that a list of certificates has been stored, you can access the recipient information when sending a document:

1. Open a file in Acrobat. Select File ➤ Document Security.

2. Select Acrobat Self-Sign Security and log in.

3. In the Encryption Settings dialog box, click a name in the Trusted Certificate pane to select it, and click Add to move that recipient to the Recipients list. Sometimes you may need to change the access rights granted to a recipient on your list.

In the next section you will learn how to manage the contents of your list.

Managing Your Recipients List

You can add, remove, and change the content of your Recipients list. Table 4-3 lists common list-management functions. In all cases, you start from the Encryption Settings dialog box, with the recipient in question selected.

Table 4-3   Managing Your Recipients List

To Do This . . .	Do This . . .
Change a recipient's access level	Click User Access. Change settings as required.
Check a certificate	Click Details. Details on the recipient's Trusted Certificate will be displayed in a window. Click Close to exit the detail window.
Delete a recipient (or more correctly, remove a recipient from a list)	Click Remove, then click OK.

Sharing Your User Certificate

In order for others to access information from your documents, you have to share your certificates as well. Sharing can be done in one of three ways:

- Exporting to a key file

- E-mailing your certificate

- Extracting from a verified signature in a document

Let's look at these three options as the grand finale to this chapter's discussions. In the first two options, you must be logged into Acrobat Self-Sign Security.

1. Select Tools ➤ Self-Sign Security ➤ User Settings.

2. Click User Information in the left pane to select it. The window shown in Figure 4-22 will open. Basic information on the certificate creator is listed in the top portion of the window.

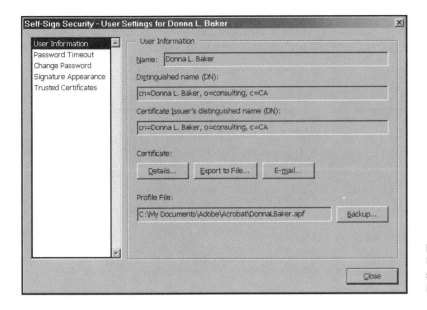

Figure 4-22
Use this dialog box to
share your certificate
information with others.

3. You'll see three buttons in the Certificate portion of the window.

   • Click Details to see all information on the certificate.

   • Click Export To File to save the certificate in an FDF format for
     sharing.

   • Click E-mail to send your certificate to another user by e-mail.

4. Click Backup to save a copy of the profile.

5. Finally, click Close (click Done on a Mac) to close the window.

The last method for getting certificate information is for a signature that
is already on a document.

Importing a Certificate from a Signature on a Document

As I noted, you can choose from three methods of certificate distribution.
We have looked at the first two. The third extracts a certificate from a
signature in a document. Logically, for this process to work, you must
have a document that contains a signature open in Acrobat.

Workflow Tip

Why Does a File Need Fingerprints?

As you can see in
Figure 4-24, two finger-
prints are listed. The
purpose of fingerprints is
to verify the identity of a
signature holder. Because
you can share certificates
easily, and recipients can
extract certificates directly
from a signature, copy and
paste the fingerprints into
a text file, and keep them
for reference. The next
time someone needs
verification of your identity,
simply send them a copy
of the fingerprint file. The
recipient can check the
content of your file against
the fingerprint strings
extracted or received.

1. Right-click (Control-click on a Mac) the signature in the Signatures palette or the document. Choose Properties from the context menu to open the dialog box shown in Figure 4-23.

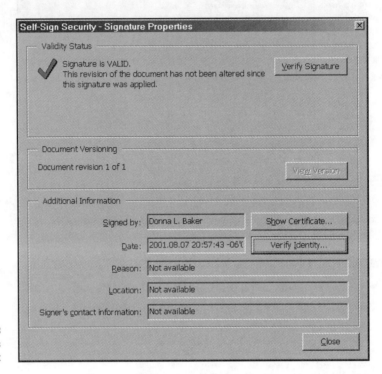

Figure 4-23
The Signature Properties
dialog box

2. Click Verify Signature if required (the signature must be valid for extraction to work).

3. Click Verify Identity to access more information on the signature. Along with stating the owner of the signature, the dialog box lists fingerprints, which are numerical strings. You can access the fingerprints as part of the information in the Certificate Attributes dialog box, which opens if you click Show Certificate. The Certificate Attributes dialog box is shown in Figure 4-24.

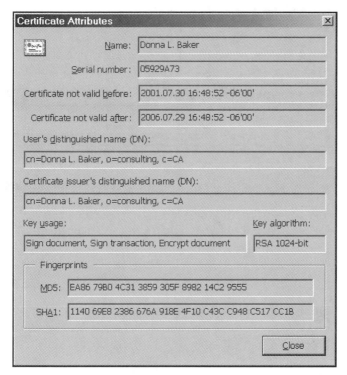

Figure 4-24
All the information stored
in a valid signature

Selecting a Signature Handler

At the beginning of the chapter, I noted that there were a number of different signature handlers. Each of these is a plug-in, and all are supported by Acrobat. What we have used in this chapter is the default plug-in, Acrobat Self-Sign Security. We have seen how to add, verify, and manage signatures using Acrobat's tools. The individual plug-in will determine how the signatures are used and managed. The signature handler used will vary depending on your work environment. For example, the VeriSign signature handler is verified online.

The Acrobat CD contains three third-party signature handler plug-ins, as well as documentation on their use:

- VeriSign Document Signer

- SignIt Document Signer and Server

- The Entrust Security plug-in

Set your default signature handler in the Digital Signatures Preferences dialog box:

1. Select Edit ➤ Preferences ➤ General.

2. Click Digital Signatures in the left pane of the Preferences dialog box. As you can see in the following figure, I have two different signature handlers installed.

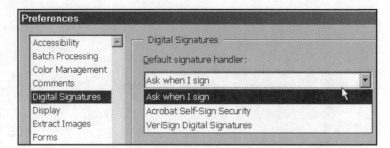

Digital signature preferences with multiple signature handler options

3. Select a default signature handler. The drop-down menu lists all handlers installed in the Acrobat Plug-ins folder.

4. Select Verify Signatures When Document Is Opened to determine if signatures will be verified automatically when a document is opened.

5. Click OK.

I think you deserve a break. Make a fresh cup of coffee, walk the dog, answer your e-mail. Then come back for the third and final project in this chapter.

Project Project 4-3. Creating and Sharing Certificates

In this project, you will create two profiles and then a set of certificates. They will be used in the next chapter when we look at collaborating on documents. You will also need the signature you created earlier in Project 4-2, which will be exported as a certificate.

Note

If you didn't do Project 4-2, there are two "spare" certificates on the CD in the Chapter 4 Projects folder, in addition to the ones created here. These additional files are named AbbyAaron.apf (for one of my dogs) and FoxMulder.apf (for the fictional TV character).

Create the New Users

Let's start with the new users' profiles. Once the profiles are created, you will import their certificates into your own profile for further use.

Monica Smith, New User

I have supplied a file, project3.pdf, which is on the CD in the Chapter 4 Projects folder. It doesn't matter what file is open in the program, however, because no work is being done to anything at the moment. In order to make the processes work, however, *something* must be open, and it must be unsigned.

1. Log into your signature handler. Select Tools ➤ Self-Sign Security ➤ Log In As Different User.

2. In the dialog box, select Acrobat Self-Sign Security from the options drop-down list. When the Self-Sign Security dialog box appears, click New User Profile.

3. You will be creating two new profiles. In the Create New User window, add the name **Monica Smith** (and for the password, use **password**).

4. Click OK. A Save dialog box will open. Leave the default name, MonicaSmith.apf, and click Save to save the profile.

5. Once the profile has been saved, you'll see the alert shown in Figure 4-25.

Note
With password protection for experimental purposes, it is often better to err on the side of caution. Hence the boring password.

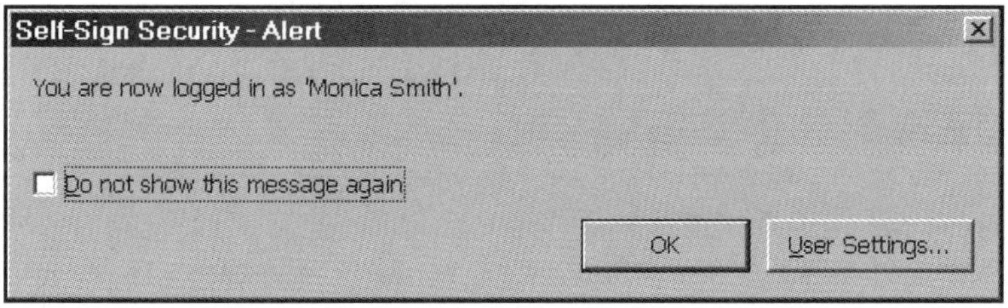

Figure 4-25
Notification of successful login as a new user

6. Click User Settings to open the window. Review the particulars of this new certificate. If you want, copy and paste the fingerprints from the certificate into a text file for storage. Figure 4-26 shows the Certificate Attributes for Monica Smith.

7. Finally, export the certificate for sharing. First, select Tools ➤ Self-Sign Security ➤ User Settings.

8. Click User Settings in the left pane. Under the Certificates portion of the right pane, click Export To File. When the Save File dialog box opens, accept the default settings.

Certificate Attributes

	_N_ame:	Monica Smith
	_S_erial number:	059E2207
Certificate not valid _b_efore:		2001.08.08 10:42:16 -06'00'
Certificate not valid a_f_ter:		2006.08.07 10:42:16 -06'00'

User's _d_istinguished name (DN):

cn=Monica Smith, c=US

Certificate _i_ssuer's distinguished name (DN):

cn=Monica Smith, c=US

Key _u_sage: _K_ey algorithm:

Sign document, Sign transaction, Encrypt document   RSA 1024-bit

Fingerprints

_M_D5:   0675 BBD4 562A 0423 39E0 0F07 651D 6BDD

S_H_A1:   7FFB FDC4 9D68 944E CB16 BD01 0A55 97D8 9214 4F2A

[_C_lose]

Figure 4-26
The certificate for the first
new user, Monica

George Burns, sans Cigar

We also need a second profile, this time for George Burns. In order to create the new profile, we have to log off Monica's settings. The Self-Sign Security menu options are shown in Figure 4-27.

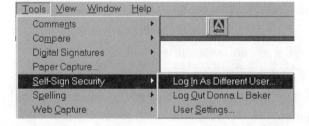

Figure 4-27
Options available to
change users associated
with a document

_T_ools   _V_iew   _W_indow   _H_elp

Comments   ▶
Co_m_pare   ▶
Digital Signatures ▶
Paper _C_apture...
_S_elf-Sign Security ▶   Log _I_n As Different User...
S_p_elling   ▶   Log _O_ut Donna L. Baker
Web _C_apture   ▶   User _S_ettings...

1. Select Tools ➤ Self-Sign Security ➤ Log Out Monica Smith.

2. Continue with the same process as that for creating Monica's profile. Use **password** as the password again (same reason, still boring). Leave the default name when saving the certificate, which will be GeorgeBurns.apf.

3. Export George's certificate using the same process as that for Monica.

Note

You can be logged in only as one user at a time. Log out from a user to clear the Self-Sign Security function altogether, or select Tools ➤ Self-Sign Security ➤ Log In As Different User and choose an alternate profile from the drop-down list.

Working As Yourself

Now you will work as yourself for a while.

1. Select Tools ➤ Self-Sign Security ➤ Log In As Different User.

2. When the Self-Sign Security dialog box appears, click the drop-down arrow and select your name from the list. You should see the other profiles you have created listed as well.

3. Enter your password and click Log In.

In this final part of the project, the new users' certificates will be imported into your list.

Bring in the Certificates

At this point, you should have the certificates belonging to Monica and George stored on your hard drive. You should also be logged into the document as yourself. Let's get the other certificates.

1. Select Tools ➤ Self-Sign Security ➤ User Settings.

2. Click Trusted Certificates to open a list of current certificates stored in your system.

3. Click Import From File (which opens a window that lets you browse for the file). Import both Monica and George into your list. My completed list is shown in Figure 4-28.

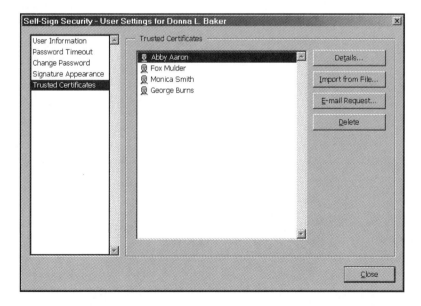

Figure 4-28
The completed certificate list. I also have some extras that were created earlier.

4. To finish the set, log out of your profile. Log in as Monica and then as George and import the certificates into each.

You should end up with three profiles, each holding two of three Trusted Certificates (for example, Monica will have George's certificate as well as yours). Interesting process, isn't it?

Up Next

This chapter has certainly been vigorous, hasn't it? A lot is involved in dealing with security, as we have certainly seen in this chapter. We looked at passwords, both user and master types. We examined different ways to protect content in a document and restrict access to functions. We learned about signatures and created a custom signature; we looked at the Acrobat Self-Sign Security plug-in and all its workings; and we covered the process of sharing documents and ways to distribute certificates.

It's time for more sharing. In Chapter 5, we will look at the processes for sharing the workload—collaborating on documents, as well as editing and distributing documents. I will be introducing a wonderful Web site we will use as source material for the projects. And lest you think you have seen the last of security, we will use the set of certificates created in this chapter as part of the collaborative process.

Chapter 5

Collaborating on Document Creation and Modification

Near the end of Chapter 4, I mentioned that sharing is a good thing. Acrobat 5 masters the concept of sharing a document among a group of people. In this chapter, we will look at collaborative processes—commenting, editing, versioning, and controlling.

Creating a Workflow

You may have noticed that I have been sprinkling Workflow Tips throughout this book. My reason for using these tips so generously has been to make things clearer for you, the reader. It is one thing for me to explain something, but it is quite another to explain how you could actually use the concept in question. It makes for a more interesting and valuable book, and it also makes it more interesting and fun for me to write. After all, along with the click-this, click-that stuff, I have to translate what I am discussing into something you can use in your workplace.

This chapter, which deals with collaborating on documents, may be treated as one big Workflow Tip. At this point, we are going beyond using the program on a solitary basis and will explore using Acrobat for sharing a document with others. Another issue that will come up in this chapter is the fact that there might be a number of approaches to achieving the same outcome. We'll discuss the options as they arise. The goal is to help you work both more efficiently and more intelligently.

What Is Collaboration?

Working on a project with others is a common occurrence. What might not be so common is how the processes you have been using can be converted into an Acrobat workflow. That is the aim of this chapter.

The projects in this chapter are an example of a collaborative process. Here's the storyline: You are The Boss. You are working with two others, Monica and George (who were first mentioned in Chapter 4). The three of you are converting a portion of a Web site into a PDF brochure. This is what happens:

1. You (The Boss) add comments to the downloaded pages and send the file to Monica and George.

2. George extracts the images and inserts them into the document Monica created using Microsoft Word. He converts the file to PDF, adds comments, signs the document, and sends it to Monica.

3. Monica, who revised the original text, reviews the changes, adds comments, and sends it to you.

4. You review their work and their comments, and determine if this is now a first draft of the brochure. You will also create a summary of the activities for reference. You sign it to approve the document going into a draft stage.

Figure 5-1 shows these processes in a flowchart format.

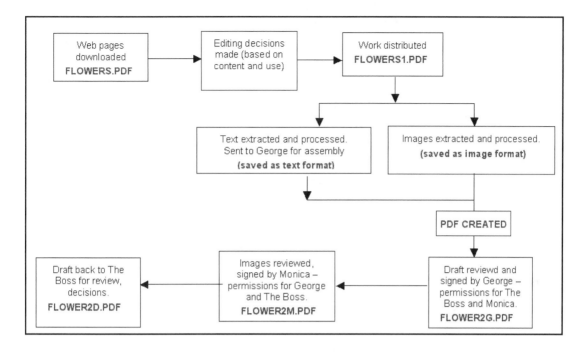

Figure 5-1
An example of
collaborating on
document creation
using signed versions

This is collaboration. Along the way, I will introduce the concepts needed for creating the brochure, including editing, managing versions, and adding security to the file.

So how do you approach working on a document in a group? Same as always. Somebody is assigned a project and provides a general starting point, and then the activities are assigned to the team members. Once everyone has done his or her work, it is all brought together for review. The only difference here is that you don't have to make any copies or walk anything to anyone's desk. We will start with editing.

Using the Editing Tools

Acrobat has a set of editing tools. You can find them by selecting Window ➤ Toolbars ➤ Editing. Let's have a look at them, what they do, and what they *don't* do.

The Editing Tools

Table 5-1 lists the eight editing tools and their primary functions. As you can see, these tools are used for quite a range of functions. Some of the tools are prominent players in other chapters, so I will simply give you an overview of them now. If a function figures prominently in another chapter, I've referenced that chapter in the table.

Table 5-1   The Editing Tools

Icon	Name	Function
▤	Movie tool	Inserts a movie into a document (see Chapter 12)
◉	Link tool	Inserts a link into a document
⟲	Article tool	Lets you create linked rectangles to connect sections of a document and control its flow (see Chapter 7)
⌗	Crop tool	Crops the margins of a page
▤	Form tool	Inserts form elements into a page (see Chapter 10)
T	TouchUp Text tool	Allows you to make minor changes to a document's text
▶	TouchUp Object tool	Allows you to export, alter, and import graphics from Acrobat
¹²₃	TouchUp Order tool	Allows you to change the order of elements in a tagged document (see Chapters 6, 7, and 8)

In this chapter, we'll deal with the three TouchUp tools, the Crop tool, and the Link. I want to start with the TouchUp tools and introduce a demo file I made about my zodiac sign, Sagittarius. Figure 5-2 shows the unedited document.

The document has some simple errors that will be corrected in Acrobat— a text error, a graphic position error, and an inappropriate layout on the page. What a coincidence! These are exactly the things I want to discuss. First, let's look at the text error and how to correct it.

Figure 5-2
The document before touchups are done

Touching Up Text in Acrobat

The most important thing to remember is that you can make changes in either the program you created the original document in or in the Acrobat PDF version. If you are making minor changes, as I will show here, use the tools. If, on the other hand, the changes required in a document are substantial—as the ones in the project certainly are—it is more practical to return to the program that created the original PDF file.

Figure 5-3 shows a block of text from the bottom of the page.

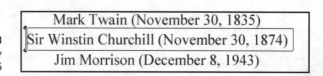

Mark Twain (November 30, 1835)
Sir Winstin Churchill (November 30, 1874)
Jim Morrison (December 8, 1943)

Figure 5-3
Typos—an easy fix in Acrobat 5

As you can see, this text contains a typo. Here's how to correct the error using the TouchUp Text tool:

1. Click the TouchUp Text tool on the Editing toolbar to activate it.
2. Click the row of text to select it. A blue box (as shown in Figure 5-3) will surround the line.
3. A cursor will appear in the line. Click to position the cursor to the correct position in the line. Type the corrected text.
4. Click the Hand tool on the Basic Tools toolbar to deselect the text line.

You can also make changes to text attributes for the line. If you right-click the selected text line and select Attributes from the context menu, the palette shown in Figure 5-4 will open. This palette is especially helpful if the fonts used in the document are not embedded.

Text Attributes
BookAntiqua-Bold
Embed
14.52 pt
100%
0 pt
125
0
179.16 pt
178.2 pt

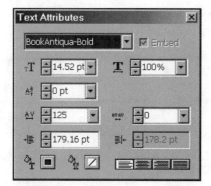

Figure 5-4
Text attributes that you can alter using the TouchUp Text tool

Other text touchups you can do in Acrobat include the following:

- Create an empty line in a document by using Ctrl-click (Option-click on a Mac).
- Remove or add embedding from a font by clicking the Embed check box on the Text Attributes palette.
- Touch up rotated text (the baseline shift will be left and right instead of up and down as for horizontal fonts).

Now let's have a look at the TouchUp Object tool.

Touching Up Graphics in Acrobat

Acrobat has very limited object editing capabilities. What you can do, though, is access the authoring application the objects were created in directly from Acrobat. You can use this technique with line art and images.

Let me show you how to use the TouchUp Object tool. The horoscope document we looked at earlier also contains a layout error. As you can see in Figure 5-5, the two arrow icons are not aligned.

Figure 5-5
With the page grid displayed, layout errors are easy to spot.

Follow these steps to correct a graphic error:

1. Click the TouchUp Object tool on the Editing toolbar.

2. Click the element to be changed. A blue bounding box will appear around the object (as shown in Figure 5-5).

3. Manipulate the object. In this case, I used the arrow keys to nudge the icon into a better alignment.

That's it for this file. You can also use other functions accessible from the context menu. These options are self-explanatory.

What if I needed to reopen the object in an authoring application like Photoshop? I could simply select the object with the TouchUp Object tool, and then choose Edit Object from the context menu—which opens the application. Maybe.

Now let's move on to page layouts and cropping.

Note

You have to assign an image editor in Acrobat. To do so, select Edit ➤ Preferences ➤ General ➤ TouchUp. In the resulting dialog box, click Choose Image Editor and browse to the location of your preferred application. Click OK to select it. You may also set a preference for a page-editing application in the same way by clicking Choose Page/Object Editor.

Cropping a Page in Acrobat

Workflow Tip

What About Other Objects?

On a page, you can select anything with the TouchUp Object tool. That doesn't mean it will do you much good. If you select a word or title, and then right-click and choose Edit Object from the context menu, a temporary file consisting of many pages of code and symbols opens. So how is this a Workflow Tip? If you are not familiar with a document and you're trying to evaluate the amount of work you have to do, you can try this technique on something that may be either text or an image. Making small corrections to text is much faster than modifying embedded images.

The Crop tool is a handy feature. If you look back at Figure 5-2, you can see that the layout of the page is uneven, with margins different on all sides and too much extra space at the bottom of the page. Here's how to fix that problem:

1. Select the Crop tool from the Editing toolbar. Click and drag a cropping rectangle on the page. The handles may be used to resize.

2. Double-click inside the rectangle to open the Crop Pages dialog box, shown in Figure 5-6.

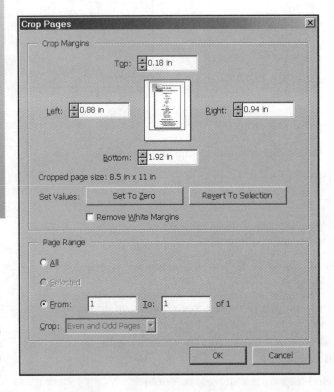

Figure 5-6
Use the Crop Pages dialog box for precise settings or multiple pages.

3. Set required margins by entering a value in the margin's box or using the arrows. The location of the margins is shown on the thumbnail. Other options are available as well:

   • Click Set To Zero to restore margins to 0; click Revert To Selection to return to the values of the original cropping rectangle; or enable the Remove White Margins option to trim the page to content.

- Select page ranges as required. My demo document has only one page.

4. Click OK to set the new margins.

My revised document is shown in Figure 5-7. I have added a border to show you the new layout.

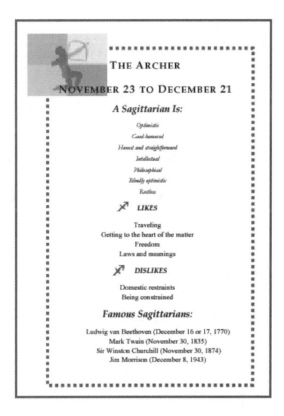

Figure 5-7
The document after cropping

Now let's move to the last editing tool we will be looking at in this chapter. Links will be used throughout the book, starting with a project in this chapter.

Working with Links

The ubiquitous link. Present everywhere you look. Terrific invention, really. Links are immediate. Your readers don't have to scroll through anything, or look for anything, or open a browser—they just click a link.

We will look at these basic functions using links in this chapter. In later chapters and projects, we will take links to their limits—for initiating such actions as submitting forms and controlling other media.

Links are extremely easy to add, and they come in two varieties: visible and invisible. I will show you how to add a link to the horoscope demo file.

1. Click the Link tool on the Editing toolbar. As you move the cursor over your document, you will notice the pointer changes to crosshairs.

2. Click the document where you want the link located. Drag the mouse to create a marquee or create a link the exact size of your text by pressing Ctrl (Option on a Mac) and selecting the text. The Link Properties dialog box will open, as shown in Figure 5-8.

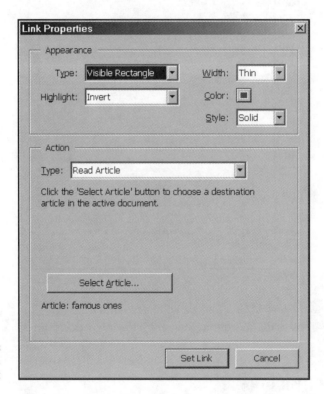

Figure 5-8
The Link Properties
dialog box

3. Select the desired appearance options:

    • From the Appearance Type drop-down list, choose Visible Rect-
      angle (then select Width, Color, and Style) or choose Invisible
      Rectangle.

    • From the Highlight drop-down list, select None (no change);
      Invert (changes the outline color to the opposite when selected);
      Outline (changes the link's color to the opposite when selected); or
      Inset (results in an embossed rectangle effect).

4. Select the desired action. I have three articles created in the doc-
    ument that correspond with the two icons and the bottom block,
    which lists famous Sagittarians. I selected the "famous ones" arti-
    cle. (More on articles in Chapter 7.)

5. Click Set Link to save the link's settings. The inserted link is shown
    in Figure 5-9. I think if I were using this as a "real" document,
    I would likely opt for invisible links, because the frame detracts
    from the layout.

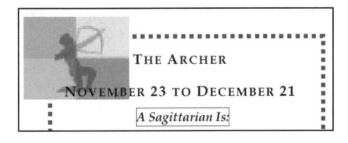

Figure 5-9
The segment of the page
showing the inserted link

Now, just a few words on commenting, and then it's time to introduce
this chapter's tutorial and project material.

Commenting

I described using Acrobat's commenting tools in Chapter 2. I will not
rehash the processes in this chapter, but I will recap what you need to do
the projects. For more information, see the section "Adding Comments
to a Document" in Chapter 2.

Just a few points as they pertain to this chapter's processes and projects:

    • Comments can be customized.

    • Comments can be used to navigate through a document.

    • Comments can be imported and exported.

Note

Because you are one person likely working with one computer and one copy of Acrobat, you will have to log out of a document as one person and log in as another. Just remember that this is totally artificial and for experimentation only. This wouldn't likely happen in a real work situation.

In other words, when it comes to workflow, comments are a good way to organize work. As we will see, because comments are customizable, the three members of our workgroup use different commenting colors. When it comes to organizing your own part of a project, the comments can be sorted based on your participation.

Project Tutorial: Distributing Source Materials

It is important for you to understand the collaborative process. It is not necessarily important for you to add the list of comments I did to create these versions of the file. To that end, I merely want to explain what happened and why, before going into an actual project.

Creating and Commenting the Source Material

If you would like, you may follow along with these processes and create the output yourself. I have made reference to appropriate files along the way, which are on the CD in the Chapter 5 Projects folder.

1. The first step is to download the source materials to be used for the brochure. The content is general information on the farm, its location, and tour and wedding information—general information that a prospective visitor could download from the Wildflower Farm's Web site.

2. The file consists of pages downloaded from the Web site, located at http://www.wildflowerfarm.com. Pages were accessed from three levels of the site and were saved as flowers.pdf.

3. As The Boss, it was my job to initially comment on the document for my group members. I added numerous comments pertaining to content, layout, images, and so forth.

4. I saved the file as flowers1.pdf. At this point the document is still unsecured (that is, it is neither password-protected nor signed).

Workflow Tip

Establish a System

As you can see in the flowers1.pdf file, I have used a system for commenting. All the comments are coded with my color (blue); I have addressed a comment to a specific member of the group as required; and I have used a stamp to simplify some commenting—in this case, one of the pointers, "Nuke This," is used instead of adding a written note.

Figure 5-10 shows page 1 of the document to give you a frame of reference. You can see the overlays of the notes I added to the page.

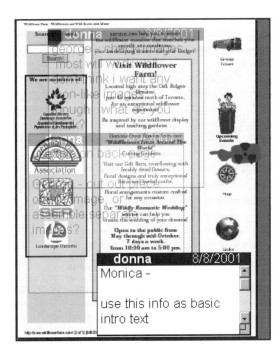

Figure 5-10
Page 1 of the
commented document

Distributing the Comments and the Work

Now that I have added comments and determined how to proceed, it is time for the members of my group to get organized and get started. Rather than sending them copies of the marked-up file, I exported the comments (by selecting File ➤ Export ➤ Comments). I left the default file name, flowers1.fdf, and saved the file. The recipients will open their unmarked file and select File ➤ Import ➤ Comments. The set of comments will then be displayed.

And now for a project.

Note

If you want to try this export and import process, make a copy of the original file, flowers.pdf, open it, and import the comments, flowers1.fdf (all files are in the Chapter 5 Projects folder). You will see it now contains all the comments in the same locations as the original.

Project Project 5-1. Editing and Signing the Document

If you have opened flowers1.pdf and looked through it, you will see that it needs a whole lotta editing. One of the things I would like you to take

Note

To create the revised document, I saved the PDF file as Rich Text Format, opened it in Microsoft Word for editing, and then exported the document as a PDF again. I extracted the images by selecting File ➤ Export ➤ Extract Images As ➤ TIFF. More on these topics in Chapter 6.

away from this chapter is the fact that Acrobat 5 is not designed to do the massive amount of editing required for a document like this.

As a result, we are going to start this project a day after the comment files were distributed to the workgroup. By this time, the document has been revised in external authoring and editing programs and converted to a new PDF file.

For this project you will start with the flowers2.pdf file, which is on the CD in the Chapter 5 Projects folder. When you open the file, you will note that it is markedly different from the flowers1.pdf file.

The Process and Files Created

There are a number of files in this project. I have included the different versions and their stage of development in Table 5-2. All files on the CD have had their password protection removed.

Note

In each case, when the next process began, I saved a version of the file with the new name.

Table 5-2   Files Used in This Chapter's Projects and Tutorials

File Name	Stage of Development
flowers.pdf	The original downloaded Web site pages
flowers1.pdf	The Web site pages with initial comments from The Boss
flowers2.pdf	The reformatted file
flowerG.pdf	The file after George has added comments and signed it
flowerM.pdf	The file after Monica has added comments and signed it
flowerD.pdf	The final file with comments added and signed by The Boss

Working on the Document As George

At the time the document is distributed by The Boss (TB), it is still unsigned. Once George has finished his work on the images and inserted them into the document, he will generate a new PDF file, add comments, sign the document, and then send it on to Monica for placement review and comments. Here are the steps:

1. Open flowers2.pdf.

2. Add the comments as listed in Table 5-3.

Table 5-3 George's Comments on His Draft

Page	Type/Location	Text
1	Note, upper page	I used .2" separation for all images. There are differences in sizes to fit page layouts.
1	Note, image block upper page	What do you think of using this entire block? Should it be rebuilt?
2	Note, upper page over color bar	Color block is subset of main graphic. Top or bottom?
8	Vertical line, last paragraph	I like this extra paragraph—but should it be more graphical?

The document must be signed and saved as another version. In order for this process to occur, George must sign in.

Signing and Saving the Document

Depending on where you are in a document process, you may have to log into a document. In this case, though, since George is the initial signer, he can log in before or after he finishes his work. Let's assume he has finished his comments and saved the document with its initial name.

1. Save the file as flowerG.pdf.

2. Select Tools ➤ Self-Sign Security ➤ Log In.

3. In the dialog box that opens, select the user profile file from the drop-down list (if necessary) and enter the password. Remember from Chapter 4 that George's password is "password". Click Log In.

4. When the Log In alert displays, click User Settings.

5. When the User Settings window opens, click Trusted Certificates in the left pane. Make sure Monica Smith and The Boss are listed. (If not, click Import From File, browse to the certificate location, and select the missing names.)

6. Select Tools ➤ Digital Signatures ➤ Sign Document.

7. Click and drag the crosshairs on the document to create a text block for George's signature. After you log into Adobe Self-Sign Security, add a reason for the signature—in this case, that the review is complete. Save the file again.

The file is now complete with comments, a signature, and rights granted to the other members of the workgroup to open and work with the document.

Note

If you would like to read along with the tutorial and project, there is a final copy of the file on the CD in the Chapter 5 Projects folder; the file is called flowerD.pdf. The file contains all the comments and changes made by the members of our workgroup. In order to open this file, you must first log in as one of the workgroup members. Earlier I discussed how to create George and Monica's signatures. To log in as one of them, select Tools ➤ Self-Sign Security ➤ Log In. Select one of their names from the User Profile drop-down list. Enter the password (all passwords are the word "password"), and then click Log In. Now you can open the file.

Note

As I said earlier, the goal here is to work through a collaborative process. As you are likely working on one machine, you will have to log out and log in as a different person.

Logging In As Monica

Before you can become Monica, you must cease to be George (they make movies about stuff like this).

1. Select Tools ➤ Self-Sign Security ➤ Log In As Different User.

2. In the dialog box that opens, select the user profile file from the drop-down list (if necessary) and enter the password. Monica's password is also "password". Click Log In.

3. When the Log In alert displays, click User Settings.

4. When the User Settings window opens, click Trusted Certificates in the left pane. Make sure George Burns and The Boss are listed. (If not, click Import From File, browse to the certificate location, and select the missing names.)

5. Add the comments as listed in Table 5-4.

Table 5-4   Add Monica's Comments

Page	Type/Location	Text
1	Highlight, over main title	Used custom colors and fonts as per Web site.
1	Note, first paragraph	Is this font punchy enough? Don't want to detract from the images.
2	Note, lower-left half of page	I kept all the content and separated the blocks as in the Web pages.
5	Rectangle, over time and cost block	Should these blocks be bold?

Workflow Tip

Save Time Communicating with Workgroup Members

Figure 5-11 shows another example of using a specific pattern of communicating with other workgroup members. Rather than respond to every comment, you can use a face stamp to indicate that you agree with comments. Where further revisions are required, you can add a note. Also, you will have noticed earlier that George and Monica added their comments as either statements or questions, implying information on some decision they made or asking for a decision on something they were unsure of. Good habits to get into.

Signing and Saving Monica's Document

This approach is a bit different from that used by George, because you would have already been signed into Adobe Self-Sign Security when starting Monica's part of the project.

1. Select Tools ➤ Digital Signatures ➤ Sign Document.

2. Click and drag the crosshairs on the document to create a text block for Monica's signature.

3. In the Sign Document dialog box, add a reason for the signature (your review is complete).

4. Click Save As, and save the file as flowerM.pdf.

Now let's move on to The Boss.

Logging In As The Boss

Repeat the same process you used for Monica. In a real situation, as workgroup leader, it would be your job to review the document, review the comments, add your comments, and sign the document. That is what I have done. To review the comments The Boss added, open flowerD.pdf (*D* as in "done"). The first page of the document, now draft 1 and commented by The Boss, is shown in Figure 5-11.

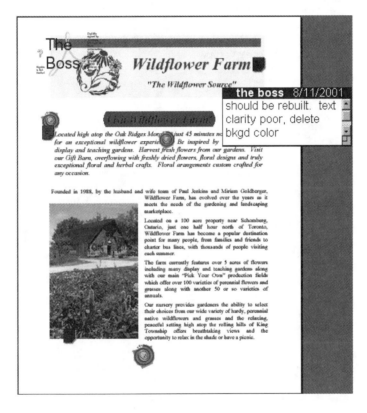

Figure 5-11
Page 1 of the
draft document

Adding Navigation

Earlier in the chapter, I described how links are used in Acrobat documents. As The Boss, you will add a link to connect the PDF file to Wildflower Farm's Web site.

1. Open flowerD.pdf.

2. Click the Links tool on the Editing toolbar. On the first page of the brochure, fence the major heading "Visit Wildflower Farm".

3. Use these settings in the Link properties dialog box (as shown in Figure 5-12):

- *Appearance Type:* Invisible Rectangle
- *Highlight:* Invert
- *Action Type:* World Wide Web Link

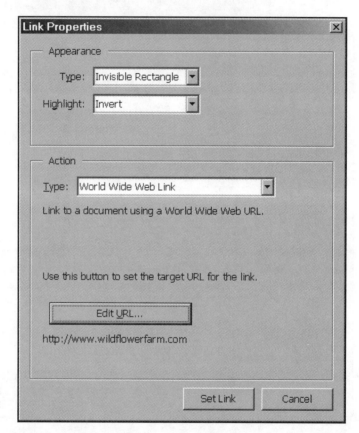

Figure 5-12
Add the details in the Link
Properties dialog box.

4. Click Edit URL. Enter this address:
   http://www.wildflowerfarm.com.

5. Click Set Link.

6. Save the file. You can do a straight save of the file at this time because you are changing neither the login nor the signature.

Creating a Summary of Comments

One last task for The Boss at this time. Create a summary of the work your group has done on the draft to date. You are still using the file flowerD.pdf.

1. Select Tools ➤ Comments ➤ Summarize.

2. Select a filtering option—by page, author, date, type. Leave the default page.

3. Click OK.

The summary will be generated.

We have seen how to create a document that a group of people then modifies and signs. Now let's look at what else can be done with this information.

Workflow Tip

Why Use a Summary Document?

Everybody has meetings. Use the summary document as reference material when you're discussing a project with your workgroup members. Also, the summary document would be a useful reference when discussing client input into a project.

When You See the Big Red X

It's interesting how you can be working merrily along, and something suddenly happens that sends a cold chill down your spine. The Big Red X is a case in point.

I am referring to invalid signatures. Look at the following image. This is a spine-chiller until you understand what is going on.

Name: Monica Smith
Date: 2001.08.10 17:53:41 -06'00'
Reason: This document is ready for review
Method: Adobe.PPKLite
Revision: Corrupt

A corrupted signature. How can this happen to me?

This actually happened. When it did, I naturally assumed that my computer had been hit by some kind of a worm or a virus at the very least, although it happened very quickly and didn't affect anything else. I then assumed, as the program indicated, that the signature file was corrupted. I investigated, and this is where the idea of copying and saving certificate fingerprints comes in. I opened the signature files I had for Monica and George, and compared them with the text file in which I had saved their fingerprints. Alas, the numbers matched. Which led me back to the Acrobat file.

I thought perhaps I just had to try to verify the signature again. The following message was displayed instead of a green check mark on the signature.

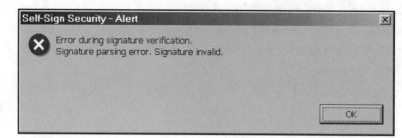

I tried to validate the
signature a second time.
No luck.

As a final recourse, I tried to open a different version of the document. Now I got the
following message.

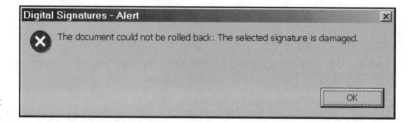

Trying to open a different
version didn't work either.

After wandering about aimlessly, I saw the light. It wasn't that the signature itself was corrupted; it
was that the program couldn't interpret the signature based on what I was giving it to work with.
Here's the problem and how to fix it.

The key to the error, and correcting it, is the way files were saved. If the workflow entails sending a
document from one user to the next, each time someone new logs into the document, makes
changes, and signs it, *it cannot be saved with the same name.*

You are a trusted user of a document. You do what you need, sign it, and save it. If the file is sent
to someone else, who then repeats the process, you are still saving the original file. Only now layers of signatures are added that can't be verified.

Consider the programming here. An original named document is just that—what existed in the file
up to the time it was first signed. To maintain version control and signature security, every time a
document is changed, the changes and the signatures are appended to the original. The original
doesn't change. Therefore, by adding changes and signatures, and saving with the same name,
you really haven't added anything. Well, nothing that the program can distinguish from the original
in a usable way.

There are two solutions: One is a workflow solution, and the other is a naming solution. If it is not
imperative that your work be signed, export the comments and send them on. The next member
of your group can import them and start from there. On the other hand, if you must sign the document, as we did in the projects in this chapter, each time a file is signed, it is saved with a different name. This way, although each new user has to validate the signatures, the signatures *can* be
validated, and the version control process is not disrupted. Whew!

One final and very sad note. If you have saved over a file and now have corrupted signatures, there
is no way to fix this. The document must be rerouted and resigned.

Using Document Versions

Why bother to sign documents? For control. Although the example used in this chapter's projects is quite simple, you can see how well the document is secured. Another major reason for signing documents is the fact that different versions of a document can be viewed and compared to other versions. All the people working on a document in a group have signed proof of the work they have contributed to a project, as well as what changes they were responsible for. Their version is signed and can be tracked. Because many projects are information-critical, this is a very valuable tool.

Acrobat has tools for using signed versions of documents. You can open earlier versions and do a visual comparison. You can also generate a report on the differences between the documents. We will look at these different versioning and comparison tools next.

Viewing Signed Document Versions

Acrobat maintains signed versions of a document in a single PDF file. Whenever a document is signed, Acrobat saves an appended version that coordinates with the work done under a specific signature. Each signature and the information about that particular version is listed in the Signatures palette.

Select the signature in the Signatures palette, and choose View Signed Version from the Signatures palette menu (or select View Signed Version from the context menu). The version corresponding with the selected signature will open in a new file window. Use this method for visually comparing two versions of a document. But what if you don't want to eyeball documents for differences? Acrobat can do it for you.

The Compare Two Versions Within A Signed Document command identifies changes made based on signatures. Here's how to use this command:

1. Select Tools ➤ Compare ➤ Two Versions Within A Signed Document. The dialog box shown in Figure 5-13 will open.

2. The document currently open will be displayed by default. Click Choose to open another document if necessary.

3. Select the two versions for comparison by clicking the Compare and To drop-down arrows.

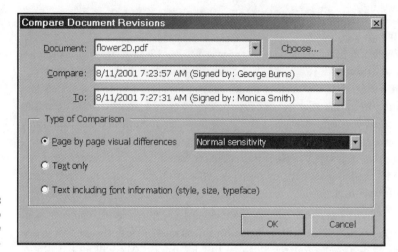

Figure 5-13
Use this dialog box to
compare versions of the
same document.

Note

I have not defined this
process as a project. You
may want to try it with
the project's document.
A copy of the file, called
comments.pdf, is on the
CD in the Chapter 5
Projects folder.

4. Select the type of comparison to be made by clicking one of the radio buttons:

   • Page By Page Visual Differences compares text and graphics pixel by pixel.

   • Text Only compares only text content changes.

   • Text Including Font Information compares fonts and font attributes in addition to text content changes.

5. Click OK. Acrobat will generate a document like the one shown in Figure 5-14.

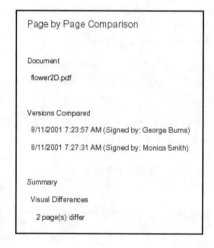

Figure 5-14
The document version
comparison output for
this chapter's project file

What if you want to compare two totally different documents? You can do that as well, as you'll see in the next section.

Comparing Two PDF Documents

Acrobat has another command, Compare Two Documents, that is similar to the one we just looked at. The Compare Two Documents command compares pages in two separate documents. The process is a bit different in that there are likely to be more discrepancies in elements such as number of pages. Follow these steps:

1. Select Tools ➤ Compare ➤ Two Documents. The Compare Documents dialog box will open, as shown in Figure 5-15.

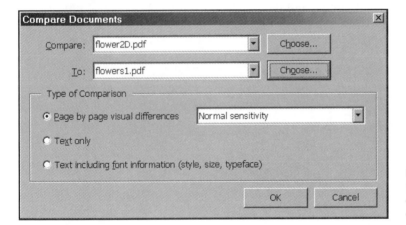

Figure 5-15
Use this command to compare two different documents.

2. Select the files to be compared. An open file is entered in the Compare text box by default.

3. Select Type Of Comparison options as you did for the earlier command.

4. Click OK.

Acrobat will create a new file that lists the comparisons. Pages will display side by side highlighting the differences. The Comments palette will list all the differences.

As an experiment, try a comparison between the original file used for this chapter's project, flowers1.pdf, and one of the later versions. There are quite substantial differences.

Note

A Special Thanks to Wildflower Farm

The materials used for the project in this chapter (and again in Chapters 6, 7, and 9) come from Wildflower Farm, located north of Toronto, Canada. The farm, owned by Miriam Goldberger and Paul Jenkins, hosts tours and weddings and sells plants, seed, flowers, and dried materials. As you will see when we get to the later projects, it is a beautiful place.

Up Next

This chapter contained a lot of information. The idea was to describe *how* a collaborative process is created and executed by creating a scenario as close to reality as possible. Along the way I showed you how some Acrobat functionality contributes to workflow. We looked at some of the editing tools and briefly discussed reusing downloaded materials.

Much of the chapter revolved around creating a PDF brochure, in the form of both a project and a tutorial. The aim was to show how the different processes contribute to advancing that goal. As I promised, we revisited the security material from Chapter 4. I also described how and why to use different versions of the same document.

In the next chapter, you will learn about repurposing content. We certainly started that in this chapter, but there is so much more to repurposing than what we have seen so far.

Chapter 6

Repurposing Content

One of Acrobat's most powerful features is its ability to repurpose content. From one document you can create a range of different types of output. Is it magic? No. It's smart software used intelligently. Let's see why you can repurpose content.

What's in a Name?

This is interesting: Five of the six dictionaries in which I searched for the term "repurposing" didn't have a definition. The closest ordinary term is something like "reusing" or "recycling"—neither of which fits what we are going to look at in this chapter and the next. Reusing, to my mind, implies simply using something again, like plastic bags. And recycling? Making something useful from something useless or discarded. Nothing at all like what Acrobat does. So I decree that henceforth the term "repurposing" shall be used to the exclusion of all others—besides, that is the term Adobe uses. Repurposing, by the new definition, means using something (in this case, a file) as the basis for creating something else that is used in an entirely different way.

The implication here is that Acrobat can do it all for you. Well, that is only partially true. It is true that Acrobat has the capacity to manipulate the structure and content of a file to create different forms of output, such as indexes or e-books. But it goes beyond that. As with all things digital, unless the user can identify what is needed and then use the capabilities of the software available to bring this about, the point is moot.

What is required, then, is a plan on several levels:

- Identify what is available.

- Understand what is required.

- Inventory what you have.

- Make the necessary modifications.

- Create the output skillfully.

I have said a few times throughout this book that my intent is not to create a click-this, click-that guide to using Acrobat, but to give you insight into how to use the program to help you work more efficiently. I never said this route would be easy. But wouldn't you rather be Picasso than a paint-by-number artist?

Planning Your Workflow

I just outlined a plan. Let's have a look at its components and see what they mean.

Identify What Is Available

Identifying what tools you have available is a fairly simple process. What I am referring to is identifying what you are using as source material. Just as you would identify source material for any other type of work—be it text, images, video, or sound clips—you now add another layer to the mix.

Not only must you consider the obvious, but you must also identify what the source materials contribute in the way of structure for the document you want to use as your PDF source.

Understand What Is Required

I will cover this in much greater depth further along in the chapter, but again, there are similarities to what you do on a regular basis now. Suppose you are building a Web page. You have several images to choose from. Some of the images are JPEG files, some are TIFF files. Do you have to convert all the images to TIFF files? Of course not. In fact, if you want to use any of the TIFF files, you have to convert them first to JPEG files. The basic concept is understanding what you need. This is a result of training and experience.

The same idea applies to document structuring. Again, just because you *can* do something doesn't mean you *must* do it.

Inventory What You Have

This step follows from understanding what you need. I am referring to an inventory of the available components in a document. To use the earlier example, suppose you have assembled all the available media for your project. The images just don't cut it, but you have a video clip that might have some promising frames.

Again, the same thing applies to document structuring. As we will see later, some file types lend themselves to creating structured documents, others can work given planning, and others will require some work on your part.

Make the Necessary Modifications

What changes will you have to make to acquire the components needed for the task at hand? Again, using our example, you might have to open a video clip in Premiere, select the frames that look promising, and export them as bitmaps. The work is still not finished, of course; the bitmaps will likely need some correction, and you will need to change their formats at the very least.

The same thing occurs with document structuring. Based on what you have, what you can get, and what you need, you might have to make changes. There are some tradeoffs in terms of different stages of the process. How you like to work, as well as other influences (such as knowing clearly what is expected of a project, which isn't always the case), might influence what kinds of modifications are required and where.

Create the Output Skillfully

Creating the output is not a job for amateurs! Just because you can finish something doesn't necessarily mean that it is a good piece of work. Compare your school portfolio with the one you have now (and everyone has a current one, right?). Although you might have two Web pages or two illustrations or two of anything else from then and now, you most likely can see differences in quality. Why? Experience and understanding. As we will see when creating different forms of outputs in Chapter 7, PDF outputs can be finessed to run better on their respective devices. With enough forethought and planning, some of the work involved in producing multiple outputs can be streamlined.

All of the elements of my grand plan are based on one requirement: understanding how a document is made. That is, it's not what you see, but more important, what you don't see. It is the underpinnings of a document that allow for all the fancy manipulation and the ability to repurpose the content.

What's in a Document?

In earlier chapters, we briefly looked at the content of converted documents. This is where we get into the heart of the matter. Look at a printed document. (At the risk of stating the obvious, if you are reading this, I guess you already are.) You see the content, whether text or tables or images. You see pagination elements, such as the page numbers and header and footer elements. You see layout elements, such as the figures.

Imagine you could see the manuscript as I was editing it. You would see editing functions, such as text and graphic markups and comments. Now imagine that you could see the pages laid out for printing. What else do you see? Crop marks, print notations, and the like.

This is a basic document. This is also a description of an unstructured document. Not that there isn't a lot of visual structure, because there certainly is. But this structure doesn't have to be programmed, nor can its source be reused automatically. Sure, I could copy and paste to my heart's content, but it is still unstructured.

The key to repurposing content lies in structure. In a PDF document, there are two levels of structured document: structured and tagged. Look at it as a continuum. At the one end is a simple text document, at the other end is a tagged document, and somewhere in between lies a structured document.

Like Leaves on a Tree

If we consider content to be the leaves of a tree, the structure would be twigs, and tags would be the branches and trunks. In the case of structured and tagged documents, all contain content, but there are additional components.

Structured Documents

Structured documents contain a structure tree in addition to the content. Content is referenced in a logical reading order, just as the pages of this book are structured. For example, this book uses a structured layout, in that different levels of headings are used. So, when you read this paragraph, which has a lower-level heading than this subsection, you know that it is part of the larger heading, which in turn is part of the main headings. Have a look at Figure 6-1. This is a screen shot of a portion of this chapter's preliminary outline view. You can easily see how the levels branch from the main level—that is, the chapter title.

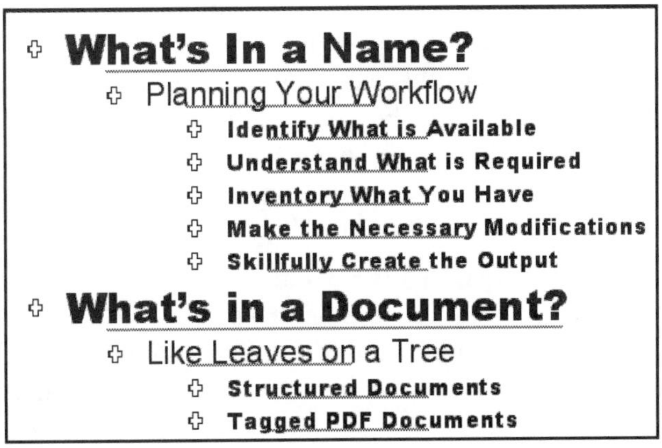

Figure 6-1
A structured document's layout

From the Acrobat perspective, a similar structure is in place. Some of the elements contained in a regular, unstructured document are not used. For example, comments or page numbers aren't translated into a structured format because they aren't considered useful structures in terms of formulating outputs. A basic structured document is one that contains bookmarks, for example. If the document I am writing were converted to a PDF and opened in Acrobat, the bookmarked structure would look like the outline structure. As you can see in Figure 6-2, I did convert the document, and this is the structure outlined in Acrobat.

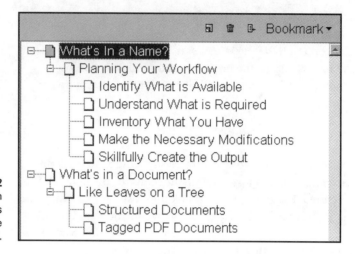

Figure 6-2
A structured document in Acrobat. The bookmarks correspond to the outline levels initially set in Word.

We will look at that structure a bit later in the chapter.

Tagged PDF Documents

The most advanced form of document we will look at in this chapter is the tagged document. In addition to the content and structure of the other two forms, other elements are defined. These other elements also relate to the content, but from a different perspective. Content, as I described earlier, relates to the words, tables, images, and so forth. In a tagged document, additional content information includes word spacing, hyphenation, and Unicode character values.

As you can see in Figure 6-3, although the Tags Root heading is present and the headings displayed in the earlier two images appear, the tags don't have anything in the document assigned to them. On the other hand, if I had chosen to have the bookmarks tagged, the document's elements would appear here. More on this later as well.

Note

Some authoring applications, such as Adobe FrameMaker 6, can produce structured PDF files. In FrameMaker, for example, you save the file by selecting File ➤ Save As and choosing settings. You can also print to PostScript and convert to PDF using Acrobat Distiller.

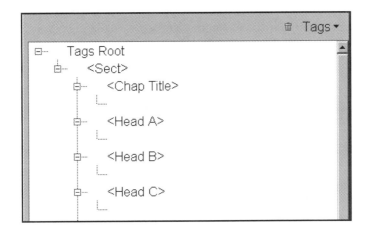

Figure 6-3
The logical (but blank)
structure tree in the
Tags palette

As I have described, depending on the characteristics of your document, you can repurpose the content in different ways. Table 6-1 lists the three document types and summarizes the features each can support.

Table 6-1 Repurposing Capabilities of Different PDF Document Types

Characteristic	Unstructured	Structured	Tagged
Save to RTF	Yes	Yes	Yes
Paragraph recognition	Yes	Yes	Yes
Text formatting	No	Yes	Yes
Lists/tables	No	No	Yes
Reflow ability	No	No	Yes
View on screen reader	No (unreliable)	Yes (unreliable)	Yes

Working with Bookmarks

As we saw earlier in this chapter, and also in Chapter 3's discussion of the stage makeup manual, bookmarks are imported and function as links. As in other forms of linking, bookmarks listed in the navigation pane link to the content in the document pane.

As we saw in Chapter 3, the table of contents in the manual became the bookmark list in Acrobat. Any desktop publishing program that can generate a table of contents will have the table converted to bookmarks in Acrobat.

Workflow Tip

Don't Use an Elephant Gun to Hunt a Fly

I'll bet that got your attention. Sometimes, depending on the source materials you have available, it can take a good deal of time to plan and produce a tagged file and finesse the compo-=nents, such as line breaks. But what if you don't need the tags? Don't use them. Again, the situation boils down to what it is you need, which I outlined in my master plan at the start of this chapter.

As with all other elements, bookmarks in Acrobat can be customized and manipulated. Bookmarks can be

- Added and deleted

- Edited

- Reorganized (in their hierarchy)

You access bookmarks by opening the Bookmarks tab (select Window ➤ Bookmarks). For each of the areas we will look at, remember that commands are available through either the context menu or by using the drop-down menu from the Bookmarks tab.

Project Tutorial: Manipulating a Set of Bookmarks

Note

This file is from a commentary I wrote for *WindoWatch* magazine, Vol. 7, No. 2, February 2001. (Copyright © 2001 by Donna L. Baker. Used with permission.)

Let's have a look at these functions. For illustration purposes, I am using a file named satellite.pdf. If you want to see what I did, the finished file is on the CD in the Chapter 6 Projects folder.

Adding and Deleting Bookmarks

A common bookmarking activity is adding and deleting bookmarks. For example, if you are using a heading or style structure as the basis for converting a PDF file from a Microsoft Word document, you might have a structure similar to the one shown in Figure 6-4. This doesn't mean that you are necessarily satisfied with the locations and numbers of bookmarks once you have the file converted. In this example, I used a Word document and selected the headings as the basis for the bookmark structure.

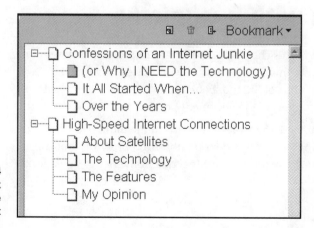

Figure 6-4
The bookmark hierarchy from the satellite.pdf document

The document has a small bio attached at the end. Because I was using headings as bookmarks, the bio wasn't added. I will add the bio to illustrate how to add a bookmark following these steps:

1. Click the bookmark above the desired location for the new one. In my example, I want to add it to the end, so I clicked on the My Opinion heading.

2. Navigate to the correct location in the document where the bookmark is to be linked—in this case, the last page (page 5).

3. Click the Create New Bookmark icon at the top of the Bookmarks tab, or select Bookmark ➤ New Bookmark from the Bookmark drop-down menu.

4. Select some text in the document to serve as the label. I entered **Donna Baker**.

5. Press Enter (or Return on a Mac).

6. I tested the bookmark by clicking a different bookmark and then clicking the new one. The first revision to the Bookmarks tab is shown in Figure 6-5.

Note

If I didn't select a location, it would be added automatically to the end of the list—which, of course, is where I want it anyway.

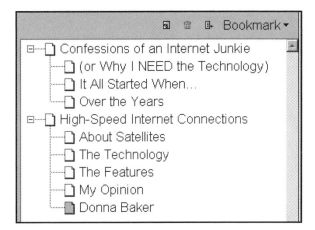

Figure 6-5
The Bookmarks tab contents after I added a bookmark

The top two bookmarks in my list are actually a title and a subtitle. I deleted the subtitle by first clicking the bookmark to select it and then pressing Delete. A confirmation window opens to confirm the deletion. I clicked Yes to delete the bookmark permanently. The bookmark list now appears as shown in Figure 6-6.

Now let's look at editing bookmarks.

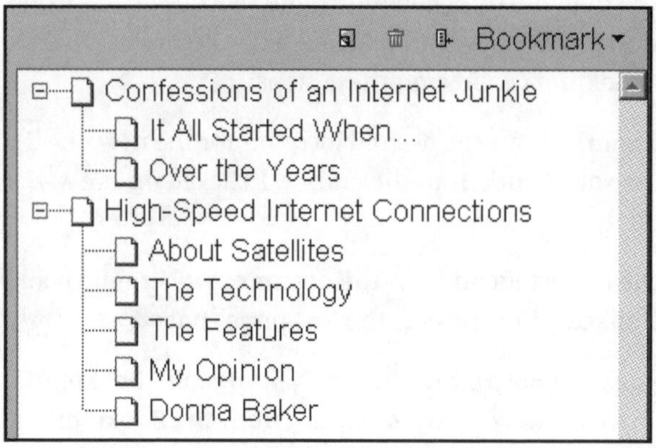

Figure 6-6
The Bookmarks tab
contents after I deleted
a pointless bookmark

Editing the Content and Appearance of Bookmarks

In the example I am using here, I want to edit text in one bookmark and change the appearance of the two main headings.

1. As you can see in Figure 6-6, there is a bookmark named "My Opinion." I want to change its name to "In My Opinion." To do this, I double-click the bookmark and change the text (I could also right-click the bookmark and select Rename).

2. Now I want to change the appearance of the text in the main heading. First, I click the bookmark to select it and then choose Bookmark Properties from the context menu or the Bookmark menu. Then, in the Bookmark Properties dialog box, I select the color and text style for the bookmark.

3. From the Bookmark Properties dialog box, I click Set Action to save the changes.

My modified bookmarks are shown in Figure 6-7. If you look at the satellite.pdf file, you will see that the headings now are the same color and font as the headings in the document.

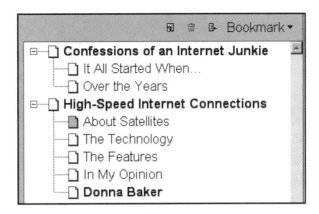

Figure 6-7
The bookmarks after
I customized text
to coordinate with
the document

Setting a Bookmark's Destination

The destination settings are the last of the editing functions we'll look at. Be careful when you use these settings; I'll explain why as we go along.

I would like to point out one thing first. The destination for a bookmark is a particular magnification of a specific area of a specific page. This is not the same as using the Destinations tab. Destinations, although they still use bookmarks and specific locations and magnifications, are used with more than one document.

1. Select the bookmark to be edited. Move to the location you want to specify as the new bookmark destination in the document pane.

2. Adjust the magnification. Select Properties from the context menu. When the Bookmark Properties dialog box opens, click Edit Destination. This button will be replaced by a Magnification drop-down list, as shown in Figure 6-8.

3. Click an option to select it. Click Set Action to close the dialog box.

4. With the bookmark still selected, select Bookmark ➤ Set Bookmark Destination (or choose Set Destination from the context menu). Click Yes in the action confirmation dialog box. The bookmark location is now set.

Note

You can also modify a bookmark's actions. In this chapter, we are restricting action to setting views within a single document. We will look at more action functions in Chapter 9 and then again in Chapter 12.

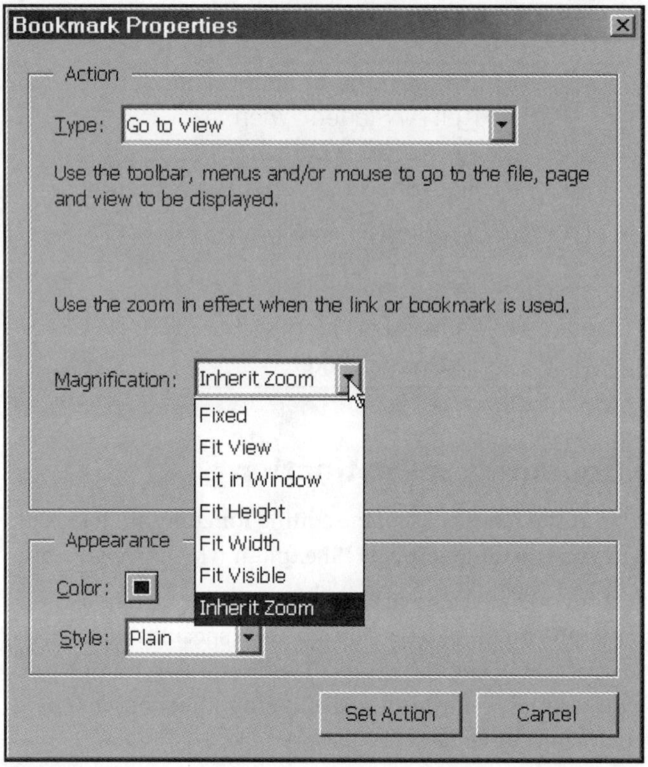

Bookmark Properties

Action

Type: Go to View

Use the toolbar, menus and/or mouse to go to the file, page and view to be displayed.

Use the zoom in effect when the link or bookmark is used.

Magnification: Inherit Zoom

- Fixed
- Fit View
- Fit in Window
- Fit Height
- Fit Width
- Fit Visible
- Inherit Zoom

Appearance

Color: ■

Style: Plain

Set Action   Cancel

Figure 6-8
In the Bookmark
Properties dialog
box, select the
Magnification
setting desired.

And here is where the caution comes. You can choose from several magnification options. I have listed them by name, along with their effect, in Table 6-2.

Table 6-2   Magnification Options

Option	Displays This . . .
Fixed	Magnification level and page position in effect when the bookmark was created
Fit View	The visible portion of the current page
Fit In Window	Current page in the destination window
Fit Width	Width of the current page in the destination window
Fit Height	Height of the current page in the destination window
Fit Visible	Width of the visible contents of the current page in the destination window (usually without margins)
Inherit Zoom	Magnification level the reader is using when he or she clicks on the link or bookmark

You are not restricted to using this method for setting how a bookmark is displayed. A convenient, quick method for bookmarking is described in the next Workflow Tip. If you have lots of time, you can also manually set the magnification and page location, right-click the bookmark, and select Set Destination.

The last stop on our bookmark trek is a look at the hierarchy structure and how to change it.

Bookmark Hierarchy

Bookmarks come in a sort of nest. There are relationships between the levels of bookmark (you can change those relationships, of course). Look at Figure 6-9 as I go through these points.

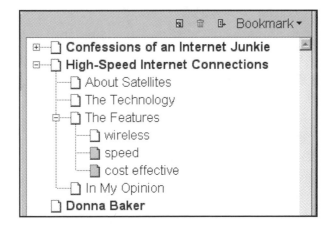

Figure 6-9
The finished hierarchy for the satellite.pdf document

- You can see in Figure 6-9 that one of the groups is open and one is closed, based on whether the title is prefaced by a plus sign (+) or a minus sign (-). The second group is expanded to show all the subtitles. This is referred to as *nesting.* The subtopics are considered children of the parent title.

- You can also see that I have added a new set of bookmarks under The Features. These are the concepts outlined in the bullets in the document. They have a parent/child relationship with The Features subtitle, which in turn has a parent/child relationship with the High-Speed Internet Connections heading.

Workflow Tip

Using Magnification Options Correctly

As with many other settings, a magnification option will apply until you next change the option. This means that each time you add a new bookmark, it will inherit the magnification you last specified. This may or may not be a problem.

Suppose you are adding several bookmarks to a document. If the setting you are using is different from the ones used with the other bookmarks, readers will find their progress through your document quite jumpy and distracting. For a good (or horrible) example of this effect, see the document I have been using for this discussion. I have purposely set the magnifications all askew to show how annoying this can be. Don't do this at home, kids.

On the other hand, the inherited magnification options can streamline your bookmarking processes. Select the first bookmark, and set the magnification options to whatever you desire. To set all subsequent bookmarks, select a bookmark, which will move the document to the appropriate place in your document, right-click the bookmark, and select Set Destination. Click OK to confirm the bookmark's destination.

- In case you were wondering earlier why I assigned the main-heading colors and text attributes to my name, here's why. I have promoted my name to a first-level position. To move a bookmark, click the name to select it, and then drag it slowly to the left (promoting it to a higher level in the hierarchy). A black bar shows the location of the icon. When you release the mouse, a confirmation dialog box will appear. Click OK to move the bookmark.

- If you look at the bookmark list again, when all the nested groups are collapsed, the two headings from before, as well as my name, will be listed. Also note that my name is not nested—that is, there are no dependencies on this heading.

- Because of the parent/child relationship of the bookmarks, if I deleted The Features, for example, the bookmarks I set for the bullets would also be deleted.

Now let's put all this newfound knowledge into practice.

Project Project 6-1. Structuring the "Applying Stage Makeup" Manual

We are going to pick up where we left off with the "Applying Stage Makeup" manual used in Chapter 3. Our area of concentration for this go-around with the manual will be the document's structure. We will use this manual again in Chapter 7. You will need the manualb.pdf file, which is on the CD in the Chapter 6 Projects folder.

Revising the Bookmark Structure

Let's see what we have:

1. Open the manualb.pdf file, and open the Bookmarks tab.

2. Click the + to the left of the bookmarks to expand any that are nested. You should see something similar to Figure 6-10.

3. The bookmark hierarchy is askew. Because we need to make a number of changes, I have listed those changes in Table 6-3, by first-level heading.

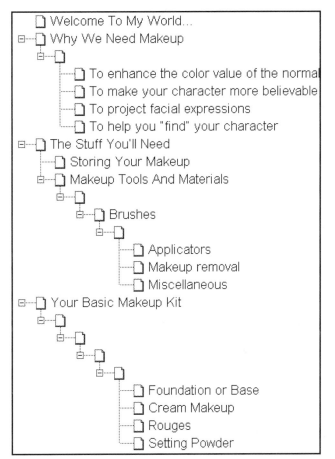

Figure 6-10
A portion of the manual's expanded bookmarks

Table 6-3   Bookmark Modifications in the Makeup Manual

Level 1 Heading	Changes
Welcome To My World...	None.
Why We Need Makeup	Promote the four bullets. Shift-click to select the set of four lines, and then drag them into position under the Why We Need Makeup heading. When the black line appears, release the mouse button.
	Delete the empty bookmark. Click it to select it, and then press Delete. Click Yes to confirm the deletion.
The Stuff You'll Need	Click and drag Brushes to a promoted position under Makeup Tools And Materials.
	Shift-click to select the set of three bullets. Drag them into a promoted position under the Brushes bookmark.
	Delete the two blank bookmarks.
Your Basic Makeup Kit	Delete all the bookmarks. (This is a list of bullets in the table.)

Table 6-3 Bookmark Modifications in the Makeup Manual (Continued)

Level 1 Heading	Changes
Applying Straight Makeup	Delete the bookmark "To get your face ready."
	Delete the two bookmarks under Applying a Base (both the blank bookmark and the one named "To apply your base").
	Shift-click the two Rouge bookmarks. Click and drag them in a promoted position under Rouge Application.
	Delete the two blank bookmarks.
All About Eye Makeup	Delete the bookmark "To create a perfect eyebrow."
	Delete the two bookmarks under Last But Not Least, Mascara.
	Delete the bookmark "To set your finished makeup."
Makeup Removal	Delete the bookmark "To remove your makeup."
Caring for Your Makeup Materials and Tools	None
Bibliography	None

Workflow Tip

Creating the Bookmark Hierarchy Before Converting the File

When I originally converted this file to PDF, I used the Word styles. I attached different outline levels to the heading styles so it would convert to PDF in this way, which allowed me to illustrate how to modify bookmarks. In real life, however, I don't recommend making this extra work for yourself. If you are converting a Word file, check the heading styles (if that is what you are using as bookmark sources) to ensure that they follow in a straightforward outline method. When the file is converted, the bookmarks are nested properly.

The finished product should be a smooth, consistent set of nested bookmarks. Now let's dress it up a bit.

Customizing the Bookmarks

Opinions on customized bookmarks vary from acceptance to annoyance. Let's go out on a limb and customize them a bit by adding color to the main titles to coordinate with the content.

1. Collapse all expanded main-level bookmarks (this is optional, but I find it easier).

2. Click the first heading to select it. Right-click and select Properties from the context menu.

3. The Bookmark Properties dialog box will open. Modify the appearance: Change the color by clicking the color icon to open the palette and selecting the dark red swatch in the top row, and select Bold from the Style drop-down list.

4. Click Set Action to make the change and close the dialog box.

5. Repeat with the other main headings. The finished set is shown in Figure 6-11.

I'd like to do a bit more to this manual at this point. Let's add some more bookmarks and custom magnifications.

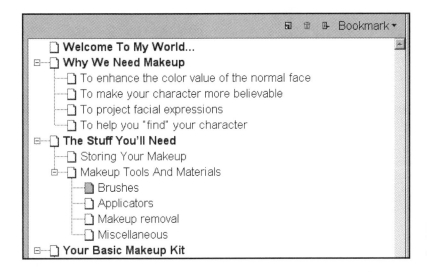

Figure 6-11
The revised bookmark list
with enhanced headings

Showing Off the Images

If you look through the manual, you will see a number of interesting
sketches that illustrate both the tools and the techniques used in
this manual.

We are going to enhance those sketches by adding new bookmarks and
custom views. This way, the manual user can both read the associated
text and have a good look at the illustrations. The finished and modified
Bookmarks tab is shown in Figure 6-12.

Adding the New Bookmarks

Again, because the list is lengthy, I have placed the details in a table.
Add each of the new bookmarks using these steps:

1. Click the bookmark above the location where you want to add
   the new bookmark to select it. (The first one is Brushes.)

2. Select Bookmark ➤ New Bookmark. An empty bookmark field
   will appear below the selected bookmark.

3. Enter the text for the new bookmark. For each, I used the same
   structure—that is, Image: <image name>.

4. Now click and drag the image bookmarks to become children of
   the topic bookmark the image is associated with.

5. Click Yes in the confirmation message window. The bookmark
   will be moved.

Use the information in Table 6-4 to add the new bookmarks.

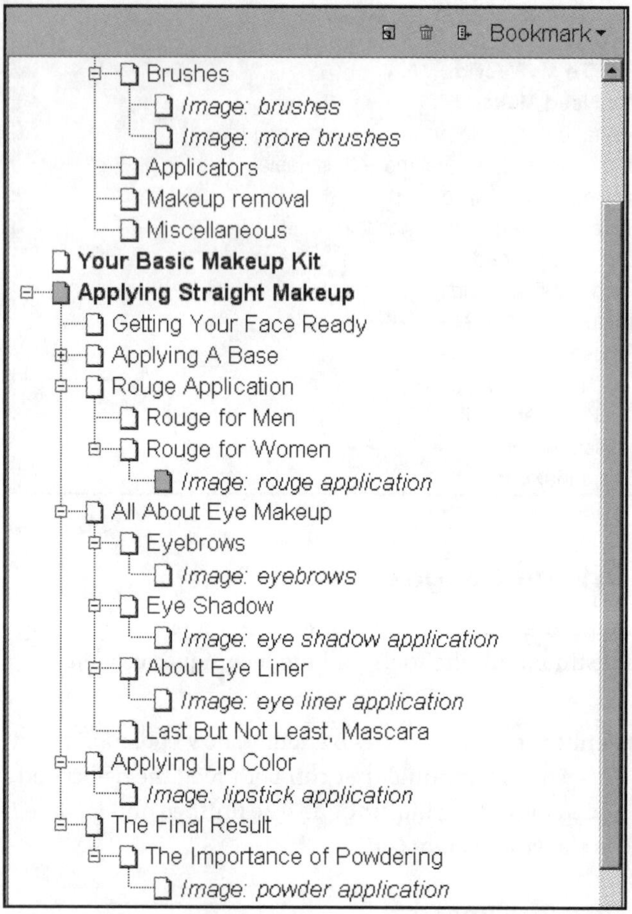

Figure 6-12
The last revision to the
Bookmarks tab

Table 6-4   Add the Image Bookmarks

Select This Bookmark for Position Reference	Add This Label
Brushes	Image: brushes
Brushes	Image: more brushes
Rouge for Women	Image: rouge application
Eyebrows	Image: eyebrows
Eye Shadow	Image: eye shadow application
About Eye Liner	Image: eye liner application
Applying Lip Color	Image: lipstick application
The Importance of Powdering	Image: powder application

Setting the Properties for the New Bookmarks

As you can see in the last bookmark revision image, Figure 6-12, the image bookmarks have been customized to some extent as well. In addition to changing their text style to italic, we must also define the destinations for the new bookmarks.

1. In the document pane, scroll to the location of the first image bookmark. Roughly center it on the page. Use the magnifying tool to resize the page in the pane.

2. In the bookmark pane, click the first image's bookmark to select it. Then right-click and select Properties from the context menu. The Bookmark Properties dialog box will open.

3. Leave the Action Type setting at its default selection, Go To View.

4. Click Edit Destination. The magnification options will replace the Edit Magnification button, as shown in Figure 6-13.

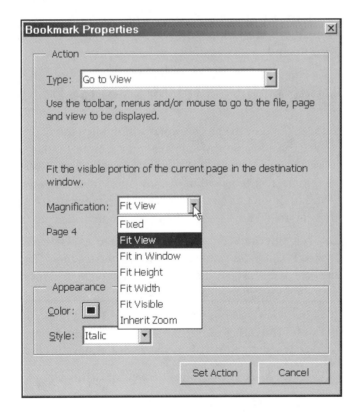

Figure 6-13
Use the Bookmark Properties dialog box to set a destination for the bookmark.

Workflow Tip

Creating a Number of Bookmarks

Each bookmark has a corresponding display in the document. After all, that is why bookmarks exist. Streamline your work by working in one pane and then the other. By that, I mean construct your set of bookmarks and modify their hierarchy and arrangement as desired. Then set the corresponding destinations and magnifications. This way, you won't be distracted moving back and forth between panes and functions.

On the other hand, adding bookmarks one at a time has its advantages. When you have added the last bookmark, the job is done. Also, when you add the first bookmark and set its properties, the magnification will default to the modified setting for all subsequent bookmarks.

The key is understanding what works best for you.

5. Select Fit View from the Magnification drop-down list. This will fit the visible portion of the page in the document pane.

6. Click Style (in the Appearance area) and select Italic from the drop-down list.

7. Click the Set Action button to set the properties for the bookmark.

Continue with the rest of the new bookmarks. Be sure to position the image in the document pane before modifying the properties. Save the file (I renamed it manualc.pdf) and test the bookmarks.

So that is everything you ever wanted to know about bookmarks and structured files. Now some more discussion on tagged files.

Creating Tagged PDF Files

You can choose one of two methods for automatically creating tagged PDF files. Source materials created in Microsoft Office 2000 applications can be converted to tagged PDF files, and so can Web pages converted in Acrobat. If you are running Office XP, you will first need the Acrobat 5.0.5 upgrade (released in December 2001).

Using a Microsoft Word Source Document

Let's look at how the process works within Microsoft Office first. Again, we will use a Microsoft Word file as an example. In Chapter 3, I described how to create PDF files by using Acrobat PDFMaker and converting the files from within the host application. I am not going to rehash that information. Instead, I want to point out a couple of details that you might have missed then but that are critical for this discussion.

Earlier in this chapter, I described the differences between structured and tagged PDF files. In Figure 6-3, I showed you a sample Tags tab from a file I created. As you could see in that figure, the file was not converted with the tags automatically present. Why not?

It all boils down to the conversion settings I used in Word. Allow me to illustrate. The earlier example used basic conversion settings. One particular setting makes all the difference. Follow this process:

1. Select Acrobat ➤ Change Conversion Settings.

2. Click the Office tab to open it.

3. Click the Embed Tags In PDF check box to activate it, as shown in Figure 6-14.

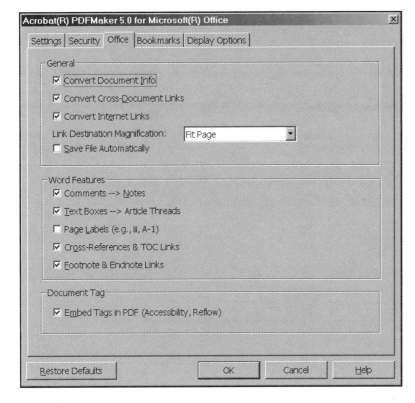

4. Click OK to close the dialog box.

5. Create the PDF file by clicking the Convert To Adobe PDF icon on the toolbar.

What effect does this have? Look at Figure 6-15. This is still the same file as the one I used earlier. You can see here that the tags are now "filled in"—that is, each element has a location in the document associated with it.

Now look at Figure 6-16 for reference. This is a portion of the first page that corresponds to the tags shown in Figure 6-15. As you can see, the tags are attached to different elements, ranging from the chapter title to body text and headings.

Figure 6-15
The Tags tab now shows
tags and their
attachments.

Figure 6-16
The tagged PDF
document. Note how the
elements are named in
the different tags
displayed in Figure 6-15.

Chapter 6 Repurposing Content

One of Acrobat's most powerful features is its ability to repurpose content. Bring in some form of a document. Presto-Chango! Create something entirely different. Is it magic? No. Smart software used intelligently.

What's In a Name?

This is interesting. Five of the six dictionaries I searched for the term "repurposing" didn't have a definition. The closest ordinary term is something like reusing or recycling. Neither of which fit what we are going to look at in this chapter and the next. Reusing, to my mind, implies simply using something again, like plastic bags. And recycling? Making something useful from something useless or discarded. Nothing at all like what Acrobat does. So I decree that henceforth the term "repurposing" shall be used to the exclusion of all others. Besides which, this is the term Adobe uses. Repurposing, by the new definition, means using something (in this case a file) as the basis for creating something else which is used in an entirely different way.

The implication here is that Acrobat can do it all for you. Well, that is only partially true. It is true that Acrobat has the capacity to manipulate the structure and content of a file to create different forms of output. But it goes beyond that. Like all things digital, unless the user can identify what is needed, and then use the capabilities of the software available to bring this about, the point is moot.

What is required, then, is a plan on several levels. Like this:

*   Identify what is available.

*   Understand what is required.

*   Inventory what you have.

*   Make the necessary modifications.

*   Skillfully create the output.

Using Web Pages As Source Documents

We have seen in other chapters that it is a slick process to create a PDF file directly in Acrobat from a Web page. To create a tagged document, you must use a specific method.

Again, as I did with the Word document, I want to illustrate the difference. Figure 6-17 shows the downloaded Web page's tags. (The file is a magazine article that I keep on my hard drive.)

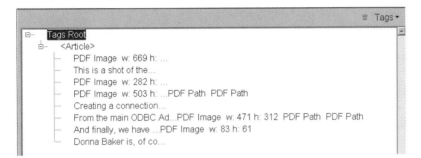

Figure 6-17
The tags from the downloaded Web page

If you look at the Tags listing, you'll find little information of much value in using the contents of the document. The Word document required specific conversion settings, and the same applies for a Web page. Here's what you do:

1. Select Tools ➤ Web Capture ➤ Open Web Page.

2. In the Open Web Page dialog box, click Conversion Settings. The dialog box shown in Figure 6-18 will open.

3. Click the Add PDF Tags option to select it.

4. Click OK to close the Conversion Settings dialog box and return to the Open Web Page dialog box. Select the file and levels to download.

5. Click Download to close the dialog box and start the conversion process.

Now look at the Tags palette. I have shown a portion of it in Figure 6-19.

Again, you can see that there are now more usable elements listed.

Workflow Tip

Develop a System for File Conversions

If there's a possibility that your work will be reused in different formats—and you might know this at the time of the initial file conversions—always include tags as part of the conversion process. That way, in the event something extra is required, you are set to go.

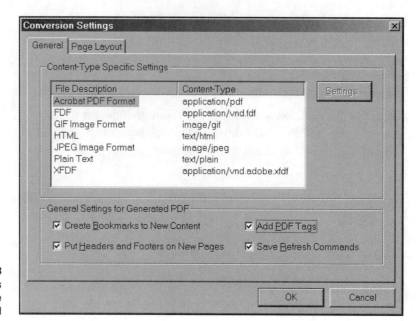

Note

In Figure 6-19, the first
entry after Tags Root is
`<Article>`. An article is a
complete Web page and
is equivalent to the
page's title. You'll find a
full discussion of articles
in Chapter 7.

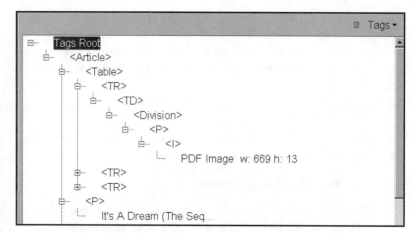

Figure 6-19
The Tags palette from the
converted Web page

Note

If you would like to see
what I am referring to in
action, the file is on the
CD in the Chapter 6
Projects folder. It is
named, appropriately,
blues.pdf.

Project Tutorial: Working with Web Pages

I want to explain more of Acrobat's ability to use Web pages, but in a less generic way. This is not your typical project; I'm not describing a step-by-step process. Rather, I have built a site to use as a frame of reference. I constructed this site by converting a Web site I built into a PDF file using the Conversion Settings dialog box for Web pages.

Want to see the file this masterpiece came from? Figure 6-20 shows the frameset. The files were originally called header.htm (the heading) and main.htm (the lower frame).

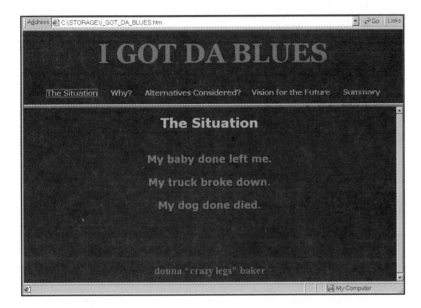

Figure 6-20
I Got Da Blues frameset—the subject of this tutorial

Web Bookmarks

Web bookmarks behave in the same fashion as regular document bookmarks, with one addition. In the context menu you'll find an extra command for downloading more Web pages. As with regular bookmarks, you can add, delete, edit, and reorganize the hierarchy of Web bookmarks.

You'll note a slight difference in the way the bookmarks look in the Bookmarks tab, however. As you can see in Figure 6-21, the icons are Web-like.

Figure 6-21
The list of bookmarks for the converted Web site

In Figure 6-21, the first bookmark represents the Web server. In this case, because the Web site is hosted locally, it is labeled Local Disk. Each bookmark following this represents one page, with the exception of the first one, I Got Da Blues. This is actually the title of the frameset used to house the other pages. As you may have surmised, the bookmark names come from the pages' titles.

These bookmarks are initially all at the same level and subordinate to the server. There are no parent/child relationships. Now let's look at the tags.

"I Got Da Blues" from the Tags Perspective

When I downloaded these files from my local server into Acrobat, I selected Add PDF Tags in the download Web page settings. This means that the file also contains tag information.

Because the PDF tags were added to the page, the structure information is stored in the PDF document. This information corresponds to the HTML structure of the original pages. I want to walk you through what you see in Figure 6-22. It will be important in future chapters for you to understand what you see in the Tags palette because it relates to the HTML structure of the original page.

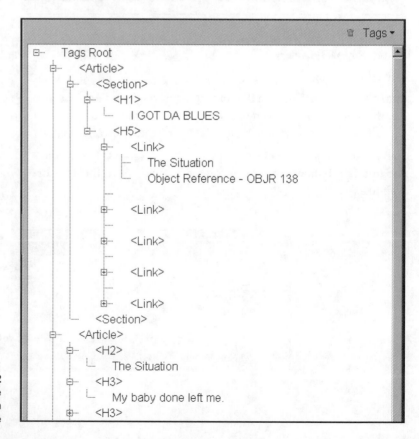

Figure 6-22
The structure of the converted "I Got Da Blues" Web site

My little Web site had a total of eight pages—five linked pages, and three pages for the frames and frameset. As you can see in Figure 6-22, the first element listed below Tags Root is an article. Each Web page is a single article. It has a structure that does not depend on something so arbitrary as the length of a page (how long is a Web page?).

The contents of the first page (or article) are different from the following pages because this is the frameset. Refer to Table 6-5 for a description of what you see.

Table 6-5 Analyzing the Tags for This Web Site

Tag (or Description)	What It Means
Tags Root	Base of file; represents the server.
<Article>	The first page. This consists of the frameset as well as its two frames, described here as separate sections.
<Section>	A section of the frameset, which was the header.htm file (where I had placed the heading and the links).
<H1>	The HTML tag for Heading 1.
I GOT DA BLUES	The content of the tag—the title of the page used the H1 style.
<H5>	The HTML tag for Heading 5.
<Link>	The tag identifying the content with the Heading 5 attribute as being linked to something.
The Situation	The content of the tag—the text used for the link.
Object Reference - OBJR 138	What the link is linked to—in this case, The Situation. You will see that below the object reference, there is a blank tag. This represents nonbreaking spaces that I added on the page between the links.
Four additional collapsed link tags	These are all nested below the <H5> tag and contain the links for the other four pages.
<Section>	A section of the frameset, which was the main.htm file (where the linked frame content would be displayed).
<Article>	This refers to another Web page, in this case, the first of the linked pages, which was situation.htm.
<H2>	The HTML tag for Heading 2.
The Situation	The heading for the first linked page.
<H3>	The HTML tag for Heading 3.
My baby done left me.	The first line of content for the linked page. This is followed by two additional <H3> tags and the two other lines of content.

If you look at the links, you will see that their content and Object References are nested within the same heading tag. Now, if you look lower down to where the first linked page is located, each line is nested within its own <H3> tag. Why? Because when I constructed the pages, I added line breaks between the lines of text. As a result, each line had its own heading tag, which was transferred to Acrobat when the files were converted.

This brings me back to what I discussed at the beginning of the chapter: Know what you have and what you plan to do with it. In the tags example, it would have been preferable to build a style for the text rather than adding the blank lines. And before we end this chapter, I have another example.

Look at Figure 6-23. This was a second variation on the Web site that I created in a much different way. Rather than using a frameset and text links to the other pages, I took the more sophisticated route. I built the first two links as images in layers (these are shown in Figure 6-23 as the first two scruffy text blocks). They were then linked to layers on the page that would be shown or hidden depending on which link was activated. As you can see in the message, Acrobat doesn't know how to interpret these links. Which shows you that simpler can sometimes be better.

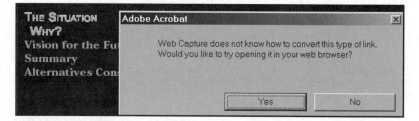

Figure 6-23
Using a different Web site layout produces different results in Acrobat.

So this wasn't a good plan. Although the links can be configured manually, imagine if this were a very complex site. It would certainly add to your workload. Adding to your workload is precisely what I am trying to prevent.

Up Next

In this chapter, we have looked "under the hood," so to speak, at the whole idea of repurposing content. I started with a game plan for planning and organizing workflow. As we saw at the very end of this chapter, this approach makes sense.

I have discussed in some detail bookmarks and tags, which are both key elements in using Acrobat intelligently. These two ideas will reappear in the next several chapters.

Throughout this chapter, I have also mentioned the term "article" a few times. Coming up in Chapter 7: everything you ever wanted to know about articles, along with a few other items used for creating different forms of output. And more on tags. We will build on what I have discussed in this chapter, and we'll look at some other interesting things.

Chapter 7

Planning and Preparing for Output

So far we have looked at different ways to access and manipulate source information. In this chapter, we will look at how to create some specific output formats. I will also give you the rundown on two functions that are new to Acrobat 5: batch commands and the PDF Consultant.

What If I Want to Make . . .?

This is where we fill in the blank. So far in this book, we have covered a lot of information—how Acrobat works, how to convert files into PDF format to work with in Acrobat, and how to manipulate and secure the Acrobat documents. I have explained how to comment and edit documents, and I've discussed how to collaborate on documents with others.

I have referred occasionally to concepts such as articles and reflowing. Well, it all comes together now. This chapter covers a number of interesting types of output. Along the way, we will look at some more information you will need to create specific output types.

Just a note before I start. Some output types have a chapter devoted to them because their requirements are specific and because they use different processes. This includes accessibility, forms, e-books, and print. In this chapter, though, we will look at several types of output that you can create using the same source material and variations on the same processes.

Along the way, we will also look at some processes that I have hinted at or even looked at briefly in earlier chapters, including using the article feature. Then, we will look at a new plug-in for saving PDF files as different types of Web page formats, and we will conclude with a look under the hood at the metadata of our documents.

Before we delve into any specific output types, I first want to show you two new features in Acrobat 5. The first, PDF Consultant, analyzes and optimizes a file. The second new feature lets you create and use automated batch functions. Both of these features come into play as you prepare a document for export to another format or as an alternate form of output.

Using PDF Consultant

What a valuable plug-in! Regardless of the type of output you are planning, your output will be more efficient and more professional if the output is as clean and focused as possible. You use the PDF Consultant plug-in to inspect, analyze, and repair documents. PDF Consultant, which works at the object level, can perform a number of functions, including the following:

- *Detect And Remove:* Lets you seek and destroy all those unnecessary elements that add weight to a file without contributing to its function.

- *Optimize Space:* Allows you to decrease the file size by removing things such as invalid bookmarks or links.

- *Audit Space Usage:* Indicates how much of the total file weight is attributed to different elements such as images, comments, fonts, and so forth. The values are expressed either in bytes or as a percentage of the entire file's size.

Let's put this feature through its paces.

Optimizing and Analyzing a Document

I will use one of the demos I designed for Chapter 6 to illustrate how these processes work. Figure 7-1 shows the Document Summary dialog box. As you can see, the file is 29.9KB. Certainly not a big file, but we are going for concept, not quantity.

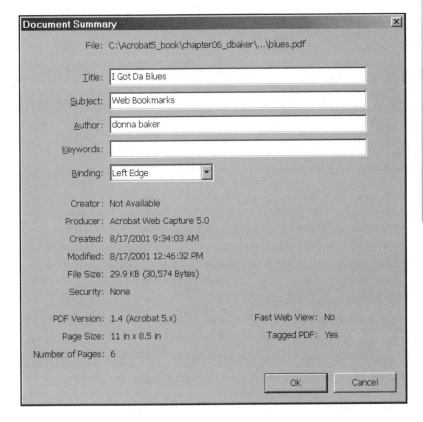

Figure 7-1
The Document Summary dialog box for this demo

You access the PDF Consultant plug-in by selecting Tools ➤ PDF Consultant and then selecting the desired option. The first option we will look at is the Detect And Remove process.

Detecting and Removing

Also known as the seek and destroy process. When you select the Detect And Remove option, the dialog box shown in Figure 7-2 opens.

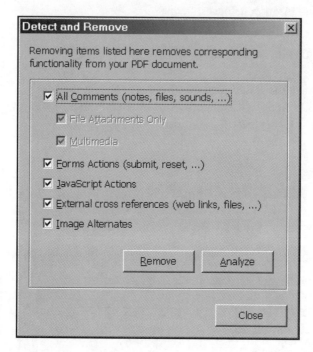

Figure 7-2
Start with the Detect
And Remove dialog box
if you know what you
want to remove.

As the dialog box warns, when you select items from this menu to remove from the document, you will lose any functionality the items provided—which only stands to reason. For example, you might choose to delete JavaScript Actions from a document. It would make sense, then, that whatever JavaScript functions had been present won't be available to you anymore.

Once you have decided what you need to strip from the file, click Remove. The job is finished. But what if you aren't sure that's what you want to do? Instead, click Analyze. The dialog box shown in Figure 7-3 will open.

As you can see in Figure 7-3, the Consultant found five comments and five Web links. Click OK to close this dialog box and return to the main Detect And Remove dialog box. Now decide what to remove and click the check boxes to select the items. Click Remove to strip the items from the document. Then click OK to close the dialog box.

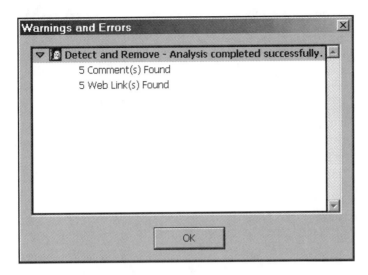

Figure 7-3
The Warnings And Errors
dialog box

Making Space

In the previous chapter, I showed you how to manipulate bookmarks
and delete the unnecessary ones by smoothing out the hierarchy.
Because the bookmarks were created automatically and converted into
bookmarks in the PDF file, in some instances I could have a bookmark
that points to nothing.

This PDF Consultant tool can remove invalid bookmarks as well as
invalid or unused links. All of these changes will contribute to a smaller
file size. Figure 7-4 shows the Optimize Space dialog box.

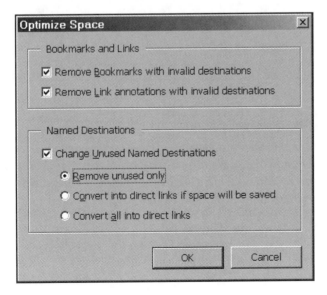

Figure 7-4
Optimizing space using the
PDF Consultant

As you can see, there are two sections: one for bookmarks and links and the other for named destinations. So, for example, if you had created internal jumps or links or targets (so many terms for the same thing!) that weren't used in the final product, rather than tracking them down individually and removing each one, you can evaluate and deal with them all at once.

To use this tool, make your selections by clicking the appropriate check boxes or radio buttons, and then click OK to run the process and display the results (shown in Figure 7-5). Click OK to close the results window. That's it.

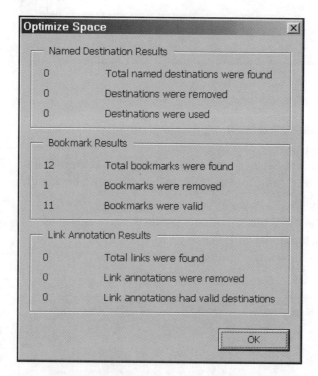

Figure 7-5
Results of the Optimize
Space process

Auditing Your File

The third tool in this set is used to perform a space audit. File size has become important in some organizations, particularly in government organizations, where literally thousands of files are being stored. By evaluating the content of a file, you can see how much space a type of object is using.

You might want to do a file audit before any of the other functions. I'll discuss that in a minute. Regardless, there is much information to digest after an audit has been completed. To initiate the process, select the Audit Space Usage option. Rather than a dialog box opening, the message shown in Figure 7-6 will be displayed.

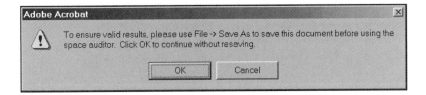

Figure 7-6
Acrobat recommends that you save your document under a different name before running an audit.

If you save the file under another name, you are assured that the file has been completely saved. An audit can be run at any time, but unless everything in the file was saved prior to starting the audit, the results may not be valid. For example, at the last minute you might decide to add some new bookmarks to a file. If you forget to save the file before running the audit, your results will be valid only to the point at which the file was last saved. Therefore, click Cancel and give the file an alternate name by selecting File ➤ Save As. Once the file has been resaved, the audit will automatically start. You won't have to restart the process again. On the other hand, if the file has been open but you are sure you haven't made any changes in it, click OK to run the audit. The finished audit for my file is shown in Figure 7-7.

Note

Depending on whether you are using an original file or one that has been through a Save As process, the message box in Figure 7-6 might appear when you select the Optimize Space tool as well as the Audit Space Usage tool.

Percentage	Bytes	Description
0.0%	0	Thumbnails
0.0%	0	Images
6.1%	1618	Bookmarks
15.5%	4091	Content Streams
13.7%	3617	Fonts
14.7%	3879	Structure Info
0.0%	0	Forms
0.0%	0	Comments
0.0%	0	Named Destinations
13.6%	3570	Cross Reference Table
36.3%	9560	Unknown
100.0%	26335	Total
	26335	File Size in Bytes

Figure 7-7
The completed audit of my file

Notice how many elements are actually in a document, even a simple one such as this. As you can see in the figure, my file has been reduced to 26.3KB. I started this demo with a file size of 29.9KB, so that is a whopping saving of 3.6K. As I said earlier, I was going for concept, not quantity.

Once you have looked at your audit results, click OK to close the window, or click Remove Elements, which will open the Detect And Remove dialog box. We have come full circle.

One final note on the PDF Consultant—and here is the most interesting feature: All of these operations can be configured in the Batch Sequences process. In other words, in addition to exporting a batch of files, you can optimize them prior to export. Isn't that convenient?

And speaking of batch processes, let's have a look at those now.

Batching Files for Conversion

Batching, as I am sure you know from experience with other programs, is a way to automate repetitive processes. In the last few years, a number of programs have been released that use JavaScript as a basis for writing custom command sequences. Acrobat 5 joins that illustrious crowd. You can use batching commands on anything from a single document to a collection of documents.

The batching process is composed of three segments:

- Defining commands
- Defining files to execute the commands on
- Defining storage locations for the converted files

Defining the Batch Commands

You can run any of a series of preconfigured commands or create custom sequences. We will look at both options. To create a new process, select File ➤ Batch Processing ➤ Edit Batch Sequences. The dialog box shown in Figure 7-8 will open. The window lists the preconfigured commands.

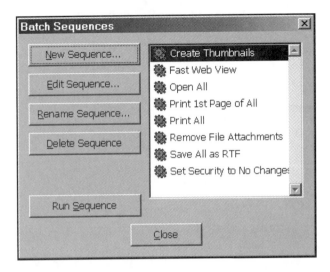

Figure 7-8
Start the batch command
process in this dialog box.

Follow these steps to define the batch commands:

1. Click New Sequence. A sequence placeholder will appear in the list
   at the right side of the window. Enter a name for the new command
   sequence in the pop-up window, and click OK to open the Batch
   Edit Sequence dialog box, shown in Figure 7-9.

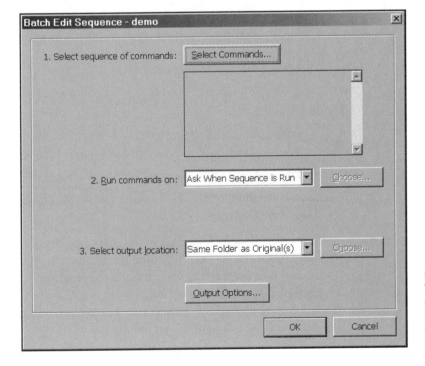

Figure 7-9
The Batch Edit Sequence
dialog box houses the
information for the
command-building
process.

2. In the Batch Edit Sequence dialog box, click Select Commands. The Edit Sequence dialog box, shown in Figure 7-10, will open. This dialog box is the heart of the process. Included are a number of commands in the following areas:

- Comments

- Documents

- JavaScript

- Page

- PDF Consultant

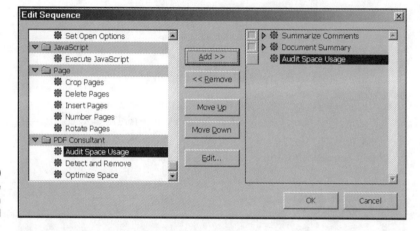

Figure 7-10
The Edit Sequence
dialog box with
commands added

3. In the Edit Sequence dialog box, configure the commands for the sequence. You can manipulate the content of this window in several ways:

- Select a command from the left pane of the dialog box and click Add. The command will be added to the sequence.

- Delete a command by selecting it and clicking Remove.

- To reorder the list, highlight the command to move, and click Move Up or Move Down.

4. Set options for each command by clicking the command in the right pane and then clicking Edit. For example, as shown in Figure 7-11, you can configure the options for the Summarize Comments command by changing the attributes in this dialog box.

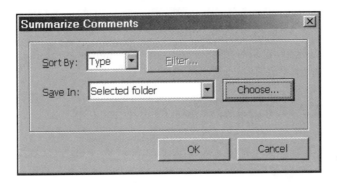

Figure 7-11
An example of command
configuration options

5. You can make some commands interactive. Click the white box to
    the left of the arrow next to the command to Toggle Interactive
    Mode. This mode pauses the batching process and allows you to
    configure options before executing the command. For example,
    look at Figure 7-12. I want to point out some details:

    - You can display the content of each command by clicking the
      arrow to the left of the command name.

    - The sequence of elements in the command is displayed, as well
      as any options.

    - The Summarize Comments command has a white box to the
      left of the arrow. Click the selection box to the left of the com-
      mand line to make a command interactive. This indicates that
      the batch process will be paused depending on what settings
      you used (as shown in Figure 7-11, I changed this setting to
      save in a selected folder).

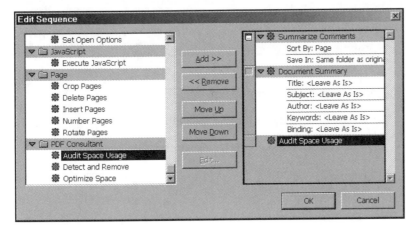

Figure 7-12
The content of the
commands. The
Summarize Contents
command is in Interactive
Mode.

6. Click OK to finish building the command sequence and return to the Batch Edit Sequence dialog box.

Once you've created a command sequence, it's time to define the target files.

Defining the Target Files

Once you've established a command sequence, the next step is to specify the files on which you want the commands to be executed. The options available are shown in Figure 7-13.

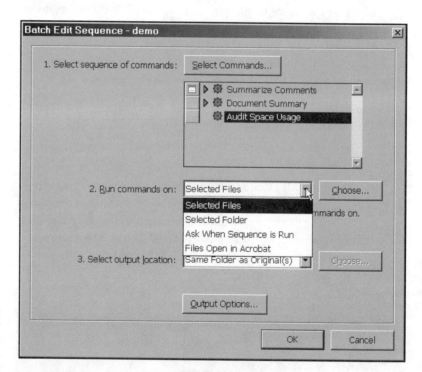

Figure 7-13
Pick the options for running the command from this drop-down list.

Note

In Windows, the files must all be in the same folder. They may be in different folders if you are using a Mac OS version.

The drop-down list contains several options:

- *Selected Files:* Select multiple individual files.

- *Selected Folder:* Select all the files in a selected folder.

- *Ask When Sequence is Run:* Allows you to select different locations and options as the situation requires.

- *Files Open in Acrobat:* Will batch any open files.

The final part of the process is defining storage options.

Selecting Storage Options

Storage options include both location and file options.

1. Select a storage location. By default, the files will be saved to their source folder. Other options are to save to a specific folder or to the same folder as the original, or to ask when the sequence is run (again for customized use of the batching process). These options are shown in Figure 7-14.

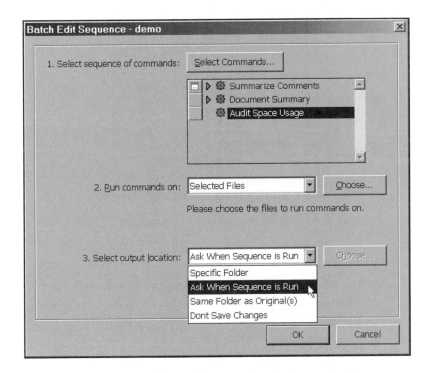

Figure 7-14
Select the location to store the output from the batch processing.

2. Define the output options. Hidden beneath the selection list in Figure 7-14 is a button called Output Options. Click it to open the dialog box shown in Figure 7-15.

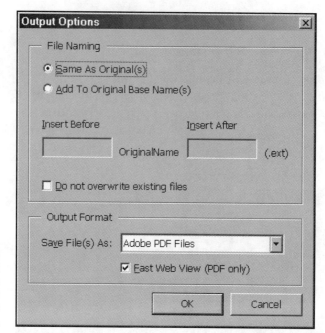

Figure 7-15
Make the final
selections for the
custom batch
commands in this
dialog box.

3. The dialog box contains these options:

- *Same As Original(s):* Uses the same filename with a PDF extension

- *Add To Original Base Name(s):* Adds a prefix or suffix to the original filename

- *Do Not Overwrite Existing Files:* Does not overwrite existing files if you are creating several similar files

- *Save File(s) As:* Lets you choose a file format before each save

- *Fast Web View:* Creates a Web page version of a document

4. Click OK to close this dialog box and return to the Batch Sequences dialog box.

Now your custom batching command sequence has been created. In the Batch Sequences dialog box, click Run to run the batch. If you need to modify any of the settings, select File ➤ Batch Processing ➤ Edit Batch Sequences and select the sequence.

Preconfigured Batch Commands

As I mentioned earlier, a number of batch commands are automatically installed with Acrobat. The menu list, which you access by selecting File ➤ Batch Processing, is shown in Figure 7-16.

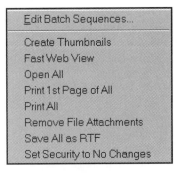

Edit Batch Sequences...

Create Thumbnails
Fast Web View
Open All
Print 1st Page of All
Print All
Remove File Attachments
Save All as RTF
Set Security to No Changes

Figure 7-16
The preconfigured
batch commands

As you can see, a number of basic processes can be accomplished quickly. If you look at the list, you will see that these are all useful ways to save time when performing the same kind of activities on a number of files.

That was quite a whirlwind tour, wasn't it? I think the best way to appreciate how this feature works is to use it. On that note, a project is up next.

Project Project 7-1. Creating a Custom Batch Process for "Manual Cleanup"

For this project, you will construct a custom batch command to run against the magazine article about satellite Internet connections we have used in other projects.

What You Will Need

For this project, you will need the internet.pdf file, which is on the CD in the Chapter 7 Projects folder. You will see that this version of the article now has a column layout. This will be important as we work through the projects in this chapter.

If you open the internet.pdf file, you will notice a few changes:

- The thumbnails are not embedded in the file.

- The text is arranged in columns (I created the columns in Word and converted the file to PDF).

What to Include in the Batch Process

The batching processes we will create here are a custom collection of cleanup and organization processes. I have decided that finalizing this article will require a number of processes as a standard cleanup workflow:

- Delete comments

- Embed thumbnails

- Add page numbers

- Audit space usage

- Detect and remove excess links, bookmarks

- Optimize space

1. Close all open files in Acrobat. Select File ➤ Batch Processing ➤ Edit Batch Sequences. In the Batch Sequences dialog box, click New Sequence. Enter the name **Article cleanup** in the pop-up window, and click OK. As shown in Figure 7-17, the new sequence will appear in the list.

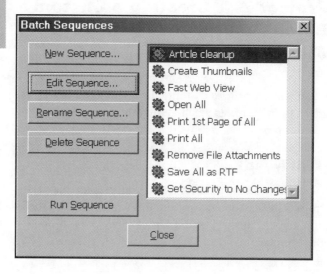

Figure 7-17
Add the new batch sequence.

2. Click Edit Sequence ➤ Select Commands. The Edit Sequence window will open, as shown in Figure 7-18. Click the names of the commands to be added, and then click Add to move them to the sequence window:
   - Delete All Comments
   - Embed All Thumbnails
   - Number Pages
   - Audit Space Usage
   - Detect And Remove
   - Optimize Space

Note

Only the Number Pages, Detect And Remove, and Optimize Space commands have configuration options, as indicated by the arrow to the left of the command line. Leave the default settings.

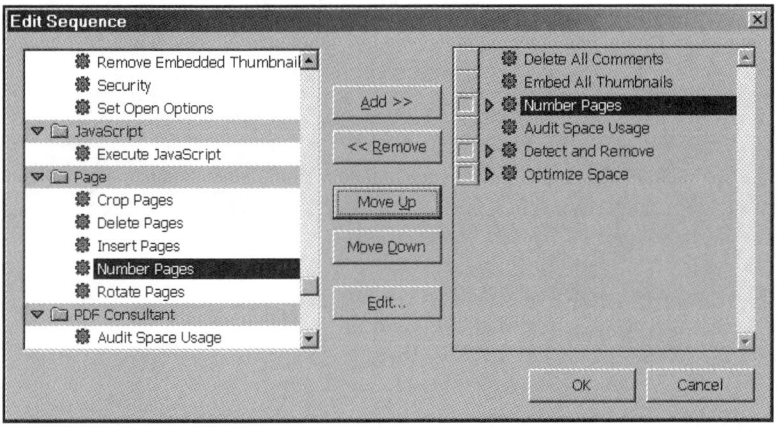

Figure 7-18
Add the commands to the sequence.

3. Click OK to close the Edit Sequence dialog box and return to the Batch Edit Sequence – Article Cleanup dialog box. The next step is to define the condition to run the sequence. From the Run Commands On drop-down list, select Ask When Sequence Is Run.
4. The final stages of the process are the storage location and output options. As you can see in Figure 7-19, I left the default storage location—that is, Same Folder as Original(s). I left the default output options. Click OK to close the Batch Edit Sequence dialog box. Click Close to close the Batch Sequences dialog box.

Note

I may have chosen the Open File option instead. After considering how I work, I decided to have the batch process prompt me as I may or may not have the file open that I want to run the batch against.

Now let's see how it works.

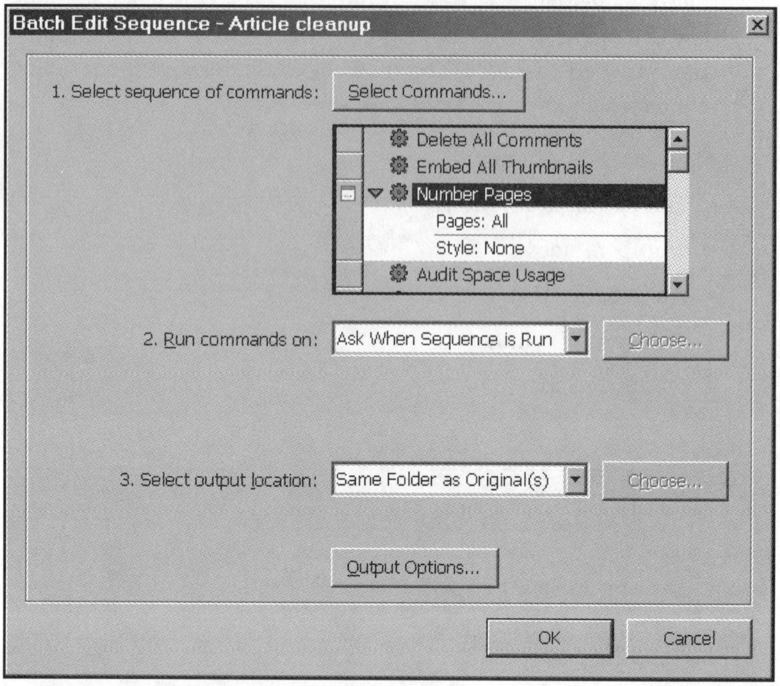

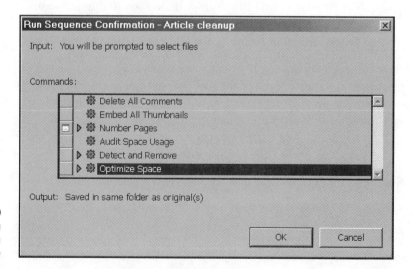

Figure 7-19
Finish selecting the batch
sequence options.

Running the Batch Sequence

Time to run this set of commands.

1. Select File ➤ Batch Processing ➤ Article Cleanup. The confirmation
    dialog box shown in Figure 7-20 will open.

Figure 7-20
Confirmation dialog
box for the custom
batch sequence

2. If necessary, review the contents of the sequence. As you can see in Figure 7-20, the Number Pages command has configuration options. Click OK to run the commands.

3. You will be prompted for the file to run the batch against. Browse to the file location and click Select. You will also be prompted when the Number Pages command is reached. Accept the defaults and click OK.

4. When the sequence has finished, the Warnings And Errors window will open. Review the results, and click OK to close the window.

Now the file is clean, organized, and numbered. We will use it again later in the chapter.

That has been a batch of information on batches, hasn't it? So far we have looked at processes applied to a document from *outside* the document. Next let's go into a document and look at organizing its content.

All About Articles

Try as we might, using a computer screen to read something just doesn't work the same way as reading magazine or newsletter articles. How often do you read articles that are in several columns, span several pages, and have advertising, images, and other nonarticle information inserted? My guess is regularly. Now translate that concept into reading the same thing on a computer screen.

It's an interesting phenomenon. We let our eyes move through pages and up and down columns, and we use our fingers to flip pages—without a second thought. It's almost as though our brains are on auto-pilot. The eye moves up and down the columns and jumps over callouts and images and advertisements until we reach "Continued on p. 79," at which point we flip through the pages to page 79 and continue. Sometimes at the top-left column, sometimes partway down the right column. No big deal.

On the other hand, if you tried to do the same thing with something on a screen, what would happen? Chaos is my guess. Why? Well, not being a neurologist, I can only hazard a guess. And here it is.

If you consider the mechanics of what you are doing when you read an article on a screen versus when you read a magazine article, there is only one difference. The magazine is a static entity, and your eyes move. When you read something on a screen, it, as well as your eyes, moves. So rather than commanding your mechanical functions to find the page

Note

When running a batch file, make sure that all files selected are closed. Batch processes run within Acrobat, not within individual files.

Workflow Tip
Who Would Use This Type of Process?

Again, as I have mentioned throughout this book, think about how you work. If you do a lot of document processing, categorize the types of work you do. For example, the batch process in this project is named "Article cleanup." Depending on what you do on a regular basis, you may have a series of custom batch processes for manuals, brochures, proposals, Web pages, and the like. Before building a batch process, review the steps you take to finish a project. Many of these things could probably be incorporated into a batch process. Not only will you save time, but also your output will be more consistent.

and the correct location, you have to scroll for it. What's the difference? The simple function is different. After all, we have had centuries to learn how to read a book, and only a few years to learn how to read a screen.

Add to the mix the ability to zoom in and out of a document, and it becomes difficult. After all, if you have zoomed in on the last part of the first column of the first page and want to continue to the second column of the next page, how do you remember where you are? Until we reach the point where on-screen reading is standard operating procedure, it behooves us to destress the on-screen reading experience for our users.

If you built a document using multiple columns, is the solution to rebuild that document if you think it will be read primarily online? Au contraire, mon ami. Acrobat has a tool designed just for this purpose.

Introducing Articles

Yes, Acrobat has an article feature. Using linked elements, you configure a path for reading a document regardless of the number of columns or pages it spans, and regardless of the zoom factor being used. This process is used for formatting articles to be read online as they are or for use with assistive reading devices. Articles are linked objects defined in a document. Have you ever spent time on message boards? One way entries can be followed is through threads. A *thread* follows the same topic throughout the content of the board regardless of posting dates or authors. When you follow a thread, you read postings on the same topic. Acrobat's version of an article thread basically follows the same idea of guiding the reader through the material.

As with some of the other structural elements we have looked at, you can either generate article threads before a file is converted to PDF or do it from within Acrobat. We will look at both of these methods. Regardless of the document origin, Acrobat provides access to an Article palette, which I will describe later in the chapter.

Creating Articles in a Document

Using text frames, and then linking the text frames together, is a common procedure in desktop publishing programs. When text is entered into the first text frame, overflow spills to the next one, and so on. The same thing happens when you create article threads in Acrobat. In this case, though, the content is already there, and then the text frames are added.

Here's how to define an article in a document:

1. Click the Article tool on the Editing toolbar to select it.

2. Click and drag the pointer crosshairs to define the first box by fencing in the text. When the marquee is complete, release the mouse button, and the text selected will be enclosed by an article box.

3. The article box will be automatically labeled with a two-part label: *<article number>-<sequence>*. For example, the first article defined would be labeled 1-1, then 1-2, and so on. As you can see in Figure 7-21, this thread has three defined articles.

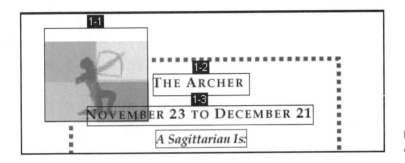

Figure 7-21
Articles defined on a page

4. Continue until you have finished (wow—is that stating the obvious). To end the numbering process, press Enter (Return on a Mac). The Article Property dialog box will open.

5. Each article has its own properties in addition to numbering. As shown in Figure 7-22, you can add a title, subject, author, and keywords in the Article Properties dialog box. Click OK to add the information and close the dialog box.

Note
You can revise the properties by clicking a box to select it and then selecting Properties from the context menu.

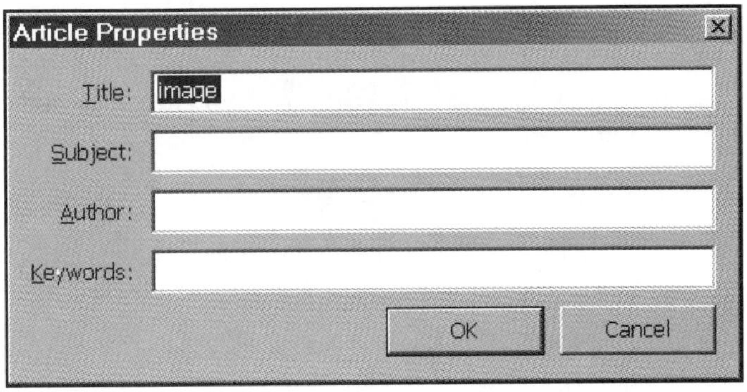

Article Properties

Title: image

Subject:

Author:

Keywords:

OK   Cancel

Figure 7-22
You can add properties to the articles. At a minimum, you should name the article.

If you have made a mistake or want to change anything in the sequence you have created, you have to end the process first. Also, in one document you might have more than one sequence. In this case, you will also have to end one thread before starting another one.

Manipulating Articles

Articles can be modified like any other kind of element you add in Acrobat. You can manipulate the articles themselves as well as the article threads. In fact, you can delete, insert, combine, move, or resize an article box, and edit an article's properties. Make sure you have the Articles palette open to see what you are doing (to display the palette, select Window ➤ Articles). In our example, there are four articles, as shown in Figure 7-23. To access these functions, click the Article tool on the Editing toolbar. The articles identified in the document will be displayed.

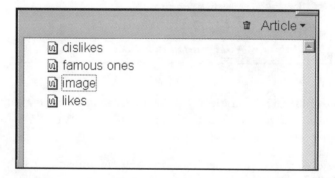

Figure 7-23
The content of
the Articles palette

Deleting Article Threads and Boxes

Remember that deleting and inserting applies to both the articles and the threads.

1. To delete an entire article thread, select the article in the Articles palette and press Delete. The remaining article threads will be renumbered.

2. To delete a box from an article:

    a. Click the box in the document to select it.

    b. Select Delete from the context menu.

    c. Select Box from the dialog box. The remaining article boxes will be renumbered.

3. Click another tool to deselect the Article tool.

Inserting an Article Box

You can add an article box to a thread. Here's how:

1. Click the article box located in the flow before the one you want to insert.

2. Click the plus sign (+) at the bottom of the selected box, as shown in Figure 7-24.

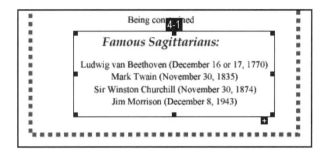

Figure 7-24
Use the + indicator to attach article boxes to a thread.

3. Click OK when prompted to drag and create a new article box.

4. The new box is inserted into the thread, and all boxes following the inserted one are renumbered automatically.

And that's not all. The boxes themselves are elements that can be moved or resized. If a box is selected, you can drag it to a new location, or resize it by dragging one of the corner handles.

That is quite enough of do-this, click-that. Time to build something.

Project **Project 7-2. Threading Your Way Through the Internet Document**

For this project, you will need the same file we used for the first project in this chapter: internet.pdf. It is located on the CD in the Chapter 7 Projects folder. You do not have to complete Project 7-1 to use the file for this project. In this project, we will create article threads in the document.

Evaluating the Document

Always best to start at the beginning. Let's see what is already there to work from. Open the internet.pdf file, and then open the Articles

Workflow Tip

Planning an Article Flow

The point of adding articles is to organize a flow for readers who may be using different devices. In order to create a readable document, we have to set a path through the document that makes the content flow from beginning to end.

You can take several different approaches. For example, you may want to add one giant article thread from page 1 to page *x*. I prefer to organize a flow of articles according to headings.

Note

You could leave the articles and attach other elements to them as you come to them, or move their boxes to the correct positions in the sequence and add to them. I find all that a waste of time. It's much simpler and quicker to delete them and start afresh.

palette. Click the Article tool to activate the articles in the document. You will see that four article threads are preformatted at conversion:

- 1-1 is the graphic on page 1.

- 2-1 is the graphic on page 5.

- 3-1 is the text box on page 2.

- 4-1 is the text box on page 5.

Delete the articles by clicking their icons in the Articles palette and pressing Delete. A confirmation dialog box will pop up. Click OK to delete the articles. The articles that were integrated in the conversion process are of little value in the workflow.

Now we need to add some article threads.

Adding Article Threads

Let's add a series of article threads corresponding with the layout of the document. Figure 7-25 shows the outline for this document from its authoring application, Microsoft Word.

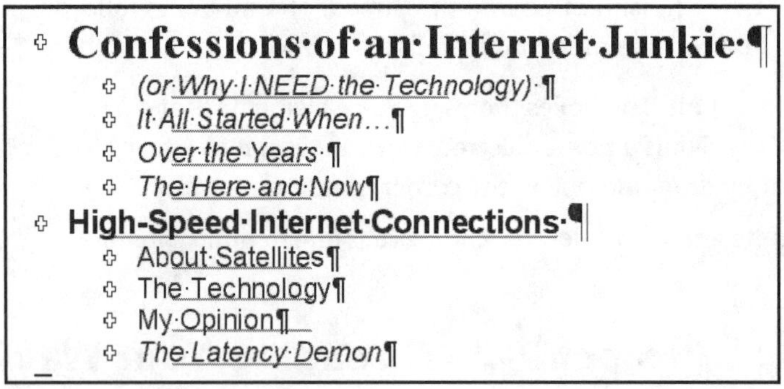

Confessions·of·an·Internet·Junkie·¶
   ⊹ *(or·Why·I·NEED·the·Technology)·¶*
   ⊹ *It·All·Started·When…¶*
   ⊹ *Over·the·Years·¶*
   ⊹ *The·Here·and·Now¶*
⊹ **High-Speed·Internet·Connections·¶**
   ⊹ About·Satellites¶
   ⊹ The·Technology¶
   ⊹ My·Opinion¶
   ⊹ The·Latency·Demon¶

Figure 7-25
The outline of the document

There are two first-level and eight second-level headings. This will correspond to ten article threads. Here's how to build them:

1. Click the Article tool to activate it. Click and drag to fence in the title text. Release the mouse.

2. Click and drag each column in reading sequence. Where you see a text box, click that in sequence as well.

3. Finally, where there are graphics, add them as the last element of the two threads in which they will appear.

4. Click another tool in the toolbar to deselect the Article tool and end the thread.

5. The Properties dialog box will appear. Enter a name for the thread and click OK.

6. Continue to the end of the document. Save the file.

The structure of each article thread in this document is listed in Table 7-1.

Table 7-1   The Article Threads Added to internet.pdf

Thread	Articles	Page	Instructions/Notes
1	2	1	Two articles, one for titles and copyright, and one for paragraph
2	4	1	Articles for head, each column, and then the graphic
3	4	2	Articles for head, each column, and then the text box
4	5	2/3	Articles for head, each column, and then paragraph-spanning columns
5	4	3	Articles for head, then the callout, and then two columns
6	2	3	Two articles for head and text
7	3	4	Articles for head and column text, then spanning paragraph
8	2	4	Two articles for head and bullet text
9	4	4	Article for head, spanning paragraph, and then the two columns
10	6	5	Article for head, two spanning paragraphs, column text, paragraph under image, graphic, and finally the last text box

Testing the Document

You can test this document's articles either in Acrobat 5 or Acrobat Reader 5. I tried it in both.

1. Click the Reflow tool (in Acrobat Reader) or select View ➤ Reflow (in Acrobat).

2. Scroll through the document. You should see that the document flows according to the articles and their sequences.

Workflow Tip
Easy Naming of Article Threads

Want an easy way to name article threads in a document such as the one we are using? Before starting a new article, click the TouchUp Text tool (or the Text Select tool), and then click and drag to select the heading text. Copy it. When the article thread is finished and the Properties dialog box opens, paste the text as the name for the thread. I use the TouchUp Text tool rather than the Text Select tool because I know for certain that only the heading line will be selected. The Text Select tool has a habit of selecting more text when I click and drag.

Note
You may find that some of the components don't look as "neat and tidy" as you may like—line lengths differ, for example. We will look further at Reflow options in Chapter 8.

To make a case in point, I want to end this project with a discussion of Figure 7-26. As you can see in the image, I have shown the article assignment for the last page of this project.

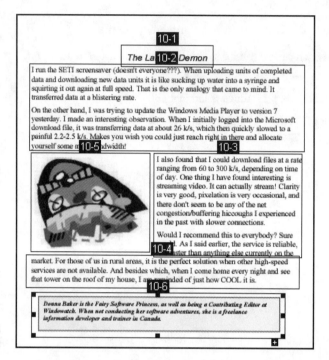

Figure 7-26
Page 5 of the project

As you can see in the image, there are six articles. The way they are assigned is a matter of personal preference to some extent. For example, I could have combined the first two articles, or I could have made the text box at the bottom a separate article. The only thing that should be standard is to have the image last—which I didn't do, by the way, because I wanted to have the image before the author bio text block. The point is, how you work with articles is customized according to both your work habits and what corporate/workgroup requirements may be in place. Many options are available.

Now let's look at another way to distribute output via Web browsers—and a new plug-in.

Creating Web Output

Adobe has produced a terrific extension for creating Web output in a variety of formats. The Save As XML plug-in for Acrobat 5 is used for repurposing content. The plug-in saves content from a tagged PDF file as XML, HTML, or plain text. At the time of this writing, the beta version was available.

Note

To get the plug-in, go to http://www.adobe.com/products/acrobat/. Click Downloads, and select the desired version of the Save As XML plug-in.

The plug-in can generate a number of formats. Depending on the intended use of the file, you may need to save a file in more than one version. The plug-in can generate these formats:

- HTML-4.01 with CSS-1.00

- HTML-3.20 without CSS

- HTML-3.20 Accessible

- XML-1.00 without styling

Let's have a look at each of these options. In all instances, I have used the same source file to compare the output.

Output in HTML with Style Sheet Information

Sometimes it is extremely valuable to export a formatted document. Think of instances when you are working with different types of documents that use specific corporate templates, colors, and so forth. This export format can save a lot of time. Figure 7-27 shows a partial page layout. I want to point out some of the translation benefits and issues.

Note

XML is a language specification developed by the World Wide Web Consortium (W3C) and designed especially for Web documents. It allows designers to create customized tags, enabling data flow between applications and between organizations.

Note

If the images look familiar, they should. It is the Applying Stage Makeup Manual I have used in other chapters. This incarnation has a column layout.

Granted, these people were not standing on a stage but quite often they were using makeup to embellish the movement, attitude and temperament required to get the message across.
One of the best ways to *get into character* is to watch the growth of that character in the mirror. Applying stage makeup is essential in the creation of your physical character and ultimately, your entire character.
Actors have been wearing makeup since the dawn of time. Picture ancient man reenacting the thrill of the hunt or an aboriginal ancestor smearing his face with war paint to instill fear in the enemy. Granted, these people were not standing on a stage but quite often they were using makeup to embellish the movement, attitude and temperament required to get the message across.

One of the best ways to *get into character* before hitting the stage is to watch the growth of that character in the mirror as you create him/her. If that physical character is the product of your search for the entire character - your performance will always be exhilarating.

HE IMPORTANCE OF MAKEUP

Imagine a performance of the 'Wizard of Oz' without makeup. Now, imagine seeing that same performance sitting in the back row of a 2,000 seat concert hall. It doesn't really paint an image of an inspiring, believable performance does it? Here are some reasons why good makeup is so important.

Figure 7-27
The exported HTML 4.01 version of the manual.pdf document

Basically, the translation worked very well, but you will still have to proofread the converted documents—special characters, such as curly apostrophes, do not translate. Image placeholders are added, of course, and I have placed the actual image next to the broken image icon for reference.

Look at the main title. The beginning of the title line is missing. And this where a word of caution comes in. Just as you plan different uses for material and design approaches to using content for multiple forms of output, think about such things as templates as well. If I were using this as a one-off process, I would adjust the content of the file. On the other hand, think how tedious it would be to adjust headings constantly every time a page had to be posted, particularly if you were posting dozens of pages a day.

Here's why this happened. In Figure 7-28, I have captured the beginning of the HTML code for the page shown in Figure 7-27.

```
<!DOCTYPE html
PUBLIC "-//W3C//DTD HTML 4.01//EN" "http://www.w3.org/TR/html40/strict.dtd">
<!--
 Created from PDF via
Acrobat 5.0 SaveAs: 'HTML-4.01 with CSS-1.00'
 Mapping Table version:
21-May-2001
-->
<HTML><HEAD><STYLE type="text/css">
DIV[class="Sect"]
{
 text-align:left;
 margin-bottom:0.00pt;
 margin-top:0.00pt;
 margin-right:0.00pt;
 margin-left:0.00pt;
 text-indent:0.00pt;
 direction:ltr
}
H1 {
 text-align:left;
 margin-bottom:12.00pt;
 margin-top:18.00pt;
 margin-right:6.50pt;
 margin-left:-35.99pt;
 text-indent:0.00pt;
 direction:ltr
}
```

Figure 7-28
A portion of the HTML
content for the manual file

This output type includes style sheet information (CSS version 1.00). After the opening <Head> tag, the first style describes the "Sect" (Section) class, followed by the <H1> class attributes. Here is the issue. If you look at the content of the style, the lines "margin-left:-35.99pt" and "text-indent:0.00pt" are the source of the problem. In order to display the main headings correctly, you have to set the margin-left in the "Sect" to a negative value, or you have to increase the text indent for the body to roughly 36 pts. to accommodate this.

Now let's look at the layout without style sheet information.

Output in HTML-3.20 Format Without CSS Information

The second option I want to look at is output converted without style sheet information. Look at Figure 7-29. You can see that the page layout is simpler. That is, no styles are carried from the PDF document to the HTML version. Unless you have a particular need for the precise layout, however, this might be a better choice for the document we are looking at.

Workflow Tip

Why Would I Use This Version If a Newer Version Is Available?

The differences between the two versions are not so great as to make this an unlikely choice for output. There would be no need for modifying any of the style sheet elements from within a Web design program, and pages could be easily converted to Web output. Using this form of HTML output would be convenient and would still allow written materials to use the original styles. Of course, in some circumstances that might not be appropriate, but I think it is acceptable in this example—depending on the client!

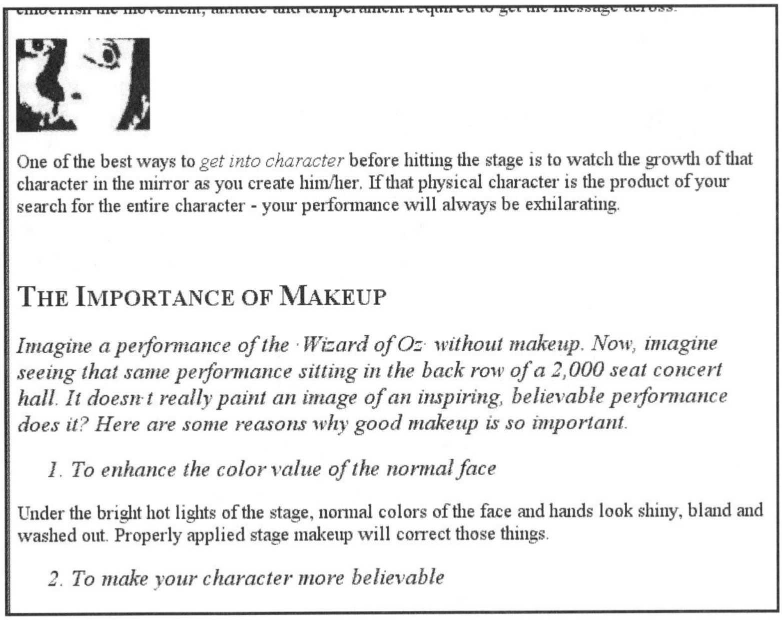

One of the best ways to *get into character* before hitting the stage is to watch the growth of that character in the mirror as you create him/her. If that physical character is the product of your search for the entire character - your performance will always be exhilarating.

THE IMPORTANCE OF MAKEUP

Imagine a performance of the ·Wizard of Oz· without makeup. Now, imagine seeing that same performance sitting in the back row of a 2,000 seat concert hall. It doesn·t really paint an image of an inspiring, believable performance does it? Here are some reasons why good makeup is so important.

1. To enhance the color value of the normal face

Under the bright hot lights of the stage, normal colors of the face and hands look shiny, bland and washed out. Properly applied stage makeup will correct those things.

2. To make your character more believable

Figure 7-29
The HTML version without style sheet information. The layout is simpler.

Another output option is available using the same HTML version designed for accessible viewing.

Output in Accessible HTML-3.20 Format

A separate option is available for making accessible HTML output. As we will see in the next chapter, a number of processes can be used with a PDF document to make them comply with accessibility standards. This option carries out that theme of streamlining processes to make information accessible. The output of the same page we used in the previous examples is shown in Figure 7-30.

embellish the movement, attitude and temperament required to get the message across.

One of the best ways to *get into character* before hitting the stage is to watch the growth of that character in the mirror as you create him/her. If that physical character is the product of your search for the entire character - your performance will always be exhilarating.

THE IMPORTANCE OF MAKEUP

Imagine a performance of the Wizard of Oz without makeup. Now, imagine seeing that same performance sitting in the back row of a 2,000 seat concert hall. It doesn't really paint an image of an inspiring, believable performance does it? Here are some reasons why good makeup is so important.

1. To enhance the color value of the normal face

Under the bright hot lights of the stage, normal colors of the face and hands look shiny, bland and washed out. Properly applied stage makeup will correct those things.

2. To make your character more believable

Unless you are playing yourself (which is unlikely) makeup is required to create highlights, shadows, shapes things that can change the characteristics of your face into your character's face.

Figure 7-30
The manual in Accessible
HTML-3.20 format

What's the difference? Well, as we will see in the next chapter, you must enter additional pieces of information in order to comply with standards and to make the file readily usable with visual assistive devices.

Here's one example. If you look at the image of the accessible-format page, you will see the image is placed correctly. I didn't add it. The conversion process will add the following lines of code to the file automatically.

```
<IMG Alt="" width="137" height="92"
 src="manual_0_img.jpg" />
```

As you can see, this is a simple image tag. Because both the tag and the source were added, however, the image is already inserted, not merely a placeholder. You will also notice that an Alt text component has been added, which is integral to the accessibility process.

The last option (or perhaps, more correctly, the first option) is XML.

Output in XML-1.00 Format

As Sgt. Joe Friday always used to say, "Just the facts, Ma'am." That is the core of XML. Simply the guts of a document, the essence of a file, elegant in its simplicity. I could go on, but I think you get the idea.

Figure 7-31 shows the XML output for the manual.pdf file.

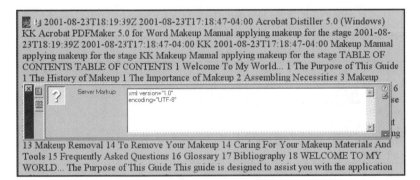

Figure 7-31
The essence of a document: XML output

Visually, there really isn't much to the document. Look at the image, though. After the metadata, beginning with the "TABLE OF CONTENTS" element, everything that must be there is there. That does not include things like links or images, which are objects added to a document, not its essence.

When the XML document is viewed in a browser, the tag structure is also included. I have shown a portion of the file, approximately the same view as the other versions, in Figure 7-32.

As an introduction to this section, I referenced XML as the last option for this discussion, but identified it as "more correctly, the first option." Regardless of the HTML/XML format in which you choose to save a PDF file, initially it will be converted to XML and then have the attributes added to it depending on the version.

Previously, as I was describing the content of the XML file, I made a reference to the metadata. Not to confuse the issue, but *metadata* is data about data. I think that deserves some explanation.

Note

More information on installation and configuring the plug-in is in Appendix B at the end of this book.

```
<Normal>One of the best ways to get into character is to watch the
  growth of that character in the mirror. Applying stage makeup is
  essential in the creation of your physical character and ultimately,
  your entire character.</Normal>
<Normal>Actors have been wearing makeup since the dawn of time.
  Picture ancient man reenacting the thrill of the hunt or an aboriginal
  ancestor smearing his face with war paint to instill fear in the
  enemy.</Normal>
<Normal>Granted, these people were not standing on a stage but quite
  often they were using makeup to embellish the movement, attitude
  and temperament required to get the message across.</Normal>
<Shape Alt="" src="manual_0_img.jpg" />
<Normal>One of the best ways to get into character before hitting the
  stage is to watch the growth of that character in the mirror as you
  create him/her. If that physical character is the product of your
  search for the entire character - your performance will always be
  exhilarating.</Normal>
<Normal />
<Heading-1>THE IMPORTANCE OF MAKEUP</Heading-1>
<Style3>Imagine a performance of the "Wizard of Oz" without makeup.
  Now, imagine seeing that same performance sitting in the back row of
  a 2,000 seat concert hall. It doesn't really paint an image of an
  inspiring, believable performance does it? Here are some reasons why
  good makeup is so important.</Style3>
- <L>
  - <LI>
    <LBody>1. To enhance the color value of the normal
```

Figure 7-32
The browser view of
the manual.xml file

Document Metadata

Metadata describes how and when and by whom a particular set of data was collected, and how the data is formatted. Acrobat PDF files use XML-formatted metadata. The metadata is the information you find in a document's properties. Whenever a change is made to the properties, changes will logically be made to its metadata. You cannot change the metadata information directly. Even if you could, it wouldn't then reflect the content of the document accurately.

You can see a document's metadata by selecting File ➤ Document Properties ➤ Document Metadata. The information window shown in Figure 7-33 will open.

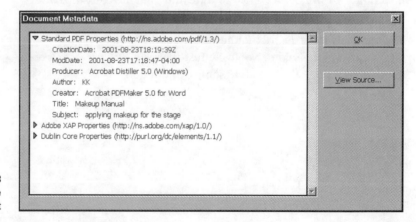

Figure 7-33
The metadata for the
manual.pdf document

All the metadata embedded in the document is organized according to different groups of properties. I have expanded the Standard PDF Properties section of Figure 7-33. From this window, you can also see the XML code. Click View Source to open the window shown in Figure 7-34.

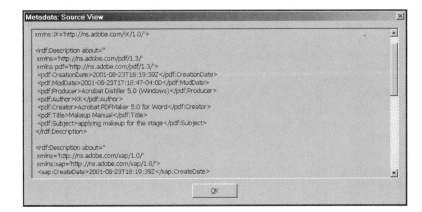

Figure 7-34
The Metadata: Source View window for the manual.pdf document

The source code can be copied and pasted (but not changed) from this view window. So why is this important, and why is it here? The metadata, as I discussed earlier, is information about the information. When a document is converted to any type of HTML, this information will be translated along with it.

Anyone who is familiar with HTML knows that metatags are included in the <Head> tags of the file. These serve the same purpose in HTML as information about the document itself. Figure 7-35 shows a portion of the HTML code for the manual.pdf saved as an HTML 3.2 version. You can see here that much of the information I have shown you in the metadata figures has been translated into metatags.

And that's it for that.

Up Next

Quite a heavy note to end a chapter on, isn't it? That is the beauty of the software we are discussing in this book. It has an inner beauty along with the cool stuff we can create on the outside. Its inner beauty is characterized by its simplicity. I like that. And I do think it is important to understand what is under the hood. It makes the wild and wonderful creations all the more awesome when you know what they are built on.

```
<!DOCTYPE HTML
PUBLIC "-//W3C//DTD HTML 3.2 FINAL //EN">
<!--
 Created from PDF via
Acrobat 5.0 SaveAs: 'HTML-3.20 Accessible'
 Mapping Table version:
19-May-2001
-->
<HTML><HEAD
><META
 name="DC.Title"
 content="Makeup Manual" />
<META
 name="DC.Contributor"
 content="KK" />
<META
 name="DC.Subject"
 content="applying makeup for the stage" />
<META
 name="DC.Creator"
 content="Acrobat PDFMaker 5.0 for Word" />
<META
 name="DC.Date"
 content="2001-08-23T18:19:39Z" />
<META
 name="DC.Date.Modified"
 content="2001-08-23T17:18:47-04:00" />
</HEAD><BODY
```

Figure 7-35
The <Head> tags for the
manual.pdf document
after saving a version in
HTML 3.2 format

In this chapter, my aim was to show you a number of types of output you can create from a single PDF document. Rather than showing you one of these and one of those, I concentrated instead on some of the processes and tools at your disposal, and the how and why of using them. I think it will give you a better sense of what can be done with Acrobat. Not only that, but by using this approach you can better understand how to adapt these processes and tools to your work.

A number of specialized types of output do exist, however. Coming up next, we will look at one of those specialized outputs. Specifically, we will learn how to make PDF documents accessible for users with special needs and assistive devices.

Chapter 8

Making Documents Accessible to Everyone

The world is full of information, and everyone has a right to access that information. Here's how to use Acrobat 5 to make your information accessible.

What Does "Accessible" Mean?

The idea of user accessibility evolved based on the statements that open this chapter. Consider what can happen when you, the average person, opens a document. You scroll down the page, change pages, use the mouse, use shortcut keys, change magnifications, activate links, and so on. If there is video, you can watch it. If there is audio, you can hear it. But what happens if you are not capable of performing any or all of these functions?

As software and presentation have become increasingly sophisticated, the need for standards has evolved, as has a greater understanding of what is required to make information accessible. Not only that, but software manufacturers have made available methods for their products' users to create accessible information.

Before we get into any specifics, let me first explain more clearly what I am referring to.

Capabilities

Basically, we are considering two separate but conjoined issues: the abilities of the user and the capabilities of devices.

A user's abilities can be restricted on the basis of movement, sight, hearing, or comprehension. A user might be able to access information only through sight, sound, or touch, or some combination of these three methods.

On the other hand, we also have to consider the capabilities of devices. After all, unless the technology exists for the user to interact with information in a meaningful way, the discussion is pointless. From a device perspective, then, we are looking at two things: screen sizes and inter-action methods. Screen size is self-explanatory. Interaction methods may include using keyboard, using voice, or using assistive devices (such as infrared pointers and the like).

That's what we are starting from. I have stressed that information should be accessible, and that the software and devices used for distrib-uting and presenting the information should also comply to standards. Let's have a look at what these standards are.

W3C Standards

In 1999, the World Wide Web Consortium (W3C) released the first-ever standards for accessibility. The initial set of standards is quite lengthy, and the items are organized according to scope and priority levels. This was followed in January 2001 by the working draft for version 2 of the guidelines, and the draft discussed here, which was released in August 2001.

W3C Guideline 1—Presentation

The first guideline deals with presentation, specifically by allowing users to control the presentation of the materials according to their needs and preferences.

- Checkpoint 1.1 Provide a text equivalent for all non-text content.

- Checkpoint 1.2 Provide synchronized media equivalents for time-dependent presentations.

- Checkpoint 1.3 Use markup or a data model to provide the logical structure of content.

- Checkpoint 1.4 Identify the primary natural language of text and text equivalents and all changes in natural language.

- Checkpoint 1.5 Separate content and structure from presentation.

W3C Guideline 2—Interaction

The second guideline deals with content design. Users must be able to interact with content according to their needs and preferences.

- Checkpoint 2.1 Provide multiple site navigation mechanisms.

- Checkpoint 2.2 Provide consistent and predictable responses to user actions.

- Checkpoint 2.3 Either give users control of mechanisms that cause extreme changes in context or warn them of pending changes.

- Checkpoint 2.4 Either give users control over how long they can interact with content that requires a timed response or give them as much time as possible.

- Checkpoint 2.5 Use device-independent event handlers.

- Checkpoint 2.6 Avoid causing the screen to flicker.

- Checkpoint 2.7 Handle input errors, such as misspellings.

Note

The content of these guidelines is taken from the draft document available at http://www.w3.org/TR/WCAG20. All of the following information, with the exception of the introduction to each of the four guidelines, is taken directly from the draft document. (Copyright © 2001 by World Wide Web Consortium. All Rights Reserved. http://www.w3.org/Consortium/Legal/.)

W3C Guideline 3—Comprehension

This guideline deals with making information as easy as possible to use and understand.

- Checkpoint 3.1 Use consistent presentation.
- Checkpoint 3.2 Emphasize structure through presentation, positioning, and labels.
- Checkpoint 3.3 Write as clearly and simply as is appropriate for the content.
- Checkpoint 3.4 Supplement text with non-text content.
- Checkpoint 3.5 Annotate complex, abbreviated, or unfamiliar information with summaries and definitions.

W3C Guideline 4—Technology Considerations

The fourth guideline considers technology, and specifies design for compatibility and interoperability.

- Checkpoint 4.1 Choose technologies that support the use of these guidelines.
- Checkpoint 4.2 Use technologies according to specification.
- Checkpoint 4.3 Design user interfaces compatible with assistive technology.
- Checkpoint 4.4 Ensure that content remains usable when technologies that modify default user agent processing or behavior are turned off or not supported.

These guidelines, as I mentioned earlier, are a working draft. By reading through the list, however, you should see many familiar elements, including some that are part of your everyday work.

An important thing to point out is that these are the guidelines from the W3C. So how are they applicable to Acrobat? If you look at the functionality of the program, its array of outputs, its integration with Internet browsers, and its use of cross-platform readers, creating materials that are not compliant with the standards is illogical—especially when so much of the work can be done for you using Acrobat's plug-ins and tools.

Before we get into the plug-ins and tools, I want to look further at some of Acrobat's elements that play a part in accessible document production.

What Acrobat Can Do

In order to meet the needs of both users and devices, Acrobat 5 has some basic as well as some not-so-basic features. For some topics, even though they are familiar, I have included them based specifically on how they contribute to meeting accessibility requirements.

General Accessibility Functions

The following functions are components of the program's structure. They do not require any particular modification on your part to use them.

- Keyboard shortcuts

- High-contrast color schemes

- Screen reader support

Keyboard Shortcuts

Acrobat uses a range of keyboard shortcuts. Users can use the program's interface without using a mouse. This also applies when using Acrobat in Microsoft Internet Explorer.

High-Contrast Color Schemes

Visually impaired users may be able to view a document if a high-contrast color scheme is used—that is, if the amount of contrast between a page's background and its text are in high contrast. Regardless of the color scheme specified in a document by its creator, users are able to override the assigned color scheme and use their own. As you can see in Figure 8-1, this amount of contrast in a document enhances the visibility.

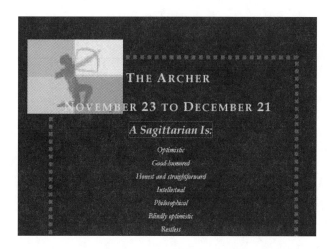

Figure 8-1
A portion of a page after a high-contrast color scheme has been applied

Here's how to set a high-contrast color scheme:

1. With the tagged file open, select Edit ➤ Preferences ➤ General.

2. Select Accessibility from the preferences list in the left pane.

3. Select Use Custom Scheme from the Color Scheme drop-down menu. (If you are using Windows and have a high-contrast viewing mode set up, you can choose Use Windows Colors.)

4. Select Text Color and Set Background Colors.

5. Select Always Overriding Document Colors from the Adjust Display Of Colors menu.

6. Click OK.

Note

You can also use these settings to test view any document in a high-contrast mode, and then return to the document colors by resetting this preference.

Screen Reader Support

Microsoft has created an application programming interface (API) called Microsoft Active Accessibility (MSAA). This API is used in Acrobat 5 for Windows. Screen readers, which use synthesized voice or Braille output, receive information on content and user interface elements of programs. Because both the screen readers and Acrobat both use the MSAA standard, PDF files are easily integrated.

Now let's look at some of the features and tools you can customize to improve and customize the accessibility features of your documents.

Acrobat's Accessibility Features

As I mentioned earlier when I introduced this section, some of these topics have been discussed elsewhere in this book. In order to give you a complete overview of what Acrobat can do, I have collected the entire list here:

- Enhanced security settings

- Reflowable text blocks (articles)

- Tagged files

- Tags palette

- Metadata

We will be looking at some of the specific features further on in this chapter.

Enhanced Security Settings

Until Acrobat 5, locking a PDF document to prevent copying and pasting of text meant that the document was inaccessible. As you can see in Figure 8-2, content can be made accessible and still have copying and extraction blocked.

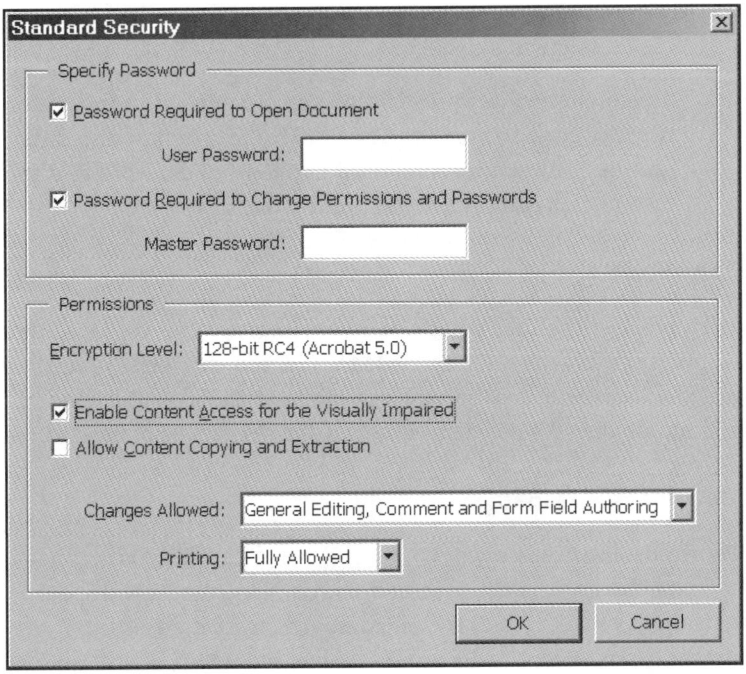

Figure 8-2
The security functions for accessible content

Reflowable Text Blocks

In the previous chapter, I introduced the subject of articles and touched on reflowing briefly. Content is reproportioned based on the zoom factor; a line that has, for example, 12 words on it at normal magnification might contain only 4 words when magnified. When the text reflows at a high magnification, the user can more easily read the content and will not have to scroll the page right and left to read the entire line. Tagged PDF documents may be reflowed. In combination with high-contrast viewing, users with limited vision can more easily read a document.

Tagged Files

We have looked at tagged files in other chapters. We will look at them again later in this chapter, specifically in terms of how to use them for optimizing accessibility in documents. From the standpoint of making a file accessible, tagged files do the following:

- Allow control over read order.

- Understand paragraph attributes.

- Support alternate text (alt text) descriptions for images.

- Allow accessible interaction with documents (filling in form fields, following links).

- Represent text as Unicode. Unicode presents all characters and words clearly to assistive devices. This text format also distinguishes between soft and hard hyphens, and a word that spans two lines is read as a single word.

Tags Palette

We have seen the Tags palette in other chapters. You will recall that it displays the structure of a tagged PDF file. You can revise and edit the palette. As we will see when we look at the Make Accessible plug-in, you can manipulate the palette to enhance the accessibility of the document.

Document Metadata

Remember this? Data about the data. When a document is manipulated by someone using assistive reading devices, the reader will speak the document's title before it is opened, saved, printed, or closed. If the document is not titled, the file name will be used. Think about some of the strange and awkward-sounding names we give to files. By adding a separate title to the metadata, the user will have a clearer understanding of what the file is about.

One last note on metadata. As shown in Figure 8-3, I have added the full description for the metadata elements of this file. In this way, the document is more readily searchable.

To add information to be stored in the document's metadata, select File ➤ Document Properties ➤ Summary. The dialog box shown in Figure 8-4 will open. Add information to complete the description of the file. Then click OK to close the dialog box.

Now let's have a look at how Acrobat's accessibility tools work.

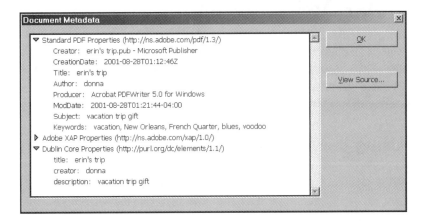

Figure 8-3
A complete metadata set

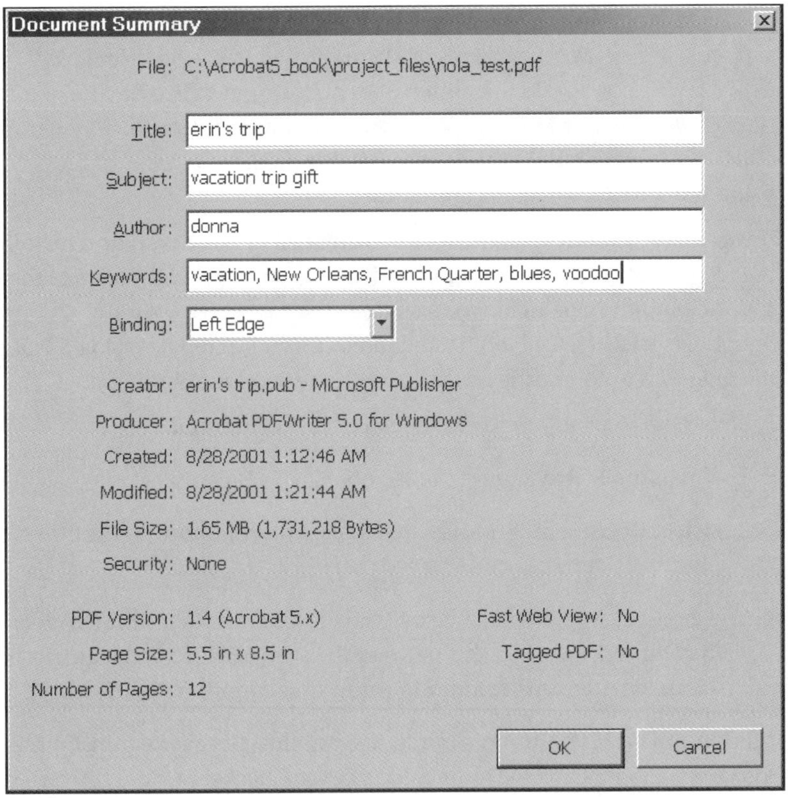

Figure 8-4
Add information to
the Document Summary
dialog box to create more
complete metadata for
the file.

Using the Accessibility Tools

Acrobat 5 offers two tools that are specifically designed for accessibility. The Make Accessible plug-in is a separate plug-in available from Adobe. The Accessibility Checker is a plug-in tool installed with Acrobat. Let's start with the Make Accessible plug-in.

Using the Make Accessible Plug-in

What if you have a document created in an older version of Acrobat? Or you have a different type of file that was converted to PDF using Acrobat Distiller? Enter the Make Accessible plug-in.

This plug-in can be used for any of these circumstances. It can also be used with files that were converted without a tagged format. The plug-in supports files created in versions of Microsoft Windows from Windows 95 OSR 2 to Windows 2000 files, but it does not support Office XP files at the time of writing, nor Mac OS. And here is an interesting note: You can either process a single document or batch-process a number of files using the Make Accessible command.

Note

In this demo, I started with alternate versions of the nola.pdf file for reference. (The project version of the file is on the CD in the Chapter 8 Projects folder.) Or use the file as a travel guide!

If you have Acrobat version 5.0, you will need to download and install the plug-in. For more information and to download the plug-in, go to the specific plug-in page at `http://www.adobe.com/support/downloads/detail.jsp?ftpID=1309`. If your installation CD is for Acrobat version 5.0.5, the plug-in is automatically installed with the regular installation.

Follow these steps to use the Make Accessible command:

1. Open the PDF document in Acrobat.

2. Select Document ➤ Make Accessible. The command will automatically start.

3. Select File ➤ Save As and save the file with another name (Adobe recommends you do this because the structure of the document is changed after this command is run and cannot be undone).

What happens if you try to run the Accessibility Checker against a file that has no tags? Look at Figure 8-5. I ran the Checker before I converted the file to see what the Accessibility Checker would do once the file was tagged. Primarily, the problem is that this document has not been tagged. Speaking of the Accessibility Checker, let's have a look at it now.

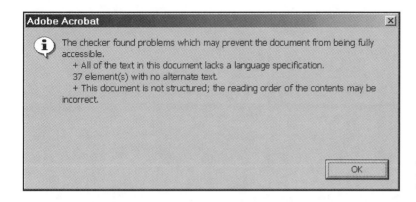

Figure 8-5
Results of running the
Accessibility Checker
against my demo version
of the nola.pdf file

Using the Accessibility Checker

The Accessibility Checker will evaluate a tagged document for compliance
with accessibility requirements. The tool checks for the elements I
described in the "What Acrobat Can Do" section, in which I discussed
Acrobat's accessibility components.

The Accessibility Checker will look for noncompliant elements such as
missing tags and incorrect or unrecognizable character encodings. Any
noncompliant elements will be logged to a file or displayed in an information window.

You can also use this tool as a controller. Run the Checker and compile
a list of problems. Correct the issues and rerun the controller to verify
your corrections and amendments. When all the problems have been
corrected, your document is ready for distribution.

Running the Accessibility Checker

Of course, you must start with a tagged PDF file. Then follow these steps:

1. Open the file in Acrobat.

2. Select Tools ➤ Accessibility Checker. The dialog box will open
   with a list of options.

3. Select the options desired. As shown in Figure 8-6, the options are
   as follows:

   • Alternate Descriptions Provided

   • Text Language Specified

   • Reliable Character Encodings

   • All Content Contained In The Document Structure

   • Form Fields Have Descriptions

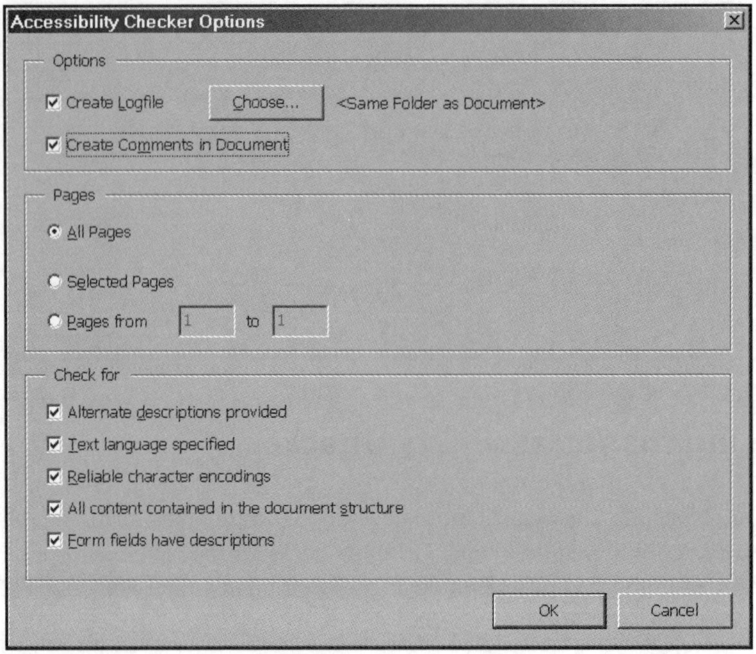

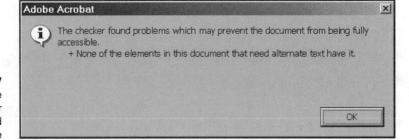

Figure 8-6
The Accessibility Checker Options dialog box

4. Click OK to run the Accessibility Checker.
5. The results will be shown in a dialog box (see Figure 8-7). As you can see in this image, aside from the `<Alt Text>` tags, the other issues have been corrected with the tagging process.

Figure 8-7
The results of running the Accessibility Checker against the tagged version of my demo file

Note

If you chose the Create Logfile option, the file cannot be opened in Acrobat. Use Notepad or a similar plain text editor to open the log file.

When I set the options for the Checker, I selected both the Create Logfile and Create Comments In Document options. As you can see in Figure 8-8, the comments on the page are in a standard format (I was logged in as The Boss). You can access the comment by double-clicking one of the graphic rectangles.

Figure 8-8
The Accessibility Checker displays comments in a standard format.

Figure 8-9 shows a portion of the Comments palette for the nola.pdf file. You will see that there are both text and graphical comments added by the Checker.

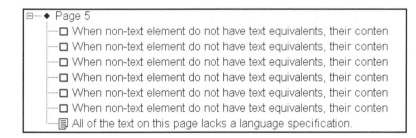

Figure 8-9
The Tags palette showing commented problem areas in the demonstration document

This is a very useful feature for finding locations in a document. Figure 8-10 shows the page from which this list of comments came. Quite a simple page. Imagine if the document were 50 pages instead of 5!

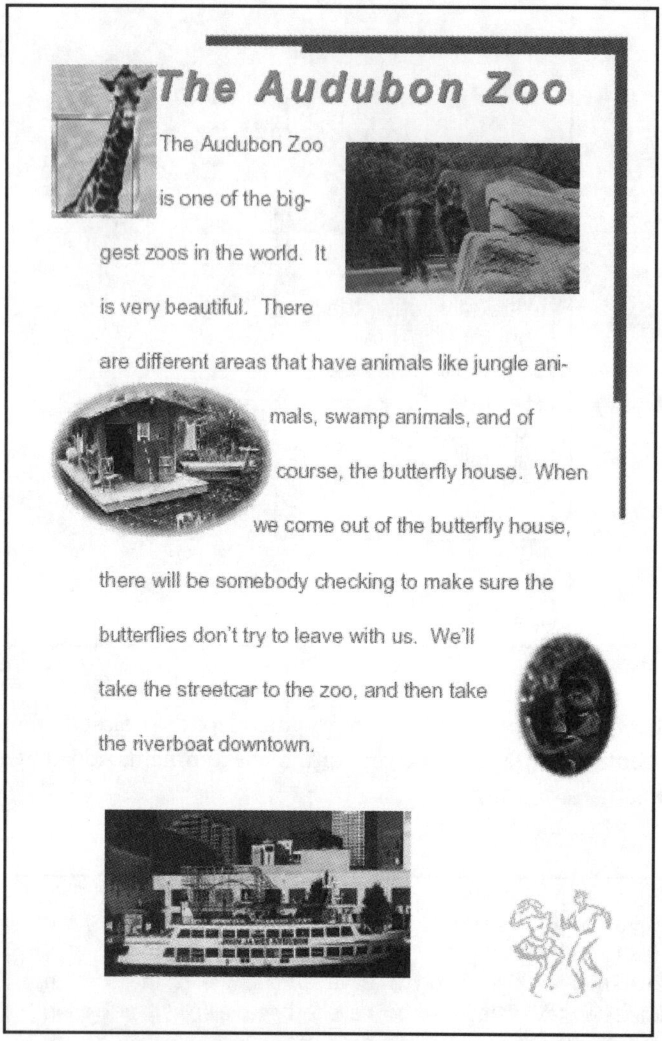

Figure 8-10
The page from the demo
file that produced the
Accessibility Checker
comments shown
in Figure 8-9

Using the Tags Palette

Some typical problems can be most easily corrected in the Tags palette.
In all instances, once you have located the element in the Tags palette, click
it to select it, and then right-click and select Element Properties from the
context menu. Be sure to select the tag, not the description of the element
itself. As shown in Figure 8-11, the image has only a size description. The
element itself is the ‹Span› tag.

Figure 8-11
Select the tag, not
the description of the
tag's content.

```
Tags Root
☐─    <Figure>
   ☐─    <Span>
          PDF Image  w: 899 h: 1015
```

The dialog box displayed will vary according to the type of element error.

To add missing alternate text (as shown in Figure 8-12):

1. Enter the alternate text in the Alternate Text text box.

2. Click OK to close the dialog box and make the change in the tag.

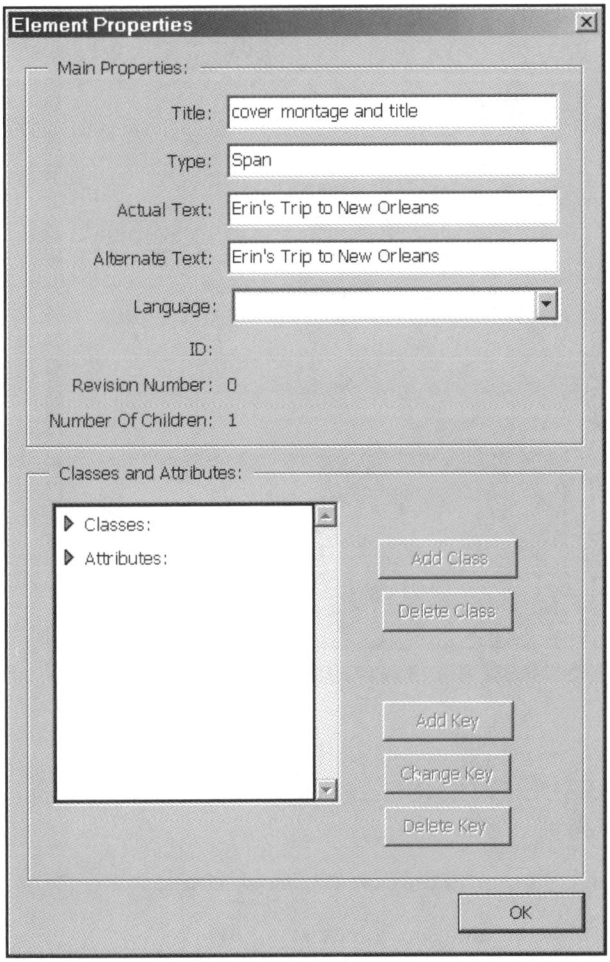

Workflow Tip

Do I Have to Make a File 100-Percent Compliant?

Not necessarily. I know this contradicts what I said in the Accessibility Checker discussion, but use your discretion. After all, what you are doing is configuring your document to be used with assistive devices. For example, the Checker might report that the file contains images that do not have alternate text. If these images are just the decorative borders on the page, as in my example, however, they would be unnecessary for someone with a vision impairment and would not require alternate text. Similarly, the Checker might report that a running header is not part of the structure tree. Again, you could leave this as is, because you don't need this information to be vocalized by a screen reader. Finally, another common error type is language specification. If language isn't an issue, don't worry about it.

Element Properties

Main Properties:

Title: cover montage and title

Type: Span

Actual Text: Erin's Trip to New Orleans

Alternate Text: Erin's Trip to New Orleans

Language:

ID:

Revision Number: 0

Number Of Children: 1

Classes and Attributes:

▶ Classes:
▶ Attributes:

Add Class

Delete Class

Add Key

Change Key

Delete Key

OK

Figure 8-12
Add missing alternate text in this dialog box.

Interpreting the Tags

Other common errors that can be corrected in this palette include tag type and language. Now let's look at a completed segment of the file. In Figure 8-13, I have shown page 4 of this file. As you can see, it has a heading, two images, one text block, and a graphic.

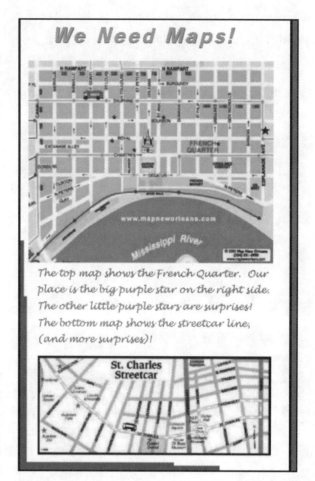

Figure 8-13
Layout of page 4
of the document

Figure 8-14 shows the portion of the Tags palette that corresponds to this page (after I have finished the modifications). I want to point out what I did:

- I named the part **We Need Maps!**

- I left the <H1> tag as is.

- I named the first <Figure> tag **border**. You see that strange description—PDF Path PDF Path PDF Path. That is not a typo! This corresponds with the border elements on the page, which are a set of three shapes.

- I named both the map images. I also changed their tags from <Span> to <Figure>.

The page will reflow in a different way. The two maps will be followed by the text. In the original layout, the maps are separated by the text.

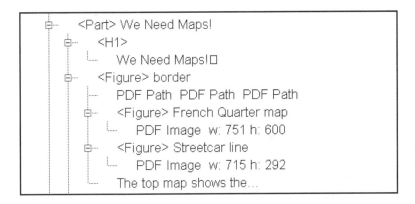

Figure 8-14
A completed segment of the Tags palette for page 4 of the document

Highlighting Content

Here's one last way to ease your way through a long list of corrections. In Figure 8-15, I have shown the Tags palette menu. Select Turn On Associated Content Highlighting. This way, the item selected in the Tags palette will highlight the corresponding element in the document. Be aware, though, that this reference process disables all the other functions in the Tags palette. Once you have highlighted an item in the page, it must be turned off to perform any other functions.

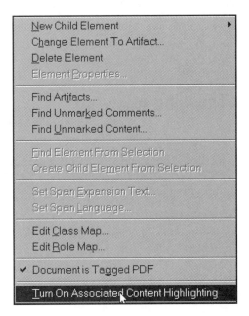

Figure 8-15
Use the content-highlighting feature to find the errors on the page.

Testing a Document

This is the final step in the accessibility workflow. You should test the document using a screen reader. Although you can see the presentation by selecting View ➤ Reflow, this is only a simulation. Only from within a reader will you be able to evaluate the actual reading order and functionality of the document.

Reflowing Tagged PDF Documents

Reflowing. The idea is that in a tagged document, the content can be laid out in such a way as to be readable regardless of the device being used to view it. That is the point of the tags. A tagged document has a highly defined structure. So, whether the reader views it on a handheld device or a large monitor, and regardless of zoom factor, it will be readable and logical.

And here is something else that is interesting. Reflowing in Acrobat is an experimental process only. You can't save a reflowed document. You wouldn't *want* to save a reflowed document. That is because your users will have the document served to them one page at a time and they will control reflowing as they view your document. Reflowing is simply a viewing option, but you can certainly reflow a document to test it and finesse the layout you have designed.

You can see the reflow of any tagged document by clicking the Reflow tool on the Editing toolbar or by selecting View ➤ Reflow. Leave this view state by clicking one of the other view buttons.

Finessing a Layout

In Chapter 7, I briefly discussed using the Reflow view to see how a document designed with columns would flow on a single page after I added articles to it. I also mentioned that you had a number of options for improving the reflowed layout.

What can you do to tweak a layout? Some touchup work, using touchup tools. Specifically the TouchUp Order, TouchUp Text, and TouchUp TextBreaks tools.

Editing Reflow Order

Editing reflow order does not change content or the actual structure of a document. Instead, this is a viewing sequence process that overlays the structure of the document. All it does is rearrange the sequence the reader experiences.

The file I have been using for this discussion, for example, has images with text wrapping around them for interest. In an on-screen use, however, that may be distracting. Change the reflow to have the image viewed at the end of the paragraph instead. Figure 8-16 shows the reflow order of a page. This page is taken from my demonstration version of the nola.pdf file. This would be hard to deal with!

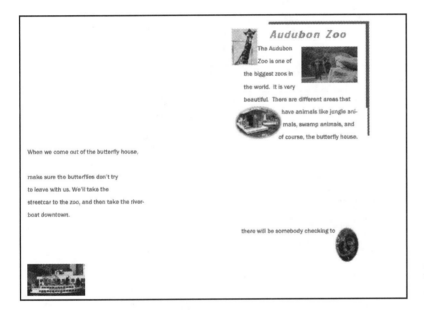

Figure 8-16
The Reflow view.
Not easy to read.

To edit the reflow order, follow these steps:

1. Click the TouchUp Order tool on the Editing toolbar to select it. All the elements on the page will be boxed and numbered with their order and position on the page (see Figure 8-17).

2. Change the order of the page's elements by clicking the numbers in the boxes in the order in which you want them to be viewed (if you make a mistake in this ordering, select a different tool from the toolbar to deactivate the TouchUp Order tool, then reselect it to start again).

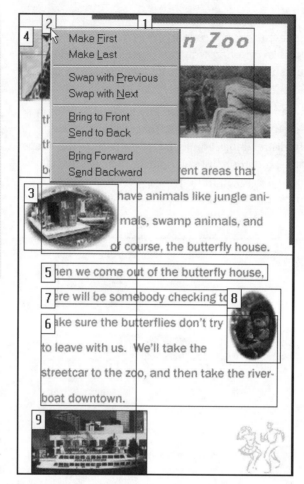

Figure 8-17
The page elements' order and the context menu

3. Save the document and then select View ➤ Reflow to test the changes you made. My output is shown in Figure 8-18. It still doesn't look great, but it is in the proper order.

Other TouchUp Options

Word sequencing includes partitioning with word and line breaks and hyphenation. Use the TouchUp Text tool to verify sequencing. After selecting a line of text, select Tools ➤ TouchUp Text ➤ Text Breaks. Make changes as required. Close the window when your review is complete.

One last area to mention. What if you want to use special characters? Using the TouchUp Text tool, click into the document to activate the text cursor. Then select Tools ➤ TouchUp Text ➤ Insert and select the character desired.

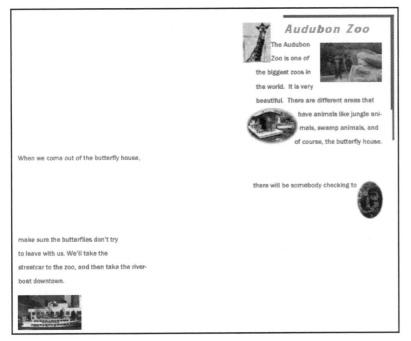

Figure 8-18
The modified reflow
of the page

Consider the Source

Consider this section a giant Workflow Tip. Rather than having to rework contents of a file once it has been converted to PDF, make some decisions in the source application that will make the file convert smoothly and save time in the long run.

- When using a document that is text-based with added elements, use Microsoft Word 2000 (Word XP if you have Acrobat 5.0.5 installed). In this version of the program, you can create tagged PDF files directly. (The demo file I used earlier in this chapter was created in Microsoft Publisher and printed to Acrobat Distiller. Once in Acrobat, I had to go through the entire accessibility process, with less than stellar results.)

- The same applies to other versions of Microsoft Word. Open and save the files in Word 2000 format.

- Use styles for format text. These styles can be converted to structural elements when converted to PDF format.

- Use the Table and Column commands instead of simulating tables or columns with tabs.

Workflow Tip
Fix It at the Source

If you look at Figure 8-18, you will see that there is still some irregularity in the Reflow view. This is not related to the reflow orders. This is how I constructed the file in the first place. When the document was originally created, I used non-breaking spaces to align elements. Text and images become reflow elements based on their arrangement. Also, the elements on the page overlap. The project at the end of the chapter deals with working smart from the start (which I obviously did not!).

- Save time required for locating and editing alternate text in Acrobat's Tag palette. Instead, add alternate text in the source program. (In Word, for example, add alternate text in the Web tab of the Properties dialog box.)

- Where practical, group a collection of illustrations using the Group command. This will require only one alternate tag and won't affect placement or reflow.

- When converting the file, ensure that, in the conversion settings, Embed Tags In PDF is turned on and Page Labels is turned off.

Let's see what differences these changes can make.

Project Project 8-1. Alternate Versions of the Same Source Material (or the Good, the Bad, and the Ugly)

I thought it would be interesting to look at a case in point to illustrate how smart construction of your source material translates into a more useful and usable PDF document. In this project, I have two versions of the same Microsoft Word document to use as source material. The files are SMD.doc and SMD1.doc. They are on the CD in the Chapter 8 Projects folder. You can also find versions of the converted document for reference. SMD.pdf and SMD1.pdf are also in the same folder on the CD.

Thanks to a Wonderful Organization

I would like to thank the Society for Manitobans with Disabilities, a 50-year-old service agency in my area. Executive Director David Steen has allowed me to use a document outlining the focus of one of its organizations as the subject material for this project. Because this chapter deals with accessibility issues, it is a fitting subject. Thanks also to Marshall Ring, CEO of AbiTech, for providing the materials used.

My apologies for using the word "ugly" in this project's title. But when you see what havoc I can wreak with this file, it is enough to give you bad dreams.

Review the Source

Let's take each file and convert it to a PDF file. There are significant differences between the two files in terms of how they are configured in Microsoft Word, and this will certainly be reflected in the converted PDF versions.

Convert the First File

We are going to start with the nonaccessibility-specific file—in other words, a document that has a number of advanced features used throughout but that has not been constructed with conversion to PDF in mind.

1. Open the SMD.doc file in Microsoft Word (either Word 97 or Word 2000; Word XP if you have installed Acrobat 5.0.5).

2. Review the document. As you can see, it is composed of six pages and includes a number of charts and different styles.

3. Open the conversion dialog box. Select Acrobat ➤ Change Conversion Settings. On the Settings tab, select Print from the Conversion Settings drop-down menu.

4. Click the Office tab. Make sure the option to create a tagged file is deselected.

5. Click the Bookmarks tab. The option to create headings from the document's headings will be selected, and Headings 1 to 4 will be selected. Leave these default settings.

6. Click the Edit Conversion Settings button to open the editing dialog boxes.

7. In the General tab, the default settings for this conversion use Acrobat 4.*x* compatible output. Leave this setting. Make sure the Embed Thumbnails option is deselected.

8. Click the Convert To Adobe PDF button on the toolbar or select Acrobat ➤ Convert To Adobe PDF.

9. Save the file with the default name in a new location (you cannot save the file to the CD).

> **Note**
>
> If someone were using this file to convert to a printable PDF file, this would be the logical choice. I would choose an alternate collection of settings or custom settings that included conversion settings.

Make This into an Accessible Document

Open the file in Acrobat. There is work to be done! Let's start at the beginning.

1. Make the document accessible (that is, add tags). Select Document ➤ Make Accessible. The prompt will request that you save the file with an alternate name. There is no need because this is a "new" file, and you have made no changes since you opened it.

2. Once the Make Accessible command has run against the file, save the file.

3. Run the Accessibility Checker. Select Tools ➤ Accessibility Checker. Select the option Create Comments In Document. Leave the other settings, and click OK to run the command. Again, if you are prompted to save the file with a different name, dismiss the prompt (provided you saved the file as previously suggested).

4. The Checker will display the results. They will be similar to those shown in Figure 8-19.

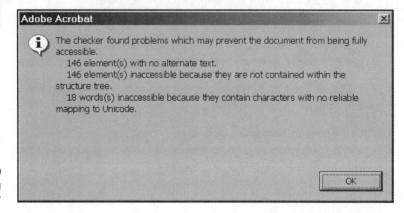

Figure 8-19
The results of running the Accessibility Checker

5. Save the file.

Now let's look at what is inside.

The Work That Has to Be Done!

This is where the "ugly" from the project's title comes into play. Not ugly in any visual sense, but the idea of having to make all these corrections manually could make one weep. Let's see what we have.

1. Open the Tabs palette. Scroll to page 1 of the document. Figure 8-20 shows the highlighting in the document pane for the logo that is in each page's header. As you can see, a number of rectangles appear, each of which represents one element of the illustration.

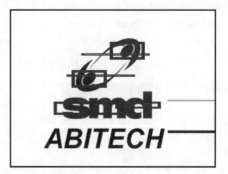

Figure 8-20
The logo's image elements

2. Scroll down the page to the flowchart. I have shown its elements selected in Figure 8-21. Again, this is a very complicated structure.

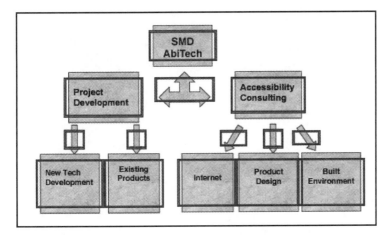

Figure 8-21
The elements of
the flowchart

3. Scroll to page 2. You will see text as shown in Figure 8-22. What you will not find, however, is a corresponding tag for the heading in the Tags palette...

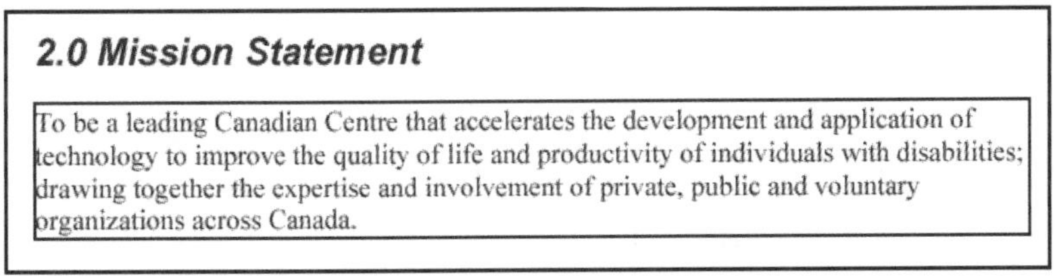

2.0 Mission Statement

To be a leading Canadian Centre that accelerates the development and application of technology to improve the quality of life and productivity of individuals with disabilities; drawing together the expertise and involvement of private, public and voluntary organizations across Canada.

Figure 8-22
Text displayed on page 2.
The title is untagged.

4. Scroll through the document. I want to show you one last issue before we look at an alternate solution to this problem. One of the charts from page 3 is shown in Figure 8-23. The chart is composed of separate elements.

Figure 8-24 shows the beginning of the tag set for this chart. It goes on and on and on....

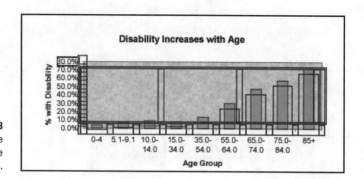

Figure 8-23
One of the charts in the
document. None of the
elements is conjoined.

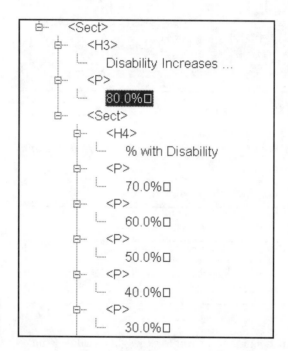

Figure 8-24
The beginning of the tags
list for the chart

And if that weren't bad enough, look at Figure 8-25. This is the Reflow
view of the page containing the chart we have been looking at. Each
and every one of these dots is a comment tied to a needed repair.

But it doesn't have to be that way. Work smart. I would like to point out
one thing before we look at an alternate version of this file. There is
nothing at all wrong with the source file. For general purposes, it is perfectly fine. It will print well, and it can be shared or e-mailed readily. By
smart, I am referring only to designing a document in a source application that minimizes the work that has to be done in Acrobat once the
file is converted. So let's go back to the source and start over again.

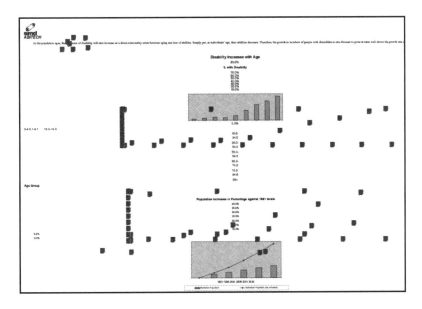

Figure 8-25
The noncompliance comments shown in the Reflow view. A nightmare!

Project **Project 8-2. The Source File Revisited**

An alternate version of this document, SMD1.doc, is on the CD in the Chapter 8 Projects folder. When you open this file, you will not see much difference visually, if any, but quite a few changes have been made to the file structurally.

Rather than outline a blow-by-blow account of the changes made to the file, I have assembled the changes in Table 8-1. I have given a short description of the original version (*Then*) as well as the changes I made (*Now*).

Note

If you would like to experiment with the changed settings, you can start from the original SMD.pdf file and attach the template file, SMD1.dot, which is also in the Projects folder.

Table 8-1   Modifications Made to the Source File

Element	Changes Made
Header	*Then*: Graphic logo, text block for title, lines. *Now*: Single graphic for logo and title. Logo and lines enclosed in text frame. Alt text added.
Styles	*Then*: Headings, body, and modified tags. *Now*: Different styles for different purposes, no styles applied and then modified.
Spacing	*Then*: Blank lines used between text blocks. *Now*: No spaces. All spacing controlled by paragraph settings in the styles.

Table 8-1   Modifications Made to the Source File (Continued)

Element	Changes Made
Charts	*Then*: Embedded spreadsheet charts. *Now*: Embedded spreadsheet charts inside text frames. Alt text added.
Image spacing	*Then*: Spaces added to align images. *Now*: No spaces used. Text frames set with specific layout settings to align and lay out images.
Spacing graphic	*Then*: Two horizontal lines. *Now*: Two lines within a text frame. Alt text added.

As I said, the template I created for the revised document is on the CD. Figure 8-26 shows the list of styles used for the revised document. As you can see, there is a style named "bullet_last". This is an example of using a style to set spacing, and the style is used for the last bullet of a set.

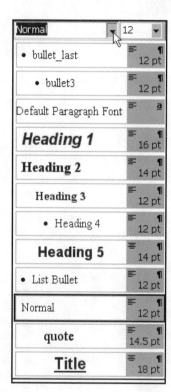

Figure 8-26
The styles used in the document. This streamlines the conversion process.

Once the file has been modified, save it. Now let's get it into a PDF format and see the changes.

Convert the File

First you have to modify the conversion settings slightly.

1. Select Acrobat ➤ Change Conversion Settings. Leave the default e-book option, and click Edit Conversion Settings.

2. When the Edit Conversion Settings dialog box opens, change the compatibility to Acrobat 5 (this option is on the General tab, which the dialog box opens to).

3. Click Save As and name the settings.

4. Back in the document window, click the Convert To Adobe PDF button on the toolbar, or select Acrobat ➤ Convert To Adobe PDF.

5. When the file is converted and opened in Acrobat, save it as a PDF file.

Now let's have a look. This is amazing.

View the Masterpiece

It's time to see what wonders we have wrought. Scroll through this version of the document. You will see very little obvious difference between the two versions. But what is under the hood? Let's see.

1. Open the Tags palette. Expand the Tags Root. As you can see in Figure 8-27, the tags are neat and tidy. The entire document is one section now, as it should be. There are no blank lines. The bullets are translated as lists and list items. It is a thing of beauty.

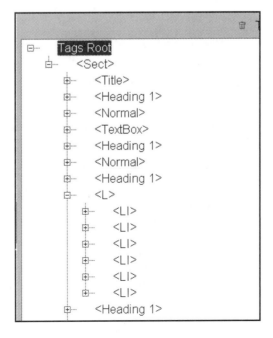

Figure 8-27
The revised Tags listing—
neat and tidy

2. Now zoom in on a page and select View ➤ Reflow. Scroll through the document. You will see that even at a high zoom factor, as shown in Figure 8-28, the text reflows well, and the entire flow-chart has resized itself accordingly. No parts missing anywhere.

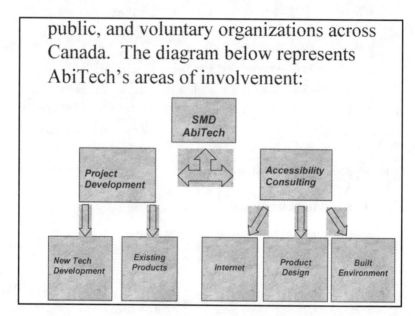

Figure 8-28
Reflow view at a
high zoom factor

3. Finally, run the Accessibility Checker. You may or may not get the same message I received, which appears in Figure 8-29.

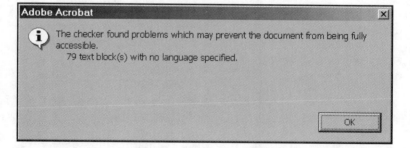

Figure 8-29
The Accessibility Checker
results for the
modified document

Up Next

As we have seen in this chapter, you have many options for making documents accessible. I have shown you what Acrobat's design functions provide. I have also described what makes a document accessible. Then we looked at ways to use Acrobat's tools to evaluate a document in terms of accessibility. I also showed you how you can "rescue" a document by changing its reflow structure. Finally, we looked at how to make alterations to the source document and save time after converting to PDF.

In the next chapter, we will look at indexing. This is not a ho-hum topic, folks. Acrobat includes some cool features that can even make this a database-driven process.

Chapter 9

Indexing and Structuring Documents

It's not an index like your mother used to make! In the old days, an index was just a way of identifying major topics in a document. Not anymore. Now we have collections, cross-document searching, databases, and navigation structures.

Indexing: More Than It Seems

I have a confession to make. I like indexes. I am not an indexer, although I have had to build my fair share of them over the years. What I am is a writer and a designer. There is something about an index, though, that seems to finish off a project. I suppose it is being able to see my work organized so neatly and knowing what each and every item means. It is almost like a summary of a part of my life, or a representation of what I have learned and shared with others. I think that is enough of the philosophy of indexing according to me—before I burst into tears and short-circuit my keyboard.

All right. I am better now. Onward and upward. For those of us who have worked in Adobe FrameMaker or even Microsoft Word, indexing is not new. Acrobat, not surprisingly, has some pretty imposing indexing capabilities. With the program, you can create a simple index for one file, create an index across a number of files, or index collections of files. You can also define and set search functions, and update and modify indexes. Using some of the navigation tools, you can create impressive ways to maneuver through documents as well.

This chapter has two projects. I have re-created the same files in much different configurations in order to illustrate some of the points I will cover. In the first project, I created a set of documents to use as a collection for indexing. In the second project, that same collection has been rolled into one document, but it has a customized index.

On that note, welcome to document collections and indexing with Acrobat.

What Indexing Can Be

The Acrobat help file index is one of the best examples of indexing I have ever seen. As a frame of reference, and to give you some context of what we will be covering in this chapter, I will walk you through some of the help files' features.

The help index is created over a single file and includes a number of navigational structures. As you can see in Figure 9-1, the document has internal links at the top of the page; the links are repeated at the bottom of the page.

The Bookmarks palette consists of four main sections, which correspond to a standard help-file design structure. These sections are divided in a logical structure, as shown in Figure 9-2. The Using Help section describes how to use and print the files. The Contents section contains the actual body of the document, which is arranged in separate sections corresponding to topic

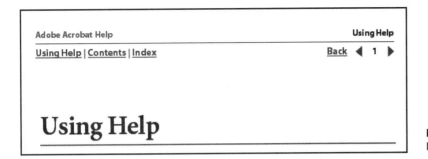

Figure 9-1
Internal links in the help file

areas. The Index is an alphabetical guide accessed by lettered bookmarks.
Legal Notices outlines copyright information.

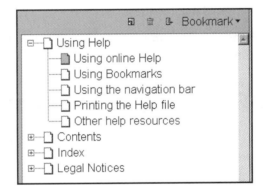

Figure 9-2
The bookmark structure

The help files also use a complete tagged structure. Figure 9-3 shows a
portion of the tag structure for the files. The components follow the
same pattern.

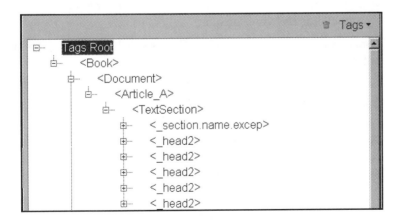

Figure 9-3
Sections added to the
document translate to
<Document> elements.

So what are we looking at here? Lots, actually. Acrobat 5 has a command named Adobe Acrobat Catalog. This command creates and manages indexes. In this chapter, we will go beyond a simple "click the button and make an index" process. I will also incorporate surrounding building and management issues that will affect how an indexed set of documents functions, and how indexed files should be handled. We will look at the following:

- Collecting source material

- Naming and storing the documents in a collection

- Designing the index content

- Creating the index

- Managing the index

And I used to think compiling an index was as simple as knowing my ABCs!

Preparing a Document Collection

As with most things in life, preparation is the key. As we have seen in other chapters, the more you take into consideration regarding the intended use of a document, the less time you'll need for time-consuming repairs.

Creating the File Structure

First things first. Define the file structure you are going to use. In this chapter, we will concentrate on creating an index from a number of documents, known as a *document collection*. To create the collection, move or copy files to the same location.

Now that the collection is assembled, let's turn to the individual documents within it.

Naming the Documents

Now that you have decided where to house the index materials, let's look at the individual documents. Some of these issues are fairly straightforward. Some are not.

Each document must be named correctly, and it must have Document Info elements and other metadata added.

MS-DOS Naming Requirements

The safest way to name documents for a collection is with MS-DOS file-naming conventions. The reasons for this are clarity and speed. Acrobat can identify formats of indexed documents, but it will take time to apply the mapping filter when conventions other than DOS conventions are applied. Therefore, the search will be slower. It might even result in inaccurate search results.

Macintosh-Specific Naming Requirements

A number of naming issues are specific to Macs:

- *Using Mac OS with an OS/2 LAN Server:* To make indexed files searchable on all PC platforms, either configure LAN Server Macintosh (LSM) to enforce MS-DOS file-naming conventions or index only File Allocation Table (FAT) volumes.

- *Using the Mac OS version of Acrobat Catalog to build a cross-platform indexed document collection:* Select Make Include/Exclude Folders DOS Compatible in the Index preferences before building the index. You won't have to change long PDF file names to MS-DOS file names, but you will have to use MS-DOS file-naming conventions for the folder names (eight digits with a three-digit extension).

- *Creating documents that will be searched only by Macintosh users:* Do not use deeply nested folders or pathnames longer than 256 characters.

- *Using ISO 9660 file names with ISO 9660-formatted discs:* In the Macintosh version of Acrobat Catalog, check Log Compatibility Warnings (in the Logging preferences) for noncompliant file names.

- *Indexing PDF documents with long file names that will be truncated for Windows use:* Use either the Windows or Mac OS version of Acrobat Catalog to build or update the index.

Note

This information on Macintosh-specific naming issues was taken from the Adobe Acrobat 5 Help file, pages 222–223.

Completing the Document Information

More information should be added to the document's metadata to allow for search access. Document information can be added either in the source application before conversion or in Acrobat after conversion. The option you choose (or both) depends on how you use your documents. For example, if you are creating a set of Word files that will only be used for source material to convert to PDF, it doesn't matter which end of the conversion process you choose. I would most likely add the information in Acrobat, as that is the only location I would be using it. On the other hand, if your source documents will also be used for other purposes, you may want to add the document information in the source documents and then convert to PDF.

Adding Document Information in Source Files

Figure 9-4 shows the Document Summary dialog box from a Word 2000 file used as source material for an online course.

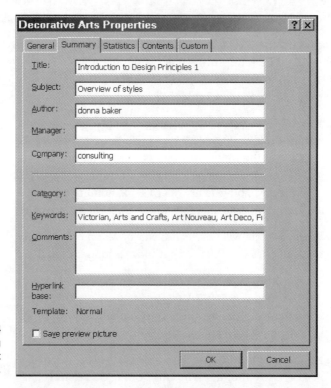

Figure 9-4
Indexing and searching requires document information.

Let's go through the dialog box and see what to do. It isn't quite as simple as it looks. You can add whatever you like to the fields, but that won't necessarily make for a good index.

- *Title:* When a search is done, the file name appears in the Search Results dialog box. The title should be descriptive and not simply an alphanumeric string used for file management.

- *Subject vs. Keywords:* Establish a pattern. Consistently use one or the other, or both. If you use both, identify keywords in advance for the entire collection so you know what to add here.

- *Author:* This entry identifies responsibility for the document's creation and management. I am responsible for my own work (sometimes to my dismay!). You may use the name of a work-group rather than an individual in this field.

- *Category:* You can use this field to categorize documents by type.

- *Comments:* Add information to describe the index. When users want to view available indexes, they can select based on the descriptions.

If I add information to the source document, there is only one conversion setting that will be affected. Regardless of the conversion settings you use, make sure the Document Information check box has been selected, as follows:

1. Select Acrobat ➤ Change Conversion Settings. The PDFMaker dialog box will open.

2. Click the Office tab shown in Figure 9-5. Make sure the Convert Document Info option in the General settings is selected (if you haven't changed your default settings, this will automatically be selected).

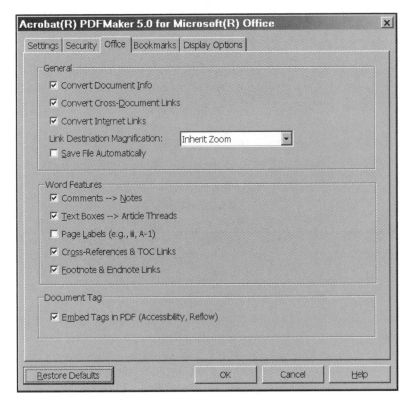

Figure 9-5
Set the Convert Document Info option.

3. Click OK to close the dialog box. Save the file, and convert it. Your information will be converted and displayed in your PDF file.

Speaking of PDF files, you can add the document information directly in Acrobat. Let's have a look at that.

Adding Document Information in Acrobat

You may not need to add document information in your source files, nor have a program that allows you to do this easily. Regardless of where your files originate, once they are open in Acrobat, information can be added or changed as necessary. Let me show you.

I described how to add document information in a source file and what was required to convert this information along with the rest of the file's information. Figure 9-6 shows the same document information, now in its PDF version.

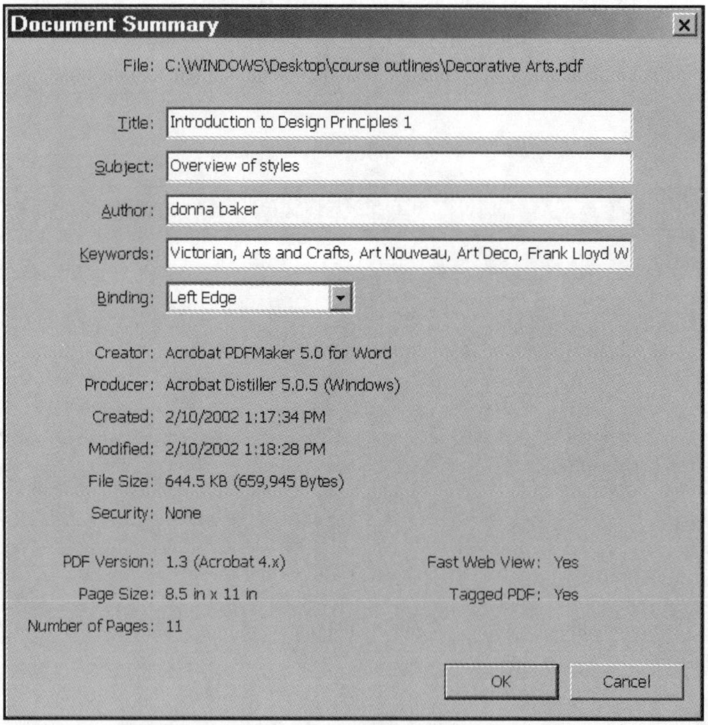

Figure 9-6
The same document information displayed in Acrobat

Select File ➤ Document Properties ➤ Document Summary to open this dialog box. The document information fields are active. You can modify the entries for title, subject, author, and keywords.

Advanced Document Management

In certain instances, it is appropriate to develop a document management system beyond what we are looking at in this chapter. To give you an idea of what can be done with and around Acrobat, consider these concepts:

- In Acrobat, you can define custom data fields to enhance searchability. This will require custom data fields in the document's properties, such as the ones shown earlier in Figure 9-5. This can be used for elements such as document identification in large systems.

- Compile information about a large index system in a readme file. This can include such elements as the scope of the documents, names and locations of folders, search options supported, stopwords used in the indexes, and so on. The first project in this chapter uses a sample readme file.

- Maintain a list of values for each document (as I described earlier to complete the document information for a file). This way, you will have a record of what has been done and used in the past, and you can use it as a frame of reference for ongoing work.

Defining and Constructing an Index

Once you've structured a set of documents correctly and have completed all its information, you can build the index using Acrobat Catalog. This same process will create a full-text index of single documents or document collections.

I will demonstrate the basic process (we will look at customizing issues later). The Adobe Catalog dialog box (shown in Figure 9-7) will open when you select Tools ➤ Catalog.

This main dialog box has a number of features. For example, the Adobe Catalog section at the left of the dialog box shows information about a selected index, or it displays information about a new index as it is being created.

To the right are three buttons. Click New Index to start a new indexing process. If you click Open Index, you will be taken to an Explorer window to browse for an index location. Clicking Preferences opens the Preferences panel for setting cataloging and searching preferences (I will

---

Workflow Tip

Working with Fewer Than Thousands of Documents

All kidding aside, it makes sense to coordinate what is going into a set of documents, even if the elements number in the single digits. Again, it all comes down to the value of preplanning. As I will show you in this chapter's projects, using even eight documents can lead to inconsistency. Using a table that lists values assigned to each document is a good way to store overall information as well as to maintain consistency. When you've finished the index, store the table in a readme file with the rest of the index materials.

Note

This is a demonstration. I want to discuss and describe the basics of indexing. In the upcoming projects, you will be able to create your own index using files from the CD.

cover this later in the chapter). Information about Acrobat Catalog
appears in the text box at the bottom of the page. Finally, click Close to
exit the plug-in.

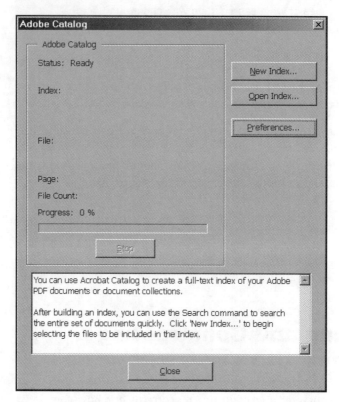

Figure 9-7
The Adobe Catalog
dialog box

Let's look at how to create a new index.

1. Start from the main Adobe Catalog dialog box. Click New Index.
   The New Index Definition dialog box will open, as shown in
   Figure 9-8. Enter a name for the index. You can save the index
   now and then configure its settings.

2. Click Save As. Once you have specified a storage location, click
   OK to return to this dialog box. Consider these points before
   deciding on a name and storage location:

   • Store the index folder on the same disk or server volume as the
     documents (Windows only). Change the preference setting to
     allow different storage locations.

   • Do not use ANSI characters with values over 128 or the slash
     (/) character in the name of the location.

3. Then add or change settings as follows (more about these options will follow this general discussion):

- *Index Description section:* Click Options to select deletions from the search functionality. Click OK to store the selections.

- *Include These Directories section:* Click Add and select the folder(s) to include. Click OK (Choose on a Mac).

- *Exclude These Subdirectories section:* Select any folders to be excluded.

4. Click Build. Leave the default naming convention. The index will be created with the .pdx extension.

Note

You cannot select individual files for exclusion. If you have to deselect a file, deselect its folder. Plan ahead and move from a directory any folders that you don't want to include before you start and save yourself time in this step.

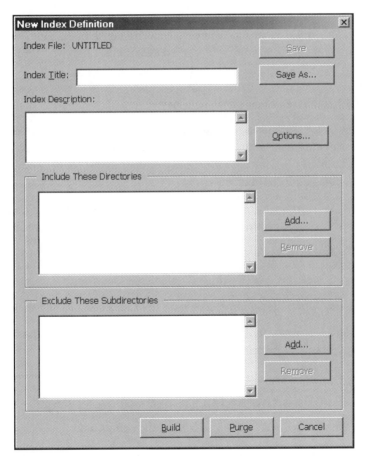

Figure 9-8
Add information in this dialog box to define a new index.

The index build will start. If you discover an error after you have started the build process, you can stop the build by clicking Stop in the dialog box. After the process is stopped, the partial build will be stored and used when you resume the build process.

Let's try this out with some project material now.

Project **Project 9-1. Building a Simple Index from a Document Collection for Wildflower Farm**

For this project, use the set of files that are on the CD in the Chapter 9 Projects folder. The subfolder named Index contains a set of nine PDF files, which we will make into a collection and index. There is also a readme file, appropriately named Readme.txt. As we go through the project, I will point out how the file was used.

Building the Collection

A collection must be in one place in a unique folder. The files are named with a number as the first character. The set of nine are numbered 1 to 9; for example, 1intro, 9index. They are numbered in the sequence they will be added to the collection.

1. Start by gathering all the files in one place. Create a new folder on your hard drive, and copy the entire set of files into the folder.

2. Open the first file, 1intro.pdf.

3. Select File ➤ Document Properties ➤ Summary. Look at the entries.

4. Open the Readme.txt file (in the Index subfolder). Read the file.

You will notice that the Readme.txt file contains information about the components added to the files, their source application, the template used, and so on.

Building the Index

We will create a simple index from the collection.

1. Open Acrobat. Select Tools ➤ Catalog. The Adobe Catalog dialog box will open.

2. Click New Index. The New Index Definition dialog box will open.

3. Name the index **index**.

4. Click Add. Browse to the location you have stored the folder and select it. It will now appear in the Include These Directories section.

5. Click Build. Catalog will prompt you for a storage location for the index.pdx file. It will default to the folder where the other files are stored. Click Save to save the file and start the index process.

6. As shown in Figure 9-9, an indicator and progress information will be displayed as the index is being created. Once the build is complete, review the information and click Close.

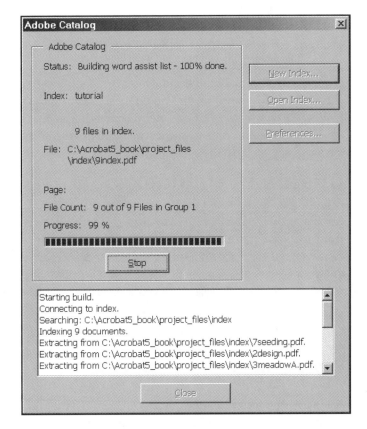

Figure 9-9
The build and progress information

Now that the index has been created, let's have a quick look at what Catalog has done. Look at Figure 9-10. As you can see in the figure, which contains a portion of my Explorer window, Acrobat Catalog has added a folder, also called "index," which contains a number of sub-folders. I have expanded one of the subfolders. You will notice a file called acrocat.cat, which is the main Acrobat Catalog file. This is the key to the whole cataloging process, and it is found in most of the sub-folders added. A log file will also be saved to the same folder location as the set of PDF files.

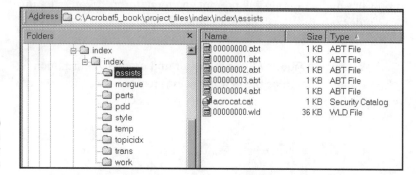

Figure 9-10
The folders and contents added by the indexing process

The index is built and has been duly examined. In order to actually search this index, however, you would have to attach it to the files. In Project 9-2, which is coming up after the next discussion, I will include search and customizing issues when we build another index.

Customizing Indexes

Acrobat features a number of custom indexing features. I want to discuss searching and optimizing options as well as storage options. In all cases, these changes are made from within the New Index Definition dialog box in Acrobat Catalog. If you want to try this with your own files, make sure the Word Options preference is set. Select Edit ➤ Preferences ➤ General ➤ Search. The top of the dialog box, Include in Query section, has several options. Make sure Word Options is selected.

Search and Optimize Options

If you are working on a large index (and even if it isn't that large), excluding words is a good idea. Using this exclusion, or *stopword*, process can make an index 10 to 15 percent smaller. You can exclude up to 500 words from an index. Common examples of excluded words include "a," "but," "the," and "for."

Note

Because there are so many ways to customize and optimize indexes, I want to demonstrate how these options work with a demo file. When we do the next project, we will use the project files. If you would like to experiment with these options, use a file of your own choice, or make a copy of the project files and keep the pristine originals for the next project.

Note

If you use stopwords, users can't search for phrases using these stopwords. You should include a list of stopwords in the index's information or readme file.

Here's how to organize a stopword list:

1. Click Options in the New Index Definition dialog box. The dialog box shown in Figure 9-11 will open.

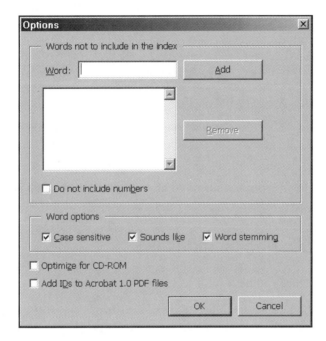

Figure 9-11
Use this dialog box to modify indexing options.

2. Enter a new word in the Word text box. Click Add. A stopword can be 26 characters long. Stopwords are case sensitive.

3. To delete a word from the list, select it from the Words To Not Include In The Index list and click Remove.

4. You can also exclude numbers by selecting the Do Not Include Numbers option in the Options dialog box. The default is to include numbers. As with stopwords, excluding numbers will decrease the size of the index. Again, if you have made this customization, the information should be included in the index's readme file.

5. Click OK to store these options.

Note

If you change this option, you must also change the option in the Catalog and Search preferences. These options are discussed later in this chapter.

Word Search Options

Acrobat Catalog includes default searching options. As shown earlier in Figure 9-11, three options are selected by default. You can use any combination of options. If you make changes, make sure the amended options are included in your readme file.

The options are

- *Case Sensitive:* Allows searching based on matched cases.

- *Sounds Like:* Searches for proper names.

- *Word Stemming:* Searches for words sharing word stems with the search term, such as "look" and "looking." This process is done by the Word Assistant in the search tool.

In all instances, once you have modified these settings, click OK to store the options.

Testing an Index

Once you have built an index, you should test it by running a search.

1. First the index has to be attached. Select Edit ➤ Search ➤ Select Index. As you can see in my demo file, shown in Figure 9-12, I have several indexes. Add other indexes by clicking Add. Browse to the location of the desired index, and then click OK.

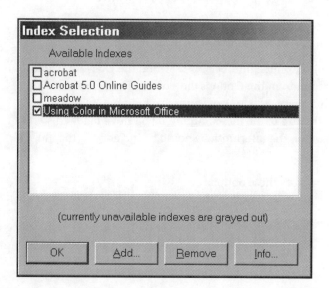

Figure 9-12
The Index Selection dialog box. Use this dialog box to attach and remove indexes from files or collections in your system.

2. Start the search process by selecting Edit ➤ Search and then the desired option. Basically, the key to testing is to run a query, so select the Query option. The Adobe Acrobat Search dialog box will open, as shown in Figure 9-13. Select or deselect options as required.

Figure 9-13
Starting a query using the basic search parameters

3. Click Search. The document will jump to the first page on which the term is found. The text will be highlighted, as you can see in Figure 9-14.

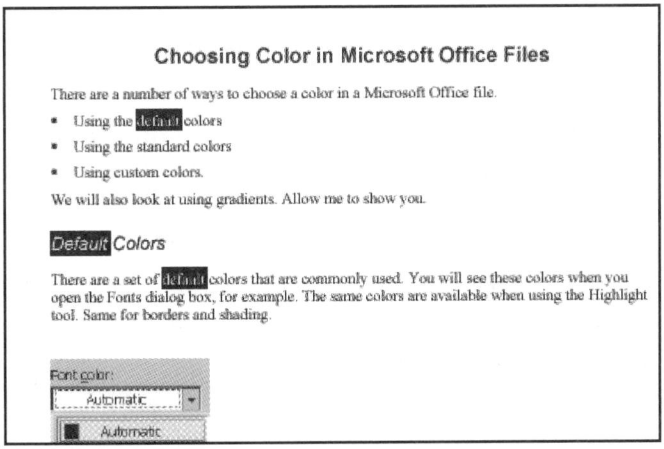

Figure 9-14
The results of the query are highlighted on the page.

The search dialog boxes default to hidden after the results are displayed. To find the next occurrence of the query, use Ctrl-], or set the search dialog box to the Shown After Results option.

Want to see this in action? Let's return one last time to the Wildflower Farm project.

Project   Project 9-2. Another Take on Building the Wildflower Farm Index

In this project, we are basically going to start all over, but with a difference. The subject material is the same as that used in the first project. The focus of this project will be on customizing the search functions rather than on the process of building the index. This time, you will need the meadow.pdf file, which is on the CD in the Chapter 9 Projects folder. Ready?

Starting the Process

Again, we have to start by defining content.

Note

As I mentioned in the discussion earlier, you must have the Word Options preference set. Select Edit ➤ Preferences ➤ General ➤ Search. The top of the dialog box, Include in Query section, has several options. Make sure Word Options is selected.

1. Copy the meadow.pdf file from the CD and store it in a new folder on your hard drive.

2. Open Acrobat. Select Tools ➤ Catalog. The Adobe Catalog dialog box will open.

3. Click New Index. The New Index Definition dialog box will open.

4. Name the index **meadow**.

5. Click Add. Browse to the location where you have stored the folder and select it. It will now appear in the Include These Directories section.

That is the basic information you need to assemble in order to build the index, but we are going to customize the search.

Setting Search Options

To customize this index, follow these steps. You should still have the New Index Definition dialog box open.

Note

When you are adding stopwords, rather than entering the word and clicking Add, press Enter to move the word to the list.

1. Click Options. The Options dialog box will open (imagine that).

2. First add some stopwords. Add any or all articles, conjunctions, and prepositions you can think of. Table 9-1 has a list to get you started.

Table 9-1   Stopwords List

a	an	and	at	but
by	for	if	in	on
or	since	the	to	when

4. Click the Do Not Include Numbers check box to select it.

5. Deselect items under Word Options. Click Case Sensitive and Sounds Like to deselect the items. Leave the Word Stemming option selected.

6. Click Optimize For CD-ROM to select it (remember the Workflow Tip?).

7. The completed dialog box is shown in Figure 9-15. Click OK to close the dialog box.

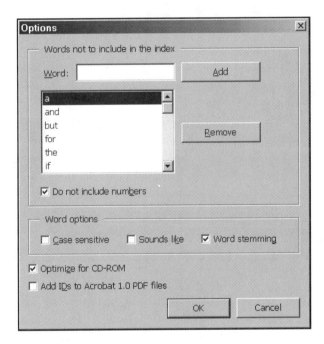

Figure 9-15
The customized options for this project

You should now be back in the New Index Definition dialog box.

Building and Attaching the Index

One last item to add, and then it's time to build the index.

1. Enter a description in the Index Description box. Click into the box and enter the text **Index of articles from Wildflower Farm describing planning, preparation, planting and maintaining a wildflower and grass meadow**. The completed New Index Definition dialog box is shown in Figure 9-16.

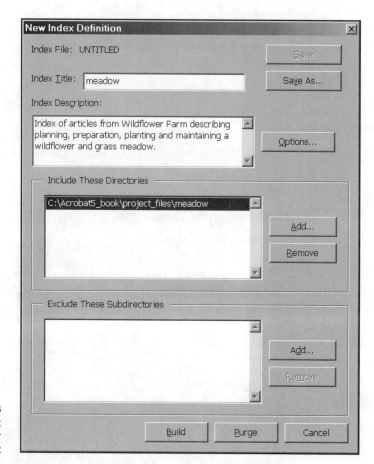

Figure 9-16
The complete index
information for
this project

Note

Don't be too hasty! You
will see that the Progress
indicator will get to 99
percent and then appear
to stop. It hasn't locked
up. This last 1 percent is
where it all happens.
Depending on the
amount of customization
and the number of
stopwords added, this
last part of the process
will take longer.

2. Click Build at the bottom of the dialog box. The New Index
   Definition dialog box will close, and you will return to the main
   Adobe Catalog dialog box. The build process will run.

3. When the Progress indicator has stopped, and the build is
   100 percent complete, the Stop button will be replaced by a
   Close button. Click Close. The index is finished.

Now to attach this index to the document.

Attaching the Index, Part 1

Depending on the number of documents associated with an index, there
are different methods of attaching an index. We have only one document
for this index.

1. Open meadow.pdf in Acrobat.

2. Select File ➤ Document Properties ➤ Associated Index.

3. The dialog box shown in Figure 9-17 will open. Click Choose to browse to the location of the meadow.pdx file. Click the file to select it.

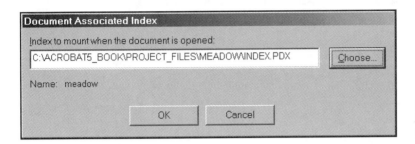

Figure 9-17
Associate the index
you created.

4. Click OK to associate the index with the document.

Attaching the Index, Part 2

The index has been associated with the file. Now we have to add the index to the search functions.

1. First add the index to the query list. Select Edit ➤ Search ➤ Select Indexes. The dialog box shown in Figure 9-18 will open.

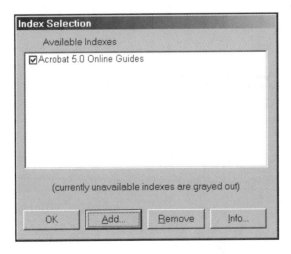

Note

You do not have to save meadow.pdf at this point. This is a process external to the file and is basically associated with the index file instead. If you are a creature of habit, however, you will likely find yourself saving the file anyway.

Figure 9-18
Use the Index Selection dialog box to attach the index to the search functions.

2. Click Add. An Explorer window will open at the location where you stored the meadow.pdx file (which was the index associated with this document—isn't that handy?).

Note

You can either remove or deselect other indexes in your system. As you can see in Figure 9-18, the help files are also listed.

3. Click OK to select the meadow.pdx file. It will now be listed.

You can also view information about the index. Click Info in the Index Selection dialog box to display this information, as shown in Figure 9-19.

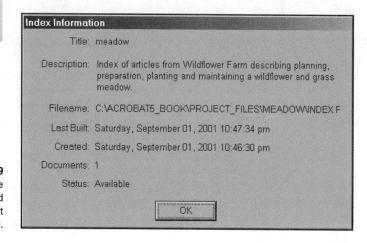

Figure 9-19
Information about the index. This was added to the source document in Word 2000.

Testing the Index

One last important step. There is very little use in creating an index unless you test to see if it works. Also, given the fact that we customized the query parameters, we should see if they work as well.

1. Select Edit ➤ Search ➤ Query. The dialog box shown in Figure 9-20 will open.

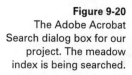

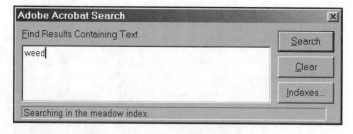

Figure 9-20
The Adobe Acrobat Search dialog box for our project. The meadow index is being searched.

2. A number of conditions were set earlier that should be tested:

    • *Numbers:* Enter a number, any number. Click Search. You should receive a message that the search term is not found.

    • *Case sensitivity:* Enter the word **weed**. Click Search. To jump through the document for subsequent matches, use Ctrl-]. You will note that both "weed" and "Weed" are highlighted.

- *Word stemming:* Move the view to page 9. That page contains two instances of the word "rototiller." Try searching with portions of the word—that is, "roto" and "tiller." No results will be found. If you enter **rototiller**, both instances on page 9 will be highlighted.

Now let's add one more twist to the search process and call it a day. Throughout this chapter I have been referring to document information. It can also be used for searching, with a bit of modification.

1. Try searching for my name, **donna baker**. You will have no result. Stands to reason, because my name doesn't appear in the document.

2. Now change the search settings. Select Edit ➤ Preferences ➤ General ➤ Search (Edit ➤ Preferences ➤ Search on a Mac).

3. Click Document Information in the Include In Query section. Click OK to change the preference.

4. Now select Edit ➤ Search ➤ Query. The reconfigured dialog box shown in Figure 9-21 will open.

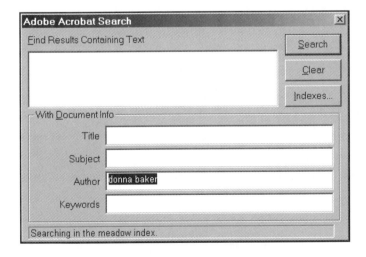

Figure 9-21
Adding document information to the search functions

5. Search for my name again. Did you see it? Me neither. All that occurs is that the document moves to the beginning of the document—which is actually what it is supposed to do.

6. If you really want to see this in action, close the meadow.pdf file. Now select Edit ➤ Search ➤ Query. Enter my name in the Author line and click Search. The meadow.pdf file will open. Cool.

Workflow Tip

When to Rebuild an Index

Depending on the kind of work you do, and the extent to which your documents are modified, you may want to define a purge-and-rebuild schedule. Also, consider rebuilding an index if you change either stopwords or optional search features.

Workflow Tip

Doing Your Work Without Ruining Anyone Else's Day

You know how sometimes you can be working away, minding your own business, and then something is ruined because you weren't warned about a network event or similar activity? Acrobat sets a default time of 15 minutes before purging. Users attempting to do a query against the index will receive a message stating the index is unavailable. With a 15-minute lead time, you will be able to broadcast a message or e-mail users to warn them.

That is the end of the information on building and using indexes. There are also management issues associated with indexes. Let's have a look.

Managing Indexes

Once you've built your index, that is not usually the end of your work. Depending on how you plan to use the material, as components and circumstances change, so must the index. Let's see how.

Purging and Rebuilding Indexes

Have you ever been to a Web site that had a bunch of broken links? Of course you have. It is one of the most irritating and annoying Web experiences.

Indexing follows the same concept. Although indexes use bookmarks rather than links, the outcome is the same. A "dirty" index will have entries for deleted documents and original versions of documents that have been changed. These entries will be marked as invalid. Now add extra time to search for entries when an index contains invalid entries and extra disk space to store extra invalid entries. All these factors can lead to incorrect search results and make for a messy situation. The solution? Periodically purge and rebuild your indexes.

Here's how to do it:

1. Select Tools ➤ Catalog and click Open Index.

2. Browse and select the PDX file for the index.

3. Click Purge. The index will be deleted.

4. Now select the PDX file by clicking the name, and then click Open.

5. Click Build.

The new "clean" index is ready to go.

Moving Collections and Indexes

Again, there are similarities between an indexed document collection and a Web site. Both can be built and tested locally, and then uploaded to a server for distribution. Both can be stored on disk. Both have dangers in doing this kind of transfer.

The basis for an index is the PDX file. This file contains relative paths between itself and the folders containing indexed documents. After moving a document collection and its corresponding PDX file, you may or may not have to rebuild the index. The index and all portions of the collection must be on the same driver or server volume. If they aren't, moving any component will break the index.

What if you didn't create the indexed collection, or you didn't store all the files in the same location? Fear not. Follow these steps:

1. Move the indexed documents.

2. Copy the PDX file to the desired folder.

3. Edit Include and Exclude lists if necessary.

I showed you how to set a preference earlier. Let's have a look at more preferences available for indexing and searching, which will wrap up this chapter.

Setting Preferences for Catalog and Searches

When you have worked with the program for a while, you will appreciate the ability to modify settings according to how you work. The hallmark of a power user! Setting preferences for searching, on the other hand, influences what your users can do with your indexes. Because they are closely related, we will look at them together.

Search Preferences

The preferences you set here will determine what options are available to your readers when they use the Acrobat Search feature. The Catalog and Search preferences are very closely related, so be sure to consider both when building your indexes.

For all options, start by selecting Tools ➤ Catalog and then clicking Preferences. Also, for all options, once you have made changes click OK to save the changes and close the dialog box.

For each preference category, I have included a figure. Rather than a step-by-step tour of each item, some of which are self-explanatory, I will discuss when and why to change some of the settings. Seems more valuable as information, don't you think? Consider this a Workflow Tip.

Workflow Tip
Moving Made Simple

Whenever possible, keep the PDX file and its folders containing indexed documents in the same folder. This way, regardless of where and how often the files are moved, the relative paths are always constant. This will prevent rebuilds and headaches.

Note

As in other customized setting dialog boxes in Acrobat, you can restore all settings to the program defaults by clicking Restore All Defaults.

General Preferences

Let's start at the beginning with the General preferences, as shown in Figure 9-22.

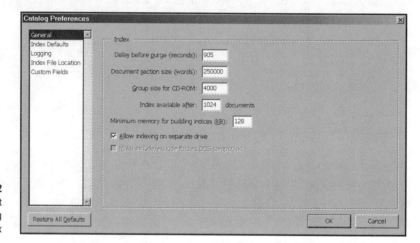

The figure shows the default settings. In general, you'll have little need to change the settings, but there are exceptions:

- The Delay Before Purge (Seconds) setting can be set in a range from 30 to 905 seconds, and it defaults to the largest value. This is about 15 minutes. As I described earlier, this long time delay would be useful for large systems. Not so if you are waiting to get something done, though. Figure 9-23 shows the message I received after resetting the purge delay to 30 seconds. Because this was a small index, and the delay is set at 30 seconds, waiting 15 minutes for a job that takes less than a minute seemed a bit silly.

Figure 9-23
Set the purge delay to a
practical length of time.

- The Document Section Size (Words) setting determines the maximum size of a document before Acrobat Catalog will split an index. My setting, the default of 250,000 words, is fairly small. The only reason to use a very low setting is if you have limited memory. The higher the value, the faster the index will update.

- The Group Size For CD-ROM setting defaults to 4000. Acrobat documentation recommends leaving this setting as is.

- Index Available After X Documents setting can be changed to optimize performance. If you are running a large number of documents through Catalog to create an index, use this setting to specify the number that will be processed before making a partial index or partial updates available. Again, this is a setting for enormous cataloging processes. The default is shown in Figure 9-22. The larger the number, the faster the search. The lower the number, the faster you serve partial indexes to your users.

- I recommend deselecting the Allow Indexing On Separate Drive option. Remember earlier when I discussed setting up indexes? If this preference is not available, there is no chance of creating an index on a volume or drive that will later cause grief.

- The Make Include/Exclude Folders DOS Compatible setting is for Mac users only (I described these Mac-specific options earlier).

Index Defaults Preferences

This panel of the Preferences dialog box is shown in Figure 9-24.

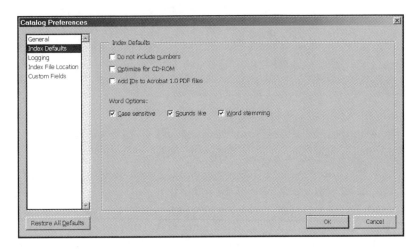

Figure 9-24
The Index Defaults settings

You use these settings for specifying default structures when you are creating and compiling an index. By default, the top set of options is deselected. Remember that any changes you make here will affect how a user can search your index. For example, if you specify the Do Not Include Numbers option, you must make this information known to your users (this prevents that annoying "this thing is garbage" response from unhappy customers). Also, remember the "Removing That Annoying 'Use This Index?' Prompt" Workflow Tip earlier? This is where you need to go to select the Optimize For CD-ROM option to remove that prompt.

The word options are used for search parameters. I recommend leaving the default settings in this window, unless you are indexing in a large system with specified indexing requirements.

Logging Preferences

The Logging preferences panel is shown in Figure 9-25.

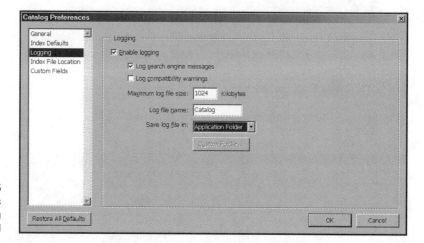

Figure 9-25
The default settings for the Logging preferences panel

These options are self-explanatory. I recommend leaving the default settings.

The last option, Save Log File In, has two choices—either in the application folder (where the rest of the index material is stored) or to a custom folder. If you are indexing in a large enterprise, your network administrator may have a requirement to have all programs with logging capabilities log activity to specific network locations, or may not want to have index logs maintained at all, in which case you'd deselect the Enable Logging option.

To select a different folder, click the drop-down arrow and select the option. Then click Custom Folder and browse to the location to store the file.

Index File Location Preferences

The Index File Location preferences panel is shown in Figure 9-26.

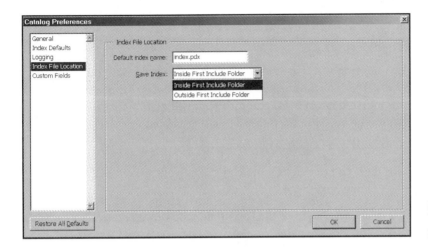

Figure 9-26
The Index File Location preferences panel

I again recommend leaving these defaults, unless you are required for corporate reasons to change them. The figure shows the Save Index drop-down list. My preference is to keep everything together whenever I can right from the start. It doesn't take any more time, and it can save you a lot of time in the long run. That goes for the index name as well.

Custom Fields Preferences

The final panel, shown in Figure 9-27, lets you create custom fields. You will notice in Figure 9-27 that I have three custom fields.

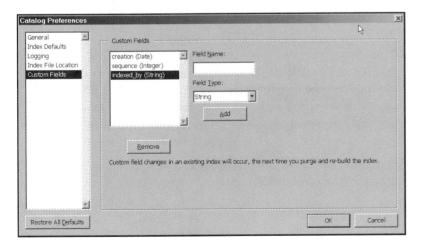

Figure 9-27
The Index File Location preferences panel

Creating custom fields is a way to incorporate more search options into your system. This is especially useful when you are working in a large enterprise. For example, if your indexing is organized using numeric sequencing, you may want to add an integer field (as I did) named "sequence." Also, from the perspective of a large enterprise, I added a string that will be used to enter the name of the person who indexed a collection.

This information is used for both ends of the process. In addition to storing this information when an index is created, the users of the index can search against these parameters. It will require that the same information be added to the index when it is created.

New fields can be added quite simply:

1. Enter a name for the new field you want to create in the Field Name box.

2. Select a type from the Field Type drop-down box (as in my examples, you have three options: Integer, Date, and String).

3. Acrobat adds the custom field.

To remove a custom field, click it in the list and then click Remove.

This concludes our tour of cataloging preferences. Coincidentally, this also concludes this chapter.

Up Next

In the introduction to this chapter, I tried to convey the idea that indexing is not dry or dull. I have to stress, though, that it is something that requires a lot of planning and preparation. Unfortunately, it is also something that is often done without enough of the aforementioned forethought.

In this chapter we have looked at indexing inside and out. We have looked at how to prepare documents, how to create an index, how to store indexes, and how to customize cataloging and searching preferences that correspond with your work environment and needs. Along the way, I discussed how to add some very nice navigation to a set of indexed documents.

Up next are forms. Not dry and dull either. Interesting, useful, and enormous time- and money-savers.

Chapter 10

Creating Forms
with Acrobat

*Is there anything you do in life that
isn't form driven at some level?
Not much. In the realms of business
and conducting day-to-day
activities, forms are ubiquitous.*

Forms, Forms, Everywhere . . .

The use of forms varies from business to business. But can you imagine interacting with anyone in government, health, banking, or virtually any other type of organization without the presence of at least one form?

As things have evolved in recent years, purchases of all types have become form driven as well. If you use a credit card or debit card for purchasing something, you had to have filled out forms for the cards at one time, and the company you purchase products from has to process your purchases by forms and order its stock using forms, and its suppliers use forms to order wholesale and. . . . That's my point.

Let's look at a real-life example. One that annoys me.

I do my banking online through an entity that doesn't even have a physical location. It does have an agreement with a national bank to use its bank machines, but that is as far as the physical elements of the bank exist. So what's the problem? The bank mails me statements every month for each of my two accounts. What does this cost?

- *Cost for two envelopes:* Let's say 4 cents each, for 8 cents.

- *Printing copies of each statement:* Let's say 4 cents each, for 8 cents.

- *Postage (this is Canadian postage at 46 cents each):* 92 cents.

- *Tax on all of this (Canadian taxes again):* 15 cents.

On a monthly basis, that is a total cost of $1.23. Per year, my bank pays $14.76 to send me statements that I don't even read most of the time. The reason I decided to use this service is because it is online. I log into my accounts when I need to, and I have absolutely no need for printed materials to be delivered to my door. How many trees does it take per year to mail statements to all of that bank's customers? Staggering.

Not only is it expensive, but also by the time a statement arrives at my door, its content is dated; meanwhile, I can access my accounts' real-time status whenever I like.

This is a typical example. If you consider all the aspects of your life that are form driven and handled in anything but an electronic format, the costs are astonishing.

Now that I am on the way to converting you to an eForm zealot, let's see what the big deal is.

So What Is a Form?

At the risk of stating the obvious, a *form* is a means of communicating specific types of information in specific formats. In database terms, a form is nothing more than an organized front end for collecting data to add to tables. For example, if you are filling in a tax form, your information is input into the form in a specific way. Of course, since the tax collection process doesn't end with filling in the form, the data collection process becomes something larger. On the other hand, if you are filling in a form to enter a contest at your local supermarket, that is it. Unless the contest organizers use the information you provide, it is wasted information.

Let's see what we have here.

Online Forms

There are millions of forms online. Online forms are HTML based and use server-side scripting to collect data, which is then transmitted to databases. What's wrong with that? Glad you asked. Nothing, except that you are beholden to an Internet connection to use one successfully. Think about some situations where it can take a very long time to complete a form—for example, submitting an online résumé. Even though you think you are prepared, depending on how the site's forms are structured, you often end up back in a word processor composing or revising a segment, and then copying it and pasting it into the appropriate field in the form.

Think about the last time you were doing something online and your Internet connection was interrupted for some reason. Unless it was something very important, the odds are pretty good that you left the site. Just one of those online things.

To prevent interruptions in the process, sites make forms available for download. But what kind of forms?

Forms vs. Smart Forms

I just mentioned the idea of downloading forms. Not many of the forms you see online are smart, however. That is, aside from providing a specific layout and other elements that the PDF file format does so well, the form is static. In all likelihood, the form was created from a paper document. Once the form is downloaded, you have to print it, fill it in, and then mail or fax it back to the source. Which leads to dead trees and high labor and other costs. The information from the form completed in this way will in all likelihood have to be reconverted into an electronic format.

Not efficient.

Now imagine that a form that could be downloaded, completed offline, and then uploaded back to the site where you originally found it. Once the file was uploaded, the form data could be parsed and processed by submitting either the form data or HTML format (depending on the form's design). In other words, a smart form.

In this chapter, we are going to look at smart forms. Creating a regular fill-in-the-blank-and-mail-it-to-me form is not the focus here. That is design and layout. This is doing more than that. Earlier in the book, I discussed the difference between a scanned document and one that was converted into a searchable PDF file. This is much the same idea. On the one hand, we have what looks like a form. On the other hand, we have what looks like a form that can be used to both configure user responses and communicate with whatever data storage processes we want to use. Cool. (I think I just heard my little geeky propeller-beanie start up).

Note

Smartness in a form, as in a human, is a matter of degree. Think about that one for a moment!

What Makes a Form Smart?

A form becomes smart when it can be used electronically for more than one stage of the collection and processing cycle. And it can get smarter and smarter. Table 10-1 shows some examples of smart functionality from the user's perspective, along with benefits to the author/designer from the same concept.

Table 10-1 User Benefits vs. Designer Benefits: Two Sides of the Same Coin

The Users . . .	Author/Designer Benefit
Can fill it out electronically.	Provides overall control of users' responses.
Are guided in their responses by different options for data entry	Provides options for the user to select from, and will decrease errors and confusion.
Are assisted by having fields configured to accept only specifically formatted responses	Ensures that the responses are entered in a format usable by the receiving system.
Navigate through the form directly (control or administration form fields are hidden)	Saves troubleshooting time in assisting users with completion problems; saves processing time by submitting calculated data.
Can submit the form electronically	Information can be entered directly into the receiving system; saves time and labor. The form can be scanned for completion prior to acceptance, saving even more time and effort.

If you look down the list, you can see a progression from filling out the form, to specific ways to collect data, to submitting the completed form. As you can see from the table, it is smart to be smart! In some circumstances, you might need analog signatures or hard-copy documents for one purpose or another. Even so, by providing smart form capability, the user can store backup copies electronically rather than having to print or copy extra files for storage.

So how do you create a form that is smart? Let's have a look. Along the way, I will provide a few projects so you can get a good handle on some of these concepts.

Go to the Source

Like virtually anything else in Acrobat, forms are based on PDF files created elsewhere. Also, as you do when converting files from other programs for other purposes, you must plan carefully before designing and converting a file with forms creation in mind.

Note

For in-depth coverage of conversion processes, refer to Chapter 3.

You may find that you have to do some experimentation to create the form output you want. When you create forms in your source application, think also of how you will be working with the basic layouts once you get into Acrobat. For example, you may want a frame structure added in the source application that will have the form fields overlaid for a 3-D effect. Plan this in advance. Modifications can be done using the TouchUp tool in Acrobat. As with other types of file conversion, however, it depends on how much work there is to do.

The second way to convert a source document is from a scanned copy. Again, there are variations in how this can be done and what type of program a scanned file should be imported into. It may or may not be necessary to scan using OCR capabilities. The form elements are added over the document in any case.

Workflow Tip
Image-Intensive Forms

If you are using a scanned image for a form background with smaller images superimposed, use a vector-based program such as Adobe Illustrator or Macromedia FreeHand to create the file. Doing so will make for a smaller file size than if you use either a pixel-based program or a Microsoft Office application. On the other hand, if your form is text intensive, use a layout application such as FrameMaker instead.

Project Tutorial: Creating and Customizing Form Fields

For the next two sections, I am using a file that is on the CD in the Chapter 10 Projects folder. Use the pens.pdf file if you would like to work along with these processes. You'll also find a second file, pens1.pdf, which is the completed forms document.

Let's get down to the heart of the matter. We have a document that has been converted and is now in Acrobat. How do we take it from this point and make it into a slick, smart application? First things first. We have to build the form fields.

If you haven't used Acrobat much, or at all, but you have experience with illustration or imaging or Web design programs, you will find that a number of activities will seem obvious. When you are venturing where you have never gone before, it's always comforting to find something familiar, don't you think? But I digress.

The key to the whole process is that one little tool on the Editing toolbar: the Form tool. To start the process, click the tool to select it, and then click and drag on the page to create the rectangle for the form field. When you release the mouse, the Field Properties dialog box will open. This dialog box contains a number of tabs, which are summarized in Table 10-2. All that is required to add a form field to a page is to name it. To do any customization or change any options for a field, select the Form tool and double-click the field.

Table 10-2   Tabs in the Field Properties Dialog Box

Tab Name	Used in Order To . . .
Appearance	Set text attributes, field attributes (border, background), and visibility
Options	Set alignment, scrolling, passwords, and so on
Actions	Set activities based on mouse interactions, and focus/blur
Format	Format content type for field as well as set special input mask options
Validate	Add script to test content entered into fields
Calculate	Add script for calculating entries to fields

I will get into the specific layouts of the tabs as we work through various processes.

Adding and Naming the Fields

This is certainly another one of those examples where spending some time designing a process saves a lot of time further down the road. In my example, I have used two types of naming conventions: one is database oriented, and the other is more programming oriented. The first choice is personal preference, and the second is ease of design. As you can see in Figure 10-1, in the sample file I have used both systems. For the general customer information, I used a database-type naming convention. That is, the fields are named according to their content using a one-word name, such as OrderBy.

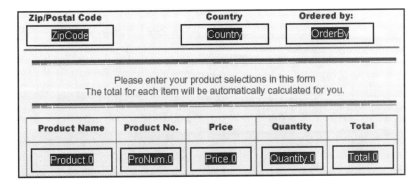

Figure 10-1
Naming conventions used in my tutorial file. I used two types of naming.

Regardless, once you have settled on a naming convention and have applied it across forms, data importing will be successful. You may find it useful to create a schema, or a table that lists all the field names you will use and what they represent.

I started by adding one field, which is named Product.0. Then I added four more fields: ProNum.0, Price.0, Quantity.0, and Total.0.

Customizing Fields

I mentioned earlier that the only information required to save a new field is a name. I want to look at the general field properties for the fields I added to pens.pdf. Figure 10-2 shows the Appearance tab in the Field Properties dialog box. You can see in the images of my table that I have used a distinctive style for the fields. This is selected from the Border options. The default size for the text is Auto. I reset my text to 10pt. to fit within the rest of the table's layout. In this tab, you set common properties such as visibility. All the fields in the table use the same Border and Text options. All are visible, but only the last column (which shows the calculated prices) is required.

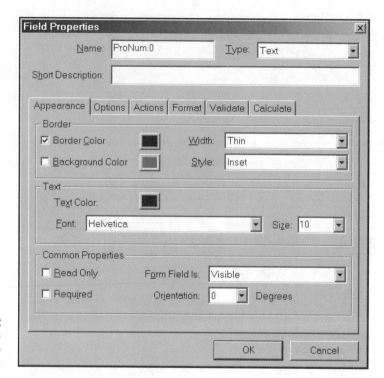

Figure 10-2
Use the Appearance tab to set the options for the overall look of your fields.

Perfecting Field Layout

We all know that layouts can be difficult to perfect. But we also know that (a) a less-than-perfect layout is extremely annoying and (b) any decent program capable of forms creation will have tools for layout tasks. Such is the case with Acrobat layout tools for forms.

Forms usually have a linear layout. Acrobat provides a system for perfecting layouts using an anchor field. This is how it works.

Figure 10-3 shows a portion of a table from the pens.pdf file. In the figure, you can see that I have added a set of five fields. No two are the same size, and they are not aligned.

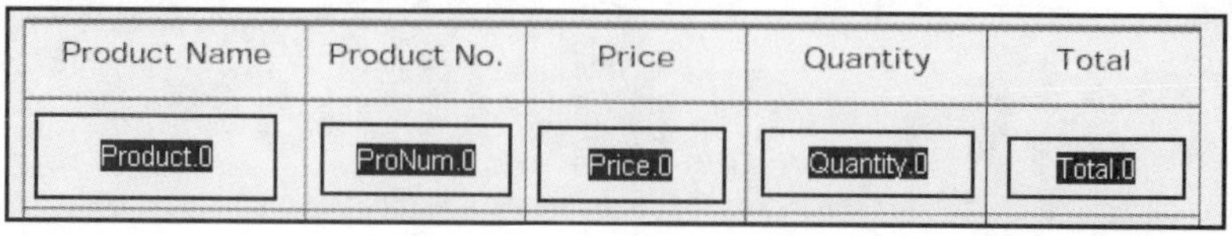

Figure 10-3
Set up the Product order fields before adjusting the layouts.

Product Name	Product No.	Price	Quantity	Total
Product.0	ProNum.0	Price.0	Quantity.0	Total.0

I want the first field to be a different width to hold the product name, but the other four fields should be sized the same. All should be aligned and distributed according to the grid I want as a backdrop. Here are the steps:

1. Select the Form tool and Shift-click to select the four fields. I start by clicking the field I want to serve as the anchor field. Look at Figure 10-4. You will see that all fields are now highlighted, and the anchor field, ProNum.0, is red (actually you will see it as a different shade of gray on this page).

Note

You can change the anchor while the fields are selected. Use Ctrl-click (Option-click on a Mac) on the field to be used for the anchor.

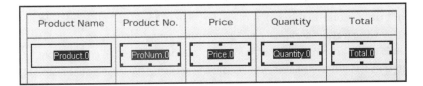

Figure 10-4
The set of fields selected. The field ProNum.0 is the anchor field.

2. Select Tools ➤ Forms ➤ Fields ➤ Size ➤ Both. All the fields will be resized to match the anchor. There are also height- or width-only options. Be sure to resize the height of the Product Name field as well to match the rest.

3. The set of fields also needs aligning. With the fields still highlighted, select Tools ➤ Forms ➤ Fields ➤ Align ➤ Bottom. Options for centering and distributing a number of fields are available. Now isn't that familiar?

4. Rather than using the Distribute command, I nudged the fields to align them to correspond with my grid background. Figure 10-5 shows the finished aligned layout of the first row.

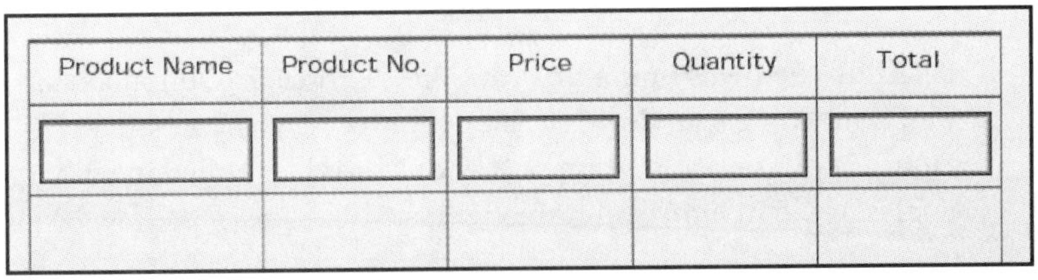

Product Name	Product No.	Price	Quantity	Total

Figure 10-5
The finished layout. Looks much better, doesn't it?

You can also use keyboard commands to nudge sizes of fields. By using the arrow keys and holding down the Shift key, you can nudge the field sizes horizontally and vertically. The sizing correlates with the direction of the arrow (for example, using the up arrow will decrease the size of the fields vertically).

Note

Again, as with any good grid, you can set preferences for the sizing and color. Select Edit ➤ Preferences ➤ General ➤ Layout Grid to change the settings.

By the way, Acrobat also has a grid feature. Select View ➤ Grid. And, as with any good grid, you can select View ➤ Snap To Grid to have all fields snap to the grid.

Now that you've laid out the fields, let's look at naming them.

Field Names for Calculations

If a form was really smart, it would do the arithmetic for me. Guess what? It can. Anyone who has used a spreadsheet knows that a computer can calculate sums. In Acrobat, you can have data fields assigned that are automatically calculated. The key to making this work relates to how the form is designed and the naming conventions used for the data fields. I also recommend that you maintain a record of the calculations used in the different fields and keep it in the same file as the field names.

If you look at a basic commercial ordering form, what kind of calculations will you find? You will likely see calculations for line totals, sales tax, shipping, a grand total, and a date. There is a way to make the field names work for you when you have to do calculations.

Consider our example again. The odds are pretty good that a product order form will have more than one row in it. After all, who would want you to buy one thing if you are willing to buy several things? Hence, several rows are the norm.

You can create a column of form fields all doing the same thing. One by one. Painfully and slowly. Or you can duplicate the fields. As we saw earlier when doing generic duplications, the first field should be complete with attributes, font size, and so on.

Back to our example. We have five columns for product name, product number, price, quantity, and total, each containing a field numbered 0. Now follow these steps to make the complete set:

1. Select all the fields in the first row. Press Ctrl-click (Option-click on a Mac) and drag down to the next row. As you can see in Figure 10-6, the top portion of the table has been filled in with copies of the first row, all named alike.

2. So what have we done so far? We have four rows with the same fields with the same names.

3. The names must be changed, which is so simple to do. Select all the fields in row 2 and press the plus sign (+) key on your keyboard. The fields will be renamed to Product.1, Price.1, and so on. Seriously.

4. Repeat for the other rows.

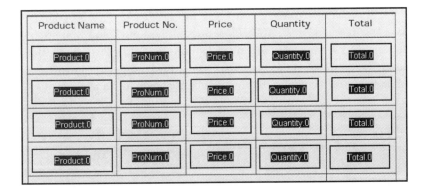

Figure 10-6
The rows duplicated through the table

Because the process is so simple, it is easy to get carried away. But after all, how many pairs of Bollé sunglasses is the average consumer likely to buy at one time? By the way, you can also decrease the values of the names by selecting the fields and pressing the minus sign (-). Now that the fields are separate entities, let's look at the calculations required.

Project Tutorial: Field Calculations 101

If you have looked at the form in pens.pdf, you will notice that a number of calculations are required. As you can see in Figure 10-7, the finished form will calculate subtotals for each line, add the totals, add tax, and produce a grand total.

Product Name	Product No.	Price	Quantity	Total
soft-grip blue / soft-grip red	11B	4.00	5	$20.00
soft-grip blue / soft-grip red	11R	4.50	5	$22.50
soft-grip red / soft-grip black	11K	4.25	5	$21.25
soft-grip blue / soft-grip red				$0.00
			Total	$63.75
		Shipping (add 8% of total cost)		$5.10
			Grand total	$68.85

Figure 10-7
The finished form with superbly correct calculations. A thing of beauty!

Before I get into the calculation processes, I did two more housekeeping steps: I set the alignment of the numbers and the field format.

Setting Alignment

As you can see in Figure 10-7, the values in the Total column are right-aligned. To set alignment, open the Options tab in the Field Properties dialog box and select the desired alignment from the drop-down Alignment list. The default value is Left, as shown in Figure 10-8.

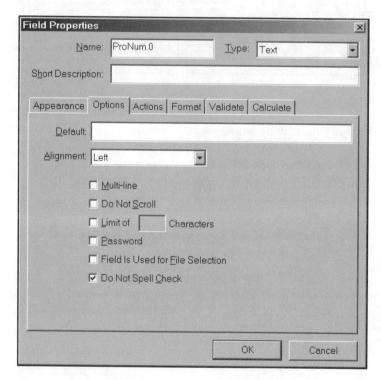

Figure 10-8
Set alignment in the Options tab.

The other requirement before doing calculations is to set the format for the fields.

Setting Field Formats

Setting the field format is very important. On the Format tab, unless the format category is set to Number, the field won't calculate your value. The default setting is None, as shown in Figure 10-9.

If you look back at the table, you will see that numbers are used in the Price, Quantity, and Total columns. Now, the calculations.

Doing Basic Calculations

The Field Properties dialog box contains a Calculate tab, as shown in Figure 10-10.

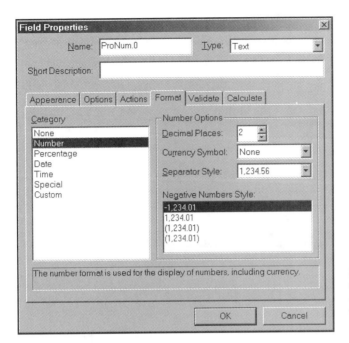

Figure 10-9
Change the format category to Number for all the fields used in calculations.

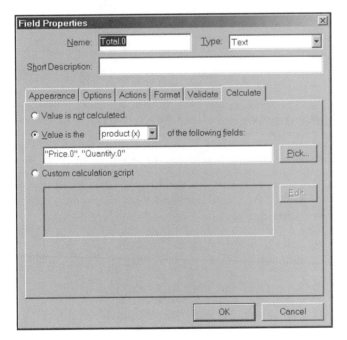

Figure 10-10
The Calculate tab showing basic calculation options

Figure 10-11
Select one of these
options for basic
calculations.

Here's how to do the basic Total calculations:

1. Double-click Total.0 with the Form tool. When the Field Properties dialog box opens, click the Calculate tab.

2. Click the second radio button to activate the calculation function.

3. Click the drop-down arrow in the Value Is The Product (*x*) Of The Following Fields: row. The options shown in Figure 10-11 will display. Select Product (x) from the list.

4. Click Pick to open a display of the fields in the table. For pens.pdf, the available fields are shown in Figure 10-12.

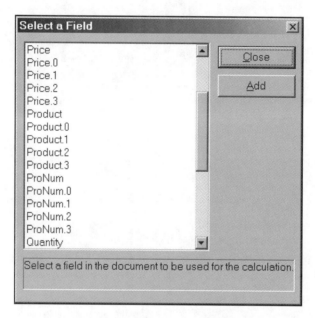

Figure 10-12
Select the fields for the
calculation from this list.

5. Click Price.0, and then click Add. Then, click Quantity.0 (not shown in the figure) and click Add. Click Close.

6. You will now see that the two field names have been added to the calculation. Click OK to close the Field Properties dialog box.

7. Repeat with the other three order rows.

8. For the subtotal field, named Total.4, select Sum (+) from the calculation type, and add the four total fields to the calculation.

What about the sales tax field? Glad I asked. This requires a custom script.

Using JavaScript for Custom Calculations

The sales tax is built on a calculation that requires using the result of another field and a specific value. With the Form tool, double-click the Total.5 (sales tax field) to open the Field Properties dialog box.

1. Click the Calculate tab. Click the Custom Calculation Script radio button. Now click Edit to open the JavaScript Edit window shown in Figure 10-13.

Figure 10-13
The JavaScript Edit window. Here we have to declare one variable and build one event.

2. We will need one line of code for each of the two issues the code will have to address.

3. Enter this code for the first line:

```
var f=this.getField("Total.4");
```

4. The variable is declared for the specific field that we want to use for calculation—that is, Total.4.

5. Enter the second line of code:

```
event.value=f.value*.08;
```

6. Watch the punctuation! This line means that we are creating a JavaScript event, a value, which is based on the variable declared in the line before; this is then multiplied by .08. Exactly what we wanted.

7. Click OK to close the JavaScript Edit window. The custom script will be displayed in the Calculate tab, as shown in Figure 10-14.

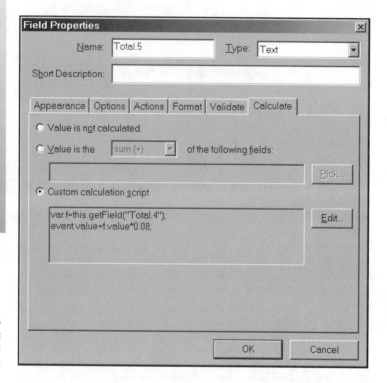

Figure 10-14
The custom script displayed in the Calculate tab

of the table is the grand total, named Total.6. Now that the custom script has been built for Total.5, add the calculation for the grand total, which will be the sum of Total.4 and Total.5.

Save the file and test the form. It may or may not work, depending on how it was built. Which brings me to field order.

Setting Field Order

There is little point in having the form calculate a sales tax amount before it calculates the totals for the individual items. Just one example of field order—more precisely, field disorder. This is easily remedied. You don't have to have the Form tool selected to use this function.

1. Select Tools ➤ Forms ➤ Set Field Calculation Order. The dialog box shown in Figure 10-15 will open.

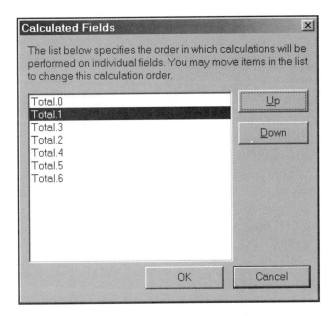

Figure 10-15
Set the order of the calculations in your table.

2. The Calculated Fields dialog box will contain only the fields that have either basic or custom calculations. As you can see in the figure, the fields are out of sequence.

3. To move a field, click its name to select it, and then click Up or Down to move it into the correct order.

4. Click OK. Your fields will now be ordered. Save the file and test it again.

You may have noticed something as you have been reading along that I haven't talked about yet. If you look again at the finished table, shown in Figure 10-7, you will see that the Product field looks different. For good reason. This is a specific field type. There are several of these field types.

Setting Field Type

Forms design in Acrobat is similar to that of many other programs. The field types are no exception. You can choose from several types. The available ones are shown in Figure 10-16.

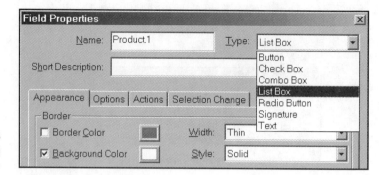

Figure 10-16
Select the field type from
the drop-down list.

The form fields on the pens.pdf file are all Text type, except for the Product list, which is a ListBox field type. You can set the field type when you create the field, or you can use the default Text type and then change the fields later. Follow these steps to modify the field type once the field has been added to the form:

1. Select the first field to change with the Form tool, and then select Properties from the context menu.

2. When the Field Properties dialog box opens, select ListBox from the Type drop-down menu. The tabs will change to the configuration shown in Figure 10-17.

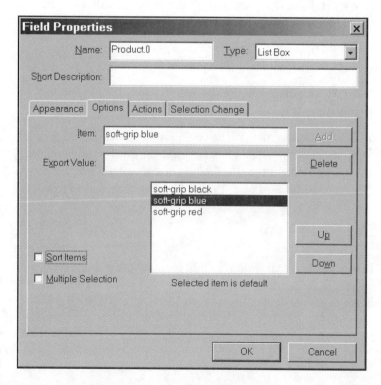

Figure 10-17
Options for a
ListBox form field

3. In the Appearance tab, set the background color to white, and deselect the border option.

4. In the Options tab, the different products that the customer will select from are listed. Click into the Item field and type the product name (maximum of 100 characters). Then click Add to move the name into the list at the lower part of the dialog box.

5. Continue adding the products until the list is complete. I added

- soft-grip black

- soft-grip blue

- soft-grip red

6. Once the items have been added to the list, you can configure the list using the two check boxes at the lower left of the dialog box:

- Click Multiple Selection if your user can select more than one item.

- Click Sort Items to rearrange the order of the items in your list. When this option is selected, click the item to be moved, and then click either Up or Down to move the item in the list.

7. Click OK to close the Field Properties dialog box and set the content of the field. As you can see in Figure 10-18, the available items are now listed in a box.

Note

There is an option on this page to enter an export value, which is used if the data from the form field is being exported to a CGI application.

Note

You can also attach mouse actions in the Actions tab, or you can attach JavaScript to individual selections. For example, you may want to write and attach a script that will open a secondary order form depending on which option is selected in the list box.

Figure 10-18
The list box fields. The top field has been selected and displays scrollbars.

Now let's look at how to organize the form for tabbing.

Setting Tab Order

If you open the finished tutorial file, pens1.pdf, you will see a tab-ordered form. That is, by using the Tab key, you can move from the top left to the bottom right of the form (with the exception of the calculated fields, which don't allow user input). It's not likely that a form is ever created this way, though.

Acrobat assigns tab order based on the order in which the fields were created. This can be easily changed. Here's how to do it:

1. Create all the fields on a form. Make sure the Form tool is selected.

2. Select Tools ➤ Forms ➤ Fields ➤ Set Tab Order. All the fields will now have a number in the top-left corner corresponding with their creation order.

3. Click the field to set as the first field, and then click subsequent fields through the form. They will be renumbered.

But what if part of the form is ordered correctly? You don't have to start at the beginning. Say the first 10 fields of a 20-field form are correctly sequenced. Hold down the Ctrl key (the Option key on the Mac) and click field 10. Then click the next one in the sequence and it will be numbered 11. Finish ordering the rest. As you can see in this order portion of the pens1.pdf form (see Figure 10-19), the tab sequence is now ordered.

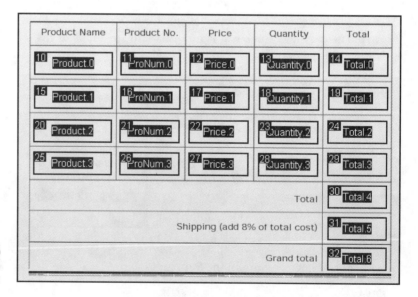

Figure 10-19
The organized tab order for the form

At this point, the form is complete. There is one last Acrobat feature I want to show you before I cover some advanced functions.

Using the Field Tab

If you have a document with fields in it, you can view the structure and layout of your fields by using the Field palette. As you do the other palettes, access it by selecting Window ➤ Field. Drag the palette's tab into the other palettes' tabs for ease of use. The contents of the Field palette for the pens1.pdf file are shown in Figure 10-20.

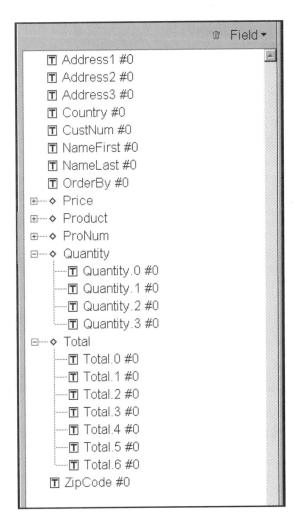

Figure 10-20
The field listing for the pens1.pdf file

If you look at Figure 10-20, you will see that there are differences between the fields that are in the table and the fields at the top of the page. This difference results from the fact that the table in which we built calculations had defined column headings, but the top customer information did not.

For any of the listings in the tab, you can select and right-click to access a context menu. As shown in Figure 10-21, this menu's options are straightforward. The Go To Field option will highlight the field on the document. The Lock option will prevent any changes from being made to the field until it is unlocked. The Properties option will open the Field Properties dialog box.

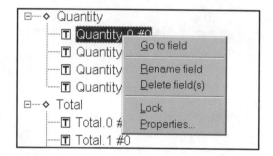

Figure 10-21
Context menu choices
for field listings

One more thing to show you. Like all the other palettes, this one offers a Field menu, shown in Figure 10-22. You can see that the processes we used earlier are accessible through this menu.

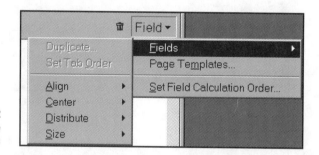

Figure 10-22
The Field palette
menu selections

Some Advanced Functions

Now that we have looked at building and customizing a basic form and accessibility issues, let's get into some of the fancy stuff. I have been waiting for this. In this section, we will look at using buttons and some navigation using JavaScript.

Fields for Buttons

You don't have to use a field just for collecting data. Fields can also be used to create buttons and to link to views. Now why would anyone want to do that? Well, it follows the same principle we applied earlier when I discussed calculating in form fields.

It goes like this. If you use the Links tool to create page and view links, the link properties cannot be copied and pasted from within Acrobat. This leads to tedious, even mind-numbing, repetition if you have to create a lot of these things. Imagine working with a 100-page document. Using a regular link-building process, you would have to build a link to the first page 100-minus-1 times (you don't need a link to the first page if you are already there). Then you would also have to rebuild the structure and add the properties and make sure the link elements are aligned the same page for page. Not so if links are created from within form elements and if a bit of JavaScript is thrown in for good measure. This is a three-stage process:

1. Create the form field.

2. Create the link.

3. Copy and reuse.

First, create a form field. To show you how it works, I have used the file from Chapter 8, nola.pdf. Open the document. If you recall, the file is a brochure for a vacation and has a 12-page book layout. If you would like to try this process, the two images I added to the nola.pdf file are on the CD in the Chapter 10 Projects folder; they are named bird1.pdf and bird2.pdf.

1. Select the Form tool, and then click and drag a rectangle for the field on your document. The Field Properties dialog box will open.

2. Name the field, and select Button from the Type drop-down list.

3. On the Appearance tab, make sure the Border and Background options are deselected.

4. I used a bird image as a button. Click the Options tab. As you can see in Figure 10-23, I chose Icon Only from the Layout drop-down list.

5. Click Select Icon and browse to the location where the image is stored.

Note

The images used for button states must be saved as PDF files.

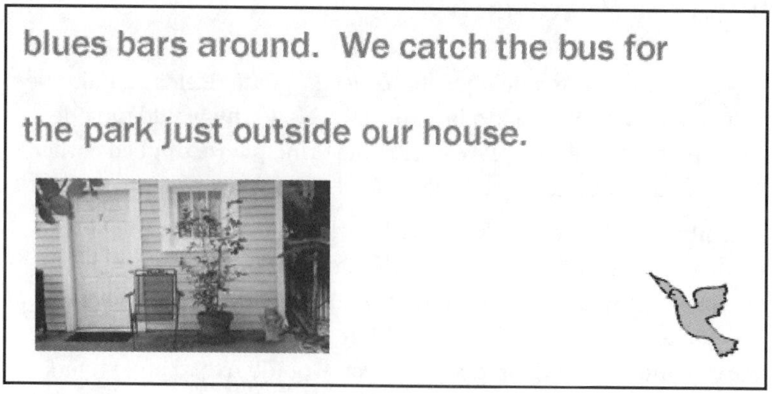

blues bars around. We catch the bus for

the park just outside our house.

Figure 10-23
Select the Icon Only
layout. This figure shows
the Down state image.

6. Use other images for other states if desired (Down or Rollover). I used the two images bird1.pdf and bird2.pdf as Down and Rollover states, respectively.

Now to build the link from these button fields. This is done in the Field Properties dialog box using the Actions tab. The link will return to the first page of the document (after the cover). As I mentioned, this link is going to be used on all right-hand pages of the document (except the first) to return to the first page. This is where the scripting comes in. Follow these steps to create the first link:

Note

Technically, we are scripting to return to page 2 of the document, given that the cover is not counted as a page but still exists. If you want to return to the cover, or page 1, enter 0 in the code line. Numbers start at 0, not 1. So the first page is page 0.

1. Click the Actions tab to open it (shown in Figure 10-24), and click the MouseDown option in the left pane. Then click Add. Select JavaScript from the Type pop-up menu and click Edit. The JavaScript window will open.

2. Enter this code in the JavaScript window:

```
this.pageNum=(1)
```

3. Click OK to close the scripting window, click Set Action, and close the Field Properties dialog box. Make sure the field is located where you want it on the page. Save the file.

That's it for the creation process. The code line simply means that when this script is run, the action is to return to whatever page is enclosed in parentheses.

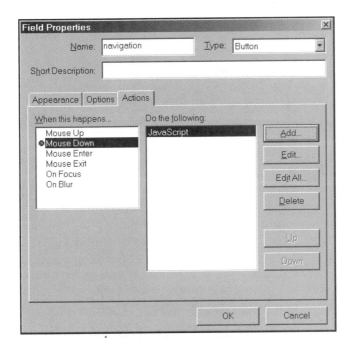

Figure 10-24
Control JavaScript actions
through the Actions tab

This document now has a form field complete with a script located in a specific location on a page, as you can see in Figure 10-25.

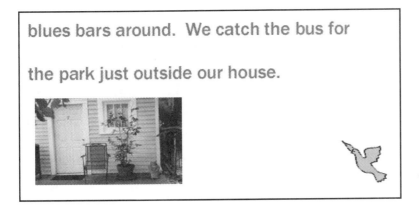

Figure 10-25
The little bird navigation
button on the page

Now for the magic. Select the button field with the Form tool. Duplicating the field is a simple process. Select Tools ➤ Forms ➤ Fields ➤ Duplicate. The dialog box shown in Figure 10-26 will open. As you can see in the figure, I didn't have an option to select every second page. To copy the field to every page, select the default All option and click OK.

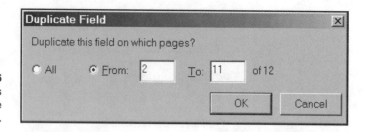

Figure 10-26
Select the range of pages
to add duplicates of the
navigation button.

The field will be duplicated to all pages and will appear in the same location on each page. It will contain the same bit of script, which will take the user back to the first page from any number of pages. (In my example, because I want the buttons to appear only on the right-hand pages, when the set was added to the document, I selected each of the ones that I wanted to remove, right-clicked, and selected Delete.)

Project Project 10-1. Creating a PDF Order Form for Wildflower Farm

> **Note**
>
> **A Special Thanks to Wildflower Farm**
>
> The materials used for the projects in this chapter (and also the projects in Chapters 6 and 9) come from Wildflower Farm, located north of Toronto, Canada. The farm, owned by Miriam Goldberger and Paul Jenkins, hosts tours and weddings, and sells plants, seed, flowers, and dried materials. As you can see in these projects, it is a beautiful place. All project source materials copyright © 2001 by Wildflower Farm.

This chapter's project again uses information from Wildflower Farm. This project is built on information taken from the Wildflower Farm Web site, which has an extensive online ordering system. In this project, you will build a simple order form in Acrobat for ordering native grasses. You will need the grass.pdf file, which is on the CD in the Chapter 10 Projects folder. The finished version of the project, grass2.pdf, is also on the CD.

What We Start With

As I mentioned, this is a simple order form. When you open the grass.pdf file, you will see that it has nine pages. It starts with an order form for native grass seed, as shown in Figure 10-27. Rather than adding fields for the user to manually enter numbers, prices, and names, these elements are already present. We will have to add fields for quantity and then a scripted calculation.

Wildflower Farm
"The Wildflower Source"

Number	Name	Price	Quantity	Total
40530	Big Bluestem	$3.75		
47590	Little Bluestem	$3.75		
41520	Sideoats Grama	$3.75		
43520	Canada Wild Rye	$3.75		
44760	Bottlebrush Grass	$3.75		
47570	Switchgrass	$3.75		
48550	Indiangrass	$3.75		
49050	Prairie Dropseed	$4.50		
			Total	
			Tax	
			Grand Total	

Figure 10-27
The order page for this project

The rest of the document consists of information on the different seed varieties. As you can see in Figure 10-28, each type has its own information page, complete with a photo.

We are going to add links from the order page to the individual information pages. Then, to prevent the user from scrolling, we will add a scripted field to return to the order form.

Then, we will add buttons to reset or print the order form. Finally, we will set the tab order. Make sure as you are working that you have the Field palette open. We will use commands from the Fields drop-down menu.

Bottlebrush Grass - Hystrix patula

This woodland grass produces delightful seedheads that resemble a bottlebrush. Growing in clumps on well drained soil, it reaches four to five feet tall and is ideal for part-shade conditions under trees where most lawn grasses fail to grow.

Colour : Green - Gold

Blooms : June - Sept.

Light : Full sun to Part shade

Height : 3'- 5'

Soil : Sand to Clay

Water : Dry to Medium

Approx. 80 seeds per pkt.

Figure 10-28
Information page for one of the available products

First Things First: Adding the Form Fields

For the eight seed varieties, you must add two fields: Quantity and Price.

Note

Refer to the tutorials earlier in this chapter for more detailed instruction if required.

1. With the Form tool selected, click and drag to create a field for the first field, Quantity.0. When the Field Properties dialog box opens, use these settings:

   - Name: Quantity.0

   - Type: Text

   - Appearance tab: No border; Text: 9 pt. Helvetica; visible

2. Now click and drag to create a field for the total field, Quantity.0. When the Field Properties dialog box opens, use these settings:

   - Name: Quantity.0

   - Type: Text

- Appearance tab: No border; Text: 9 pt. Helvetica; visible

- Options tab: Right alignment

- Format tab: Category: Number; 2 decimal places; Currency symbol: Dollar

- Calculate tab: Add the custom calculation script. Click Edit to open the JavaScript window. Add these two lines of code:

```
var a = this.getField("Quantity.0");
event.value = a.value *3.75
```

3. Click OK to accept the changes.

4. Click the Quantity.0 form field and Ctrl-drag to copy it down the entire column (you will end up with eight in total). Rename the cells. You will have a range from Quantity.0 to Quantity.7.

5. Repeat with the Total column. In addition to changing the names of the fields, you will have to change the content of the script. Table 10-3 lists the changes for each line of code, corresponding with the renamed fields.

Table 10-3   Code Changes Required for the Total Fields

Field Name	Change "Quantity.0" To	Calculation
Total.1	Quantity.1	a.value *3.75
Total.2	Quantity.2	a.value *3.75
Total.3	Quantity.3	a.value *3.75
Total.4	Quantity.4	a.value *3.75
Total.5	Quantity.5	a.value *3.75
Total.6	Quantity.6	a.value *3.75
Total.7	Quantity.7	a.value *4.50

6. Save the file.

Fields for Special Totals

You will also have to add fields for the subtotal of the order, the sales tax, and the grand total. Copy the Total.7 field, and change the copies to Total.8, Total.9, and Total.10.

1. Total.8 (subtotal of the ordered seed): Select Value is the sum (+) of the fields, and add the following:

   ```
   "Total.0","Total.1", "Total.2", "Total.3", "Total.4", "Total.5",
      "Total.6", "Total.7"
   ```

2. Total.9 (tax at 9%): Select Custom Calculation Script. Click Edit to open the JavaScript window. Add these two lines of code:

   ```
   var a = this.getField("Total.8");
   event.value = a.value *0.09;
   ```

3. Total.10 (grand total): Select Value is the sum (+) of the fields, and add these fields:

   ```
   "Total.8", "Total.9"
   ```

4. Deselect the Form tool and test the form. You may find that some of your calculations are out of whack. That is related to order of calculations. Check them as follows:

   a. Select Field ➤ Set Field Calculation Order.

   b. When the Calculated Fields window opens, reorder the list to read from Total.0 to Total.10 (top to bottom).

   c. Click OK to close the Calculated Fields window.

4. Save the file and test it again. Your calculations should work correctly now.

Note

In rows where you did not enter a quantity, the price will display "$0.00"—which makes sense.

Adding Button Fields

Next up, let's add the Reset and Print buttons to the form. I added these two form elements to the front page, as shown in Figure 10-29. First I'll explain how to build the buttons, and then I'll discuss the action settings for each.

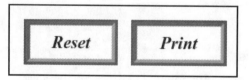

Figure 10-29
Add these functions to the front page.

1. Click and drag to create a new field. Name it **clear**. Select the Button Type. Use these settings in the Appearance tab:

1. Click and drag to create a new field. Name it **clear**. Select the Button Type. Use these settings in the Appearance tab:

   - Border color: top right in palette (shown in Figure 10-30)

   - Background color: white

   - Width: Thick

   - Style: Inset

   - Text: color dark purple, Times Bold-Italic 18pt.

2. In the Options tab, select Text Only from the Layout drop-down list. Enter **Reset** for the Button Face Attributes text.

3. Click OK to close the window.

4. Click and drag to create the second button. Name it **print**. It will contain the same properties. Change the text for the Button Face Attributes to **Print**. Click OK to close the window.

Figure 10-30
Choose a pea green or similar subdued color for the button frame.

Adding Actions to the Buttons

You now have two very pretty buttons on the page that do nothing. Let's remedy that. Start with the Reset button.

1. Double-click the field with the Form tool to open the Field Properties dialog box. Click the Actions tab.

2. Select Mouse Down from the When This Happens drop-down list.

3. Click Add. The Add An Action dialog box will open. Select Reset Form from the Type drop-down menu.

4. Click Select Fields. When the Field Selection dialog box opens, its default selection is All Fields. Click OK to accept the default and close the dialog box.

5. When you return to the Add An Action dialog box, click Set Action. Reset Form will now appear in the Do The Following list. Click OK to close the Field Properties dialog box.

Now for the print field:

1. Double-click the field with the Form tool to open the Field Properties dialog box. Click the Actions tab.

2. Select Mouse Down from the When This Happens drop-down list.

3. Click Add. The Add An Action dialog box will open. Select Execute Menu Item from the Type drop-down menu.

4. Click Edit Menu Item. The dialog box shown in Figure 10-31 will open. Select File ➤ Print from the Menu Item Selection dialog box. Click OK to close the dialog box.

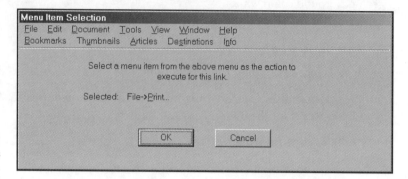

Figure 10-31
Select menu commands from this dialog box.

5. When you return to the Add An Action dialog box, click Set Action. Execute Menu Item will now appear in the Do The Following list. Click OK to close the Field Properties dialog box.

6. Save the file. Now enter some test data and try out the new functions. The final layout of the order page should look like Figure 10-32.

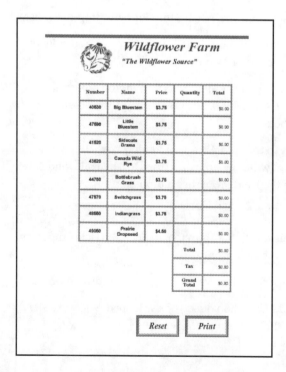

Figure 10-32
The final layout for the order form

Adding Some Navigation to the Form

We are more than half done. Let's add one more button, this time as part of navigation. The navigation for this document is composed of links from the names of the varieties in the form to descriptions of the varieties. We will add a button on each page that will return the user to the form once the information has been read. The button looks like Figure 10-33.

Figure 10-33
Add this form button to return the user to the order form.

1. Click and drag a new form element below the text and to the right of the image on page 2. The button frame should line up approximately evenly with the border at the top of the page, as shown in Figure 10-34.

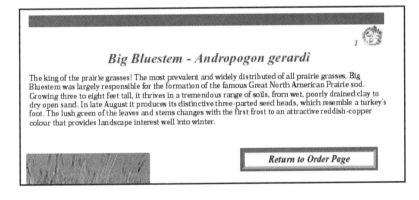

Figure 10-34
Positioning for the navigation button

2. Name the button **return**. The type will default to Button. Leave the settings in the Appearance tab, except increase the font size to 12pt.

3. On the Options tab, enter **Return to Order Page** in the Button Face Attributes text line.

4. On the Actions tab, add a JavaScript for the Mouse Down state. Click Mouse Down in the left pane, and click Add. When the Add An Action dialog box opens, select JavaScript from the drop-down menu. Click Edit to open the JavaScript Edit window. Enter this line of code:

```
this.pageNum=(0)
```

5. Click OK to return to the Add An Action dialog box, click Set Action to close the dialog box, and then click Add to close the Field Properties dialog box.

6. Duplicate the field. From the Fields palette, select Field ➤ Fields ➤ Duplicate. (You can also select Tools ➤ Forms ➤ Fields ➤ Duplicate.) When the Duplicate Field dialog box opens, select pages 2 to 9 (we have set the action to return to page 1, so including an action to return to itself would be redundant).

7. Save the file. You can test the file, since I usually say that right about now, but that is a lot of scrolling!

Let's add the links first, and then we'll test it.

Adding the Links from the Order Form

We have added buttons to return to the first page. Stands to reason we should build something to get the user off the first page. Before starting, make sure the file is in Single Page view mode (set this on the Status Bar below the Document Pane).

1. Using the Link tool, click and drag a rectangle around the first name, Big Bluestem. The Link Properties dialog box will open. Use these settings:

   - Type: Invisible Rectangle
   - Highlight: Invert
   - Action Type: Go To View (select from the drop-down menu)

2. Move through the document to page 2, which is the page to be linked. Set the view with the zoom tools or shortcut keys. If you prefer, you can use the Magnification settings on the Link Properties dialog box that appear when you choose the Go To View action. The page selected will also be shown on the Link Properties dialog box below the Magnification drop-down box.

3. Click the Set Link button on the Link Properties dialog box to attach the view to the link, and close the dialog box. You will be automatically returned to the first page (where the link was set).

4. Continue with the other varieties. When all eight varieties have been linked to their information pages, save the file.

5. Now test the links and also the return buttons.

A work of art, isn't it? One last topic and then, sadly, this chapter is finished.

Note

If you have to make any adjustments, click the link with the Link Tool and select Properties from the context menu. When the Link Properties dialog box opens, a new button, Edit Destination, will be displayed. Click this button to go to the view you set initially, and make any changes you require. Click Set Link to close the dialog box and change your settings.

Creating Accessible Adobe PDF Files

If you have been reading along with this book, you will have already read Chapter 8, which dealt with making documents accessible to users with disabilities. I mentioned in that chapter that I would cover accessible forms in this chapter. And so I shall.

When you make a form accessible, you want two things to occur:

- Field information will be useful to the user.

- The fields will be read in the correct order.

In the previous section, I showed you how to set tab orders. Let's look at the field information and also how to write descriptive tags.

As with any other kind of document that you are trying to make accessible, the file must be tagged. If you start with a tagged file, it will be simpler to make the modifications needed for full accessibility.

Completing Field Information

First, let's go back to the fields one last time. One piece of information will be required to make the field information comply with accessibility standards. In Figure 10-35, you see the Field Properties dialog box displaying information for the OrderBy field. Under the Name field, I have added **name of person placing order**. A screen reader will read this as the user tabs into the field.

To give you a frame of reference, I will refer back to the tutorial file. You may recall that form had 30-odd form fields. In another version of the pens1.pdf file (I am using it only for discussion—it is not included on the CD) I added descriptions to the entire customer information section at the top of the page. When I ran the Accessibility Checker, using only the Form Fields Have Descriptions option, the results reflect the efforts I have made (shown in Figure 10-36). Only 23 form fields left to go!

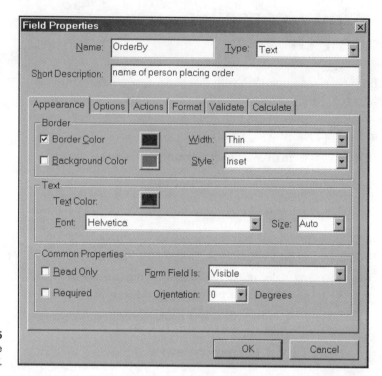

Figure 10-35
Add descriptions to the
fields for a screen reader.

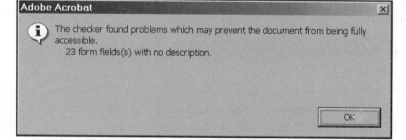

Figure 10-35
Add descriptions to the
fields for a screen reader.

Figure 10-36
The results of running
the Accessibility Checker
against the file

Correcting and Adding Tag Information

Once you have entered all the form fields and tested the form, you can
enter the additional materials required for accessibility.

Figure 10-37 shows the Tags palette from my discussion version of the
tutorial file. You can see that a multitude of tags are listed. And they are
not too tidy. For example, if you look under the ⟨TR⟩ tag, under the first
⟨TD⟩ tag, two ⟨Normal⟩ tags appear. The first one is named "Name," and
the second one is blank. That is because we added two separate form
fields in that element. There are no object references either.

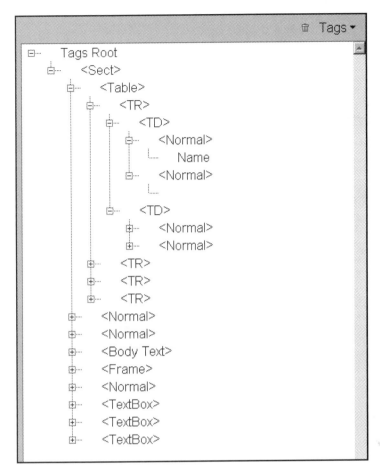

Figure 10-37
The Tags listing for the discussion version of the tutorial file

Here's how to make the modifications:

1. Click the first tag you want to alter in the Tags palette.

2. Select Tags ➤ Find Unmarked Comments. The dialog box shown in Figure 10-38 will open.

3. Select Current Page For Unmarked Comments. Click Find Next.

Note

Be careful what you select. There are two options in the Tab menu: one for comments and one for content. If you choose the content option, you will be running through many graphical elements of some objects if they aren't grouped.

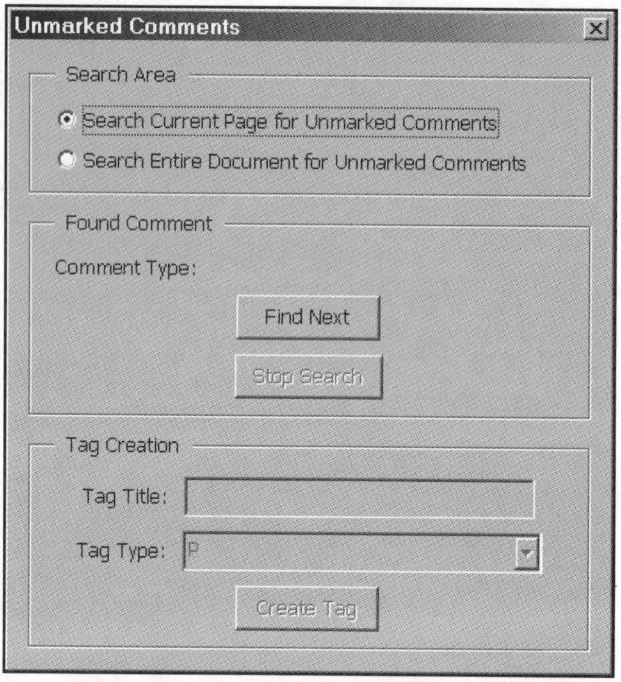

Figure 10-38
Use this dialog box to add form fields to your tags manually.

Note

Although the Tag Title is not required for a screen reader to function correctly, it can be required for authoring and modifying the document. Simply makes it easier to use.

4. The fields will highlight in their tab sequence order. Enter the following information in the dialog box:

- Tag Title
- Tag Type: Enter **Form**.

5. Continue this process with the other elements in your form. Save the file periodically as you add the tags. (Just a personal phobia and response to frozen programs and files over the years.)

Now contrast this with the next image. In Figure 10-39, you can see that I have cleaned up and corrected some of the code.

Once you have completed the entire process, test your file. Which brings this chapter to a close.

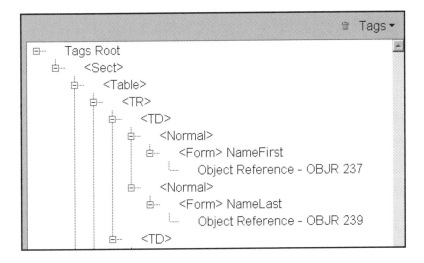

Figure 10-39
The Tags listing after I added the field information

Up Next

This has been so much fun for me. I hope you found it informative and useful. Forms are such useful creations. In this chapter, I covered the basics of building and organizing a form. I also touched on accessibility issues and templates.

I am serious when I say I covered only the basics. There are so very many forms issues that couldn't be covered here. You can consult some tutorials on the Acrobat installation CD for more information. Other Acrobat features that deal with importing and exporting data and templates will be covered in Chapters 12 and 14, when we look at advanced functionality and network issues.

Coming up next, though, we will have a look at print issues. As anyone who uses Acrobat for printing knows, print work always has issues!

Chapter 11

Print It!

One of Acrobat's strongest features is its capability to produce documents that print exactly like the original across a great many systems. To design intelligently, however, you need much more information than just where the Print button is located.

Enhancing Print Workflow

Designers design. Regardless of your medium of choice, all designers understand the advantages of using different programs for vector, bitmap, and layout production. Another inescapable truth we all share is that the clearer the communications between us and our clients, the better the relationships are and will be.

The quicker the feedback, the smoother the proofing cycle. Acrobat is a very useful tool in this process. What Acrobat can do, in addition to communication, is shorten production cycles (and costs). You can use the same format for display, preflight, proofing, editing, archiving, transport, and printing.

Designer Advantages

I hate having somebody touch my work. Look at it, admire it, hate it, make suggestions, but don't mess with the material. Sound familiar? Of course, by using the security settings in Acrobat, you can prevent anyone from modifying your work. But what other advantages are there to incorporating Acrobat into your workflow?

I have compiled a list of benefits. The items in this list are designed to set off those little mental lightbulbs. Everyone will have different experiences and backgrounds, but my aim is to offer some points to ponder.

- Proofing is very accurate. Colors can be manipulated to appear as the printed output would. Reviewers can zoom in to a factor of 1600 percent—you can't miss a detail at that magnification. The more accurate the proof, the less chance of proofing error.

- Vector graphics and embedded fonts are always at full resolution. This means you will not have any second-generation quality loss, as would occur from faxing a proof.

- Speaking of graphics, transparency is supported, so layered Illustrator and Photoshop images can be fully integrated.

- Layouts can be displayed as they will be printed. This version of Acrobat supports multiple page sizes, even in the same document.

- Work can be distributed to many people at once. You can effectively poll an entire workgroup with one e-mail. The same applies for client distribution.

- Matchprints or paper color proofs can be substituted by PDF-proofing transfers. This soft-proofing process helps to maintain integrity and saves time and money in this portion of the cycle—you don't have to send a file for printing, review it, and ship it.

- When a proof is signed off, the same PostScript file can be used and the PDF prepress version can be created by changing the Distiller Press settings. This saves time in final prepress delivery (depending on your printing services company).

Once a file is out of your hands, using a PDF-assisted workflow still has its advantages.

The Ripple Effect

The efficiencies of using PDF for production have a ripple effect. For example, because later press deadlines are possible, advertising has more time to adjust for changes in costs or pricing or other corrections, without incurring additional costs for couriers or mailing. Digital distribution is instant. Speaking of instant, from an ad agency perspective, PDF pages can be used as "tear sheets." E-mailing the page to the client on the day of publication provides the verification of a traditional tear sheet and speeds up revenue collection.

PDF files maintain corporate identity and branding. PDF files, unlike other less-consistent formats, can be printed exactly as intended.

What about prepress shops? Whether they are printers or imaging service bureaus, there are benefits. You can see content and determine immediately if you have the right components—images, fonts, and graphics. And you can do it in composite color. Not only that, but the TouchUp tools will allow you to make last-minute changes without having to redistill the source documents.

It Is an Impressive System

How's that for a buildup? As you would expect, you must deal with a number of issues to make PDF files work for your print output.

In this chapter, I will cover a number of print-related issues. Remember that, regardless of the approach you take to translating a source document into PDF format, the processes will be the same. We will first look at Distiller, and then we will learn how to set some common print output settings. I will show you how to create watched folders, and we will examine color settings in Acrobat. Following that is an in-depth discussion on fonts and color issues, and we will also look at exporting files as PostScript or EPS files.

The whole thing hinges on Acrobat Distiller, so that's where we will start.

A Run Through Distiller

Acrobat Distiller is installed as part of the Acrobat 5 installation process. Use Distiller to create a PDF from graphics programs such as PageMaker, QuarkXPress, FrameMaker, Illustrator, FreeHand, or CorelDRAW. Any program, for that matter, that can print to Distiller. Distiller is its own program, but its functionality is integrated both into authoring programs as a printer option and into Acrobat proper. Whether you convert a file to PDF using PDFMaker or write to Distiller as a printer option, you will encounter the same issues. If you are designing work intended for high-end print output, go the Distiller route rather than convert the files using macros.

So let's see what is inside the Distiller box. Before we do, though, here is a summary of some of the biggest features of Distiller 5:

- DeviceN color space, smooth shading, and masked images are supported.

- Pages can be up to 200 inches in either dimension.

- Document length is limited only by disk space and memory.

- Double-byte fonts can be embedded.

- TrueType fonts can be searchable.

The Distiller Interface

This part of the discussion will center on the program itself. Access Distiller from your desktop by selecting Start ➤ Programs ➤ Adobe ➤ Acrobat Distiller (or a similar path you assigned at installation). The interface, as shown in Figure 11-1, is deceptively simple.

Before I tiptoe through the settings, just a point about the main interface. Each time the program is launched, the fonts table is created. I will return to that later. The Job Options drop-down list contains the list of .joboptions files I have created in my system. In this example, I have shown the default Print option, which is compatible with Acrobat 4.

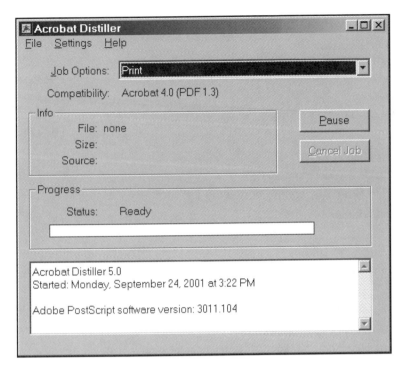

Figure 11-1
Distiller's interface

File Settings

The File options are basic. Select File ➤ Open to access any PostScript files in your system that you want to distill into a PDF format. Select File ➤ Preferences to open the Preferences dialog box. I will come back to this dialog box once the Distiller overview is finished.

Settings Options

These functions are the heart of Distiller. In this collection of options, you will find font locations, watched folders, job options, and security settings.

- Select Settings ➤ Font Locations to open the dialog box shown in Figure 11-2. In this dialog box, you can add and remove folders that Distiller will check to find fonts on your system.

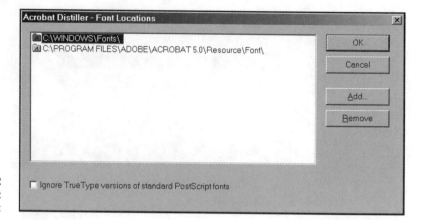

Figure 11-2
Distiller's Font
Locations dialog box

Where Have All My Fonts Gone?

Distiller gives priority to fonts embedded in a PostScript file. Then it will search through fonts in assigned folders (PSFonts folder in Windows, System Folder:Fonts on Mac), and Acrobat standard fonts (in the Font subfolder of Acrobat's Resource folder).

Set other locations using Settings ➤ Font Locations. All fonts must be in folders, not in subfolders. The easy solution? Embed the fonts you are using.

- Select Settings ➤ Watched Folders to set up a system to look in certain folders on a certain schedule for PostScript files—much more on that coming up.

- Select Settings ➤ Job Options to open the Job Options dialog box, with its set of five tabs. Again, more on that coming up.

- Select Settings ➤ Security to open a basic security settings dialog box. As you can see in Figure 11-3, you can set both passwords and encryption. The figure reflects settings for Acrobat 4, which allows only for 40-bit encryption.

Help!

I can't leave this walk-through without showing you what is available in Help. The different Help options for Distiller are shown in Figure 11-4.

As you can see in the figure, you have several options. I want to point out one file in particular. The Distiller Parameters Guide is a 60-page PDF file that covers the Distiller information in this chapter, but to a very great depth. If you are working on a project with complex output requirements, look in this file for more information.

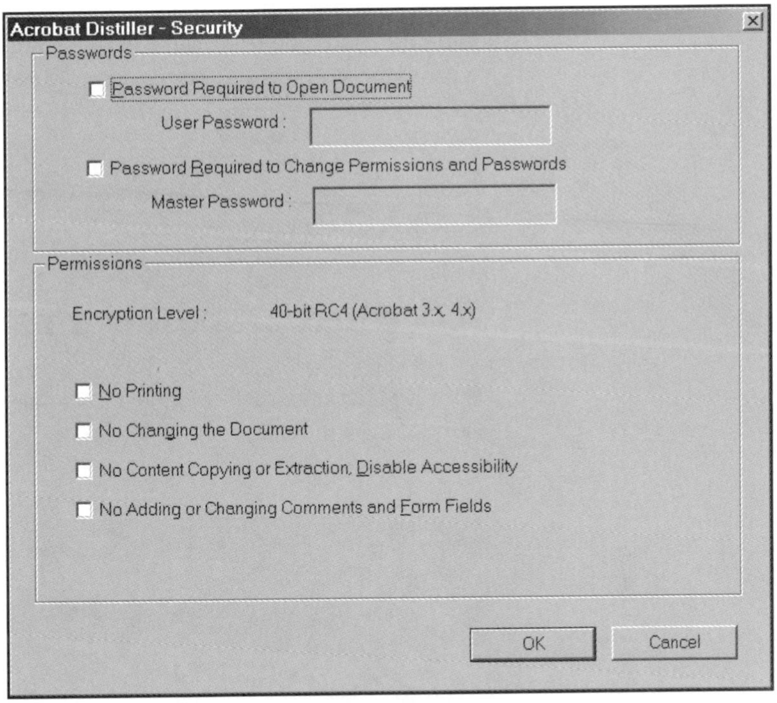

Figure 11-3
Security settings
for Distiller

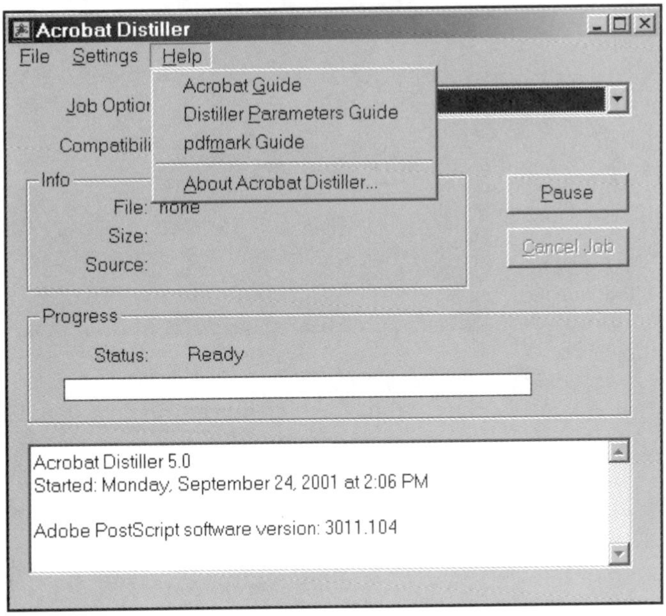

Figure 11-4
Distiller Help options

The first listing, Acrobat Guide, opens the help files for Acrobat. The pdfmark Guide is a technical programming document. It describes the syntax and use of the pdfmark operator and how to use it for coding purposes. The final option on the menu gives you the Distiller version information.

That completes the orientation of Distiller's interface. Let's look more closely at Distiller preferences.

Acrobat Distiller Preferences

With Distiller open, select File ➤ Preferences. The dialog box shown in Figure 11-5 will open.

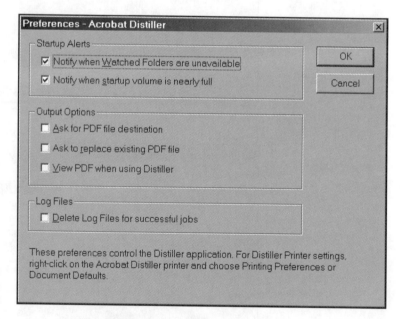

Figure 11-5
The Distiller Preferences
dialog box

Here's what the preferences will do:

- *Notify When Watched Folders Are Unavailable:* Notifies you if a folder on your list becomes unavailable or if Distiller cannot find it (more on watched folders next)

- *Notify When Startup Volume Is Nearly Full:* Warns you if less than 1MB of space is available on the hard disk where Distiller is installed

- *Ask For PDF File Destination:* Displays a dialog box that lets you name and specify a location for files when you use drag-and-drop or the Print command with Distiller (Windows only)

- *Ask To Replace Existing PDF File:* Displays a dialog box that warns you when you are about to overwrite an existing PDF file with a file of the same name (Windows only)

- *View PDF When Using Distiller:* Automatically displays a converted PDF file when you convert a document with Distiller (Windows only)

- *Delete Log Files For Successful Jobs:* Deletes log files unless the job failed

Click OK to set the preferences and close the dialog box.

As I mentioned earlier, Distiller can use watched folders. Let's have a look.

Project Tutorial: Setting Up Watched Folders

Distiller can be configured to look in a certain folder on a certain schedule for PostScript files. When it finds a file in the In folder, it converts the file to PDF and moves it to the Out folder. You can have up to 100 watched folders being monitored by Distiller at the same time, and you can create watched folders based on any criteria, such as customer or level of compression.

Here's how to set up watched folders:

1. Open Acrobat Distiller. In the dialog box, select Settings ➤ Watched Folders. The Watched Folders dialog box shown in Figure 11-6 will open.

2. To add folders, click Add. Browse to select the folder, and click OK. The In and Out folders will automatically be added by Distiller, as shown in Figure 11-7. Folders can be added at any level in your directory structure.

Note

Distiller does not convert a PostScript file in a watched folder if the file is read-only.

Note

To remove a folder, click the name, and then click Remove. The In and Out folders, their contents, and the Folder.JobOptions file must be deleted manually.

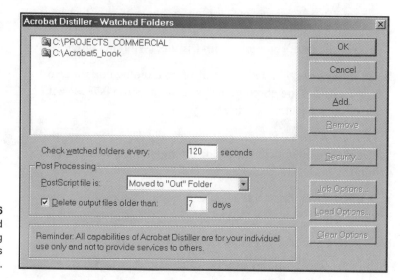

Figure 11-6
Set up the watched
folders in this dialog
box. My system has
two folders.

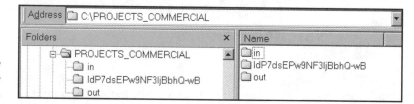

Figure 11-7
Distiller automatically
adds files to the directory.

Folder Options

As I mentioned earlier, you can set the options for the content of the watched folders. These options cover conversion processes, management, and time frames. The functions correspond to the grayed-out buttons shown in Figure 11-6.

1. Click Security to open the dialog box shown in Figure 11-8.

2. Click Job Options to open the dialog box shown in Figure 11-9. This dialog box contains the same set of options available for creating job options in other areas, such as creating custom job options in authoring programs.

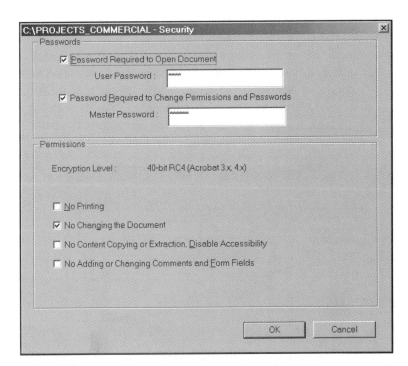

Figure 11-8
Setting security for the watched folder's contents

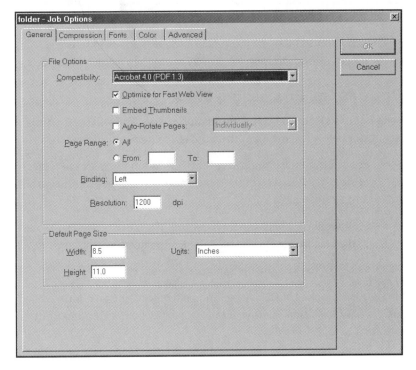

Figure 11-9
Create a new set of job options.

3. Click Load Options to load a set of options you have configured elsewhere. As you can see in Figure 11-10, I have several sets of custom job options, many of which were constructed before I converted files in authoring applications. When you select an existing set of job options, the file is saved to the watched folder as folder.joboptions. The original job options file is not changed or moved.

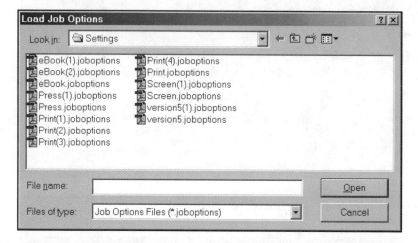

Figure 11-10
Select any of the job options files available on your system.

4. Click a folder to select it, and click Clear Options to return a folder's settings to those originally set in the Distiller dialog box.

Options for Processing Files

Refer again to Figure 11-6 (the main dialog box). You will see a number of settings below the listing of the watched folders.

- Enter a time in seconds to specify how often to check the folders. Mine is set at 120 seconds (2 minutes). The value can range from 1 to 9999 seconds.

- Set options for the file after processing. The file can be either moved to the Out folder or deleted. Also, set the deleting options.

- Click OK to close the dialog box.

Now we have looked at Distiller, setting preferences, and creating watched folders. Think it's time to have a look at particulars of creating print output? Me too.

Print Job Options

Where to start? We all know settings can be tweaked until the cows come home, but you still need a starting point. I have assembled a collection of settings and hints that you might find useful to begin your quest for the perfect output. You can create these settings in Distiller by selecting Settings ➤ Job Options.

General Settings

Use these settings from the General tab (shown in Figure 11-11):

- Select a Compatibility setting of at least Acrobat 4.

- Deselect the Optimize For Fast Web View and Embed Thumbnails options. These options add to file size but have no print output purpose, and enabling them will lengthen the Distiller process.

- Set your desired resolution, but it will be activated only if the PostScript file doesn't contain a defined resolution.

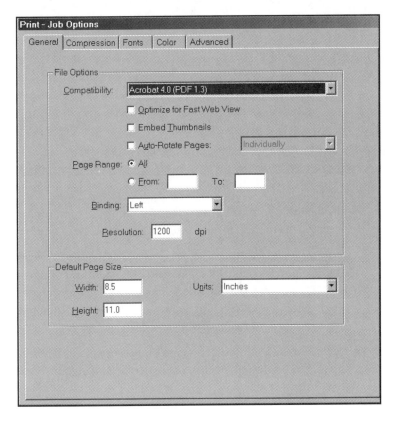

Figure 11-11
Start with modified settings on the General tab.

Compression Settings

Next up are the compression options. The Compression tab, with its default settings, is shown in Figure 11-12. There is no practical way to give you a list of optimal settings, of course. Rather, I have some tips and points to ponder.

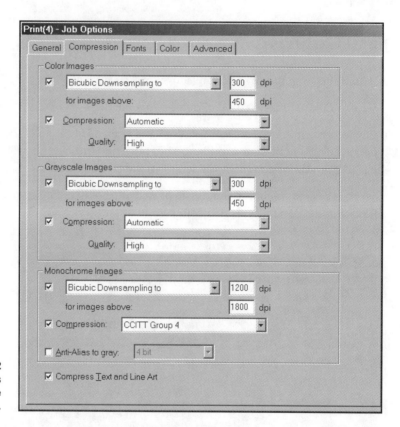

Figure 11-12
Compression options depend on the content of the file.

- The default Compression setting is Automatic at Maximum quality. This usually results in minimal compression and large file size.

- Compression is done using JPEG and ZIP algorithms. There are five JPEG quality levels. For imaging output, leave the High setting selected from the Quality drop-down list. JPEG is lossy compression; ZIP is lossless, but not as efficient as JPEG.

- Downsampling is often necessary. Images are often digitized at too high a resolution, or they are scaled during layout.

- If a file will be reused for subsequent work, use bicubic down-sampling. Although it is the slowest, it results in the best quality.

- Target resolutions depend on the screen ruling of whatever imaging process the output is planned for.

- The resolution will be downsampled only if the image's resolution is at least 50 percent higher than the target resolution.

Fonts Settings

The Fonts tab is shown in Figure 11-13. I will discuss fonts in depth later, but I want to point out some features on this tab. You have two options regarding embedding: You can embed all fonts or only subsets of fonts, and you can also define actions when embedding fails in a document.

Note

Use 250–300 dpi for contone images for offset printing. *Contone* refers to a type of printer that uses a combination of dithering and printing at different levels of intensity to produce different colors and different shades of lightness and darkness. Contone printers lay down ink using a few different levels of intensity (usually 8). Dithering is required to produce the range of colors our eyes can see.

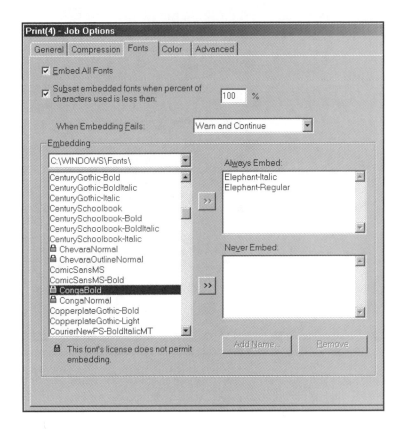

Figure 11-13
The Fonts tab

As you can see in the figure, I have specified that Elephant always be embedded. Second, I have selected a font named CongaBold. When the font is selected, the message regarding the font's license is displayed.

Workflow Tip
RGB vs. CMYK Color

If you are creating documents for both Web and print, use CMYK. CMYK documents convert quite well to RGB. The reverse is not necessarily true. Converting high-resolution PDF images into low-resolution images for the Web is not a problem.

Sadly, although it is a very attractive font, it cannot be embedded. If you look at the figure, you can see there is an icon of a lock before the name of the font. This means that it is a font with license restrictions (which is also described at the bottom of the dialog box).

Color Settings

Next up is the Color tab, which is shown in Figure 11-14. Much information is coming up in this chapter on color, but again I have a couple of points.

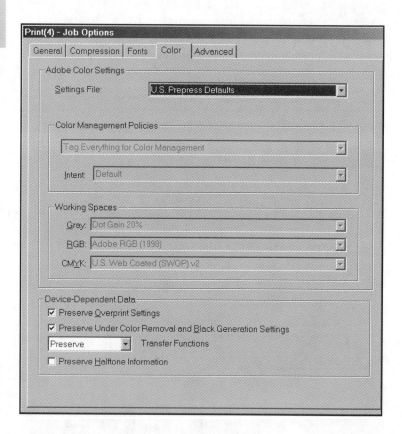

Figure 11-14
Color settings using the U.S. Prepress Defaults color settings

The figure shows the default settings for U.S. Prepress work. The options are selected as part of the profile for the Settings File, and they cannot be changed in this dialog box.

Advanced Settings

The final tab, Advanced, lists advanced settings. The advanced default settings for U.S. Prepress Defaults are shown in Figure 11-15. In general, leave the default settings, unless modifications are required by your printer.

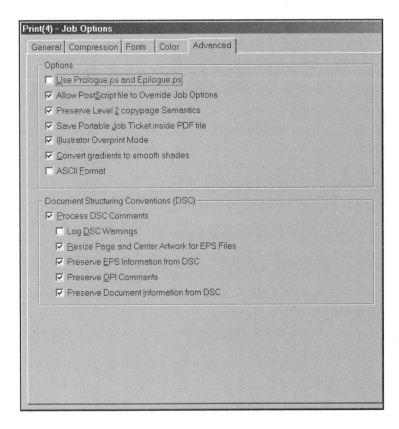

Figure 11-15
Advanced settings for prepress output

I indicated that I would return to fonts and cover some of these issues in detail. On that note, everything you want to know about fonts is up next.

Fonts

Fonts are somewhat of a personal matter. Some designers search for the perfect font (me among them). Others are satisfied to focus on content. Your choice will always depend on the purpose of your document. Regardless of which camp you are in, fonts can be easily embedded into PDF files.

What Does Embedding Do?

At the risk of stating the obvious, *embedded fonts* means the definitions of those fonts are included in the PDF file. You may create your own settings and embed, subset, or choose not to embed any font depending on your particular requirements.

In general terms, you should always embed fonts unless the file size is a primary consideration or you are creating screen output. Embedding is useful if you are working in an environment where you characteristically use the same fonts for the same types of work. In fact, you may want to create different custom settings for different types of work, different clients, and the like.

If you have an embedded font, and the user has a font with the same name installed on his or her system, the file will be read with the user's system fonts, even if they are from a different foundry. The Impact fonts come immediately to my mind.

Acrobat tries to simulate fonts not embedded in the PDF and not installed on the computer with Adobe sans MM or Adobe serif MM fonts. It reads the font metrics from the SuperATM database, which is included in the Acrobat installation process. A simulated font uses the same width and has a similar appearance. Simulation works only for relatively normal-appearing fonts. Logically, many decorative or unusual fonts cannot be simulated correctly.

What do you do if you want to ensure the user uses your fonts? You have to subset them.

Subsetting Fonts

Subsetting is different from embedding. *Subsetting* makes sure each font used is included (subset) in the file. On the Fonts tab, there is a subset setting: Subset at 100%. This setting will ensure that your desired font is actually the one used. Why? It's all in the name. When a subset is embedded, Distiller assigns a unique name to the font derived from the name of the original. This name will never match a font on the host system, and your version will always be used.

Subsetting is especially important for press work. The lower the subset percentage value, the smaller the file size because only the characters used in the file are subset. Another reason for subsetting at 100% relates to editing your document in Acrobat. You can use the TouchUp Text tool for small repairs. With a font subset at 100%, the entire font is embedded and you can then touch up the text at will. If you subset a font at a lower percentage, only the characters actually used in the document are included.

Project Tutorial: Keep an Eye on Your Fonts

In Acrobat, you can check what fonts are being used for display. This process requires using two different commands, but it is worth the few minutes it will take you to complete, especially in appearance-critical documents.

Look at Figure 11-16. In this image, I have shown a portion of a page, as well as the Text Attributes dialog box for the heading, which was selected with the TouchUp Text tool. You can see that the font is HelmetBoldItalic.

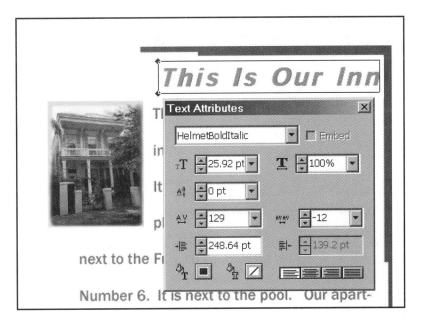

Figure 11-16
A heading displaying its text attributes

I can check to see what is in my file by selecting File ➤ Document Info ➤ Fonts. As you can see in Figure 11-17, the dialog box lists the fonts in my document, including the HelmetBoldItalic font.

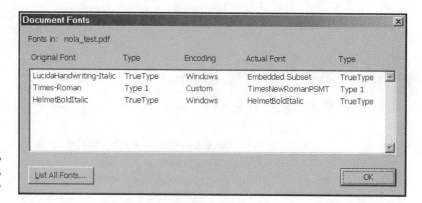

Figure 11-17
The fonts in my
document. Or are they?

But is this actually what a user would see if I ship the file elsewhere? No. Here's why. When I check what is actually in the file, the results can be deceptive, unless I set the view options first. Select View, and make sure Use Local Fonts is disabled. Then look at the Document Fonts dialog box again, as shown in Figure 11-18.

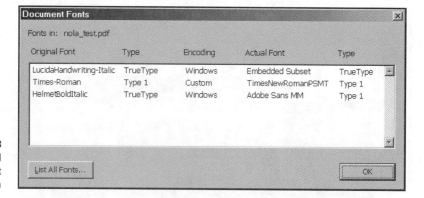

Figure 11-18
The actual fonts that will
be used in this document
after distribution

As you can see in this second dialog box, the Actual Font listed for HelmetBoldItalic is now Adobe Sans MM, meaning that I didn't embed the font correctly. What is the impact of this? Look at Figure 11-19. As you can see, there is very little difference, so I would not likely redefine and redistill the source document. Whether to redo the conversion or not is a judgment call.

Figure 11-19
The substituted font.
The most obvious
difference is spacing.

Speaking of judgment calls, let's get into color management.

Managing Color in Acrobat

Acrobat provides a number of profiles to use for converting color models in your files. In addition to choosing a color model, you can use the soft-proofing feature, which gives you a simulation of rendered output.

You can choose from a number of common color settings optimized for various workflows and prepress options. Each color settings file (CSF) has associated values for the working spaces and color management engine; these values are preselected. The CSF you choose preselects the other options. A Custom Settings option is available that allows you to edit the Working Spaces settings. Any embedded color information will take precedence over the CSF settings.

Let's look at the components and options available. Select Edit ➤ Preferences ➤ General. Select Color Management in the left pane of the Preferences dialog box. The dialog box shown in Figure 11-20 will open.

Note

Acrobat does not allow you to save custom CSF files. If you need a custom file, create it in Photoshop or Illustrator. The CSFs used in Acrobat are a subset of the Photoshop and Illustrator ones.

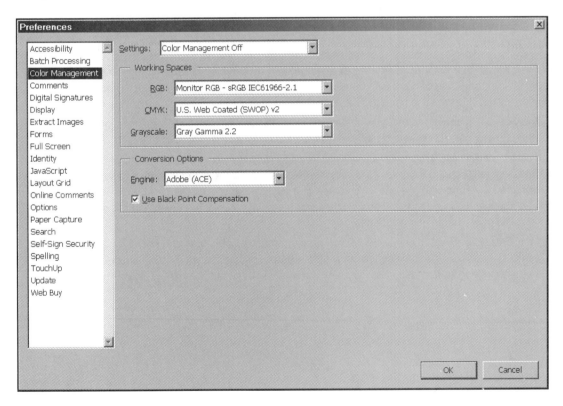

Figure 11-20
Set color preferences in this dialog box.

Click the Settings drop-down list and select Color Management Off. The options available are shown in Figure 11-21.

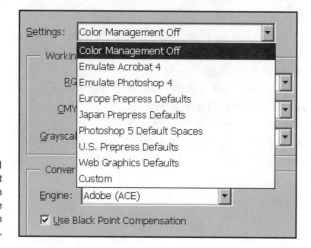

Figure 11-21
The Color Management options. Choosing an option will preselect the working space options in the dialog box.

Using ICC and CMYK Profiles

The International Color Consortium (ICC) has defined ICC color—a system used to separate creation from rendering of color information. You use a profile to map source colors into an absolute color space. Then you use other profiles to map out of this absolute color space to destination colors.

The way ICC is converted to CMYK is defined through the profiles and tools that create them. With standard profiles, there is no guarantee that gray text will be constrained to the black channel.

Do you need to use ICC color? Not necessarily. CMYK is the common data path for all PDF color data destined for print. Your primary decision is whether to use the standard CMYK or an ICC-managed workflow. It is simpler to use one or the other. If your files are often received from external sources, pre-flight them and convert to your internal standards first thing. A standard CMYK workflow is easier to manage, understand, and troubleshoot.

An ICC workflow (specifically CIEXYZ) will result in more reliably reproducible color. It is recommended when using color graphics for multiple purposes, if different printing presses are used, or if you're printing to domestic and international presses because it is device-independent.

Settings Options

As I mentioned, when you select any of the settings except for Custom, the other settings will be preselected.

- *Color Management Off:* Use this option for video and on-screen output. Documents created with this setting have no profile tags. Using this option emulates behavior of applications that do not support color. You can also use this option when you want to pass through color management information from other non-Adobe applications, such as Quark. If you are in an Adobe environment, the color management settings (working spaces) should be set the same as in the original program.

- *Emulate Photoshop 4:* Use this option if you want to match the color workflow of the Mac version of Photoshop 4 or earlier.

- *Prepress Defaults: Europe; Japan; U.S.:* Use these options for output under common press conditions in the respective regions.

- *Photoshop 5 Default Spaces:* Use this option if you prefer default color settings from Photoshop 5. If you modify any of the RGB, CMYK, or Grayscale settings, the Settings selection will change to Custom.

- *Web Graphics Defaults:* Use this option for Web-based output.

Note

A ColorSync Workflow (Mac OS only) option is also available that uses the ColorSync CMS with profiles set in ColorSync (version 3 or later). A ColorSync Workflow option is used for work containing a mix of Adobe and non-Adobe applications.

Working Spaces

When you select one of the settings options, the working spaces will default according to that setting. Experiment with the settings to see what options are associated with each settings choice. For example, I have chosen the U.S. Prepress Defaults. Let's look at the content from the respective drop-down lists. Figure 11-22 shows the default RGB option.

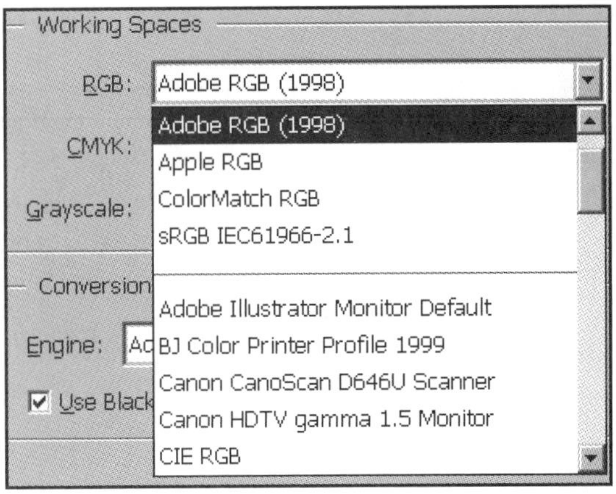

Figure 11-22
The RGB working space default for U.S. Prepress settings

Choosing the U.S. Prepress settings will set U.S. Web Coated (SWOP) v2 as the default CMYK space (see Figure 11-23).

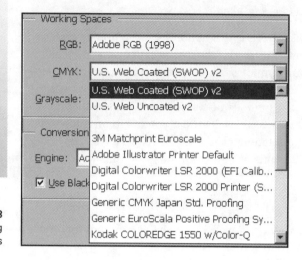

Figure 11-23
The CMYK default setting for U.S. Prepress options

Finally, the grayscale space will be set, as shown in Figure 11-24. The default value is a Dot Gain setting of 20%.

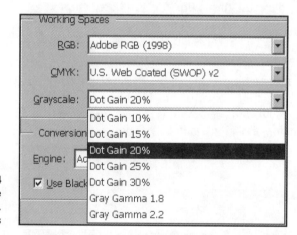

Figure 11-24
The Grayscale space default setting for U.S. Prepress options

Specifying a Color Management Engine

Acrobat ships with color management engine support. The engine specifies the system and color matching method. Acrobat uses industry-standard engines.

- *Adobe Color Engine (ACE):* Uses the Adobe system and engine. This is the default.

- *Microsoft ICM (Windows):* This option can be used with Microsoft Windows 98, 2000, and XP.

- *Mac OS:* Offers Apple ColorSync, Apple CMM, or Heidelberg CMM.

Any installed third-party color management engines will also be displayed.

Black-Point Compensation

This option is selected by default. It is used to adjust for differences in black points when you're converting colors between color spaces. When it is selected, the full range of the source space is mapped into the full space of the destination space. In general, leave this option selected. The only exception is when you're printing to a PostScript printer using Raster Image Processor (RIP) management.

Once you have selected a set of options, click OK to close the Preferences dialog box. Remember that whatever settings you have chosen will remain until you reset the preference again.

Advanced Print Settings

Color management may be either host-based or printer-based. We have concentrated on document-based color. Let's have a look at the printer options. These settings are made in the Advanced Print Settings dialog box. In addition to color management, you can define such options as tiling and transparency. Here's how to do it:

1. In the Print dialog box, click Advanced. The Print Settings dialog box shown in Figure 11-25 will open. These settings are available only for PostScript printers.

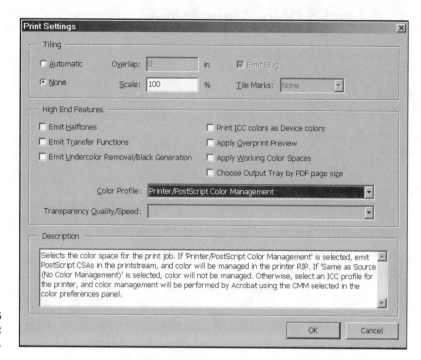

Figure 11-25
Set advanced print
settings in this dialog box.

2. Select a color profile from the Color Profile drop-down list. In general, use the color profile for your selected printer.

3. Select from the High End Features as required:

- *Emit Halftones:* Use the halftones from the PDF file, not the printer. Having all the same halftoning will minimize moiré on the press. Select this option to preserve halftone information for reproducing special effects for single page output.

- *Emit Transfer Functions:* Use the transfer functions in the PDF file, not from the printer.

- *Emit Undercolor Removal/Black Generation:* Use the UCR and black generation functions from the file, not from the printer. This option provides instructions for a PostScript RIP to convert RGB to CMYK with varying degrees of rich black.

- *Print ICC Colors As Device Colors:* Use the inherent gray, RGB, CMYK values instead of those from an ICC profile.

- *Apply Overprint Preview:* Simulate appearance of overprinted and spot colors using composite colors. Although printing time may be increased, it can be previewed on-screen. Select View ➤ Overprint Preview to toggle the preview mode on and off.

- *Apply Working Color Spaces:* The Working Color Spaces set in the Color Management Preferences are applied when printing.

- *Choose Output Tray By PDF Page Size:* The paper tray is picked by PDF page sizes, not by the Page Setup.

4. Select a Transparency Quality/Speed setting for rasterization.

5. Click OK to set the options and return to the Print dialog box.

Trapping

You may have noticed that there are no references to *trapping* in the print dialog boxes or discussions. For files being sent to a service bureau, you should declare the presence of trapping information to prevent conflicts. Trapping is not created in Acrobat but is imported into it with other PostScript file information from your authoring application. With the file open in Acrobat, select File ➤ Document Properties ➤ Trapping Key. Select a trapping option, and then click OK.

Exporting to PostScript

Once you have finished work on a file in Acrobat, it can be exported as a PostScript file for printing or prepress use. The file will be exported with advanced information such as Document Structuring Conventions. You will find that many of the options are identical to those displayed in the Print Settings dialog box.

Here's how to do it:

1. With the file open in Acrobat, select File ➤ Save As.

2. Select PostScript File (*.ps) as the Save As type, and click Settings.

3. Select a PostScript language level.

4. Choose either ASCII or Binary output format for the image data. Where possible, use binary output for smaller files.

5. Select Include Preview to generate a TIFF thumbnail preview.

6. Set the level of font embedding (None, All Embedded, or All Referenced).

7. If your file contains transparency, select quality/speed values. The options range from Lowest/Fastest to Highest/Slowest.

Note

Lowest/Fastest will rasterize all objects. Use it with very complex artwork containing many objects. Highest/Slowest will maintain the most vector artwork, but may still rasterize complex artwork. This setting produces the highest-quality output, and generally takes the most time and memory.

Note

Click Printing Tips in the Print dialog box. You will be connected to the Adobe Web site for information on troubleshooting printing problems in Acrobat.

8. Select other options as desired—for example, converting TrueType fonts and including images, comments, halftone screens, and the like.

9. Click OK to set the options, name the file, and click Save.

The process of saving EPS files is similar.

Exporting to EPS

When creating EPS files for separations, all image color spaces should be CMYK.

1. Select File ➤ Save As, and select Encapsulated PostScript (*.eps) as the Save As type. Click Settings. The dialog box shown in Figure 11-26 will open.

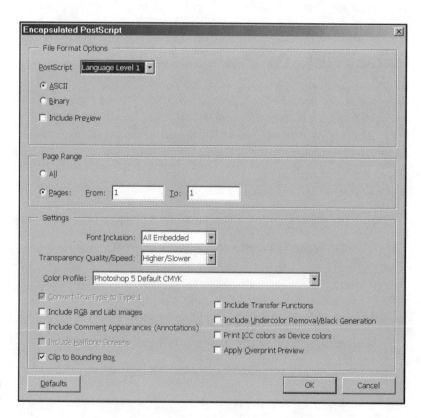

Figure 11-26
EPS output options

2. Select a PostScript language level. Use Language Level 1 for EPS files that will be used and color-separated as part of another document. You can't create color separations from a file based on Language Level 3 settings (for smooth shading or masked images).

3. Choose either ASCII or Binary output format for the image data. Select Include Preview to generate a TIFF thumbnail preview.

4. Set the level of font embedding (None, All Embedded, or All Referenced).

5. If your file contains transparency, select quality/speed values. The options range from Lowest/Fastest to Highest/Slowest—descriptions were included in the section on PostScript export.

6. Select other options as desired—for example, converting TrueType fonts and including images, comments, halftone screens, and the like. Pay particular attention to the Include RGB and Lab Images option. Why? Look at Figure 11-27.

> **Note**
> With EPS output, each page will be saved as a separate EPS file, so there is no need to select page ranges.

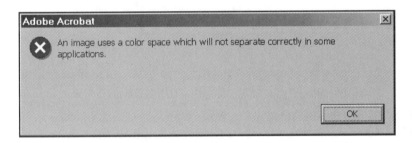

Figure 11-27
Error message for images

7. This message will appear if you have forgotten about any of these image types, and it will stop your saving process dead in its tracks.

8. The Clip To Bounding Box setting is selected by default. There is no practical reason to deselect this option.

9. Click OK to set the options, name the file, and click Save.

So we've gone from distilling to saving and covered everything in between—which brings us near to the close of this chapter.

One last thing before we end this chapter, however: soft-proofing.

Soft-Proofing Colors

I mentioned in the workflow discussion at the beginning of the chapter that you can use Acrobat to soft-proof your document's colors—that is, display a simulated output of your document on your screen. Remember that your soft-proof will depend on how good your monitor represents color, as well as how it is calibrated. Here's how to do it:

1. Select View ➤ Proof Setup ➤ Custom. The dialog box shown in Figure 11-28 will open.

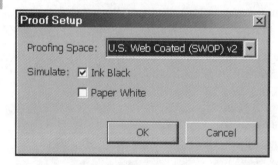

Figure 11-28
Set proof options in this dialog box.

2. Select a proofing space. You can choose either a profile or None to proof only for Ink Black or Paper White.

3. Select either Ink Black or Paper White simulation (if you select the latter, Ink Black is selected and grayed out because it is required).

4. Click OK. As you can see in Figure 11-29, you can toggle the proof display by selecting View ➤ Proof Colors.

Figure 11-29
Toggle soft-proofing options

Up Next

At the beginning of this chapter, I said that there was much more to this printing process than finding the print button on the toolbar. I wasn't kidding! As with almost everything in this book, you need a good understanding of what you are designing and a good understanding of the software you are using for designing. From the software perspective, as we have also seen in other chapters, planning in the authoring environment is important to good output.

I gave you my interpretation of print workflows using Acrobat. Then we had a look at Distiller and print output options. I also discussed fonts and color in some depth. I could only scratch the surface here. I think the important thing to take away from this chapter is that print output is a complex interaction of many different elements. The key to success will be experimentation.

Speaking of which, in Chapter 12 you'll learn how to take your experimentation to the power-user level. We will look at video, destinations, and date stamping, among other things. Stay tuned.

Chapter 12

Using Advanced Acrobat Activities

This chapter contains an avalanche
of advanced activities that will
turn you into a power user.

For All the Mighty Brains Out There

This chapter is different from many of the ones that came before. First, it doesn't cover any one specific topic. Second, the intent of this chapter is to show you some advanced ways of working with Acrobat. Some of these features are Web related; some are static. Some are functions; some are settings.

The idea is that by the time you reach this stage in the book, you should be familiar with many of the more basic and functional uses of Acrobat. This chapter's content will help to bump you to the power-user level.

In all honesty, I designed this chapter with me in mind. I have a need to be a power user for virtually any application I set my mighty brain to. So I look specifically for the types of activities that streamline my production cycle or file size. I also have a tendency to dig to the bottom of most functional areas. In this kind of book, I know in advance that I will likely cover the basics and advanced uses of some functions. I also know that I will dig too much and write too much. Because what I learn is too doggone good to keep to myself, I have to find a home for it. This is it.

This chapter, then, is dedicated to all of you who, with your own mighty brains, have a need to see what you can do with a piece of software.

What You Will Learn

As I mentioned, this chapter isn't something that is highly structured in terms of presentation. I have tried to make some sense of how I present things to you. Some of the topics are real discussions, complete with a demonstration, tutorials, and even a project. Other topics are fat Workflow Tips. Some may elicit the "Ah hah!" response. All are geared toward using Acrobat at a higher level of sophistication.

It Goes Like This

The topics in this chapter share one of two common themes. Either they are about a more advanced use of the software, or they are intended to discuss or show you how to use the software more efficiently. Enhanced efficiency means an advanced use of a piece of software, in my opinion. Here are the topics that are coming up:

- Using PDF files versus other file formats

- Working with video files (a tutorial)

- Working with destinations (discussion and project)

- Adding date stamps (a tutorial)

- Using byte-serving files on the Web

- Reducing file size

Up first is when and how to use PDF files.

Using PDFs vs. Other Media Formats

What's one of the key benefits of PDF documents? Rhetorical question. PDF formats are especially conducive to producing documents that are both cross-platform and cross-media.

What does this mean? Basically, we are looking at a format or collection process that will allow information to be used as text and graphics; for multimedia; for use on kiosks and in presentations; and for printing, online and offline. Most of these things can be done with Acrobat. But does that mean they *should* be done?

Your Basic Big Multimedia Piece

Technically, I am referring to project architecture. Consider the types of material you deal with on a regular basis: software installations, marketing pieces, learning materials . . . The list is endless. Most of these outputs include common structures. How can PDF files be added to the project, how should they be added, and what are the criteria for their use? Read on.

A large multimedia project includes these common elements:

- *Installation:* Installation is not a topic of Acrobat conversation.

- *Introduction:* Many CD pieces launch with an autorun introduction. This is usually highly visual, active content.

- *Navigation:* In addition to the ubiquitous navigation panel, there are many other navigation options—for example, thumbnailing images or video clips, or special panels to control video and talking heads.

- *Content:* The reason for opening the CD in the first place, of course, is content, and it takes virtually unlimited forms. The only comment I would like to make here is that you should consider what is required for the user to use your content. That is, will other plug-ins or extensions be required? This can be a determining factor when you're deciding on one format over another.

Let's see when to use one format or the other.

The Power of PDFs

Many times a PDF file will be the ideal medium for distribution of your work. For example:

- *When you're printing:* You can't beat the PDF format for reliable printed output.

- *When you're using source material from a variety of different authoring programs:* PDFs can be created from virtually any program that can print to Distiller or a PostScript printer.

- *When you're using cross-platform files:* PDFs work well on ISO 9660 cross-platform formatted CD-ROMs.

- *For security reasons:* PDFs are easily saved with password encryption settings.

- *For interactivity purposes:* Acrobat readily handles different types of actions smoothly and simply. These actions can be attached to a variety of handlers, including links and pages. I provide a project for adding multimedia later in this chapter.

The Power of Multimedia

Adobe Premiere and Macromedia Director are two of the big guys used for designing multimedia presentations. Depending on the structure of a piece, you may likely use both programs. Use these types of programs when the following issues are important:

- *Audio and video synchronization:* Depending on the sophistication, you will have much better results (use Acrobat to embed files that launch on specific actions only).

- *Lingo programming (Macromedia Director):* Use Director to program interactive navigation controls and other elements. Again, this depends on the level of sophistication you require.

- *Animation:* I need say no more.

CD-ROM Distribution

In other areas both of this chapter and this book, I have discussed using the Web as a medium for delivering PDFs. That is not the only option for how to deliver PDFs, and sometimes it's not even the best option. In several situations, it might be better to publish to CD-ROM. Consider these ideas:

- Suppose you have to deliver large files, movies, executable files, and the like. Internet delivery is not efficient; CD delivery is. On the same topic, Internet and/or intranet speeds may be too slow to deliver efficient and quick navigation tools and information.

- How are your users accessing material? If they ordinarily work offline, a CD is much more convenient than finding a laptop connection.

- For highly secure documents, burning a specific number of CDs for distribution will help to control access to your information.

Project Tutorial: Adding Video to PDFs Efficiently

I have neglected to show you any of the groovy things you can do with Acrobat in deference to the work-based, serious things. Time to change that. And it's a good topic to follow multimedia discussion.

Inserting a Movie into a PDF Document

You can add two types of video files to Acrobat, as you can with many applications: AVI and MOV. I will discuss how to add a movie to a PDF file and offer some tips for using video file formats.

There is a file on the CD in the Chapter 12 Projects folder named movie.pdf. This file, it will come as no surprise to you, is the basic framework to which you will add a movie (shown in Figure 12-1). You must insert the movie yourself to ensure that the storage locations for the PDF file and the MOV file are the same.

Note
You will require QuickTime to complete this tutorial. It is available for download at http://www.apple.com/quicktime/download/.

Note
The movie is a nursery rhyme—the one about the little girl with a little curl. I have no idea where the inspiration came from. Perhaps a recent shopping trip with my own little girl?

Figure 12-1
The finished document
displaying the movie

1. Open the movie.pdf file. Click the Movie tool on the Editing tool-bar to select it, and then click the document page. The dialog box shown in Figure 12-2 will open.

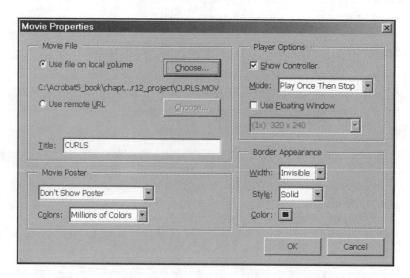

Figure 12-2
The Movie Properties
dialog box

2. Click Choose, and browse for the file to use, named CURLS.MOV (as I said, to make the file run properly on your computer, you will have to attach the file yourself).

3. In the bottom-left portion of the dialog box, Movie Poster, you can select options for the placement structure of the movie on the page. In my example, I had created the file with a window for the movie. If you are adding a movie to a document that doesn't have any placement outlines built into it, select a poster option from the drop-down list. It will display a white box the size of the movie, as shown in Figure 12-3. You can also select two color options in the same area. There is no difference in file size between the two different color options (256 versus millions of colors).

Note

You can also set border options on the right side of the dialog box to further frame out your placement guide.

Figure 12-3
A portion of the document showing the Movie Poster placement

4. Select player options from the Mode drop-down list, as shown in Figure 12-4. There are a number of different settings depending on your use. If you leave the Show Controller option selected, the user can manipulate the movie in any case. You may also choose the floating window option—when the movie area is clicked on with the mouse, a movie player (set to one of the size options) will appear on the page.

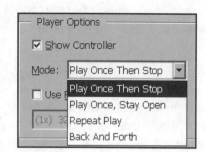

Figure 12-4
Select a mode
for the controller.

Workflow Tip

**For the Premiere Fans
Out There . . .**

. . . from a Premiere fan
over here. I always like to
know what and how a file
is composed. I have this
movie optimized for
desktop/kiosk delivery on
midrange machines. It is
in QuickTime format. I
used a Sorenson Video
Compression codec
rendered at 30fps. The
frame size was
320×240pi.

5. Save the file. Deselect the Movie tool by clicking the Hand tool. Move your mouse over the movie area of the page. You will see the hand icon change to a movie icon. Click to run the movie.

So far we have looked at multimedia issues. Up next is the first of three topics dealing with time: how to save it, how to display it, and how to serve it.

Working with Destinations

A *destination* is a link represented by text in the Destinations palette. If you look at the Acrobat help files, for example, you will find that the Destinations palette has no entries. This is because the help files are all in one document.

Creating and Linking Destinations

Before destinations can be linked, they have to be created and named in the place where they are being housed (the source document). This process can be complex. In order to make using destinations more understandable, I have built a project. But first some general discussion on how Destinations work.

For these general instructions, you must have the Destinations palette open. At the lower part of the palette, you will see a message that reads "Document Not Scanned." You must scan the document each time you open the file when working with destinations. It's akin to setting baselines. To scan a document, open the file, and select Destination ➤ Scan Document from the palette's drop-down menu. Once the scan is complete, any destinations in the document will be listed in the palette. If you have no destinations, the message that was previously displayed at the bottom of the palette will disappear.

Using destinations is a three-stage process involving a minimum of two different documents: the source document (where the links are created) and the target document (which houses the links to the source document). Follow these steps:

1. Open the target document (the document that will be linked to the source). Set the desired location and view.

2. Select Destinations ➤ New Destination in the Destination palette, or click the Create New Destination button at the top of the palette.

3. Name the destination, and press Enter (Return on a Mac).

4. Now open the source document. Select the Link tool.

5. Click and drag a rectangle to define a link location.

6. Set the options for the link:

   a. Select Go To View as the action type. (This action makes a link to a destination.)

   b. Select a magnification option.

7. With both documents open, and the Link dialog box still open, switch to the target document and select the destination to be linked. When the page is displayed, click Set Link.

8. The Link dialog box will display the file name and selected destination name from the target document.

The link is complete. Next is a project that shows how to use these destination-building ideas.

Project **Project 12-1. Adding Destinations to the Makeup Manual**

In Chapter 3, I introduced the Manual for Applying Stage Makeup project. In this project, I have made a document collection from the manual's materials. This project has two phases. First, the smaller documents will be attached to the table of contents of the main manual document. In the second phase, elements within the text of the main manual will be linked to elements in the glossary.

Workflow Tip
Why Use Destinations Instead of Regular Links?

The name of the game is efficiency. If you added normal links to pages across documents, the links will be broken if pages are added or deleted from the target document. Destinations, which reside in source documents, are not affected by changes in target documents. It might take more time to initially create destinations. In the long run, however, they can save you lots of time.

Workflow Tip
Keeping Destinations on the Straight and Narrow

Two points to remember. First, the destination names must be unique. Second, decide on a naming convention and stick to it. When working in the target document, or troubleshooting any errors, you will be able to understand the structure by looking at it in the source document's Destinations palette.

The CD contains a set of four "raw" files in the Chapter 12 Projects folder. These files are as follows:

- *manual.pdf:* The main manual document.

- *biblio.pdf:* A bibliography for the manual.

- *FAQ.pdf:* Guess what? A FAQ file.

- *gloss.pdf:* A glossary of terms.

The CD also includes a second set of files, named the same, but each file's name includes "1," as in "manual1.pdf." These four files together make up the completed project.

You will need the Destinations palette open. Also, select Destinations ➤ Scan Document every time you open one of the files.

Part 1: Linking the Accessory Files to the Makeup Manual

First, the extra files will be connected to the main manual's table of contents. The portion of the table of contents used for the destinations is shown in Figure 12-5.

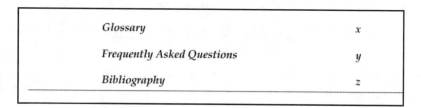

Figure 12-5
The table of contents will have files attached to these entries.

Add these elements.

1. Open the first target document: gloss.pdf.

2. Set the magnification for the glossary. Select View ➤ Actual Size.

3. Select Destinations ➤ New Destination.

4. As shown in Figure 12-6, name the new destination glossary, and press Enter (Return on a Mac).

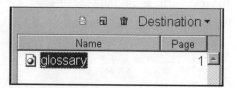

Figure 12-6
Add and name a destination in the target document.

5. Repeat this process for the other two target files:

    a. *biblio.pdf:* Name the destination bibliography.

    b. *FAQ.pdf:* Name the destination FAQ.

6. Don't forget to set the magnification to actual size.

7. Save the files.

Build the Links in the Source

Now we have to connect the target destinations to the manual.

1. Open manual.pdf.

2. Set the view mode in the bottom taskbar to Single Page.

3. Add the first link with these properties:

    a. Click the Link tool, and then click and drag a rectangle around the *x* page number for the Glossary row.

    b. Select Invisible as the link appearance.

    c. Select Go To View as the action type.

    d. Select a magnification option.

4. Leave the Link Properties palette open as it is. Now open the gloss.pdf document (if it isn't open).

5. In the gloss.pdf file, open the Destinations palette, select Scan Document, and then click the glossary destination we set earlier.

6. As you can see in Figure 12-7, which shows the lower portion of the Link Properties dialog box, the file name and the named destination are now displayed in the Link Properties palette from the manual.pdf document.

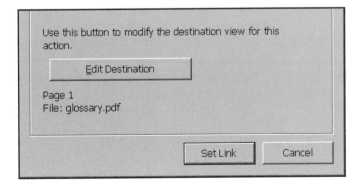

Figure 12-7
The external link has now been identified.

7. Click Set Link. The view will switch back to the manual.pdf document. Save the file and test the link.

8. Repeat the process with the destinations for the other two files.

9. Save the manual.pdf file.

Now for Part 2. Adding one destination per file is easy. What if a list of destinations is required for a list of targets, all from the same files? Read (and work) on.

Part 2: Linking Glossary Definitions to the Manual's Pages

The stage makeup manual has a total of 14 pages. Sprinkled throughout are a number of terms that are defined in the glossary. We will set definitions for the glossary terms and then set links from the terms in the manual document.

Start with the Glossary

As the heading states, start with the glossary. This is the target document, so the destinations have to be set here first.

1. Open gloss.pdf. Select Destination ➤ Scan Document. The glossary destination set earlier should be displayed.

2. Set the destinations. Name each destination according to the glossary term. There will be 13 terms and the destination for the page itself, as you can see in Figure 12-8.

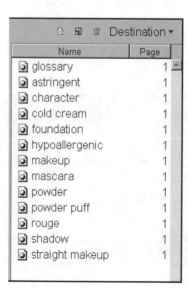

Figure 12-8
The completed destinations for the glossary file

3. Set the view for the destinations with the named term displayed the full width of the window and the term at the upper portion of the window (this will not work with the terms closer to the bottom of the page). I have shown one destination, "character," in Figure 12-9.

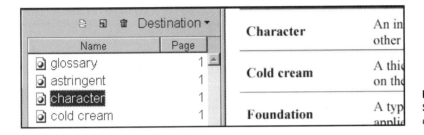

Figure 12-9
Set the view for the destinations similar to this.

4. Save the gloss.pdf file.

5. Open the manual.pdf document. Glossary terms are usually identified in some way based on their first occurrence. For this reason, I have listed the location where each term first appears in the manual in Table 12-1.

Note

The page numbers listed in the table are the actual page numbers of the document, not the pagination assignment.

Table 12-1   Link the Destinations from the Glossary to These Areas of the Manual

Glossary Term	Location
astringent	Page 8, second paragraph, first line
character	Page 3, last paragraph, first line
cold cream	Page 6, second row of top table
foundation	Page 7, first row of table
hypoallergenic	Page 5, second paragraph, last line
makeup	Page 3, first sentence of first paragraph
mascara	Page 7, second-to-last row of table
powder	Page 7, second row of table
powder puff	Page 13, second bullet in right column at bottom of page
rouge	Page 5, under brush heading, flat brushes listing
shadow	Page 10, lower heading
straight makeup	Page 3, first sentence of first paragraph

6. Using the information in the table, add links to the locations listed in the table. Use the same link properties and process described in the last section.

7. Save the manual.pdf file.

Part 3: Because I Can't Stand Things That Aren't Finished Properly

I simply could not leave this project without making it more convenient to use. It is far too irksome. On that note, we will next add one simple field to each glossary term that will return the user to the previous view. A portion of the finished glossary file is shown in Figure 12-10.

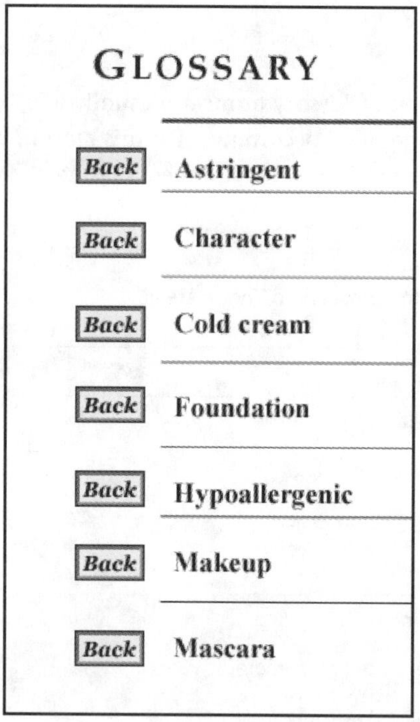

Figure 12-10
Part of the finished glossary file with back buttons added to the terms

Here's how to do it.

1. Insert the first form field. In the Field Properties dialog box, name the field **Back** and set its type as Button. Set these appearance characteristics:

   a. Border color: dark red

   b. Background color: custom color, RGB values of 255/251/234

   c. Border width: thin; border style: inset

   d. Text: black, Georgia Bold Italic, size 9pt. (or substitute a similar font)

2. Click the Options tab. Set the layout as text only, and add **Back** as text for the button face in the Up position.

3. Click the Actions tab. Select the Mouse Down state in the action list. Click Add and select Open File.

4. When the Add An Action dialog box opens, select Open File from the type drop-down box. Click Select File and select manual.pdf. Click Set Action.

5. When you return to the Field Properties dialog box, click OK to close the dialog box. The first button is built.

6. Copy the form element down the page corresponding to each glossary entry. Align the buttons. I set the buttons to be roughly centered vertically with the glossary terms.

7. Save and test the file.

Isn't that better? One last detail. Just as the Back buttons were required for the glossary terms to return to the manual, you need to add the same button to the bibliography and FAQ pages. You can add a button to the glossary page itself to make the sequence consistent. I made the same button in a larger size and changed the label, as you can see in Figure 12-11.

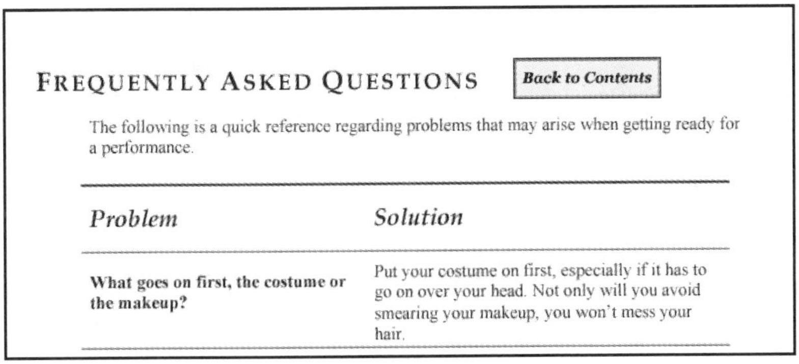

FREQUENTLY ASKED QUESTIONS   Back to Contents

The following is a quick reference regarding problems that may arise when getting ready for a performance.

Problem	Solution
What goes on first, the costume or the makeup?	Put your costume on first, especially if it has to go on over your head. Not only will you avoid smearing your makeup, you won't mess your hair.

Figure 12-11
The last detail: adding navigation back from the documents to the collection

The project is finished. This is a good way to use a simple form field to make document navigation a simpler task.

Speaking of form fields, what about using a field on a document (it doesn't have to be a form) to add a date automatically? That's coming up next.

Project Tutorial: Date Stamping

One of the really interesting features you can add to a form, or any other kind of document, is a date stamp. We will look at how to add a date to a form when it is opened. To complete this tutorial, you will need the form.pdf file, which is on the CD in the Chapter 12 Projects folder.

It all hinges on a single form field. The form field will use the current date from the computer clock, and the date will be added when the form is opened. Here's how it works:

1. Add a new text form field anywhere on the document. Name it **Date**. On the Appearance tab, select Read Only under the Common Properties section. Deselect any background or border color options.

2. Click the Format tab. Select Date from the options, and choose one of the format options on the right side of the tab, as shown in Figure 12-12. Click OK, and save the file.

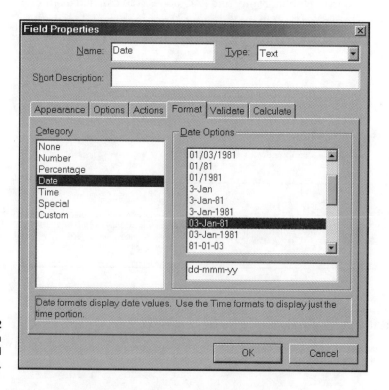

Figure 12-12
Set these date options on the Format tab of the Field Properties dialog box.

3. Now we need a document-level script that will execute each time the document opens. Select Tools ➤ JavaScript ➤ Document JavaScripts. Name the script **Date** and click Add.

Note

When the JavaScript Functions dialog box opens, some text will be present. Select and delete it.

4. Enter the following script in the JavaScript Edit dialog box within the JavaScript Functions dialog box, as shown in Figure 12-13:

```
var d = this.getField("Date");
d.value = util.printd("dd/mmm/yy", new Date());
```

Note

This script is made up of several parts. The Date field is bound to the variable, d, which is then calculated. The new expression is based on the date. The utility object (util.printd) formats the date into the format selected.

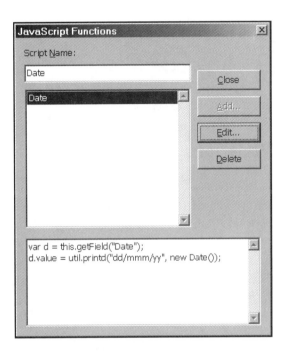

Figure 12-13
Add a document-level script.

5. Click OK in the JavaScript Edit dialog box, and then click Close in the JavaScript Functions dialog box.

6. Save the file. If you deselect the Form tool, you will see that the field now contains the date, as shown in Figure 12-14.

To view the date, select the Hand tool from the Acrobat toolbar; the date will be displayed in your new field.

Note

Be careful with this process. The field name must be exactly the same (including capitalization) in the Field Properties dialog box and the script; the same date format must be used in the Field properties dialog box and the script. If you receive errors when you try this, check these elements.

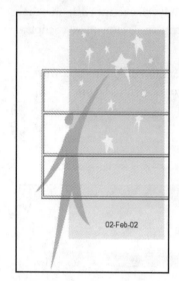

Figure 12-14
A portion of a form
showing the automatic
date entry

Variations on This Theme

You can also add different date or time formats to your form. Change
the visibility on the Appearance tab to Hidden, for example, to hide the
date field from view. When the file is printed, it will be displayed. As you
can see in Figure 12-15, you have several options.

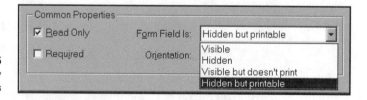

Figure 12-15
Different visibility
options for form fields

Using JavaScript in Acrobat Documents

As you have seen in several chapters, particularly with regard to forms, there are many ways to
use Adobe JavaScript to configure and customize your work. There are just as many ways to botch
it up. The date stamp discussion is a case in point. The process seems so simple: Configure the
field and its content and then write a script to input the date. The following image shows what can
happen, though.

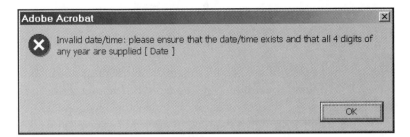

Invalid date and time error

Well, just what does "invalid date/time" mean? Date and time certainly does exist. I know this. My system clock is running, the clock on my wall is running. So why shouldn't a date and time exist? After considering and dismissing the thought that I had finally made it into the Twilight Zone, I discovered the scripted format differed from that selected in the Form dialog box, as you can see in the following image.

Make sure the JavaScript is the same as the Field Properties chosen.

The key is to be careful. When you receive a message, consider the obvious—such as punctuation and descriptions—before science fiction events.

And now for the last of our series of time issues.

Byte-Serving PDF Files on the Web

Byte-serving starts the view of a file before the entire file is downloaded, one page at a time by default. Depending on the Internet connection speed and the size of the file in question, unless the download is served in chunks, it can take a l-o-o-n-g time to serve an entire document—long enough, of course, for your reader to get bored and surf away.

Preparing the Files

Files should be cleaned, optimized, and saved with the Fast Web View options. Once a document is completed, save a version to be used for online viewing.

Check your preference settings. Figure 12-16 shows the preferences settings that will optimize browser display. Select Edit ➤ Preferences ➤ General. Click Options. As you can see, I have selected all four of the Web Browser Options.

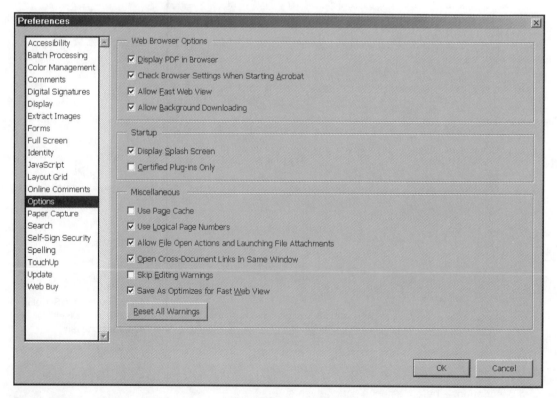

Figure 12-16
Select all of the Web Browser Options in this dialog box

While you are in this file-cleaning mode, check for the features that can be deleted from the Web-served version. Remove bookmarks, articles, and comments. This makes the file much smaller and, because these features are likely invisible to the average user, why include them?

That completes my trio of time-centric topics. For the grand finale, some tips.

Reducing File Size

Sometimes it doesn't matter how big a PDF file is. On the other hand, sometimes it is critical. Consider online files, or ones that are being shared in a workgroup. Although some elements must remain, a good understanding of how to use Acrobat will go a long way toward making file sizes more efficient. Check for these problems before throwing your hands up in disgust or moving to an isolated location without Internet access or indoor plumbing.

Here is a collection of tips for reducing the size of your files:

- Embed subsets of fonts rather than the entire font. To be safe, you can set the percentage at which the entire font is embedded.

- Watch out for crop marks and prepress information. Depending on the authoring application you use for creating source files, items such as color bars or crop marks may still be present in the converted file. Remove any of these items before converting the file to PDF.

- Consider custom PDF creators. As an experiment, export a source document using different options. If you are using a program with a custom PDF exporting utility, test it. Also create a version using Acrobat Distiller and/or PDFMaker. Check the sizes of the different versions. You may be surprised.

- Watch those graphics. Compress objects through Distiller job options. Whenever possible, use vector graphics over bitmaps. Base text on fonts, not bitmaps. Check for downsampling.

- Periodically use the Save As function instead of Save. You can use the same name and overwrite the original file. Using Save As will remove deleted objects, optimize the file, and store identical items like backgrounds, which can make an enormous difference in your file size. For example, while constructing my movie.pdf file, I saved it several times, for a final size of 61.6KB. When I used Save As, it dropped in size to 39.5KB—a drop of over 40 percent.

Workflow Tip

Beware of the Optimize Space Function

The PDF Consultant option for optimizing space analyzes the open document. When you select the Remove Unused Named Destinations option, the program doesn't check to see if the destinations in the open document are used by links in other files. In a document collection, destinations to links in other files will become invalid. Use this function only on single files with no cross-PDF links.

- Save file size for buttons by attaching actions to pages instead. Selecting Document ➤ Set Page Action opens the dialog box shown in Figure 12-17. The interface is the same as that in the Field Properties dialog box for mouse states.

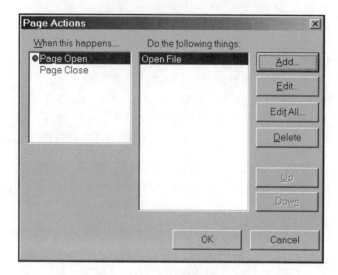

Figure 12-17
Set a page action.

- As you can see in Figure 12-18, choosing one of these actions opens the same dialog box as for other action types.

Figure 12-18
Add a page action.

- Check the named destinations set in a file. Each destination is about 100 bytes. If you are using many paragraphs, such as with an index or tables, much of the file size can be attributed to destinations.

Up Next

I introduced this chapter as a profusion of different ideas, techniques, and functions. Some of the topics were extensions of previous chapters' content or new timesaving topics. Still others presented ideas and issues rather than any specific technique.

As I mentioned, many of the concepts presented in this chapter were aimed at taking your use of Acrobat to the power-user level. Although this book isn't the forum for exhaustive discussion of any one topic, I think I gave you enough information to both stimulate your imagination and open other avenues of exploration.

And now for something completely different. Unlike this chapter, the next one is very specific and most intriguing—all about e-books.

Chapter 13

All About E-Books

The revolution is here. Have you ever wondered what goes into creating an e-book? Here it is. Find out what it takes to create, format, distribute, and secure e-books.

The E-Book Story

One of the most revolutionary concepts in recent publishing history is the e-book (also known as EBook, eBook, and e-Book). For years, reading books on a screen rather than by turning pages has eluded us, primarily because there was nothing "booklike" about reading a document on a screen—no real concept of pages, certainly nothing like turning pages, and as for indexes and tables of contents, they weren't useful either. E-books and e-book readers are changing that. The increased sophistication of the readers, the capability to create content using Acrobat, and the constantly improving security systems all contribute to e-books becoming a viable content-distribution method.

As with most developments, you will find different offerings from all the players in the game. Remember VHS versus beta? Thank goodness an organized body is working toward achieving some sense of unity among the various companies and their readers.

Just as the World Wide Web Consortium (W3C) evolved and developed standards as the Internet developed, so too has the Open Electronic Book Forum (OEBF). This group, conceived in 1998, has developed standards for electronic publishing. The group became the OEBF in January 2000. The specifications for version 1 were released in September 1999, and version 1.0.1 was released in July 2001.

This group has developed the Open eBook Publication Structure specification. The scope of the standard is to provide specifications for both content and tool providers to develop consistent materials and platforms. The specification is based on HTML and XML.

The specification outlines standards to use for creating e-book content. Using the standards, a publisher can format a title, and the content will be compatible with different readers. If you consider the number of readers on the market now, each using slightly different formatting, you will see that publishing decisions are made as much on the basis of corporate loyalty as on anything else.

By adopting the standards, however, publishers can distribute works to a diverse audience without reformatting titles for different flavors of reader—or even different devices.

Basically, e-books come in two varieties: the conventional screen and the handheld device. Dedicated e-book readers are also available. I am waiting for the *Star Trek* series to be developed (so far it exists only in my imagination!).

In this chapter, we will go through the steps used for a conventional screen, and then I will show you how to create an e-book for a handheld device. Now, after this historical buildup, let's have a look at what it takes to create an e-book and then build one. The basic stages are as follows:

1. Create a template and format the source material.

2. Convert the file using settings optimized for on-screen use.

3. Add navigational elements.

Creating an E-Book Template

An e-book template is not built in Acrobat. Rather, the template is created in an authoring program. Many of the elements are familiar to anyone who has built word processing or print-layout templates. As with any kind of template, differences exist based on the use of the template. Here, we are trying to optimize the use of the material on screen, so the elements are a bit different than the usual.

As you do when designing anything, you will have to use a combination of experience, a good eye, and design sense. If it looks good, and it's legible, it will likely work.

Format the Page Size

Unless you know for certain what page sizes your readers will use, it is best to design to the lowest common denominator—in this case, a page size about 6×9 inches, or even smaller.

Set the Margins

In an ordinary document, margins are used to frame the text. The same is true for e-books. They are used in the same way as ordinary margins—that is, to give the eyes a place to rest and set off the content. Margins also ensure that appropriate spacing exists around graphic elements.

Note

Remember that readers can use the zoom capabilities in the reader to customize their views.

Note

Adobe has a collection of 12 typefaces, the Adobe WebType Collection, which are optimized for on-screen use. More information on the collection is available at http://www.adobe.com/ type/browser/P/ P_911.html.

Define Styles

Fonts look different on screen than in print. Thin strokes are often difficult to read on screen. So are fonts with heavy strokes. Fonts of 11 to 13 points are the best sizes for on-screen viewing.

Use leading and tracking as required. Try to design pages legible at 100 percent page view. Use tracking instead of kerning where possible. Kerning contributes to file size with little noticeable on-screen impact.

Converting Source Material to E-Book Format

Source material for e-books can come from the same programs as for any other type of PDF file use. In addition, you convert material to PDF format in the same way. For example, from within Microsoft Word 2000, I use the Convert To Adobe PDF command and print to Distiller through the command's structure.

The command features a number of custom conversion settings, including settings for e-books. Let's have a look at these preformatted settings. I will also point out some changes I have found useful when creating e-book output. Later, when I discuss handhelds, I will outline another group of custom settings for that purpose.

Note

I haven't described any of the content of the Conversion Settings basic tabs. We will look at these as we work through the different types of output.

E-Book Conversion Settings

From a Microsoft Office application, you can access the conversion settings through the Acrobat menu. Select Acrobat ➤ Change Conversion Settings. In the resulting dialog box, select the e-book setting from the Conversion Settings drop-down list, as shown in Figure 13-1. As you can see in the figure, I have created a custom e-book setting as well.

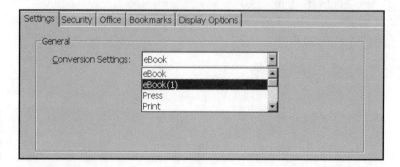

Figure 13-1
Some of the available conversion settings

Click Edit Conversion Settings to open the e-book Job Options dialog box. The General tab is shown in Figure 13-2.

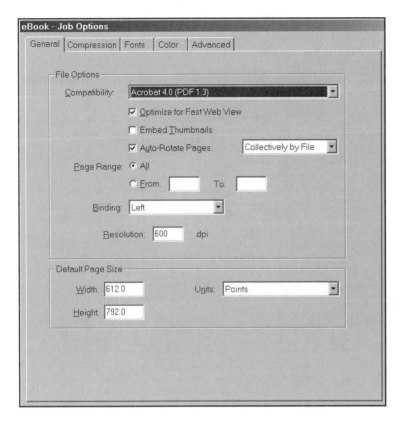

Figure 13-2
The General tab settings

Figure 13-2 shows the default settings for e-book conversion. I would like to point out three settings. First, the Compatibility setting defaults to Acrobat 4, which is based on the PDF 1.3 format. If you are designing material for a controlled environment and know that your readers will use Acrobat 5 (based on PDF 1.4), you may want to save an alternate version. Another setting I want to point out on this tab is the Embed Thumbnails option. As we will see later in the chapter, selecting this option may be appropriate for some types of work. Finally, on this tab you also set the default size of the page. This setting may be customized as well depending on your planned output and type of project.

Now let's look at compression. Figure 13-3 shows the Compression tab. This tab lists parameters for downsampling color, grayscale, and mono-chrome images. We will adjust these settings later for handhelds.

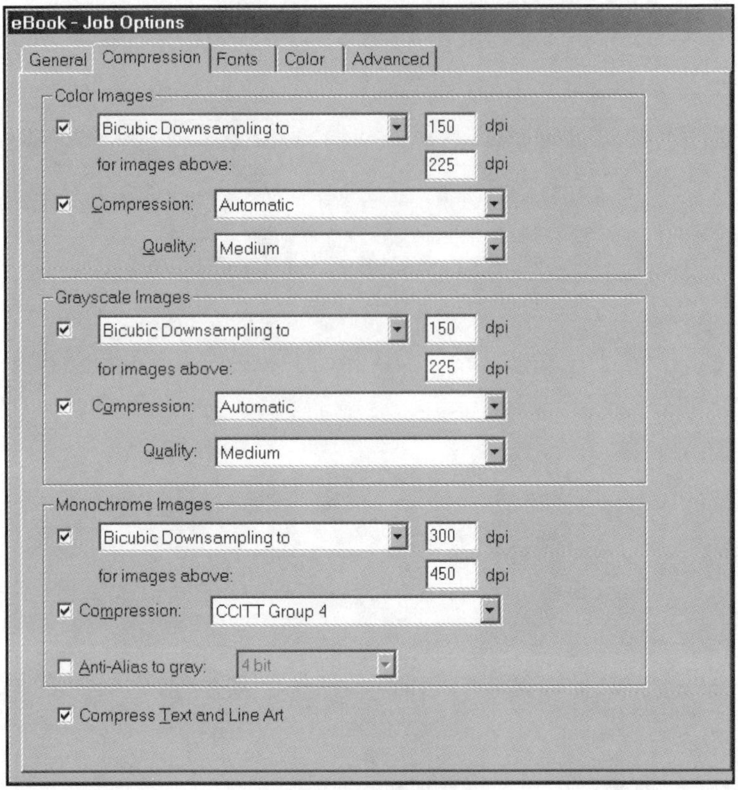

Figure 13-3
Compression settings
for e-book conversion

Up next is the Fonts tab, shown in Figure 13-4. Depending on the type of output you are creating, you may or may not want to change these settings. For example, with handhelds it is recommended to use Base 14 fonts only. For building a "traditional" e-book, that isn't necessary.

Let's have a look at the color settings next. Figure 13-5 shows the Color tab, with default settings. Depending on what you are creating, you may or may not have a need to alter these settings. For example, the Settings File option defaults to None. If you are working with full-color images, you will certainly want to change these options to ensure that the color settings displayed in your PDF file correlate with the color of your original work. The same may apply with overprinting, under color removal (UCR), and other print output settings if you allow your readers to print the file.

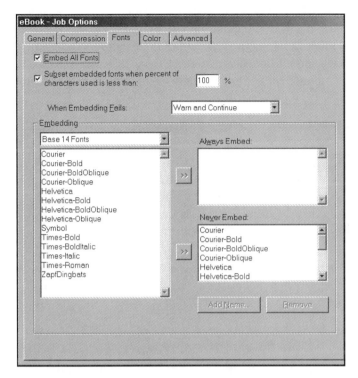

Figure 13-4
The Fonts tab

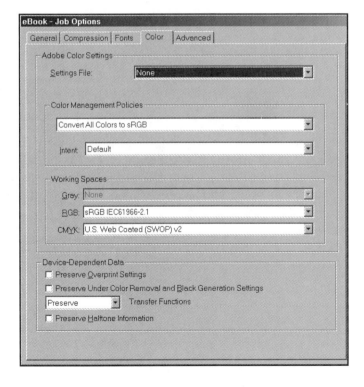

Figure 13-5
Change color settings
depending on the type of
work you are converting.

The last tab, Advanced, is shown in Figure 13-6. In general, you can leave the default options, unless you have very specific output or print options in mind. The only option I may be willing to change readily is Save Portable Job Ticket Inside PDF File. If I wanted to store information in a particular version of a document, this would be a useful feature.

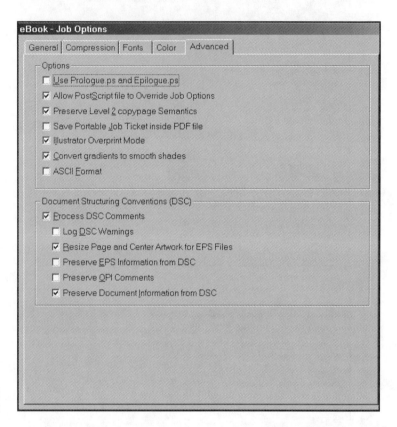

Figure 13-6
The Advanced tab

If you have made any changes to the tabs, you will be prompted to save the changes as a custom job option. Once you have reviewed the settings and made any changes you need, run the macro as usual to convert the file.

Navigation Design Issues

Navigation is a necessary part of digital life. Imagine what it would be like if there were no hyperlinks! Has the world ever really existed before hyperlinks? Sometimes I wonder.

When building an e-book, you can use one of four methods to add navigation: thumbnails, bookmarks, hyperlinks, and pagination. The processes are a bit different for e-books, however, so we will have another look at them shortly. Before I get into particulars, I want to talk about using e-book navigation in general. Remember, as with other forms of output, the easier it is for your user to access the material, the more likely your material will be used. But you don't want to overdo it either.

Let's look at three examples: a novel, a technical manual, and a complex business report. All of these examples will need page numbering of some form, but the other navigation aids will depend on the output.

The Novel

Whether or not it is the "Great American Novel," your book will need some logical navigation. Similar to paper books, e-book readers let you bookmark a page. Pagination is going to be key. You may choose to divide the book into a chapter format (for example, 1-1, or Chapter 1, page 1), or you may decide to use simple pagination.

Thumbnails would not be particularly useful for this type of output. The pages are so similar as to be basically useless for visual navigation. Bookmark listings would be useful, with the first pages of each chapter listed. As for hyperlinks, their usefulness would depend on some element, such as bibliographic references, links to publisher outlets for other works by the author, and the like.

A Technical Manual

Suppose you are building an e-book for troubleshooting an electronic device. The odds are good that the manual will contain a mixture of text, lists, tables, schematics, and diagrams. Again, pagination is required, and I would likely lean toward a sectioned format (1-1 or 1-A) for clarity.

This type of e-book would also benefit from hyperlinking within the document as well as linking to external sources of information, such as suppliers. For example, instructions for performing a task could be

Workflow Tip

Build Several Custom Conversion Sets

As we will see later in this chapter, there are different reasons to use different settings and types of navigation. If you are working in an enterprise where you regularly create documents to be used with an e-book reader for different audiences, create specific job options for each. For example, if you create both technical manuals and business reports in e-book formats, you may use thumbnails in one version and not in the other. Create a separate set of options for each variation. It will take a few minutes to create the custom settings, but you will save revision time each time you use them.

hyperlinked to schematics or diagrams, which are then linked to spec sheets or other tables of information. Internal hyperlinking from an index may also be practical, depending on the size and complexity of the project.

Bookmarking would be very useful as a navigation reference. Special care would be required in the design of the structure. You might also lay out the bookmark structure differently from the pagination of the document. For example, rather than list the elements in a sequential fashion, you could group the elements pertaining to one process into a nested set of bookmarks.

Thumbnails may or may not be useful, again depending on how the manual is to be used. For example, if the elements were distinctive enough to be visually obvious in the thumbnail view, you might include them as a navigation option.

A Complex Business Document

The key to deciding how to design navigation for this type of output will be the users of the document. If you are designing your project as an internal document only, you may tend to spend less time on visual materials than if it is aimed at external users, such as stockholders. Pagination for an e-book version of this sort of document can easily emulate other forms of output. For example, if a company normally produces a printed report with simple pagination, the same could be used in this format. On the other hand, if the corporate style is to use sectioned pagination, then use the same thing in the e-book format.

The visual components of the project will determine the logic of using thumbnails. For example, in a 60-page prospectus divided into four sections, distinctive designs for the front pages of each section would identify the four section thumbnails. Overall, though, I don't think I would use thumbnails in this type of application because there simply isn't enough difference in the material to make the thumbnails visually different.

Bookmarking would be a logical navigation method. For this type of output, I recommend a fairly complete bookmark structure. If you consider a traditional business document, it is usually prefaced by a fairly extensive table of contents. Bookmarks are representative of a table of contents.

Speaking of which, you might also consider adding a hyperlinked table of contents to the document. You can use this approach if you are building a document for a group of people who most often use a traditional type of output, such as a printed report. Although the bookmark structure resembles a table of contents in many ways, for the more traditional user it will not be intuitive. You might want to include a hyperlinked index, again based on the familiarity factor for the less technologically savvy user.

Hyperlinking inside this kind of document might be desirable for linking reference materials to text. For example, summaries of sales can be readily linked to spreadsheets. External hyperlinking would depend on the document's content. For example, you might need to link to external sources, such as suppliers' Web sites.

It is interesting to note how the complexity of these decisions increased from the first example to the last. Whereas a novel or similar document generally has one type of content, manuals and complex reports can have many different types of content, and they can be used in very different ways by their readers.

As you can see, deciding which and how much navigation is required takes a lot of thought. After all, we are discussing design issues, not word-processing details.

Navigation Elements

Now that we have looked at the design aspects of e-book navigation options, let's have a look at the particulars of the different formats. I will start with the most basic and work up from there.

Page Numbers

How much more basic can you get than page numbers? Rhetorical question. Regardless of output format, page numbers are basic—and also the most "booklike."

Depending on the source material you are converting, the page numbers may not be correct when you correlate them with the thumbnails in Acrobat. This can happen when you are converting a large document, for example, that uses front matter, such as a table of contents or summaries. In Acrobat, the pages will be numbered starting at page 1.

Within Acrobat, you can add page numbers or renumber pages according to your layout and style guides. You can use a combination of numbering styles for page ranges as well, so you can simulate a printed document's pagination.

You can renumber pages through the Thumbnails palette. Select Thumbnails ➤ Number Pages. Select either the entire document or portions of it. You can also select different numbering sequences.

Workflow Tip

Planning Navigation

Use the information in this section the next time you are planning a large project, even if the distribution is not necessarily going to be an e-book. Weigh the value of the navigation to the intended user against the size of the additional components in the file. The more tailored the navigation is to users, the easier it will be for them to use the document. That's the hallmark of a good designer.

Note

I am concentrating my discussion on Adobe Acrobat eBook Reader. A number of different readers are available; owing to space constraints, however, I can't cover all of them in this book. The design processes will be similar regardless of the reader you are designing for.

Renumbering E-Book Pages

When users launch the Acrobat eBook Reader, a page navigator bar appears that allows them to navigate to any page by choosing the page number. Another option is to display two pages at once. In order to have the pages display correctly in the two-page view, you may have to add blank pages in the PDF file. This will then require renumbering the document, of course. Otherwise, the pages appearing in the reader's navigation bar will not correlate with those on the pages of the e-book itself.

An Adobe e-book includes four sections:

- Front cover

- Inside front cover

- Front matter

- Body pages

Each section uses a different page-numbering convention. To paginate the document, you will have to divide it into four sections. I will cover each briefly. To maintain a smooth flow and to minimize error, start with the cover and work toward the back of the book. As I go through the steps, I will assume that the document is already open and that the Navigation palette is open as well, with the Thumbnail tab displayed.

Numbering the Cover and Inside Front Cover Pages

Don't use numbers for the cover and inside front cover. Adobe recommends using letters for these pages: "C" for the cover, and "c" for the inside front cover. Makes sense to me. Here's how to do it:

1. Select Thumbnail ➤ Number Pages ➤ Pages From: To:.

2. Enter **1** in both the Pages From and To fields. In the Numbering portion, select the Begin New Section option.

3. Select A, B, C, . . . from the Style drop-down list. Enter **3** in the Start field. (In this case, "3" refers to the third letter in the alphabet, not to the number.)

4. Click OK.

The front cover is now numbered. Repeat the process for the inside front cover. Again, enter **1** in the Pages From and To fields, because the front cover now is numbered "C." Choose a, b, c, . . . from the Style drop-down list.

Now you have the first two pages numbered "C" and "c," and the front matter starts at page 1.

Numbering the Front Matter

By convention, front matter is numbered with lowercase roman numerals. You can follow the same process in numbering with these changes:

- Enter **1** in the Pages From field and the last page of your front matter in the To field.

- Select Begin New Section, and select the i, ii, iii, . . . style from the Style drop-down list.

- Enter either **i** or **iii** as the Start page (depending on whether you require counting the cover and inside cover as front matter for paging).

Numbering E-Book Content

Again, numbering the content will use the same basic method. How you decide to section the material will depend on the type of document you are working with, however. For a novel, the entire body of the work could easily be paginated as one section. In the case of other types of documents—manuals or reports, for example—it will depend on your requirements and how it makes the most sense structurally.

You will also be able to define styles for the body of the work. For example, if you are working with a technical manual and want to name the pages according to the section of the manual, break the manual into sections and apply numbering that uses a chapter prefix.

Bookmarks

Bookmarks are another "booklike" element. Although using bookmarks does require referring to a specific navigation view, the process will seem familiar to the user.

In my earlier discussion of navigation design issues, I mentioned that bookmarking may play a pivotal role in how your user is able to interact with your document. I also mentioned that bookmarking does not have to be restricted to a specific table of contents layout but can be added to depending on materials you want to draw attention to and make available through this navigation tool.

> **Note**
>
> To view customized page numbers, your readers must have the Use Logical Page Numbers option selected in the Options section of the General Preferences panel. If this option is not selected, Acrobat will number the pages with Arabic numbers starting at page 1.

Workflow Tip

Minimizing the File Strain of Thumbnails

The official word is that you must use thumbnails for a project. A big project. So be sure to embed all the thumbnails. Select Thumbnails ➤ Embed All Thumbnails. Doing so won't cut down on the final file size, but at least you will cut down on redraw time.

Here's a summary of the bookmark-building process:

1. Open the page you want to bookmark in the document pane, and then open the Bookmark palette.

2. Select Bookmark ➤ New Bookmark. Enter a name for the bookmark's label, and press Enter.

In Chapter 6, I described some of the design issues surrounding bookmarking. This is where they come into play. Once you have completed the set of bookmarks for the document, you can rearrange the order for ease of use—for example, to correlate different pages with a topic.

You might also want to use bookmarks as links to actions, such as launching media or changing the zoom factor. Again, this will be a design decision. Adding an action to a bookmark is a smooth process. Select the bookmark, and then choose Bookmark ➤ Bookmark Properties. Set the action in the Bookmark Properties dialog box.

Thumbnails

Thumbnails are a highly visual means of navigation. As I mentioned earlier, you might not need to use thumbnails, depending on the audience and use for the e-book. Thumbnails can increase file size dramatically.

You can add thumbnails when you convert the source, for example, via Distiller, or you can add them in Acrobat. When creating e-books, you will also need special image thumbnails (more on that later).

Creating Thumbnails inside of Acrobat couldn't be simpler. Select Window ➤ Show Thumbnails. From the Thumbnails palette menu, select Create All Thumbnails.

Creating the Cover Thumbnails

For e-book distribution, you will need thumbnail images of the covers to be used for identification and advertising. Use a thumbnail if you are using the Adobe Content Server or other distribution system to serve your e-book. The Adobe Content Server is a system that packages, protects, and distributes Adobe PDF eBooks directly from a Web site. Users with the Acrobat eBook Reader can purchase product directly through this server system. If you are distributing the file yourself, you won't have to create a cover thumbnail. A thumbnail of the cover is automatically displayed in the eBook Reader library.

For the Adobe Content Server, create an image of your cover. This image should be in GIF format, 100 pixels wide. It should also have a resolution of 96 dpi. Upload this image to the server for online identification of your e-book.

Hypertext Links

Different approaches seem to be developing in the digital world. Although it is commonplace to have hyperlinks in documents underlined and in a different color from the rest of the material, that is becoming increasingly passé. And good riddance, I say. I suppose it is based on our level of familiarity with the idea of hyperlinking. In the past, we had to have something blue and underlined to identify it as hypertext. Didn't do much for design, though, did it?

This move from blatant display to sophisticated design applies in e-books as well. In general, e-books do not have overt hyperlink text attributes. This makes the document look more like a printed version as well.

You might find in some documents that you want to use a fair number of hyperlinks, perhaps to correspond with any hypertext bookmarking you have done. You might also want to differentiate internal hyperlinks by using bookmarks and using external hyperlinks as hyperlinks.

One of the most common e-book uses of hypertext is the table of contents.

Linking the Table of Contents

Wait until your final pagination is complete before linking the table of contents (if you are using one). You can add the table of contents in the source application, but you might run into pagination issues once you have finished working on the file in Acrobat. In addition, Acrobat does not provide a simple way to update the fields, as you can in a source application such as Microsoft Word 2000.

We have covered adding these types of links in other chapters. For context, here is the short list:

1. On the table of contents page, click and drag with the Link tool selected.

2. When the Create Link dialog box opens, use these settings:

   - Invisible Rectangle (Appearance Type)

   - Invert (Highlight)

   - Go To View (Action Type)

   - Fit In Window (Magnification)

Workflow Tip
Plan a Table of Contents in Advance

Whether you include a table of contents depends on your intended reader. If you are planning to use one, check the settings in the Conversion Settings dialog box to make sure the Cross-reference And Table of Contents feature is selected on the Office tab. Enabling this option will not necessarily make the output perfect at the other end, but a bit of tweaking will be faster than a major redo. Alternatively, you might want to add links to content without using page numbers. Nothing to fix that way.

3. Open the page to which you which you are linking.

4. Click Set Link.

5. Return to the table of contents page, and repeat.

Project **Project 13-1. Building the Great American Novel**

Well, maybe we don't have the Great American Novel here, but it's an interesting story anyway. On the CD in the Chapter 13 Projects folder, you will find alternate versions of both the Word document and the PDF document we will use for this project. Use the files according to your time and preferences, as follows:

- *book.doc:* The document without formatted sizes

- *book1.doc:* The document after changing page settings

- *book.pdf:* The document after conversion

- *book1.pdf:* The finished document

I will start with the raw document: book.doc.

Formatting and Converting the Masterpiece

As I described earlier, formatting and converting will require some coordination between the source application and the conversion settings you choose.

1. Open book.doc in Microsoft Word. Change the settings for the document as follows:

- Set the margins to 0.8/0.8/1/1 inches.

- Set the page size to a custom setting of 6×9 inches.

2. Save the file.

Now, you will need to customize the conversion settings. The default e-book settings are the place from which to start.

Note

Thanks to the Author

My thanks to Terry Dyck for allowing me to use the first chapter of his as-yet-incomplete novel. You can e-mail him (if you're a publisher—or even if you're not!) at tdyck@skyweb.ca. The e-book *Monday* is copyright © 2001 by Terry Dyck.

Note

You will see that I have added a copyright information page before the first page of the chapter, which will serve as the inside cover. I have also added a drop cap for the first page.

1. Select Acrobat ➤ Change Conversion Settings. Select eBook from the General drop-down list. Click Edit Conversion Settings. Make the changes as shown in Figure 13-7.

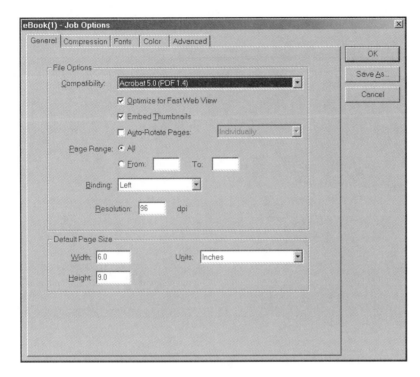

Figure 13-7
Custom General
tab settings

2. On the General tab, change these settings:

   • Select Acrobat 5.0 from the Compatibility drop-down list.

   • Click Embed Thumbnails to select it.

   • Set the Resolution option to 96 dpi.

   • Change the default page size to 6×9 inches.

3. Click the Security tab. As shown in Figure 13-8, make some permission changes:

   • Select None from the Changes Allowed drop-down list.

   • Select Fully Allowed from the Printing drop-down list.

4. Save the new settings. Click Save As, and save the settings as eBook(1).joboptions.

5. Convert the file.

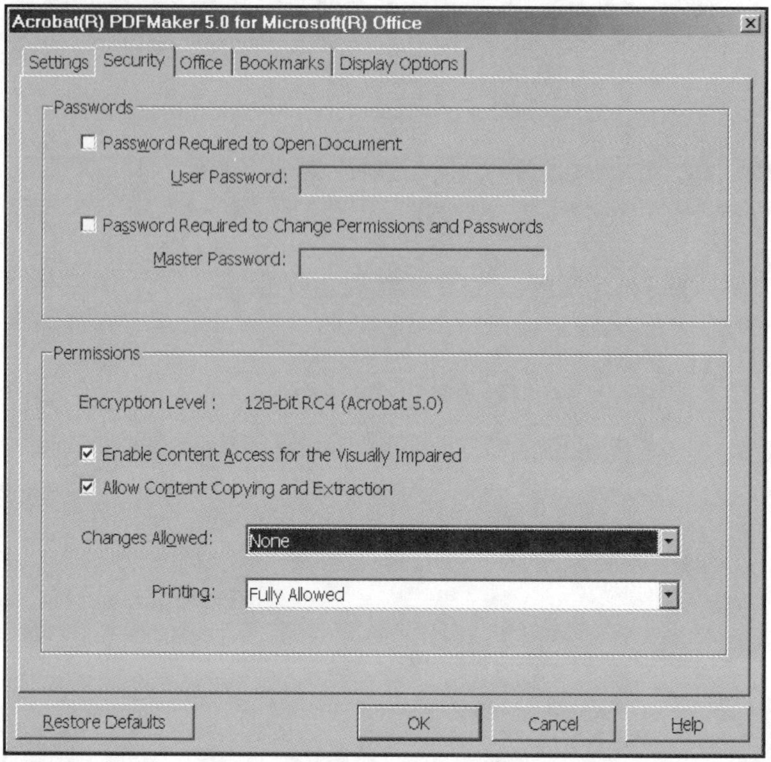

Figure 13-8
Custom security settings

I found that I had variable results using the Convert To Adobe PDF macro, but I had no problems with printing to Distiller. If you choose to use the Distiller method, do the following:

1. Select File ➤ Print, and select Acrobat Distiller from the Printer drop-down list. You will have to define the custom page size, as shown in Figure 13-9.

2. Set the width at 6 inches and the length at 9 inches. Click OK.

3. From the main Print dialog box, click Properties, and make sure that the custom e-book settings you created are selected in the Adobe PDF Settings tab. Click OK to close the Properties dialog box and return to the Print window.

4. Click OK to print the file.

So far, so good.

Note

As I mentioned, I had issues with the conversion macro, but I'm not really sure why. Although I could reproduce the same errors, which were related to margins outside the printed page, I could not repair them! Distiller worked every time. You may or may not experience similar issues.

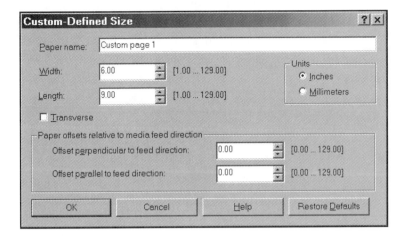

Figure 13-9
Acrobat Distiller's Custom-Defined Size dialog box

Making an E-Book

Now comes the fun stuff. We will need to add a cover, paginate the file, and build some bookmarks—in other words, make it into a real book.

1. Open the document in Acrobat, and then open the Thumbnail palette. Click page 1 (the copyright page).

2. Select Document ➤ Insert Pages. When the File Select dialog box opens, select cover.pdf. The Insert Pages dialog box will open. Select "before" from the Location drop-down menu, and select the Page 1 of 12 radio button. Click OK. The cover will be imported into the document. As you can see in Figure 13-10, the layout is correct—that is, the cover is a right-hand page, as is page 1—just like a book.

Figure 13-10
The book layout is complete.

3. Set the page numbers. Click the cover thumbnail. Select Thumbnail ➤ Number Pages. In the Page Numbers dialog box, for the selected page option, use these Numbering settings:

- Begin New Section
- Style: A,B,C, . . .
- Start: 3

4. Click OK to close the Page Numbers dialog box. The cover will now be named "C," and the page numbers will start from 1 at the inside cover.

5. Repeat the numbering process for the inside cover. Substitute "a, b, c, . . ." for the uppercase numbering used for the cover. The two sides of the cover page will now be named "C" and "c," and the document page numbering will start at 1 with the first page of the chapter—which is what we want.

6. Save the file.

Finishing Details

Now for some bookmarks. This book is so simple, it really doesn't need much in the way of bookmarks. I added three (shown in Figure 13-11): for the cover, the copyright info, and the beginning page of the book.

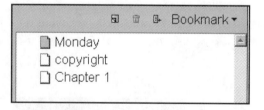

Figure 13-11
Bookmarks for the e-book

1. Open the Bookmark palette. Select Bookmark ➤ New Bookmark.

2. When the bookmark is added, enter the name. The first bookmark is named **Monday**.

3. With the cover displayed in the document pane and the bookmark selected, select Bookmark ➤ Set Bookmark Destination. Click Yes to confirm the location.

4. Continue with the other two bookmarks for the copyright page and the beginning page of Chapter 1. Make sure the appropriate pages are displayed in the document pane before setting the destinations.

5. Save the file. Open Acrobat eBook Reader. Click Open File, and select the file from the Explorer window. Click OK to open the file in the reader.

You can see the thumbnail for the book, shown in Figure 13-12, by selecting Library.

Figure 13-12
The content of the library after we added the book project.

Security and Distribution Options

E-book security has been a hot topic in recent years—and with good reason. I covered security of other formats in depth in Chapters 4 and 5. Here it is again. I suppose you must be getting the message loud and clear by now that Acrobat's security capabilities are valuable, not to mention pervasive. Well, let's look at another security feature. This one is tailored for secure content distribution.

On the one hand, being able to distribute content electronically is revolutionizing publishing. On the other hand, the need for secure istribution is increasing at the same rate. Acrobat 5 contains a plug-in from InterTrust named docBox. With it, you obtain rights to access, open, and use encrypted documents. It all comes down to DRM.

And What, Pray Tell, Is DRM?

DRM is *document rights management*. Remember back in Chapters 4 and 5 when I discussed adding signatures to documents and then sharing trusted certificates with a workgroup? This is the next step. Rather than having the intimacy of sharing a document on which to collaborate, you use DRM to share the finished work with others, in a very controlled fashion.

The docBox plug-in is automatically installed with both Acrobat 5 and Acrobat Reader 5. It controls the viewing, printing, and copying of a file. You can set access rights that can start and stop on particular days, even at particular times. You can also specify how you want the file to be distributed by establishing recipient rights.

How It Works

This process involves several parts, as well as several interested parties. Let's have a look at how this system works from the perspective of these interested parties. To simplify the process, imagine you are an independent writer.

First is the creator: you. You are responsible for two elements that together make up the package: the PDF document you want to distribute, and the usage and pricing rules you set on the document. Once the document is configured to an e-book format and you have attached the usage and pricing criteria, your role is complete—as is the package for distribution.

Part two of the process is the server. It is commonly a storefront and processes two separate transactions. The first is the commerce transaction: receiving user payment or identity information, and serving the PDF product. The second transaction delivers usage rights to the user.

Part three logically must be the user. The user transfers payment and/or identity information. If distribution is based only on payment, once payment has been received by the document server, it is downloaded to the user. If distribution is based also on rights, in addition to serving the document, the server site delivers usage rights and receipts to the user (the complexity of this process depends on what rules you, as the creator, have set on the package).

Let's have a look at some of the different ways content is distributed. Then we'll look at the docBox plug-in and see it in action.

How Content Is Distributed

Content is generally distributed in one of three ways. Of course, for each of these areas, infinite combinations and permutations exist. The reason I am including this information is because it is thought-provoking. When you look through the list, you will see what I mean. The three models are promotional, subscription, and direct-selling.

Promotional distribution is the "free" stuff that is not always free! However, it is a wonderful way to gain exposure for a particular product. Common types of promotional distribution are time-restricted content (this is common with software), sample chapters with links to retailers to buy the entire product, and free download of product in exchange for completing some sort of survey.

Subscriptions are similar to magazine subscriptions, with a few digital twists. For example, you might buy an online subscription, which is commonplace with online newsletters in many industries. You might also find subscriptions that are time limited. The user buys digital keys to content for specific lengths of time.

The last model is direct-selling. You pay me, and I send you a key that allows you to download my book. Again, there are digital twists. You might have product that has different pricing depending on whether you give the user print or save rights, or whether you are selling single or site licenses. You might also have an individual product option that allows the user to customize the content. I can see this being a logical type of product for something such as technical manuals. Different users will have different needs and can download only the components they require.

I have discussed different methods for distributing, but how is it actually done? We're coming right up with the answer to that burning question.

Serving the Document

Maybe I should have said *answers* to that burning question. Distributing e-book material for serving to end users requires an intermediary. This server setup controls the permission to access material (supplying and redeeming them), as well as serving the document once a permission receipt has been processed.

A number of companies, including Adobe, will encrypt, store, and serve your documents for public distribution. Many of these companies will do the formatting for your document as well. Interesting, isn't it? Now let's have a look at the plug-in that can make this work for you: docBox.

Using the docBox Plug-In

The docBox plug-in is included with Acrobat 5 and Acrobat Reader 5.

Is there a difference between this and other types of security we have looked at in earlier chapters? Quite a bit, actually. When we looked at trusted certificates earlier in this book, we were looking at public/private key (PPK) encryption. This type of encryption is designed primarily to collaborate securely on documents. The author encrypts the document with the recipient's public key. The recipient, using his or her private key, decrypts the document. docBox security is used for distribution. That is, the author sets encryption parameters for the recipients, who then decrypt the document with their key. All recipients can use the same key, and there is no exchange with the author. On that note, let's see how it works in Acrobat.

What's in the Box?

Let me take you on a visual tour of how the plug-in works. I am using the plug-in to access a file from InterTrust's docBox Showcase at `http://pdf.intertrust.com`. You can download a number of files from this site.

1. Within the server site, click the document you want to download. The first dialog box (see Figure 13-13) will open. This demo material is accompanied by receipts. Alternatively, click Scan to search for other receipts on your computer, or click Browse to find receipts manually.

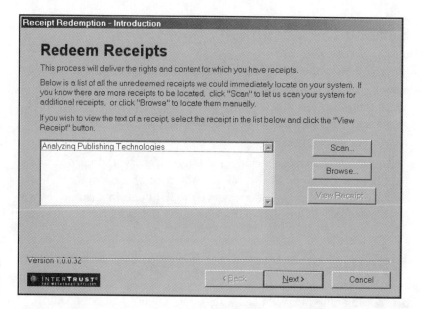

Figure 13-13
The process starts with redeeming a receipt.

2. Click the file name in the window. The third button, View Receipt, will be activated. Click View Receipt for information on the certificate. As you can see in Figure 13-14, information on the receipt and the content is included. The dialog box is named with the file name. Click OK to close the information box. Then click Next in the Redeem Receipts dialog box to move to the next window.

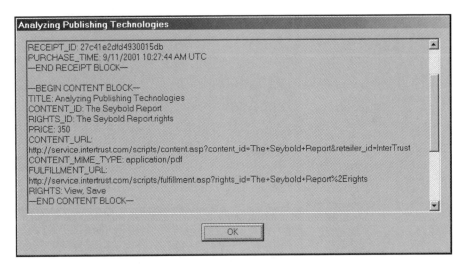

Figure 13-14
Technical information on the content is included.

3. The next window, shown in Figure 13-15, lists items for download. Items To Retrieve will list both rights and publication downloads. Their icons differentiate the two elements. You can deselect an item by clicking its check box. Click Next.

4. The next window outlines Device Parameters. If this is the first time you have attempted to redeem digital receipts, you must complete this process to determine the ability of your configuration to accept encrypted information. As you can see in Figure 13-16, you have the option to download the content to a removable disk (if you have one available). Once this process is complete, click Next.

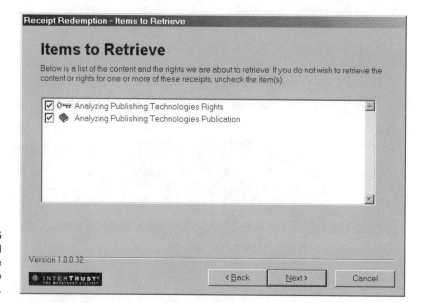

Figure 13-15
The rights and
publications are
listed in the Items To
Retrieve dialog box.

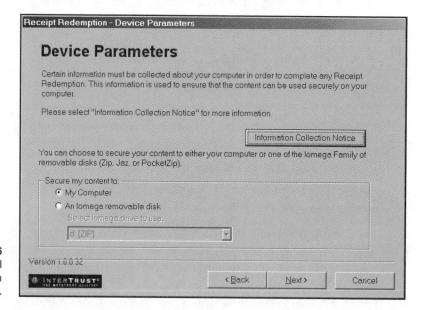

Figure 13-16
The DRM system will
evaluate your system
before downloading files.

5. The next window, shown in Figure 13-17, is an optional download for the management tool for the system. If you want to download the tool, click the Yes radio button. (The tool will be downloaded as a separate operation.) For a basic file download, click the No radio button, and then click Next to move to the next window.

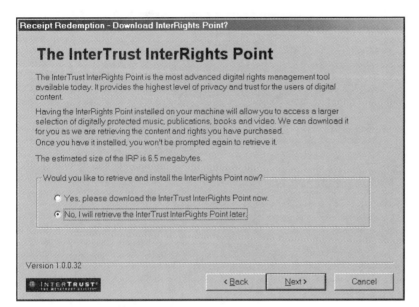

Figure 13-17
This dialog box gives you the option to download a management tool to maintain your secure downloads.

6. Finally, the files will be downloaded. You will first see a download progress window, followed by notification of completion. Acrobat will display your new document.

7. As you can see in Figure 13-18, both the document and receipt files are stored in the My eBooks directory by default.

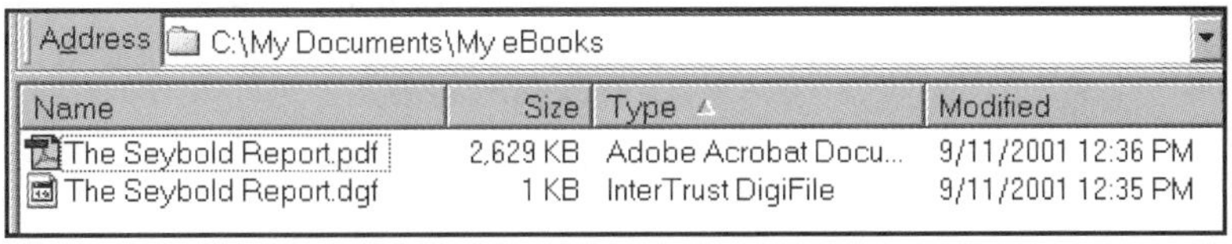

Address	C:\My Documents\My eBooks			
Name	Size	Type △	Modified	
The Seybold Report.pdf	2,629 KB	Adobe Acrobat Docu...	9/11/2001 12:36 PM	
The Seybold Report.dgf	1 KB	InterTrust DigiFile	9/11/2001 12:35 PM	

Figure 13-18
The default storage location of the downloaded files

The file that I downloaded in this example is highly encrypted. As you can see in Figure 13-19, which shows the PDF Properties tab of the Properties dialog box for this file, everything from the title to the creation date is encrypted. Now this is security!

Note

In order for the docBox-administered document to be displayed in Acrobat, the program may relaunch itself if you are running any plug-ins that are not Adobe certified.

Note

To see the process in action and download additional material, visit the docBox Showcase at http:// pdf.intertrust.com. You will also find an update to the plug-in on the site. The current version of docBox at the time of writing was 1.0.0.35.

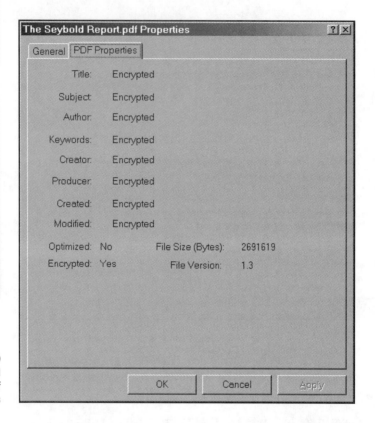

Figure 13-19
The downloaded document's list of encrypted elements

So now we seen how to format and create an e-book. We have seen how to add and customize navigation. We have also seen how to access a secure e-book using docBox. Let's look at one more topic before we leave this introduction to the world of e-books: the design of output for handheld devices.

Handheld Devices: A Special Case

There will be times when you know that the output for a specific document will be used on a handheld device. Or you may want to make a separate version of a document for use on a handheld. You must consider a number of details that will make this process smoother and produce better results.

Source Document Formatting

Like everything else we have considered in this book, understanding the importance of preplanning at the source document stage applies to handheld output as well. When creating the source materials, keep these issues in mind:

- Image display
- Fonts
- Layout

Let's have a look at these features.

Image Display

There is absolutely no need for high resolution or large-scale images for a handheld. That is wasteful, both of time and storage space. Images should be converted to grayscale, resized, and downsampled to target screen size. This will decrease the file size.

Fonts and Layout

Fonts should be scaled back as well. It is generally recommended that you use the common Base 14 system fonts that are installed on your computer. I know, how archaic. But consider the output device. Not that it is archaic, but it certainly has its own requirements. At this time, this means sacrificing snazzy layouts for content. Since the primary use of handhelds is getting information, I am sure the user would rather be able to read the content clearly and quickly without font-handling issues. Save the fancy stuff for print layouts.

From the layout perspective, set paragraph spacing equivalent to an extra line height. This will clearly separate the paragraphs on the tiny handheld screen.

Before converting the file to PDF, you will also want to have a look at the conversion settings and make some custom changes.

Conversion Settings for Handheld Devices

Note

These settings are optimized for Palm OS handhelds. Although these settings are fairly generic, you might have to experiment with them for other handheld systems.

Acrobat 5 comes with standard e-book conversion settings. You will need to make a few modifications for handhelds.

From the source application (such as Microsoft Word 2000), the settings are available by selecting Acrobat ➤ Change Conversion Settings. Select eBook from the drop-down Conversions Settings list, and click Edit Conversion Settings to open the Job Options dialog box.

Now make these changes to the settings:

1. On the General tab, in the File Options section, set Compatibility to Acrobat 4.0 (PDF 1.3). Set the resolution to 72 dpi. Leave the other default values.

2. On the Compression tab, in the Grayscale Images section, select Bicubic Downsampling, and change resolution settings to 72 dpi. Make sure the Compression is set to Automatic/Medium Quality.

3. On the Fonts tab, deselect font embedding options. The handheld will substitute its fonts.

4. On the Color and Advanced tabs, leave the default settings.

5. Save the settings. Click Save As, enter a file name, and click Save.

That, in essence, is how to create a handheld-specific document. You may find that the users of your PDA can readily handle color. In that case, change the settings to reflect the capabilities of the device.

Up Next

This has been a whirlwind tour. In this chapter, I covered the ins and outs of e-books. I considered source document formatting and custom conversion settings. I discussed navigation design based on the needs and expectations of the user, in addition to the material. I presented you with an interesting book project and walked through yet another security system. Finally, I briefly discussed output for handheld devices.

Up next is the story of network publishing. In Chapter 14, we will examine some of the topics we have already seen from a network perspective and look at a few new ideas as well.

Chapter 14

Collaborating over Networks

*The capability to work online using a Web
browser is one of Acrobat 5's most
powerful features. Have a look.*

That's Collaboration with a Capital "C"

This chapter is a bit different from many of the others. For one thing, there is no specific element or collection of commands in Acrobat that can be called "Network something." For another thing, this chapter is more an accumulation of workflow processes and tips than anything else—which makes sense when you think about it.

My goal in writing this book is to explain to you how to use Acrobat and ways I have used it over the years that have been useful and that can save both time and money. Given the fact that so many different combinations and permutations of network design and structure exist, it would be pointless to try a specific approach.

Instead, I'll give you some general information on how Acrobat behaves over networks. I'll examine some processes that work especially well over networks. Along the way, I'll describe some specific conditions that affect how well Acrobat will work in a networked environment. And I'll also look at some specific tasks and processes specific to networks.

Coming Up

Way back in Chapter 1, I introduced the idea of network publishing. Here, in this chapter, is where I want to show you some of the processes that are tailor-made for networks. In this chapter, I will discuss a number of topics:

- Using Acrobat with networks

- Setting up and using network folders

- Using online commenting

- Using forms online

- Importing and exporting data

- Creating profiles

Just a note before I start. Some of these topics are a bit more technical than others in the book have been, for good reason: The information is sophisticated. I am doing it for a particular purpose, however. If you are a designer, it isn't necessary to also be a network administrator. That is not my goal. But I think it is important to have an understanding of why and how the environment works the way it does to be a *great* designer. The more general understanding you have of what your IT colleagues do, the better you are able to design within that system and convey advanced requirements of your software to others. Also, because you work with a specific goal in mind, knowing what is possible is a great advantage in communicating your requirements to others.

Knowledge is power, after all!

So here comes a heaping spoonful of power.

On Using Networks

I mentioned in the earlier chapters of this book that online commenting can be used by multiple users. Commenting may take place either online, in real time, or offline, with the comments uploaded to a server storage location for use by others. This is the essence of collaboration. This process uses a storage process of some type.

If you recall from Chapter 2 when I introduced commenting, and later in Chapter 5 when we looked at commenting from a security perspective, the original document is not altered by users as they are commenting. The comments for a group of users can be saved in a different location and appended to the original document. In Acrobat, this external location (repository) can be a database, a network folder, or a Web folder.

Although Acrobat can be used with four repository types, I will discuss only one in detail. I will give you briefer information on the other types. The available repository types are as follows:

- Network folder

- Database

- WebDAV

- Web discussions

Regardless of which system you are working within, there are common functions. Because online commenting is one of the most common types of collaboration over networks, let's look at these commonalities from that perspective. We will examine identification, security, and data structures first. I will also add a sprinkling of tips.

Who Are You?

We have seen that several users can comment on a single document. Each set of comments belonging to an individual must be identified.

Workflow Tip
Use Unique Names

If you have ever worked with versioning software, you will be familiar with the idea of file checkouts or locking systems. These features don't exist in Acrobat. To prevent overwriting comments, make sure everyone has a different username.

What happens when you open a document? Acrobat automatically adds names to a file. Very handy. If you open the Note Properties dialog box, you will see that the Author name is already present, as shown in Figure 14-1. Acrobat uses the Windows login name (obviously on Windows). For the Mac, the name will be taken from either the login name or the file-sharing name.

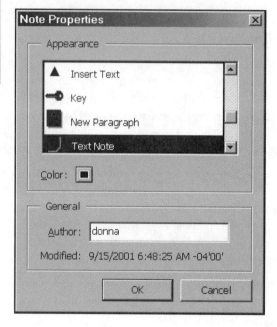

Figure 14-1
Note properties are automatically named.

You will also find that the same name appears in the title bar of the note pop-up, which is shown in Figure 14-2.

Figure 14-2
Note titles also use the name automatically.

What Can You Do?

So far, so good. You have a name. Acrobat recognizes the name and adds it to properties in your document. Next, you have to look at what your server will allow you to do. There are two parts to this. First, you must use your login name to upload comments. This is the only way Acrobat will function. Second, you must have permission to create files on the server to which you want to upload the file.

Imagine you are working merrily along. Whistling a tune. (Maybe that's a bit over the top. How's this: You are slogging along, bleary-eyed, deadline looming. . . .) Your group leader has given you one more assignment. Yippee! You open the file, do your thing, and then try to save the comments. They won't save.

Do not panic. Instead, check for two things:

- First, see whether the directory in which you are trying to save the file actually exists. Seriously. These things can easily happen. Suppose your team leader had walked the file over to you on a floppy or Zip disk.

- Second, if you find the file on the network, check its properties to see if you have write permission. You can find out by clicking the folder to select it, and then right-clicking and selecting Properties ➤ Sharing. If you don't have permission, go directly to your network administrator and get it fixed.

Sharing Web Folders

A word of caution before I describe these shared settings. If you are in a networked environment, you won't likely have access to Web sharing, and your write permissions may be restricted as well. I think it is still a good idea for you to know where permissions come from and what to look for.

For projects that are being shared over a browser, you must also have rights to Web Sharing to access the folder. I have given myself rights to my own folder, as you can see in Figure 14-3. Kind of me, I thought.

Once you have seen whether you have sharing rights to the folder, check to see what kind of rights you have. Click the name of the alias, and then click Edit Properties. The Edit Alias dialog box will open (see Figure 14-4).

Again, if the folder is one you need to use, you will have to have the permissions granted to you by your administrator.

Note

If you are in a networked environment, you aren't likely to have access to these dialog boxes, but I wanted to show you where the permissions come from and what to look for.

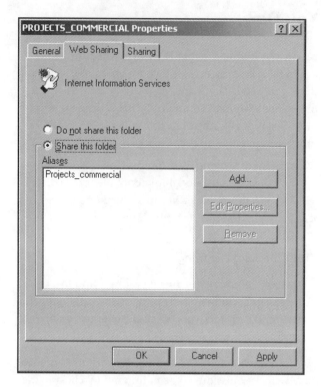

Figure 14-3
Check for access rights on the Web Sharing tab.

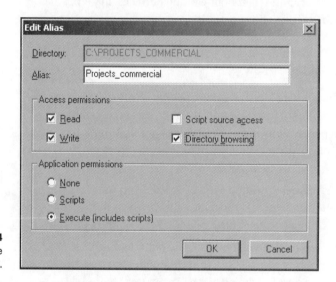

Figure 14-4
Check for write permissions for the file.

Using Shared Files

Here is an extremely important question to consider: What happens if a file is moved after some, but not all, people have added their comments? There will be a sprinkling of comment files, that's what. Not a happytime. Here's why.

When you open a PDF file in a browser, a few things happen. First, Acrobat will read the URL for the file from the network layer. It will then use the Domain Name System (DNS) protocol to translate the name to an IP address. This way, the comments will be stored in the correct location regardless of where you access the file. This is the essence of network access for collaborating on files.

If you change the document's location, the whole system breaks down. The access, which is based on the URL of the original location, will address the file differently, and any comments added once the file has been moved will be stored in the new location.

This can be repaired, of course. It isn't quick, and it is annoying. Erring on the side of caution is a good thing. That doesn't mean you can't ever move a file. On the contrary. But wait until all the comments have been added.

I will return to commenting specifically a bit later, but first I want to touch on the different types of network situations that you may be working within.

Network Options

As I have said, you don't need to become a network administrator to use Acrobat. It is important to understand "where" you are working and what kinds of things to look out for. Let's have a brief look at the options I listed early in the chapter.

Network Folders

This type of repository is the simplest to set up. I referred to this format in my earlier discussion. Material is saved to a network volume or hard drive instead of to a Web server or a database. Users open and comment on a document. Acrobat then creates a version of the document and saves each user's comments as a separate Forms Data Format (FDF) file.

Following from my earlier discussion, in order for this to work, the server must

Workflow Tip
Maintaining Control

As some of this chapter's figures show, a third option is available. Rather than using a network volume for storage, you can create a file on your local hard drive. If this file is then shared with the network, others can access the file. If you are responsible for managing the file, by storing the file locally you can make sure it isn't moved.

Note

This is a very brief overview. You can find much more information, including server requirements, online at Adobe (http://www.adobe.com). Look for developer documentation. The installation CD also contains a file that discusses some of these issues. You will find it at Acrobat 5\Collaboration\Online Comments in your Explorer.

- Have a network folder to store comments that is accessible and allows write access to users

- Allow access to the location the document is stored in

Web Discussions

You can set up a different type of commenting system using Microsoft Web Discussions. This system is similar to a threaded discussion. Users can both create topics and reply to others.

In order to use this system, the server must have Microsoft Office Server Extensions installed. All users must have access to the server being used as the discussion server.

Database Repository

The database repository is the enterprise-strength solution for online activity. Users communicate directly with a SQL database using a new technology called Acrobat Database Connectivity (ADBC). This is similar to Open Database Connectivity (ODBC), and it allows Acrobat JavaScript access to a SQL database.

This is a neat process. Acrobat creates a table containing five types of information for the document. The table is constructed as shown in Table 14-1.

Table 14-1   Structuring Comments As a Database Table

Author	Page	Name	Contents	Data
Identity of the commenter	Page number of the comment	Name generated by Acrobat	JavaScript description of the comment	Stores binary data such as sound or file attachments

WebDAV

Finally, we have the WebDAV option. WebDAV (that's Web Distributed Authoring and Versioning) is a protocol that allows for remote collaborative authoring of Web resources. WebDAV can use a Microsoft FrontPage Extended server or an FTP server to serve comments, as long as the users are running Windows 2000. This system can also be used with Apache servers or Internet Information Server (IIS) 5.

Making Acrobat Work Better for You

It's certainly not that the program doesn't work well as it is. This section, which is the last before I go into a few specific types of networked activity, covers two other topics that are important as information, but don't necessarily fit in anywhere else. I am referring to deployment systems and types of software.

Sharing and Organizing Plug-ins

As you have worked through the book, you have seen a number of Acrobat plug-ins. These are very good utilities that expand or add extra functionality to the software. Some will be required for users to access your documents fully. Some are loaded automatically as the program is installed. Others, such as the Paper Capture plug-in, are available as separate downloads from Adobe. Still others are purchased plug-ins. How to keep this straight? Well, as I noted in the chapter on indexing (Chapter 9), information is key. I would suggest a simple method to make sure everyone who needs access to a plug-in has that access.

Have your network or systems administrator set up a folder on your intranet. Include additional plug-ins (depending on your distribution agreement) in this folder. Also include a readme file outlining the content of the folder and what the plug-ins are used for. This way, you can take advantage of the functionality of the plug-ins, and your users can appreciate the sheer magnificence of your talent.

Workflow Tip

Managing Several Locations

If you are working in a group, and your group members will use more than one server setting or location, it may be practical to set up a series of FDF files. These files can be stored on your intranet. This way, whenever you have to change settings, click the required FDF file and the settings will be loaded.

Software Types

How do you know if a user needs a full-blown version of Acrobat 5, or if he can use the Acrobat Reader 5 instead? And let's complicate the matter even further. In 2001 Adobe launched a new product. Acrobat Approval 5 is more than Acrobat Reader, but it's less than the full product. This is actually a very good idea. There is no reason for all the staff in an entire organization to have the full product, based both on the cost of the software and the uses of it. If you are in a design shop, not everyone will need Photoshop or Dreamweaver, for example, just as not everyone will need Excel or Access. At the risk of sounding like an Adobe spokesperson, however, I think that any company that is moving to an eForm workflow structure would benefit greatly from using Approval over the Reader. It all comes down to time and process.

As you will see later in this chapter when I show you even more ways to use forms, managing many processes in a business can be facilitated by using this product. For example, if a certain group within an organization uses Acrobat to create forms for the entire organization, these forms can be used by everyone through Approval.

This intermediate product allows the user to access, complete, sign, and submit forms. I have included a comparison of the three products in Table 14-2. You can see that anyone whose work involves commenting will still need the full version of Acrobat, as will anyone who is involved in any design processes.

Table 14-2   Varying Functionality of the Acrobat Products

Features	Acrobat	Approval	Reader
Read and print PDF files	Yes	Yes	Yes
Fill in and submit PDF forms from a browser	Yes	Yes	Yes
Sign PDF forms	Yes	Yes	No
Save PDF forms to your hard drive	Yes	Yes	No
Add security settings	Yes	Yes	No
Spell check PDF forms	Yes	Yes	No
Create accessible PDF forms	Yes	No	No
Create interactive PDF forms	Yes	No	No
Convert any document to a PDF file	Yes	No	No
Create e-signature fields	Yes	No	No
Add comments	Yes	No	No

As you can see from the table, if you are using any forms-driven processes, you have options. If you are using either Acrobat or Approval, you can collaborate on commenting processes online. Let's have a look at that now.

Online Commenting

Unlike regular commenting—that is, commenting done on your computer, which is then distributed to others (as I showed you in earlier chapters)—online commenting requires a specific set of preference settings. Otherwise, when you try to work online, you will see the message shown in Figure 14-5.

Figure 14-5
You have to set
preferences in Acrobat
to use commenting
functions online.

Setting Your Preferences

Preferences can be easily set. Follow these steps:

1. Open Acrobat. Select Edit ➤ Preferences ➤ General ➤ Online
   Comments. The dialog box shown in Figure 14-6 will open.

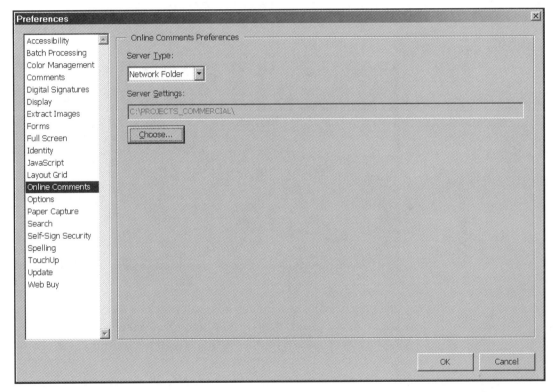

Figure 14-6
Set preferences for
commenting online
in this dialog box.

Workflow Tip

Check Your Settings

Here are a couple of
pointers on using online
comments for a number
of users. First, each user
must have the same
preferences set. If you
can't access your file
correctly, check the
settings in Acrobat. Your
preferences may be set
for a different location.
Like other settings,
preferences will remain
the same until you
change them again.

2. Select the Server Type from the drop-down list (this is the set of four alternate types I discussed earlier).

3. Click Choose to browse to the location where the network folder is stored. Select the file.

4. Click OK to save the settings.

Now, when you launch a PDF file from within a Web browser, the commenting tools will be activated.

Online Commenting

Online commenting is very similar to the process used from within Acrobat itself. As you can see in Figure 14-7, a range of commenting tools is available. I must admit a fondness for some of the little face stamps.

Figure 14-7
The comments
added online

You only have to open the file from within a browser to work with it online. As you can see in Figure 14-8, the online commenting tools are now functional, as indicated by the coloring of the icons (and the absence of the earlier request to set preferences).

The tools on the toolbar, from left to right, are

Figure 14-8
Once the preferences are set, the commenting tools will function.

- Upload And Download Comments (moves data in both directions).

- Upload Comments.

- Download Comments.

- Hide/Show Comments. (Be careful with this function. Clicking this button will hide all comments on the document. If you upload comments to the server and are in Hide Comments mode, all your comments will be cleared from the server location.)

Note

The comments I created in this demo are saved in a separate subfolder, which is an alphanumeric string called a *hash string*. Acrobat converts the location of the original file into this string.

How are your comments saved? They are automatically loaded to the storage location if you leave your present browser view, either by navigating to a different URL or by closing the browser or Acrobat. As you can see in Figure 14-9, the comments file is now stored in the network folder I set up earlier.

Figure 14-9
The comments are stored in my network folder.

Offline Commenting

You might have a group of people who need to work on a common document, but under different circumstances. For example, someone may not be able to use a document in a particular session or location. The file can be used offline and then uploaded to the server when it is convenient. Here's how to do it:

Note

If you are working with several computers, you can work on a document anywhere you like, but you must upload your comments from the same computer you used to download the copy to work with offline. Otherwise, when you try to select File ➤ Upload Comments, the option will be disabled.

1. Open the document in a Web browser.

2. Save the document to your hard drive. Click the Save A Copy Of The File icon on the Acrobat toolbar.

3. Open the file in Acrobat at your convenience, and do your thing. Save the file.

4. Select File ➤ Upload Comments. Your comments will be stored as earlier in the same designated network file.

Now that we have investigated commenting processes online, let's switch to the other main online function: *forms*.

Importing and Exporting Form Data

Note

This is another one of those instances where Acrobat Reader just won't do. Unless Acrobat 5 is installed, you can't export form information.

If you are working in a controlled system (that is, you know who is accessing forms and what kind of software they are using), you don't have to export and import entire files. Instead, only the data has to be moved. This is a slick process.

Data can be exported from a PDF file. It will be saved as a FDF file. The FDF files can also be used for archiving data. They contain the contents of a form, but not the form container itself, so they are very small files. To export form data to a file, select File ➤ Export ➤ Form Data. Name the file and click Save.

Another neat thing you can do with this data is to import it into another form. This will require that the form have fields with the same names (another good reason to take the time to set up a naming-convention system). Any form fields that do not match are ignored. To import form data from a file, select File ➤ Import ➤ Form Data. Select the file and open it. (We will look at a specific case later in this chapter.)

One last concept on form data. You can also import data from a text file. The data must be configured like this:

Workflow Tip
Make It a Habit

There are specific processes you should get into the habit of following if you are working with commented documents offline and online—such as remembering to save and upload comments whenever you have finished. When you open a document online, click Upload And Download Comments before you start working to see what progress has been made with the document if you're working in a group.

- Each row must be tab delimited.

- The first row is the column names (which are the names of the form fields).

- The content of each row's tab section is a cell in the table. When the data is imported into a table, each cell is the value for the form field corresponding to the column name.

Now, when this text file is imported into a form, the form will be automatically filled in. Isn't that slick?

Field-Naming Conventions

This is certainly another one of those examples where spending some time designing a process saves a lot of time further down the road. For example, if a group of forms use a consistent layout and naming structure, this will save you time in the design process. It will also save the user time. Close to the end of this chapter, I discuss moving data in and out of forms, but for now I want to consider what has to be done in the design and development phase to make this happen.

Suppose you are responsible for converting all the forms used by the human resources (HR) department of your organization to online smart forms. Where do you start? If you look at a basic set of HR forms, you will notice some constants. As an illustration, let's imagine you have to convert four forms:

- Medication reimbursement form

- Request for vacation form

- Expense reimbursement form

- Dental treatment reimbursement form

Although the particulars of the forms will be different, they all share some common fields. For example, the user's name and address, phone number, job classification, and employee number will all likely appear on these forms.

Making all these forms work in a similar fashion requires planning. Set up a field-naming system that makes sense and stick to it. For example, you may want to use field names such as FirstName or first.name. Your choice depends on what feels more natural to you; I go for the first option for general information because I have some database background, and I use the second one for fields that contain numerical data to be calculated. It is more programmer oriented to my mind. We will see shortly that this also helps to simplify the creation/calculation process. As you can see in Figure 14-10 (an image from the sample file used in Chapter 10), I have used both systems.

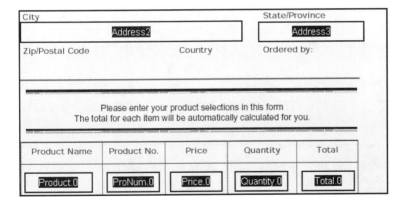

Figure 14-10
Two different naming conventions used in a form, depending on their use

Regardless, once you have settled on a naming convention and have applied it across forms, data importing will be successful. You might find it useful to create a schema or table that lists all the field names you will use and what they represent.

Filling Out Forms

As if anyone needs instruction on how to fill out forms! I do want to cover a few details when using forms from inside a Web browser. Consider these functions when you are designing this type of form.

1. When the form is opened in a Web browser, you can

   • Tab from field to field top-left to bottom-right if the tabbing sequence has been set correctly.

   • Print the form.

   • Save the file to your hard drive if you are using Acrobat or Approval (the Adobe product similar to Acrobat Reader that allows for form filling).

   • Export the data.

2. When the form is complete, you can

   • Submit the form using whatever submission tool is on the form (such as a Submit button).

   • Select File ➤ Export ➤ Form Data to save the form data in an FDF file. Enter a file name in the dialog box and click Save. When you open the FDF file, the container PDF file will be opened automatically.

3. To clear a form in a browser window, you must click the Reset button (if there is one) or exit without saving the file and start again. Using browser toolbar buttons such as Reload or Go Back, or going to another URL, will not clear a form. You can select the File ➤ Revert option.

The moral of this little story? Consider how your users will be working with the forms, don't assume they have a great deal of familiarity with how Acrobat works, and design accordingly.

Project Tutorial: Using Personal Profiles

Direct to you from Adobe. I want to discuss a process that is available for use on the installation CD. The process creates Personal Field Name (PFN)–compliant forms. We will later build a form using this information.

If you look on the Acrobat installation CD, you will find a folder containing a set of profile management tools. You will find it by selecting Acrobat 5\Forms\PFN in your Explorer. It has sample forms and materials for creating personal profile forms. I discussed field naming and forms data earlier. This is an example of how these things actually work. But it goes beyond what I outlined. Rather than you having to add fields and then name them, there is an EPS file for each field, which you can use for creating the source document for your form. The entire personal profile flow uses a few steps. Let's see how this works.

The Process

First, create your own profile.

1. Open the file on the Acrobat installation CD named PFNFORM.PDF (located in the Forms folder). Fill in the form fields in the Acrobat Forms file, the top portion of which is shown in Figure 14-11.

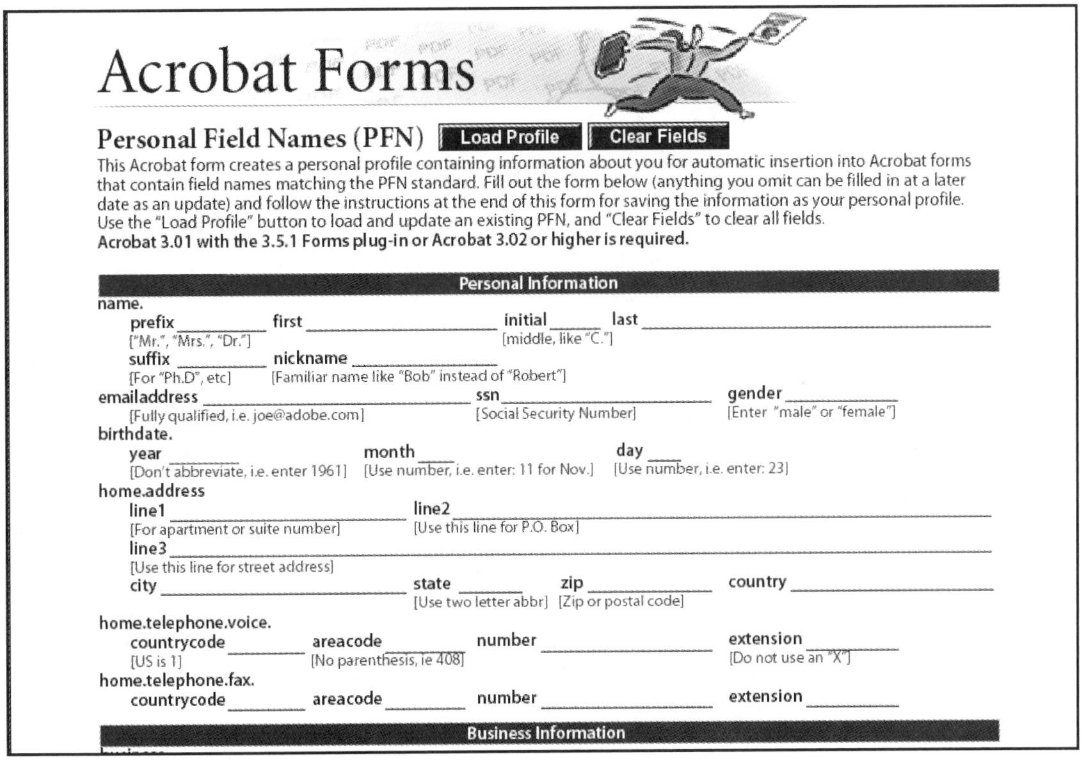

Acrobat Forms

Personal Field Names (PFN) | Load Profile | Clear Fields |

This Acrobat form creates a personal profile containing information about you for automatic insertion into Acrobat forms that contain field names matching the PFN standard. Fill out the form below (anything you omit can be filled in at a later date as an update) and follow the instructions at the end of this form for saving the information as your personal profile. Use the "Load Profile" button to load and update an existing PFN, and "Clear Fields" to clear all fields. **Acrobat 3.01 with the 3.5.1 Forms plug-in or Acrobat 3.02 or higher is required.**

Personal Information

name.
prefix _____ first _____ initial _____ last _____
["Mr.", "Mrs.", "Dr."]   [middle, like "C."]
suffix _____ nickname _____
[For "Ph.D", etc]   [Familiar name like "Bob" instead of "Robert"]
emailaddress _____ ssn _____ gender _____
[Fully qualified, i.e. joe@adobe.com]   [Social Security Number]   [Enter "male" or "female"]
birthdate.
year _____ month ____ day ____
[Don't abbreviate, i.e. enter 1961] [Use number, i.e. enter: 11 for Nov.] [Use number, i.e. enter: 23]
home.address
line1 _____ line2 _____
[For apartment or suite number]   [Use this line for P.O. Box]
line3 _____
[Use this line for street address]
city _____ state _____ zip _____ country _____
[Use two letter abbr] [Zip or postal code]
home.telephone.voice.
countrycode _____ areacode _____ number _____ extension _____
[US is 1]   [No parenthesis, ie 408]   [Do not use an "X"]
home.telephone.fax.
countrycode _____ areacode _____ number _____ extension _____

Business Information

Figure 14-11
Enter the information into this form.

2. Once the form is complete, click Save. The information must be stored in the folder Acrobat uses as an exchange folder. As you can see in Figure 14-12, the storage location on my computer is C:\My Documents\Adobe\Acrobat. This is the same folder where we stored security certificates in Chapters 4 and 5. Name the file, which must use the .fdf extension, and click Save to store the file.

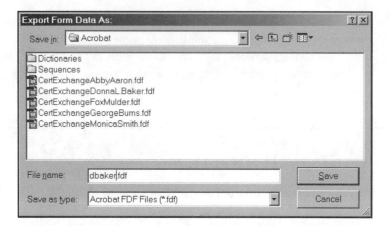

Figure 14-12
Storage location for the certificate information

3. Now back to Acrobat. Open the file on the Acrobat installation CD named PFNSAMP.PDF (located in the Forms folder). This is a sample form, shown in Figure 14-13. You will see a logo at the top of the form. This indicates that the form is PFN compliant. Use it when creating this specific type of form file.

Rather than manually entering information, click the Import Profile button. Your profile information will be automatically entered into the fields that correspond with what you saved originally. You may also click the Import Any button. Rather than autofilling your form, this button will open a browser dialog box that lets you find a specific profile.

That's how to create a personal profile and then load it into a form configured for this purpose. But that's not all there is to it, of course.

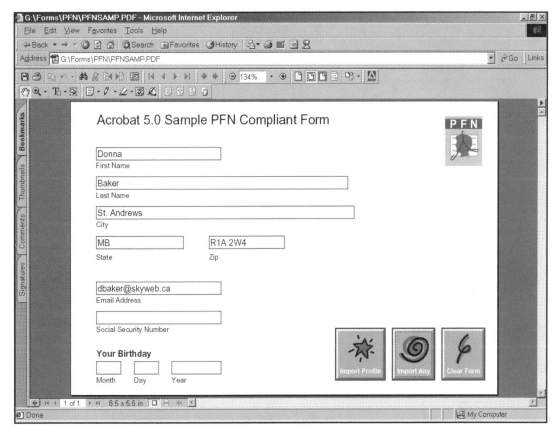

Figure 14-13
The new form, completed
by clicking one button

EPS Files

There is another subfolder on the installation CD. This one is named
PFNEPS. In this folder you will find a set of 45 EPS files. You can use these
files to make your life a lot simpler (well, the forms-creation part of it,
anyway). Look at this version of the sample form I showed earlier. In
Figure 14-14, I have selected the Form tool in Acrobat while the file was
open, so the fields are highlighted.

Before we finish this chapter, let's build and test a simple form using
this process.

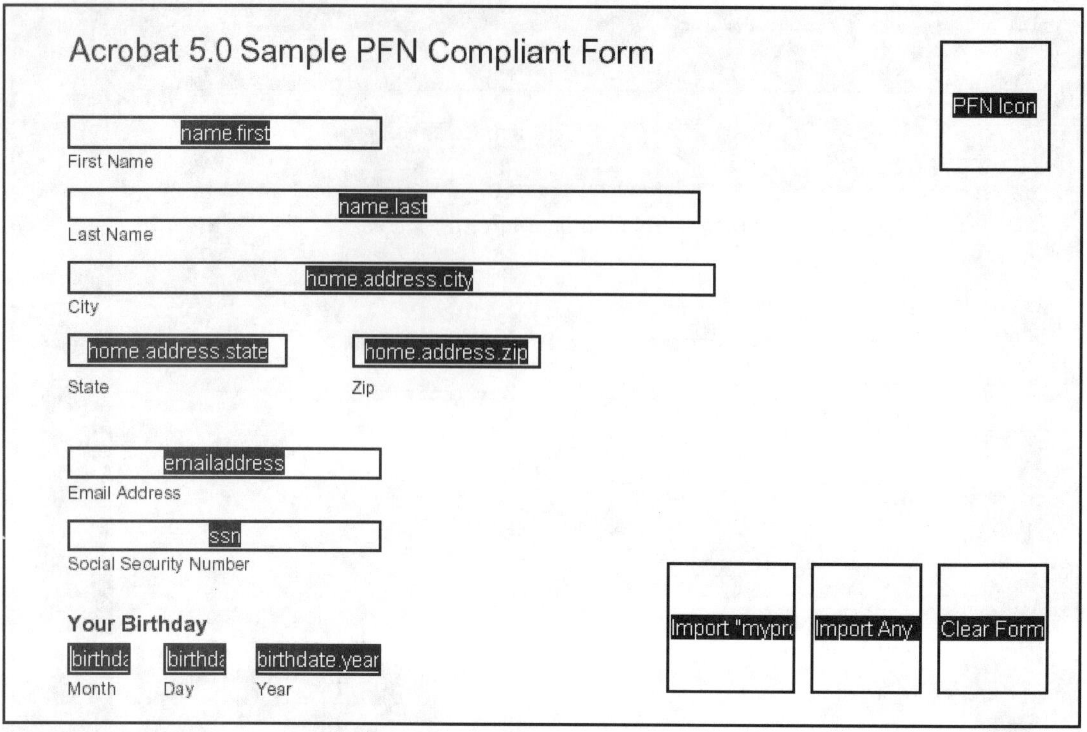

Figure 14-14
The sample form displaying the form field

Working with EPS Field Files

Here are some tips on how to use these files to create a PFN-compliant form:

- The EPS files can be used in any type of authoring application that supports the EPS format.

- No preview images are available for the EPS files.

- The files can be customized in a text editor.

- Whenever you use this creation system, you must place the file AFRMDICT.EPS on page 1 of the document (this is a forms dictionary file).

- There is a separate EPS file for each field.

Project Project 14-1. Purple Owl Press: The PFN-Compliant Form

In this project, you will build a simple form. The idea is not to slog through creating a multipage form with hundreds of fields. Instead, the purpose is to show you how to build a PFN-compliant form using the EPS files. You will need the files from the book's CD as well as the EPS files on the Acrobat installation CD.

There are a number of files on the CD in the Chapter 14 Projects folder that represent the different stages in this process:

- *form.doc:* The "raw" document before adding EPS files to it
- *form1.doc:* The completed Word file before conversion
- *form1.pdf:* The converted Word file before adding controls
- *form2.pdf:* The final output

Creating the Source Document

Any authoring program that can read EPS files can be used for creating the source document. Again, the source file we will use is created in Microsoft Word 2000. This is a sample book order form. You will need form.doc, one of the project files (shown in Figure 14-15).

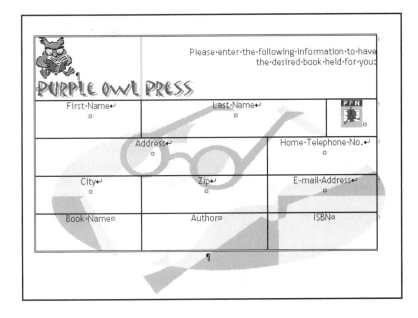

Figure 14-15
The form in its simple layout design phase

Note

For your form-building pleasure, the Chapter 14 Projects folder contains a file named EPSfiles.doc. This is a list of the EPS files from the Acrobat installation CD and their field contents.

1. Open form.doc. You will see that most of the form fields are named. The bottom row of cells will be used in Acrobat for buttons.

2. Insert the EPS files from the installation CD (they are in the Forms\PFN\PFNEPS folder). The field name, the file to insert, and the form field label are listed in Table 14-3. Note the following:

   • The Icon is located in the Forms\PFN folder.

   • The book fields will be added in Acrobat.

   • The Dictionary file, AFRMDICT.EPS, doesn't have a named field; add it to the cell displaying the purple owl.

Table 14-3   The EPS Files You Need to Enter in the Form

Field Name	Add This EPS File:	Which Is Labeled:
First Name	NF.EPS	name.first
Last Name	NL.EPS	name.last
Address	HAL1.EPS	home.address.line1
Home Telephone No.	HTVA.EPS	home.telephone.voice.areacode
Home Telephone No.	BTVN.EPS	business.telephone.voice.number
City	HAC1.EPS	home.address.city
Zip	HAZ.EPS	home.address.zip
E-mail Address	EMAIL.EPS	emailaddress
Book Name	None	None
Author	None	None
ISBN	None	None
-	AFRMDICT.EPS	Dictionary file—not labeled

3. Manipulate the image sizes once the files are imported. Click and drag to generally resize the images. Leave the tweaking until the form is converted to PDF. Do not attempt to format the pictures. Why? Refer to Figure 14-16. As you can see in the dialog box, by manipulating the file itself, you will destroy the PostScript information attached to the file.

Figure 14-16
The message box cautioning against converting the EPS file to a drawing object

Microsoft Word ⌧

? The picture contains embedded PostScript information. Converting it to Word drawing objects will discard any data not seen in the visible metafile. Do you want to proceed anyway?

[OK]   [Cancel]

4. Remove all the table borders. Select the table, and then choose Format ➤ Borders And Shading. In the dialog box, select the None setting on the Borders tab.

5. Save the file as form1.doc. The form is shown in Figure 14-17.

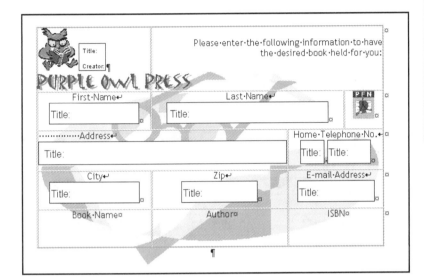

Workflow Tip
Think Before You Work

Beware. Before you convert to PDF and start the customizing process, review the form very, very carefully. Once it is converted and saved, you can't redo any of the EPS files added. The only option is to redo the file in the source application, convert to PDF, and start over with the customizing.

Figure 14-17
The form after we added EPS files

Converting to PDF

Check the settings before you convert the file.

1. Select Acrobat ➤ Change Conversion Settings. Select the Screen option.

2. Click Edit Conversion Settings. When the dialog box opens, change the settings as follows:

   - On the General tab, change the resolution to 300 dpi.

   - On the General tab, change the Compatibility setting to Acrobat 5.

   - On the General tab, ensure the Auto-Rotate option is selected.

   - On the Fonts tab, select the Embed all Fonts option.

3. Save the new settings as Screen(1).

4. In the main PDFMaker dialog box, make these changes:

   - On the General tab, deselect any bookmark options.

   - On the Display tab, select Fit In Window from the Magnification options.

5. Close the Conversion Settings dialog box.

6. Click the Convert To Adobe PDF button, or select Acrobat ➤ Convert To Adobe PDF.

7. When the file launches in Acrobat, save it as form1.pdf. The converted file is shown in Figure 14-18.

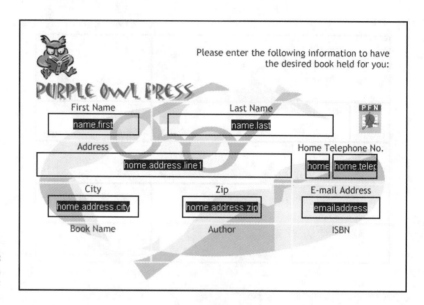

Figure 14-18
The form after we converted it to PDF

Now to finish this form.

Adding Controls and Details

We will add some control buttons to use for managing the form, and some other fields specific to this form.

1. Select all the form fields currently added and resize/align.

2. Reset the layout of the form fields. With all the fields selected, right-click and select Properties. In the Properties dialog box, do the following:

   • Change the border color to dark blue, and deselect the Fill option.

   • Leave the thin border option, and select Beveled from the Style drop-down list.

Adding the Other Fields

Now add the three additional fields that were named in the Word
version of the form.

1. Using the default settings created for the other fields, create three
   additional fields for the book information.

2. Name the fields as listed here:

   a. Book Name: book.name

   b. Author: book.author

   c. ISBN: book.ISBN

The Control Buttons

Now add the three control buttons at the bottom of the form. These
buttons will be used for importing your custom profile, locating and
importing any profile, and clearing the form.

1. Create the three buttons. Distribute them evenly below the book
   information row. Name the buttons ImportSelf, ImportAnyProfile,
   and ClearForm.

2. Set these visual options:

   • Type: button.

   • Border color, width, and style as set for the other fields.

   • Background color: Custom color with RGB value of 254/243/201.

   • Set the Text Color to dark blue, and select Matisse font, size 14 pt.
     (If you don't have Matisse on your system, substitute another
     angular font that is compatible with the logo font.)

3. Name the buttons:

   a. Name the ImportSelf button **Import Profile**.

   b. Name the ImportAnyProfile button **Find A Profile**.

   c. Name the ClearForm button **Clear Form**.

Finally, Some Action (and Some Details)

The last step in finishing the buttons is to add actions. In all three cases,
on the Actions tab, one action triggered by Mouse Up is required.

1. Add the action to the My Profile button.

   a. Click Mouse Up, and then click Add.

   b. Select Import Form Data from the Type drop-down list.

Note

The location of your personal profile will depend on your system settings, as discussed earlier.

c. Click Select File to browse for the location of your profile FDF file location. Select the file and click OK to set the Location.

d. Click Set Action to set the action for the button.

2. Add the action to the Find A Profile button.

a. Click Mouse Up, and then click Add.

b. Select Execute Menu Item from the Type drop-down list.

c. Click Edit Menu Item. Select an execute path of File ➤ Import ➤ Form Data. Click OK.

d. Click Set Action to set the action for the button.

3. Add the action to the Clear Form button.

a. Click Mouse Up, and then click Add.

b. Select Reset Form from the Type drop-down list.

c. Click Select fields, and make sure that All Fields is selected in the Field Selection dialog box. Click OK.

d. Click Set Action to set the action for the button.

4. Check the tab order and make sure it is correct.

5. Crop the page. Select Document ➤ Crop Pages. Set the top margin at 3 in. and the bottom margin at 1 in. Click OK.

6. Save the file as form2.pdf.

Testing the Form

Note

If you are using my copy of the form, you will have a message window instead asking to browse for the file location. My custom settings are not on your computer!

There's not much sense in doing all this work unless we know the thing works. So let's test the form.

1. Click the Import Profile button. The data from the profile you created earlier will automatically be loaded.

2. Click the Clear Form button. The data should be deleted.

3. Click the Find A Profile button. The Explorer dialog box should open to allow you to find a profile to load. Browse to the location, click the FDF file to select it, and click OK. The data should be loaded.

4. Test the tab order, and print a copy. The final version of the form, complete with the profile contents, is shown in Figure 14-19.

And that brings this form-creation process to an end. And the whole chapter, as a matter of fact.

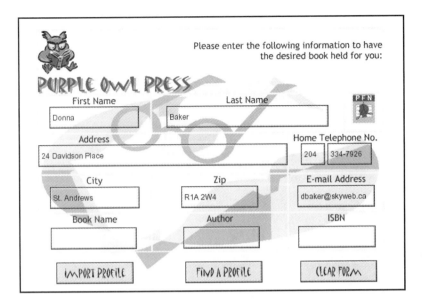

Figure 14-19
The final product, complete
with automatically
entered data

Up Next

Networked workplaces are pervasive. In this chapter, I have shown you
how Acrobat behaves in a networked environment. I touched on the different ways Acrobat can be configured to work in a network. I showed
you how commenting works through a browser in a collaborative process.
And we also looked at forms one last time. I think the PFN-compliant
form is going to be prevalent in the near future. If you have worked
through the project and tutorial in this chapter, you have reached the
cutting edge in online form development. Congratulations!

Up next is a project chapter. Chapter 15 doesn't present any new information. Instead, it integrates many of the functions we have looked at in
previous chapters into one unit. I have developed a case study, workflow,
and projects to give you an idea of how to use Acrobat to its fullest.

Chapter 15

Putting It All Together

Throughout this book, I have shown you many ways to use Acrobat and to integrate processes and principles into the way you work. Here is a sample of what you can do.

Advanced Workflow

In most of the chapters in this book, I have discussed how to do things. Tips for incorporating ideas into your workflow have accompanied the instructions in many cases. In some chapters, I have discussed work-flows at length. That is all well and good if you are working in an environment where Acrobat is part of your arsenal of tools. But what happens if you are not in such an enlightened environment? Or if you are tasked with making the decisions on how to structure and change the way work is being done in your business or organization? The word *daunting* comes to mind.

This kind of involved project requires a specific approach. Like other things in life, complex projects and issues are just a bunch of smaller projects and issues (I usually tell myself that when embarking on a large task). Let me show you how to do it.

What We Are Going to Do

In this chapter, I will take you on a step-by-step journey through a mega project. First, I will give you the scenario we are working with, both as the client and as the information developer, consultant, designer (pick a label). I have developed an outline for defining the scope and parameters of this kind of work, which I will share a bit later.

Then, we will look at the specific elements involved. Basically, the process breaks down into a series of steps:

1. Plan the work to be done.

2. Define the outputs and workflow required.

3. Analyze the available materials for input, and define the conversion workflow.

4. Develop conversion processes.

5. Consider collaboration processes and requirements.

6. Build the final assembly.

7. Make distribution decisions.

Before we get into the projects, though, let's identify the mythical participants in this process: the consultant (you) and the client.

☙ Project ❧ Tutorial: The Plan for This Event

Regardless of the scenario, you are the key to solving the issues. Your expertise, objectivity, and skill are what will make something like this work. It takes a plan. Let's start there.

The Story

You have been hired by a company named Middle Earth AgriProducts.

Welcome to Middle Earth AgriProducts.

The company, based in St. Louis, Missouri, is a distributor of agrichemical products. The company has a small headquarters but a large mobile sales staff. Up to this point, the company's processes have worked fairly well. Two events have occurred in the last year that are changing this scenario, however. First, the company has bought up a number of smaller distributorships, which has increased its sales staff from 12 to 40. Second, it has hired a new CEO, who is technically in tune with what a mobile sales staff can accomplish with the right type of technical support. (And no, his name is not Frodo, or that of any other Tolkien character.)

Your mission (and here is where that catchy tune from the TV series and film starts) is to take this need for better control and management of communications and turn it into a twenty-first–century reality.

Your efforts as an information developer will be done in concert with a significant expansion of the company's use of the Internet. To this point, Middle Earth has only had a brochureware Web site. The new Internet guru is expanding the Web presence, as well as integrating an extranet to be used by the external sales staff, and an intranet for the office staff.

The Planning Process

It's hard to work on a project of any size unless you have planned it first. By way of introduction to this project's scenario, as well as to give you a framework for the subsequent projects, use the template file. On the CD in the Chapter 15 Projects folder, you'll find a planning file, plan.doc. I suggest you print the document so you can refer to it as you work through this chapter. Here is a summary of what is on the finished project outline.

Scenario

The scenario, given in the earlier sidebar "The Story," describes the company, what it needs, and why.

Objectives

Objectives define what we will do. To facilitate technological advances in communication within the company, we will design some online forms and support materials for different processes, as well as instructional materials. We are bound by time and design constraints.

Workflow and Responsibilities

This section defines what has to be done in addition to the design and construction itself. Responsibilities include information gathering, information design, mockups, and consultation with the company's key personnel. Workflow includes the sign-off processes (editing, collaboration, and approval).

Inputs

Inputs tell us what is available. Frankly, we don't have much. The company has used a fax form for ordering, as well as an expense sheet that is photocopied and submitted with expense receipts.

Note

There are other elements I have not included in the project plan because they are beyond the scope of this chapter. Training issues, user guides, and schedules are not included. Nor have I covered hardware/ software purchases and implementations, which I would do in a commercial project.

Outputs

Outputs represent the deliverables. In this project, there are several—specifically:

- Information flow diagrams for the proposed process

- New forms: the Order form and Expense form

- New form data input forms: customers, sales staff

- Database for product information (which is not addressed in this chapter)

So, it's time for the next step.

Project Tutorial: Information Flow Design

This section is a show and tell. In addition to completing the plan document, which is the first step of any project process, it is equally important to understand how information is flowing through a system.

A visual representation of what you understand the situation to be and the changes you are planning—similar to a storyboard—is a very useful tool. To start with, let's establish the current information flow for the two main structures we will be building.

The Current Situation

Nothing in the current workings of Middle Earth can be classified as streamlined. In fact, the case is just the opposite. Let's look first at the order process, and then we will examine the expense claims process.

Order Up

First, let's consider the situation as it currently exists. In Figure 15-1, I have created an information flow. I'll go through what you see in the flowchart.

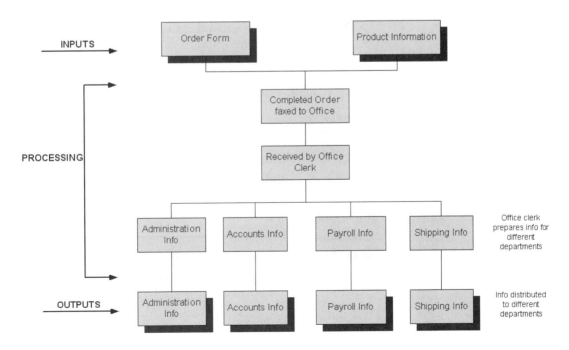

Figure 15-1
The current status of the ordering process

The process is labor intensive and time intensive—as well as inefficient. The flowcharts are broken into three components: inputs, processing, and outputs.

- *Inputs:* Salespeople manually fill in an order form. To complete an order form, they must manually enter product information from their reference materials. They must also add customer information and their own identification information.

- *Processing:* The completed order form is faxed to the head office. A clerk at the office transfers the material from the fax to a number of other internal forms for internal distribution. Based on the workflow, the clerk will have to transfer the information to four separate documents.

- *Outputs:* The separate forms are sent to the different departments for action:

  - Administration (sales) will have information on the entire sale for reference.

  - Accounts will have information on both the sale to the customer for billing, as well as product information to use for supplier accounts.

  - Payroll will need the amount of the sale to use for calculating the salesperson's commission.

  - Shipping will need product order and customer information for shipping product.

Now, isn't that complicated? No, not complicated in terms of the use of the information, but in terms of the need to re-create the same data over and over for different users.

Let's now have a look at the salesperson's expense-claim process.

Making a Claim

The salesperson's expense-claim process is no less convoluted than the ordering process. I have it mapped out in Figure 15-2. Let's go through it.

Again, we are looking at significant inefficiencies.

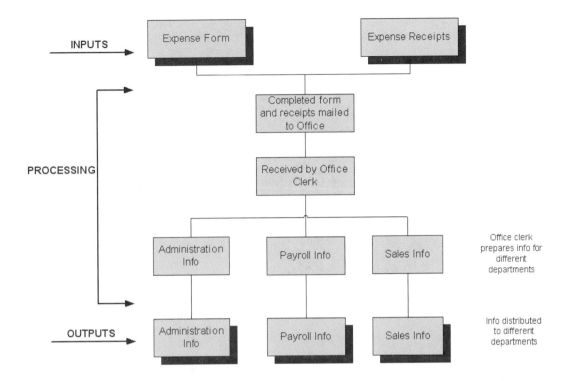

Figure 15-2
The current expense claim process

- *Input:* The salesperson must manually complete an expense form with employee information, collect receipts, and manually enter the information on the expense form.

- *Processing:* Once completed, the form and receipts are mailed to the office. Again, the office clerk has to sort and forward the information, and prepare information for different areas. General administration gets some information, the sales department will approve the expenses, and payroll is responsible for accounting processes and reimbursing expenses.

Contrast that process with what we are about to create.

Why Use a PDF-Based Workflow Instead of an HTML-Based Workflow?

Because that's the subject of another book! Seriously, though, there are significant advantages to using PDF instead of HTML. Once the forms are redesigned, they can be used either online or offline. The project plan contains a section at the end outlining a second phase where the customers can actually place their own orders. The form format will remain constant. The forms also look the same printed as online, of course, which complies with Middle Earth's desire to maintain its corporate identity.

Forms are easier to update in PDF than in HTML, and the Form Data Format (FDF) data source is easily updateable as well. As we will see in Chapter 16, the JavaScript used in Acrobat forms is different from that used in HTML forms, which is an added security feature. Finally, because the forms use JavaScript scripting, server-side scripts can still be used.

New and Improved Information Workflows

Now let's see what happens when Acrobat is introduced into the mix. First, we will look at the order process.

Streamline the Order Process

Figure 15-3 shows the revamped information flow plan for this process. As you can see, there are a number of differences.

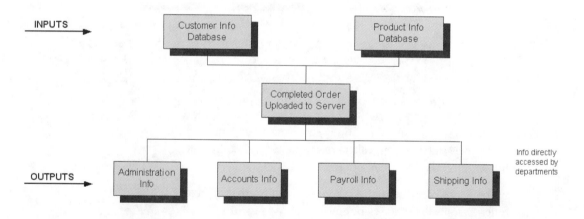

Figure 15-3
The modified order process

Note

We are not constructing the product database in this chapter, due to space constraints and unknown server capabilities.

The most noticeable change is that the hierarchy is flattened. There is no "middleman" in this process and no processing of any kind. The inputs are not added manually. Consider how much time will be saved over the course of even a single month. Once the name of the product is entered, the rest of the information will be automatically entered from the database. The same thing applies to the customer information as well.

At the other end, the process is equally enhanced from a time perspective. Anyone authorized to use the information from the order can access it directly. The company will benefit from the shortened communication cycle in a number of ways, ranging from enhanced customer relations to more efficient supplier payments.

Now, let's have a look at the modified expense claim process.

Pay Up

Figure 15-4 shows the modified salesperson expense process. Again, you can see that the process is flattened considerably.

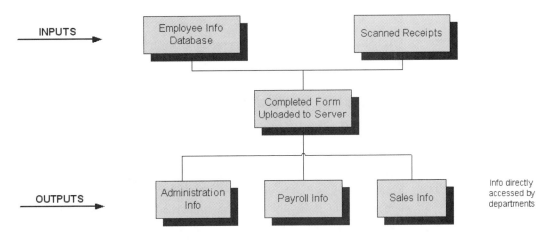

Figure 15-4
The new and improved employee-expense form process

Again, the employee information can be autofilled in the form. Depending on circumstances, expenses such as mileage can be drawn from an FDF file source as well. This process will require that salespeople have access to a scanner. Considering the current prices for scanners, that isn't an unreasonable expense, even with an increased sales force of 40.

Once the input has been completed by the salesperson and uploaded to the server, it is again available by those areas directly involved. The advantages? Aside from decreased processing time in the head office, the salesperson will likely find a faster turnaround from submitting to receiving reimbursement—all without depending on mail systems.

Training Requirements

The new processes will require the sales staff to learn to use a scanner, Acrobat Reader, and the Internet. This is in addition to general computer use training, which may be required for some staff. Headquarters staff will have to learn to use Acrobat, in particular the commenting and security features. And someone (perhaps the nearly displaced office clerk) will have to learn how to work with the form files and to use and maintain the FDF files and the product database, which store the data for the different input components.

Tackling the Project Construction

The actual work schedule you decide on is based as much on how you like to work as it is on the work and approval processes themselves. Incorporate how you work from the initial planning stage. You will likely have to coordinate your preferences with information gathering, information design, mockups, and approval processes.

Following the Data

Let's follow a single file element through this series of projects. In Chapter 14, I discussed the Personal Field Name (PFN) type of forms. Rather than having to link form data with tables using scripting or code, you use EPS files that have code elements bound to them. These elements are referred to as *widgets*. The whole thing is administered by another EPS file, which is a dictionary. Here's how the process works through the system:

1. First the widget called FN.EPS (first name) is inserted in the Staff Information data entry form, which is then converted to PDF, translating the embedded pdfmark code.

2. Data is entered in the form and then exported to an FDF file for storage.

3. The FN.EPS widget is again inserted on the Customer Order form, the salesperson's first name file is again inserted into a name block, and the name is translated when the file is converted to PDF.

4. A button on the order form will run an Insert Form Data command. The file is selected. Information from the selected file that corresponds with the FN.EPS (first name) field is automatically entered.

5. A button with the same actions is also on the Expense form. Clicking this button will import the same information from the same field into the converted FN.EPS field in this table.

If more forms were created for this company—for example, payroll, benefits, and the like—the same two processes would apply: You'd embed the same EPS file and then import the data. It takes more time to plan this type of form set, but it saves a lot of time for users.

One more short discussion, and then it's building time.

Design the Information Content

You may want to refer to information in earlier chapters, particularly Chapters 10 and 14. The Acrobat installation CD contains many EPS files that can be customized and used for other purposes. Here's how I did it:

1. In Notepad (or another text editor), open any of the EPS files but the dictionary. I have selected NF.EPS, as shown in Figure 15-5. You will have to select the All Files option from the Files Of Type drop-down list.

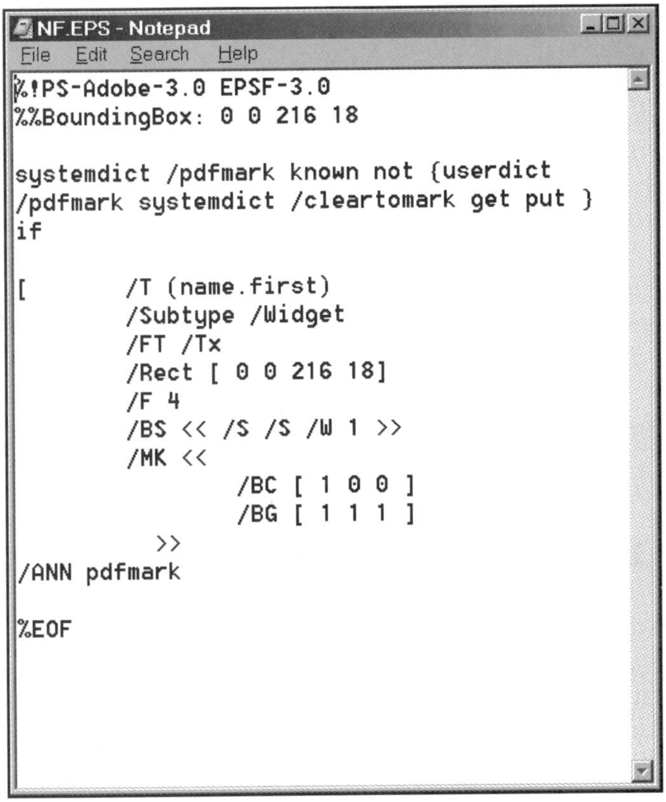

```
NF.EPS - Notepad                              _ □ X
 File   Edit   Search   Help
%!PS-Adobe-3.0 EPSF-3.0
%%BoundingBox: 0 0 216 18

systemdict /pdfmark known not {userdict
/pdfmark systemdict /cleartomark get put }
if

[       /T (name.first)
        /Subtype /Widget
        /FT /Tx
        /Rect [ 0 0 216 18]
        /F 4
        /BS << /S /S /W 1 >>
        /MK <<
                /BC [ 1 0 0 ]
                /BG [ 1 1 1 ]
        >>
/ANN pdfmark

%EOF
```

Figure 15-5
The original EPS file

2. Change the field name, as shown in Figure 15-6. Use a name from a common root, and then add a description. In the figure, the new field name is (business.contact.name).

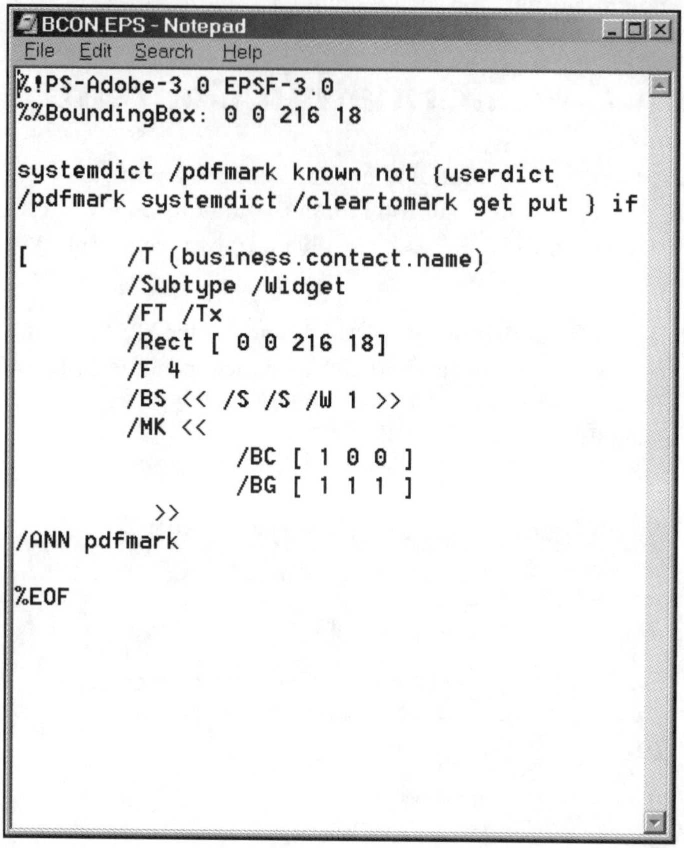

```
BCON.EPS - Notepad                                    _ □ ×
File   Edit   Search   Help
%!PS-Adobe-3.0 EPSF-3.0
%%BoundingBox: 0 0 216 18

systemdict /pdfmark known not {userdict
/pdfmark systemdict /cleartomark get put } if

[          /T (business.contact.name)
           /Subtype /Widget
           /FT /Tx
           /Rect [ 0 0 216 18]
           /F 4
           /BS << /S /S /W 1 >>
           /MK <<
                    /BC [ 1 0 0 ]
                    /BG [ 1 1 1 ]
               >>
/ANN pdfmark

%EOF
```

Figure 15-6
The modified EPS file

3. Save the file using the naming structure of the EPS file system. I named the file BCON.EPS, because several custom fields are required.

Organizing Your Information

I can't stress organization enough. You have to consider many things when building something complex. These are some of the most important, at least from the perspective of making these files actually work. After all, they can be stunning visually, but if they don't work. . . .

We are going to use the files provided by Acrobat in constructing these forms. Is this the best way to go? Not necessarily. We are using them in the interest of expediency and to demonstrate how the entire interrelated system works.

In a large project, you may want to go an alternate route. A large project, one in which you were building this information from very large tables using hundreds of products, and as many employees and customers, would not be served by this set of files.

Alternate Approaches

In all likelihood, I would use one of two approaches, depending on what the client wants (which it always boils down to). The form data could be coded, named, and coordinated with a database administrator (DBA). This would make my role more graphic design–oriented. In all likelihood, I would use a DBA for design of the product information database, because it requires a fair amount of custom scripting. If I were responsible for the design of the entire project, I would rebuild the set of EPS files.

If I were designing the entire process from scratch, I would rename all the files, resize them (the current size is too awkward for my liking), and rename all the fields according to the layouts of the table I was creating. For example, I would establish three roots:

- business

- staff

- product

Using these three roots, I would add the specific fields, such as names, telephone numbers, and the like. That is beyond what I want to show you here, though.

Project Files

Rather than listing all the files as they appear, here is an outline of the scheme I used. All the files you will need are on the CD in the Chapter 15 Projects folder.

- *Data entry forms:* These two forms have both XLS and PDF versions. In Acrobat, I have two versions: one that I started out with on conversion, and one that is completed.

- *EPS files:* A collection of standard Adobe and custom form field EPS files is available.

- *Customer Order and Employee Expense forms:* Both DOC and PDF versions of these files are available. Again, there are two PDF versions: one that I started out with on conversion, and one that is completed.

Now let's do the first project.

Project Project 15-1. Forms for Information Gathering

Note

I used Excel to create these forms for three reasons. First, this is a working document, so it doesn't need to have an enormous amount of formatting. Second, by building the form as I did, I could very clearly see what I was doing—the focus is on content, not appearance. Third, I could easily select all the EPS files to resize them as a group in this layout.

This chapter's first hands-on project involves building the data entry forms that are used to create the profiles. You will need a set of two forms for this: staff and customer.

Build the Data Entry Forms

In the form, as shown in Figure 15-7, I have included two columns: one for the EPS file name and the other for the Field name. This is more for demonstration purposes than an actual design requirement, but it does show you how they are constructed. To build these forms yourself, you may exclude the two columns. The content for each file is included in forms.doc, which is on the CD in the Chapter 15 Projects folder. The forms.doc file also includes some sample data to use for the product form, which we will use in the next project.

EPS files are inserted in Column B (which you can see by the Title appearing in the cells).

For each form, follow these steps:

1. Open a new Excel worksheet.

2. Insert the logo.tif file from the CD (Column A, Row 1).

3. Enter the field names that will appear on the forms (Column A).

4. Insert and resize the matching EPS files from the CD (Column B).

5. Insert the Acrobat form dictionary file, AFRMDICT.EPS, from the CD. It may be located anywhere on the page. I inserted it after the other rows.

6. Save the files as staff.xls and customer.xls.

Now print the files to Distiller.

Figure 15-7
The customer data entry form

1. The Edit Conversion Settings dialog box will open. Make these changes:

   - *General tab:* Acrobat 5 compatibility; select Fast Web View and Embed Thumbnails; deselect Auto Rotate.

   - *Compression tab:* Leave screen settings, but change Color images to 300dpi (this is beyond screen resolution requirements, but it will suffice for printing).

   - *Fonts tab:* Select both options (to embed all fonts and to subset fonts); set the subset value at 100%.

   - *Color tab:* Use the Web Graphics Default setting.

   - *Advanced tab:* Leave the default settings; make sure Convert Gradients To Smooth Shades is selected.

2. Click Save As, and save the new settings as screen(1).joboptions. Click OK. When you click back to the main Print dialog box, click OK to convert the file.

3. At the Print Save prompt, accept the default name.

You will finish with two PDF files: staff.pdf and customer.pdf.

Note

You will see that the page is displayed in CMYK using US Web Coated (SWOP) v2 settings—these were carried over from Photoshop with the logo.

Using the Forms

This project deals with sales staff, but the form could easily be used for any employees. I suggest that if you are building it as a working system, include other information about dental and medical plans, deductions, payroll plans, and the like. That will give you the maximum use of the form data regardless of what form is accessing it.

Each form may be used many times. This way, you can add as many staff, customers, or products as you need. Make sure you also develop a naming system for the FDF to make the files easy to access and manage.

Now we have the two files created for adding form data. Let's modify the forms in Acrobat and create some sample data to use later in the chapter.

Project **Project 15-2. Adding Sample Data**

For this project, you will need the two Acrobat files you created in the last project: staff.pdf and customer.pdf. Remember that these forms will be used only for creating FDF files that Middle Earth's staff can use later for completing customer orders or expense forms.

Finishing Touches on the Forms

Again, let's batch these processes, starting with the staff.pdf file.

1. Open customer.pdf in Acrobat. The file will look like the one shown in Figure 15-8.

2. Resize the fields as necessary to fit within the boundaries of the cells.

3. Select all form fields, and set the font size to Helvetica 9 pt.

4. Add three buttons: for resetting the form, for printing, and for exporting. Use these settings for the Reset button:

   - *Name:* **reset**; *Type:* Button

   - *Appearance tab:* Border Color: dark red; Background Color: white; Width: Medium; Style: Beveled; Text Color: Black, Arial Bold Italic, 10 pt.

   - *Options tab:* Text: **Reset**

   - *Actions tab:* Add an action on Mouse Up: Reset Form. Select the option to reset all fields. Click Set Action.

5. Click OK to close the Field Properties dialog box.

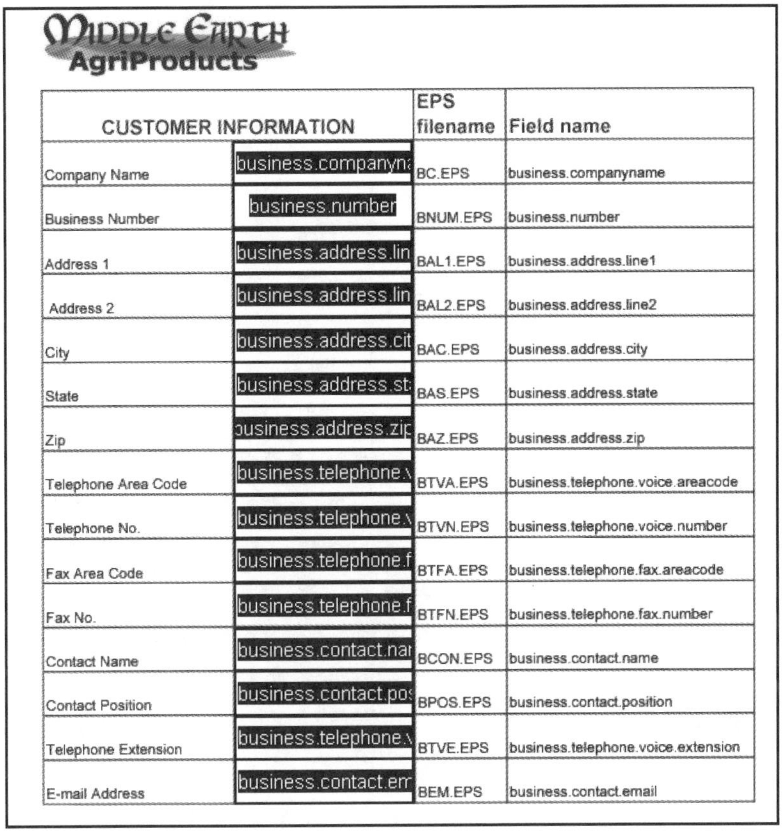

Figure 15-8
The Customer Information data entry file

6. Use the same settings for the Print button except

- *Name:* **print**

- *Options tab:* Text: **Print**

- *Actions tab:* Add an action on Mouse Up: Execute Menu Item. Select File ➤ Print. Click Set Action.

7. Use the same settings for the Export button except

- *Name:* **export**

- *Options tab:* Text: **Export**

- *Actions tab:* Add an action on Mouse Up: Execute Menu Item. Select File ➤ Export ➤ Form Data. Click Set Action.

8. Check the tab order to make sure it is correct. Save the file as product1.pdf. The finished version is shown in Figure 15-9. It isn't fancy, but it will certainly do the job. As you can see in the figure, I have created the file using the file name columns, again for illustration.

Workflow Tip

Make the Files Secure

This would be the time to secure the files as well. Protect the file by adding passwords. I have not added security to the sample files.

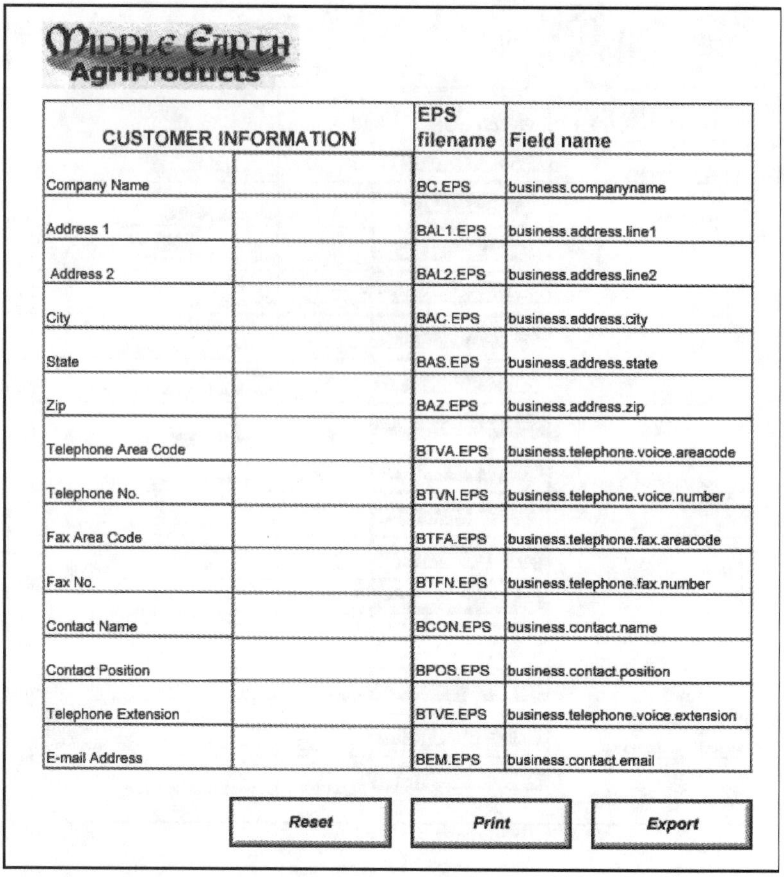

Middle Earth AgriProducts

CUSTOMER INFORMATION		EPS filename	Field name
Company Name		BC.EPS	business.companyname
Address 1		BAL1.EPS	business.address.line1
Address 2		BAL2.EPS	business.address.line2
City		BAC.EPS	business.address.city
State		BAS.EPS	business.address.state
Zip		BAZ.EPS	business.address.zip
Telephone Area Code		BTVA.EPS	business.telephone.voice.areacode
Telephone No.		BTVN.EPS	business.telephone.voice.number
Fax Area Code		BTFA.EPS	business.telephone.fax.areacode
Fax No.		BTFN.EPS	business.telephone.fax.number
Contact Name		BCON.EPS	business.contact.name
Contact Position		BPOS.EPS	business.contact.position
Telephone Extension		BTVE.EPS	business.telephone.voice.extension
E-mail Address		BEM.EPS	business.contact.email

Reset Print Export

Figure 15-9 The finished customer data input form

Repeat the process with the other file. Finished copies of the files—custom1.pdf and staff1.pdf—are on the CD.

Note

Although these forms use PFD Compliant content, I have not included the logo on the data entry forms. I have used a fair number of custom elements, and I could not determine if this was within the scope of the logo's usage.

Adding Sample Data

One last process before we get back to the pretty forms. We need some sample data. I have included sample content for the custom1.pdf file. It is available on the CD in a file named GBAir.fdf. The data added to the form is shown in Figure 15-10.

Use any kind of imaginary staff data for the files. Since this is a PFD Compliant form, you may choose to use the FDF file created in Chapter 14 rather than adding information to this chapter's staff1.pdf form.

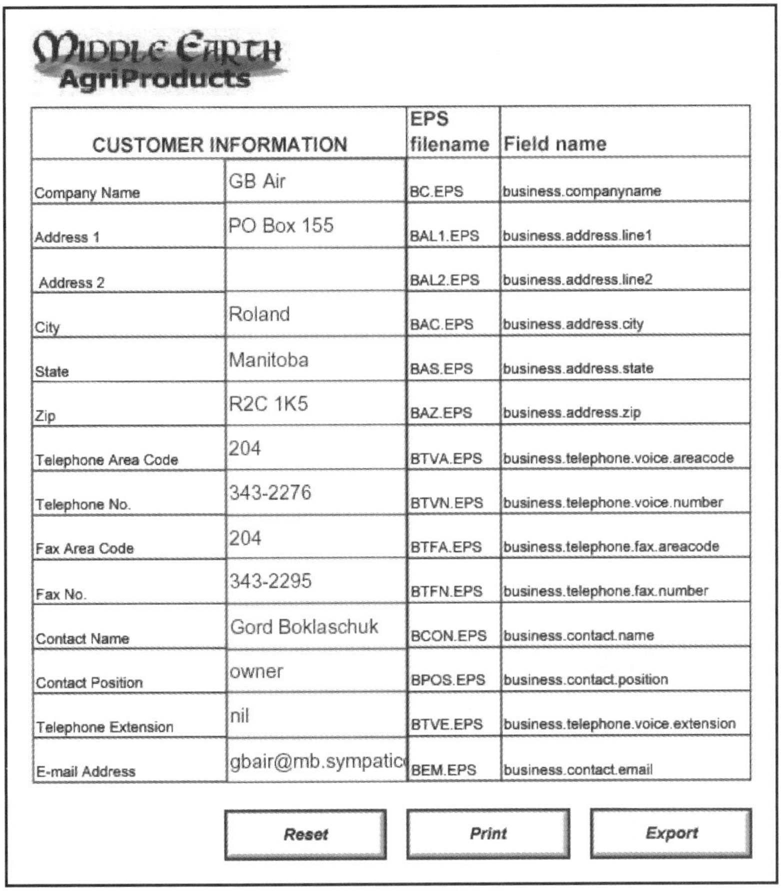

CUSTOMER INFORMATION		EPS filename	Field name
Company Name	GB Air	BC.EPS	business.companyname
Address 1	PO Box 155	BAL1.EPS	business.address.line1
Address 2		BAL2.EPS	business.address.line2
City	Roland	BAC.EPS	business.address.city
State	Manitoba	BAS.EPS	business.address.state
Zip	R2C 1K5	BAZ.EPS	business.address.zip
Telephone Area Code	204	BTVA.EPS	business.telephone.voice.areacode
Telephone No.	343-2276	BTVN.EPS	business.telephone.voice.number
Fax Area Code	204	BTFA.EPS	business.telephone.fax.areacode
Fax No.	343-2295	BTFN.EPS	business.telephone.fax.number
Contact Name	Gord Boklaschuk	BCON.EPS	business.contact.name
Contact Position	owner	BPOS.EPS	business.contact.position
Telephone Extension	nil	BTVE.EPS	business.telephone.voice.extension
E-mail Address	gbair@mb.sympatic	BEM.EPS	business.contact.email

Reset	Print	Export

Figure 15-10
The form with the sample data entered

Project Project 15-3. Back to the Original Forms

To continue with our scenario, I said that the order form had a digital format, and the expense form was a photocopied form whose origins are lost in history. For the sake of simplicity, I have re-created both forms. Let's take care of the product ordering form first. You will need the source file, which is called order.doc.

Preparing the Order Form

Convert the file using Acrobat Distiller. The logo.tif file is already embedded in the file. The layout of the basic form is shown in Figure 15-11.

Product Order Form

4500 McDonnell Blvd. St. Louis, MI 63134

(314) 422-5915   fax (314) 427-4326

Title:

Creator:

Customer No.	
Invoice No.	

Customer Information

Company Name			
Street Address		Fax No.	
City		Phone No.	
State		Contact Name:	
Zip		Extension:	
Shipping Instructions:			

Order Information

Product Name	Product No.	Unit	Unit Price	Quantity	Subtotal
				Subtotal	
				Tax	
				Shipping Cost	
				Grand Total	

Ordered By:	Date:	Signature:
Comments:		

Figure 15-11

The Product Order Form before modification and conversion

To prepare this file for conversion, follow these steps:

1. Resize the columns in the Order Information table. Select all columns except the Product Name column, and click the Distribute Columns Evenly button on the Table toolbar.

2. Resize the text heading for the Product No. column. Select the text, and then choose Format ➤ Font ➤ Character Spacing. Set the Condensed setting to 1 pt. Click OK and close the dialog box.

Finishing the Product Order Form

This is the same general process as the one used for the data entry forms. Complete the sections using the information from the figures.

1. Refer to Figure 15-12. I have added the names of the EPS files you will need to add to the file.

MIDDLE EARTH AgriProducts

4500 McDonnell Blvd. St. Louis, MI 63134

(314) 422-5915   fax (314) 427-4326

Product Order Form

Customer No.	BNUM.EPS
Invoice No.	

Customer Information

Company Name	BC.EPS		
Street Address	BAL1.EPS	Fax No.	BTFA.EPS BTFN.EPS
City	BAC.EPS	Phone No.	BTVA.EPS BTVN.EPS
State	BAS.EPS	Contact Name:	BCON.EPS (BPOS.EPS)
Zip	BAZ.EPS	Extension:	BTVE.EPS
Shipping Instructions:			

Figure 15-12
The named customer EPS files

2. In addition to the files shown in Figure 15-12, you will need to insert the first.name and last.name files in the Ordered By field at the lower part of the form (the file names are NF.EPS and NL.EPS).

3. Resize the EPS file sizes to correspond with the cell size.

4. Save the file as order1.doc.

5. Select File ➤ Print and select Acrobat Distiller from the drop-down list of printers.

6. Click Properties. Then click the Adobe PDF Settings tab. From the drop-down list, select the custom settings file created earlier named screen(1).joboptions.

7. Click Apply to apply the settings and close the dialog box. Then click OK in the Print dialog box.

8. At the Save As prompt, name the file order.pdf. Save the file.

Tagging the File

We have to make one change in the PDF file at this point. We converted the file using Distiller, so it is untagged. Adding tags from within Acrobat makes the process much cleaner.

1. Select Document ➤ Make Accessible.

2. Open the Tags palette. As shown in Figure 15-13, the file now includes a set of tags.

Note

You will need to download and install the Make Accessible plug-in, which was described in Chapter 8.

Note

Figure 15-13 shows an alternate tags layout based on another version of the file. I grouped the color bars and text in Word. When the files are converted to PDF, these grouped images will convert as one PDF image.

```
⊟    Tags Root
  ⊟      <Figure>
    └       PDF Image  w: 205 h: 57
  ⊟      <Part>
    ⊟      <H1>
      └       Product Order Form
    ⊞      <P>
    ⊞      <P>
    ⊟      <Sect>
      ⊞      <P>
      ⊟      <Figure>
        └       PDF Image  w: 469 h: 27
      ⊟      <P>
        └       Company Name ☐Street …
      ⊟      <Figure>
        └       PDF Image  w: 469 h: 27
      ⊞      <P>
      ⊞      <P>
      ⊞      <P>
```

Figure 15-13
The file is now tagged.

3. Save the file as order1.pdf.

Now for the Expense form.

Preparing the Expense Form

To prepare this file for conversion, follow these steps:

1. Resize the columns in the Expense Information table. Set the width of each column as shown in Table 15-1. Select the column, and then select Table ➤ Table Properties ➤ Column and set the column width in inches.

Table 15-1 Settings for Column Widths

Column	✓	Date	Type	Description	Amount	Cost	Subtotal
width	0.38 in.	0.7 in.	0.7 in.	2.6 in.	0.7 in.	0.7 in.	0.7 in.

2. Again, the point is to have as many columns as practical of equal widths to simplify the field insertion in Acrobat.

3. Reset any text headings that need condensing.

4. Insert the EPS files into their respective locations, as shown in Figure 15-14. Again, don't forget the AFRMDICT.EPS dictionary file (not shown in the figure).

5. Resize the EPS file sizes to correspond with the cell size.

6. Save the file as expense1.doc.

Finally, convert the file to PDF, using the same process and settings as you did with the Order Form. Again, once the file is open in Acrobat, select Document ➤ Make Accessible. The tags will now be added to the file. Save the file as expense1.pdf.

Workflow Tip
Working in Batches

You may have been wondering why I have developed these forms and converted them in concert. I had two reasons for doing this. First, I prefer to work in batches. Once I have built something to my satisfaction, I prefer to do the same thing throughout. Second, when the settings are still fresh in my mind, if something I hadn't anticipated occurs further down the conversion process, I can more readily go back to other components and change them if need be.

Employee Expense Form

Employee No.	ENUM.EPS
Expense Period	

4500 McDonnell Blvd. St. Louis, MI 63134

(314) 422-5915   fax (314) 427-4326

Employee Information

Employee Name NF.EPS   NI.EPS   NL.EPS

Street Address HAL1.EPS

City HACI.EPS	Phone No. HTVA.EPS HTVN.EPS

State HAS.EPS	Zip HAZ.EPS	Email EMAIL.EPS

Figure 15-14
Place the EPS files as shown in this figure.

Project Project 15-4. The Final Order Form

This project picks up where the last one left off, and we will work in concert with the two files again. Start with your version of the Product Order Form. Or you can follow along with order1.pdf, the completed version on the CD. To finish this form, we have to do the following:

- Modify the imported EPS fields.

- Add product fields.

- Add calculated fields.

- Add control buttons.

Modifying the imported fields is simple.

1. Select all the fields.

2. Right-click, and then select Properties from the context menu.

3. Change the appearance by deselecting the border option and selecting a pale version of the dark gold color (such as RGB 245/242/237) for the background.
4. Change the font to Helvetica 9 pt.
5. Click OK. Save the file as order2.pdf.

> **Note**
> Don't leave the fields totally invisible because some lines contain more than one field, such as the name. Also, if you want, you may resize and move the fields to your own preferences.

Adding the Product Fields to the Order Form

The PDF file contains all the customer information required. The only task remaining is to add the fields in the product section, as well as some buttons. The section of the form complete with all its fields is shown in Figure 15-15.

> **Note**
> The Invoice No. will change each time a new invoice is generated by the company. This number will be manually entered, as will the shipping instructions.

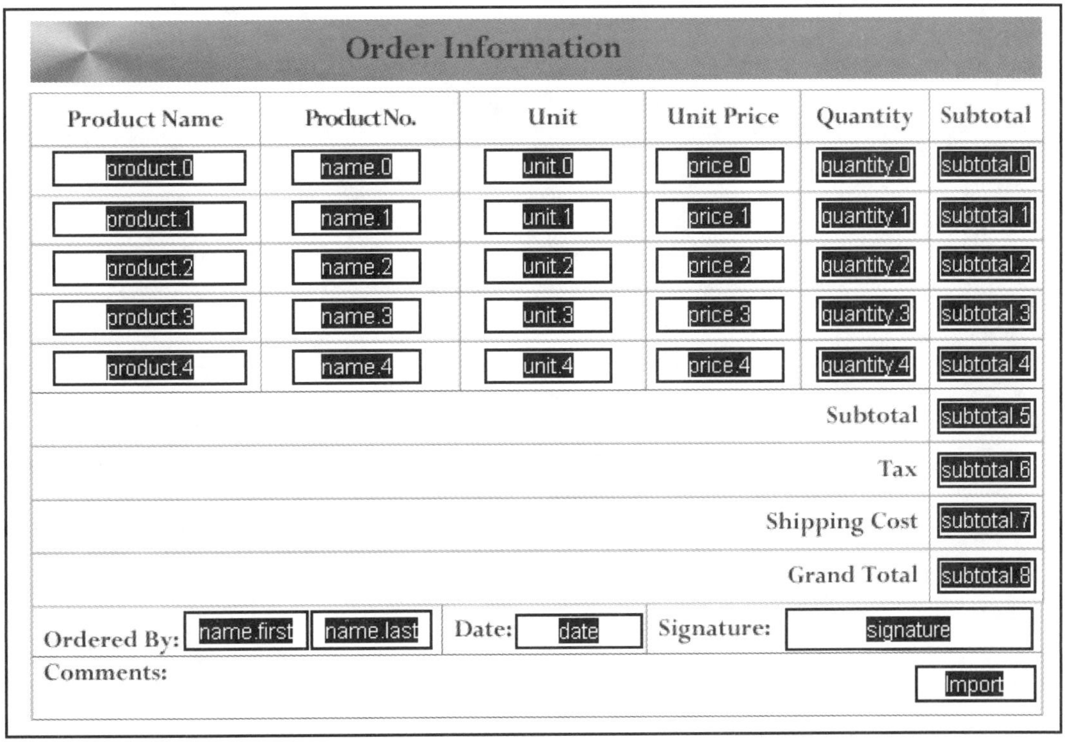

Order Information

Product Name	Product No.	Unit	Unit Price	Quantity	Subtotal
product.0	name.0	unit.0	price.0	quantity.0	subtotal.0
product.1	name.1	unit.1	price.1	quantity.1	subtotal.1
product.2	name.2	unit.2	price.2	quantity.2	subtotal.2
product.3	name.3	unit.3	price.3	quantity.3	subtotal.3
product.4	name.4	unit.4	price.4	quantity.4	subtotal.4
				Subtotal	subtotal.5
				Tax	subtotal.6
				Shipping Cost	subtotal.7
				Grand Total	subtotal.8

Ordered By: name.first name.last Date: date Signature: signature

Comments: Import

Figure 15-15
The completed product component of the Customer Order Form

1. Add the first field, product.0. The first four columns will be combo boxes.

2. Set these Appearance settings for the first field, as shown in Figure 15-16:

   - *Background Color:* Should default to the earlier color

   - *Font:* Helvetica 8 pt.

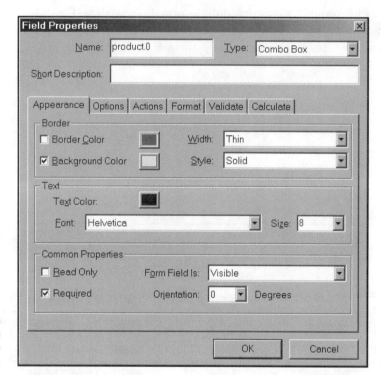

Figure 15-16
Use these Appearance
settings for the
Combo Box fields.

3. Add the following to the Options tab, as shown in Figure 15-17:

   - Add three items: a blank (add by pressing the spacebar and then clicking Add), Roundup Brush Killer, and Roundup Sure Shot Foam.

4. Click OK to set the properties.

5. Copy and rename the remaining four fields in that column.

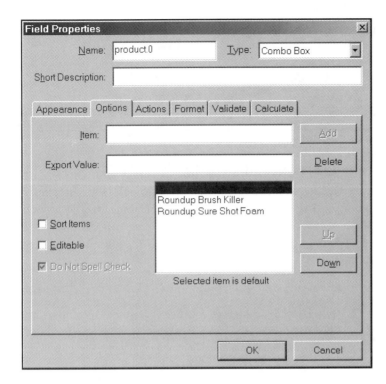

Figure 15-17
Add the Combo
Box options.

The other Combo Box fields will be formatted in the same way. Change the specific values as shown in Table 15-2.

Table 15-2   The Settings for the Remaining Combo Box Fields

Column	Field Name	Option 1	Option 2
Product No.	name	MR-BK	MR-SSF
Unit	unit	quart	pound
Unit Price	price	17.00	19.50

Now save the file. As shown in Figure 15-18, the options are available from drop-down lists.

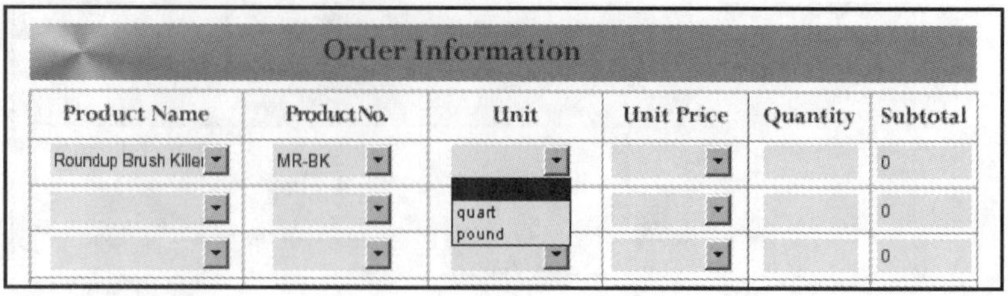

Figure 15-18
The combo box in action

Adding Fields for Special Totals

Now add fields for the subtotal of the order, sales tax, shipping, and the grand total. Copy the subtotal.4 field, and change the copies to subtotal.5, subtotal.6, subtotal.7, and subtotal.8. The only field properties that will need changing are the calculations. Refer to Figure 15-15 if necessary.

1. *For subtotal.5:* Set Value is the sum (+) of the following fields: "subtotal.0", "subtotal.1", "subtotal.2", "subtotal.3", "subtotal.4".

2. *For subtotal.6 (tax at 9 percent):* Select Custom Calculation Script. Click Edit to open the JavaScript window. Add these two lines of code:

```
var a = this.getField("subtotal.5");
event.value = a.value *0.09;
```

3. *For subtotal.7 (shipping at 10 percent):* Select Custom Calculation Script. Click Edit to open the JavaScript window. Add these two lines of code:

```
var a = this.getField("subtotal.5");
event.value = a.value*0.10;
```

4. *For subtotal.8:* Add the Currency symbol: Dollar in the Format tab. In the Calculate tab, Set Value is the sum (+) of the following fields: "subtotal.5", "subtotal.6", "subtotal.7".

5. Save the form and test it with some test data. You may have to set the calculation order. If so, select Field ➤ Set Field Calculation Order and order the list.

Adding Button Fields

Next up, let's add Import Info and Clear buttons to the form. I added these two form elements to the front page, as shown in Figure 15-19.

> **Note**
>
> For different taxation in different regions of the country, make alternate versions of this form available, or add another field for the salesperson to manually enter the sales tax amount, which is then calculated as the product of the sales tax and the subtotal.

> **Note**
>
> You can find more information on calculating fields in Chapter 16.

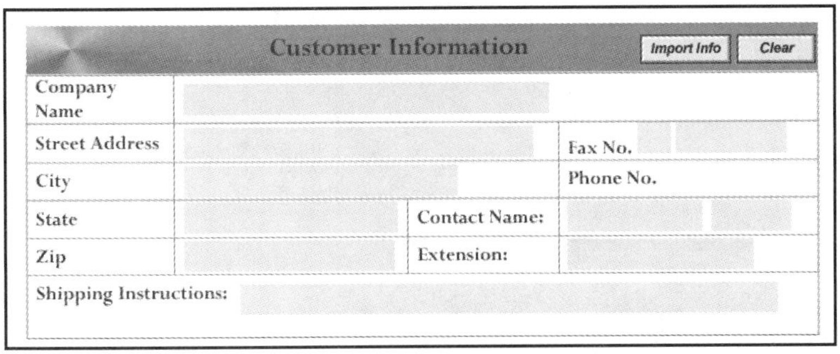

Figure 15-19
Add form elements to the Customer Information section.

1. Click and drag to create a new field. Name it **Info**. Select the Button Type. Use these settings in the Appearance tab:

   - *Border Color:* dark red

   - *Background Color:* Defaults to the beige set much earlier

   - *Width:* Thin

   - *Style:* Beveled

   - *Text:* color black, Arial Bold Italic 8 pt.

2. On the Options tab, enter **Import Info** for the Button Face Attributes text.

3. On the Actions tab, add a Mouse Up action: Execute Menu Item. Select File ➤ Import ➤ Form Data as the menu item.

4. Click Set Action to close the Action dialog box. Click OK to set the properties for the button.

5. Save the file.

Now add the second button:

1. Click and drag the Info button. Open the Field Properties dialog box. Name this button **clear**.

2. Leave the Appearance tab settings as they are. Click the Options tab and change the Text to **Clear**.

3. Click the Actions tab. Delete the action displayed. Click Add, and select Reset Form from the Type drop-down list.

4. Double-click the Select Fields button to open the options list shown in Figure 15-20. Select the Only These radio button, and click Select Fields again.

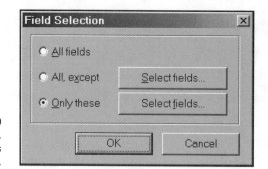

Figure 15-20
Select the last option.
There are too many fields
to exclude from the list.

5. The Field Selection dialog box shown in Figure 15-21 will open. As you can see, all the fields that belong to the business root are included.

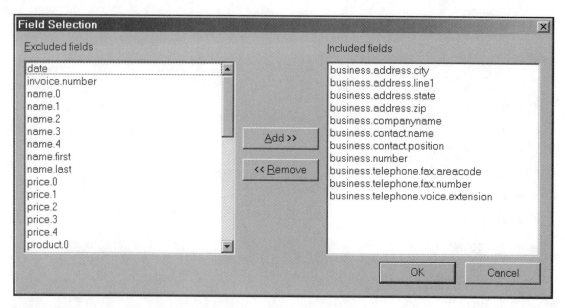

Figure 15-21
Select the list of fields to clear with the action.

6. Click OK twice, and then click Set Action to set the action. Click OK to close the Field Properties dialog box.

One final button for this form. At the bottom of the form, as shown in Figure 15-22, I have added another button to use for importing salesperson information. The button is named Import, and I added **PFN** as the text. It uses the same Execute Menu Item command for the Mouse Up action as the earlier data import button—that is, File ➤ Import ➤ Form Data.

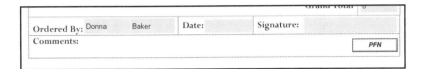

Figure 15-22
The final button in position

Save the file. Now enter some test data and try out the new functions.

Jazzing It Up

Want to do more with this file? Here are some possible enhancements:

- Format the date field using a Document JavaScript to enter the date automatically.

- Program the combo boxes in the Product Ordering section to automatically pull the values for each option.

- Add more buttons, clear the PFN data entered, add Print options, and the like.

By the way, I will show you how to do these kinds of form enhancements in Chapter 16. The point of this form was to show you how to use different data sources in one file, and then to be able to manipulate the information selectively. I think we have achieved that. Now to finish up the Expense Form.

Project Project 15-5. Final Round for the Expense Form

You can use different methods for completing the form and its calculations. We'll start with the Expense entry section because it's the most involved. The fields are shown in Figure 15-23.

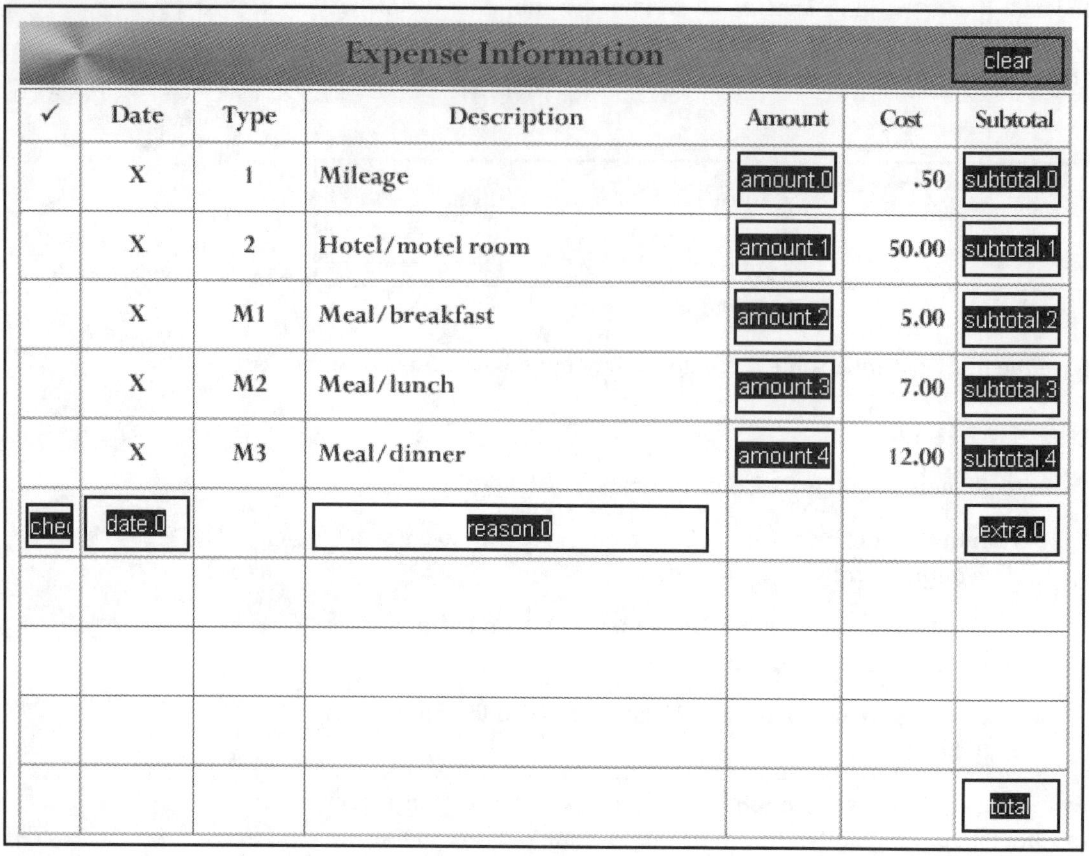
Expense Information
clear
✓
Date
Type
Description
Amount
Cost
Subtotal
X
1
Mileage
amount.0
.50
subtotal.0
X
2
Hotel/motel room
amount.1
50.00
subtotal.1
X
M1
Meal/breakfast
amount.2
5.00
subtotal.2
X
M2
Meal/lunch
amount.3
7.00
subtotal.3
X
M3
Meal/dinner
amount.4
12.00
subtotal.4
chec
date.0
reason.0
extra.0
total

Figure 15-23
Select the list of fields to clear with the action.

As you can see, there are far fewer form fields here than in other forms. This is because so much of this information is routine.

1. Add the form fields for the Amount column as usual.

2. Add the Subtotal field structure as usual—with one exception. Rather than using a product of two fields, you will need a custom calculation script. Use the scripts listed in Table 15-3 for each of the five subtotal fields.

Table 15-3   Add These Custom Scripts for the Subtotal Fields

Field	Script
subtotal.0	var a = this.getField("amount.0"); event.value = a.value *0.50;
subtotal.1	var a = this.getField("amount.1"); event.value = a.value *50.00;
subtotal.2	var a = this.getField("amount.2"); event.value = a.value *5.00;
subtotal.3	var a = this.getField("amount.3"); event.value = a.value *7.00;
subtotal.4	var a = this.getField("amount.4"); event.value = a.value *12.00;

3. The scripts bind the amount in the corresponding amount field to the variable, which is then multiplied by the value entered in the Amount column.

4. Add fields for the extra expense line:

   - In the Checkmark column, add a check mark field.

   - Add a text field in the Date column, formatted for date entry.

   - Omit the Type column.

   - In the Description field, add a Text form element.

   - Omit the Amount and Cost columns.

   - Add an amount into the Subtotal field; name the field **extra.0**.

5. Add a total field at the bottom of the Subtotal column. This is a standard calculation type, the sum of the other fields in this column.

6. Now add the button to clear the entries. The button will use the default settings again. Name the button **clear**. Select a subset of the entries to clear, as shown in Figure 15-24 (these are all the fields added to the document in Acrobat).

7. Save the file. Test the form. I have added some sample data, as shown in Figure 15-25. Reset the calculation order if necessary.

Now to finish up the top of the form, which needs only buttons.

Note

If you'd like, add more rows, and add a numbering structure to this series.

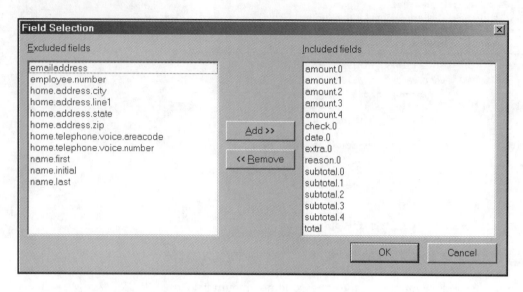

Figure 15-24
The exclusion list for the Clear function

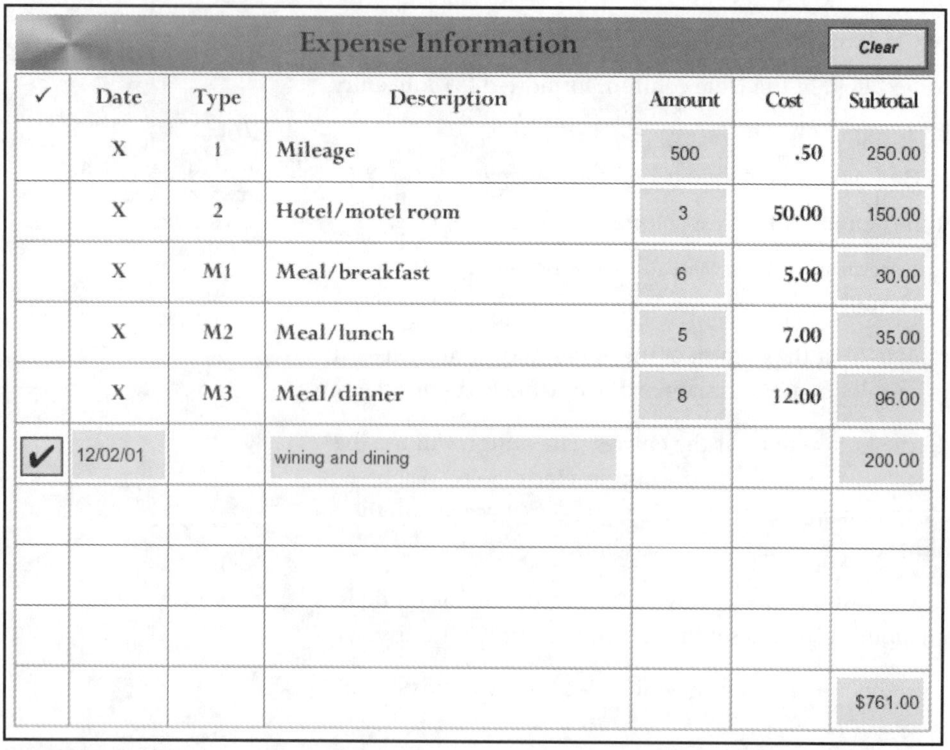

	Date	Type	Description	Amount	Cost	Subtotal	
X		1	Mileage	500	.50	250.00	
X		2	Hotel/motel room	3	50.00	150.00	
X		M1	Meal/breakfast	6	5.00	30.00	
X		M2	Meal/lunch	5	7.00	35.00	
X		M3	Meal/dinner	8	12.00	96.00	
✔	12/02/01		wining and dining			200.00	
							$761.00

Expense Information **Clear**

Figure 15-25
The completed expense portion of the form

Finishing the Employee Information Section

Not only is it easy for users to fill out a form using their own personal data file, but it is also very easy to complete the design of a form when the data fields are added using the EPS file method. All we need for this section are two buttons. The completed buttons are shown in Figure 15-26.

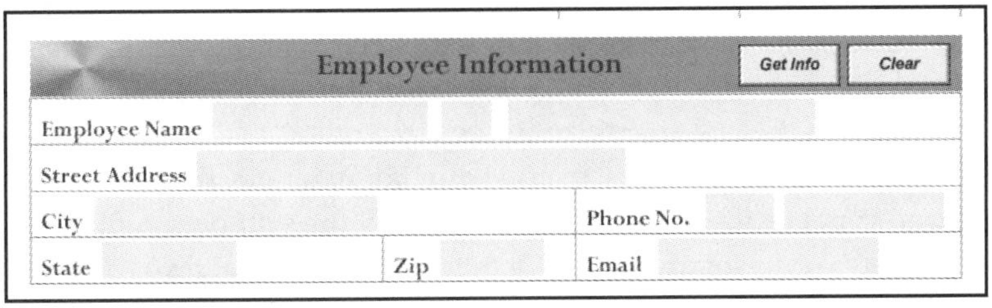

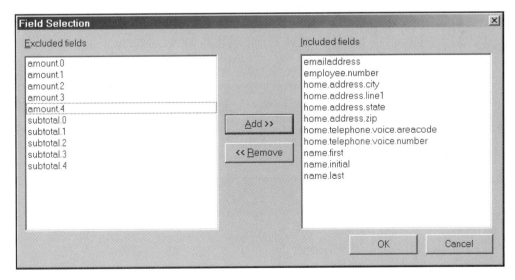

Figure 15-26
Add the same two buttons as in the last project.

Insert the two buttons described in Project 15-4 in the Add Button fields, with these minor changes:

- On the Options tab, enter **Get Info** for the Button Face Attributes text (Get Info button).

- For the Clear button, select the fields as shown in Figure 15-27 (these are all the fields that were imported into Acrobat).

Save and test the entire form.

Figure 15-27
Exclude the fields for the expense entry portion of the form.

The Big Question

Have we achieved the aims of this exercise? Well, I think so. I did not spend much time discussing collaborative processes as the materials were being designed. Rather, I concentrated on how to build the materials with the minimum of effort and the maximum of usability. While I did cover them in the introductory tutorials in this chapter, I didn't think it would be a useful exercise to go through adding comments and markups; that has been covered in several chapters and projects. (There is no reason any of these elements cannot have comments attached to them, however. In the case of the Expense Form, for example, the validation column could be formatted to be unusable by the staff person filling it out and used only for accounting or administrative purposes as a means of confirming expense claims.)

What about security issues? I haven't locked any of the files used in this chapter. You should include appropriate restrictions on access to both the forms and the content of the FDF files.

Up Next

At this point we have basically covered Acrobat from front to back. For many of you, I have covered more than enough material to make a difference in your workday. This, of course, is one of my primary goals. By including this comprehensive project chapter, I hope I have also shown you how to use the power of the program in a number of ways.

There is that other group, however, that has to go further. For you inquisitive souls, I have included a chapter covering JavaScript. That is up next.

Chapter 16

More on JavaScript

In the beginning, there was Netscape.
Netscape Communications created the
JavaScript language to make Web pages
interactive. Then Adobe said, "Let's see
what we can do with this language," and
Adobe-enhanced JavaScript was born,
bringing interactivity to PDF pages.
It is a good thing.

JavaScript and Socks

This is not really the place for an in-depth discussion of the JavaScript language. However, as many folks reading this book have not ventured too far into code-writing territory, I will give you the cook's tour of basic JavaScript. This introduction is important on two levels: first, to understand how I have used JavaScript in other chapters in this book (particularly everything dealing with forms), and second, to give you a foundation to expand your own use of Acrobat JavaScript.

One little story before we go on. This is for the die-hard designers who have never done any scripting or code before. Don't be surprised if it makes no sense to you whatsoever. Several years ago, I took four weeks' vacation from my teaching gig to learn JavaScript. (Note to self: Get a life.) The first week was absolutely horrible. My brain physically hurt. It rebelled. For days I stared at these pages blindly, reacting like a hardcore designer. What did I see? Nothing in the words and letters at all, as I couldn't process it at that level. Instead, I did see how nicely the rows of text lined up, and how the white space made a pattern, and how the repetition of some words and letters made secondary patterns on the page . . .

So, how did I turn the corner, you may well ask? I used two pieces of cardboard as visual aids in a negative sense—not to enhance my view of what I was reading, but to restrict it to a line-by-line view. I also persisted through the next three weeks, and by the end of the month I could concatenate a string with the best of them. But it still hurt.

The point is, don't sweat it. Either it comes to you, or it doesn't. Give it a chance, though shifting from right-brain to left-brain thinking is no mean feat. Regardless, reading through this chapter may give you incentive enough to try some of these things using the scripts provided. No need to start from scratch in any case, and the results may stimulate you to bigger and better coding efforts.

If all else fails, find some cardboard. Those little inserts that come with socks are a good size!

Let's Start at the Beginning

Okay. Time for some JavaScript. No cardboard required.

JavaScript is not a programming language per se, but a scripting language. The difference lies in how it works. JavaScript is loosely typed, meaning that objects can be readily converted from one form to another;

and its syntax, or phrase structure, is more forgiving to new programmers than a traditional programming language.

JavaScript uses object-oriented programming (OOP) techniques. This type of approach simplifies programming by using three basic concepts: objects, properties, and methods. *Objects* are basically lumps of data with attributes (named values directly associated with them). *Properties* are information about the object. *Methods* perform operations on or with an object.

Data can be accessed through either properties or methods. "Good programming" uses properties as much as possible. For example, consider a rectangle. JavaScript can be written about a rectangle as either a property or a method. As a property, it is written as the "rectangle" property. If a method is used, this is written as a "getRectangle()" method. If you are working with static information, and have a choice between using a property and using a method, use the property. In some cases, the information is not so straightforward. Where a set of parameters is necessary to obtain the correct information or the information is transitory, you must use a method instead. For example, if the size of a rectangle depends on user input, using a method is necessary.

An example is in order. A real-life example. So let's go shopping. A bit of imagination may be required, but I think it works.

I have to go to the grocery store (against my better judgment, given how much I loathe shopping). I make a list, which includes eggs, apples, oranges, and peanut butter. The list is an object. I can describe its properties—torn-off piece of an envelope from the phone bill, written with red pencil crayon. Each word on the paper is also an object, with its own properties—letters, descriptions. I can alter these at will. For example, I decide that my husband needs more fiber in his diet, and add the word "crunchy" to the object "peanut butter."

But are these objects usable in their present state? Well, yes and no. Yes, because I can use them as mental prompts. No, because you really shouldn't eat paper, and it is hard to make omelets with. Therefore, I must employ a method to convert the objects into usable results. That is, I must brave the elements and the humans, and make the journey to the grocery store, pick out the items, pay for them, and bring them home. By employing this method, I have converted the written "egg" object into a usable object; that is, I have modified its properties.

Now, more grocery talk. I have the items home, and I have an equivalent collection of objects in my paper bag (paper, not plastic). What do we have now? Four object types—apples, oranges, eggs, and crunchy peanut butter—for the fiber. Again we can look at their properties. First

Note

By the way, because there is more than one apple, egg, and orange, each subset (a group of apples, a carton of eggs) is technically an array. That is, apple1, apple2, apple3 is an array of apples, and so on.

the apples. Golden Delicious. Their properties include the color, size, scent, firmness, and whether or not they have stems. How are their properties accessed? Directly. You can visualize the apple's properties and simply bite into the apple to access all its properties. On the other hand, the eggs, oranges, and peanut butter will require using a method to access their properties—cracking, peeling, or opening the lid. Once the method has been employed, the results can be described.

Now let's convert this all into something written.

Objects and Properties, Apples and Oranges

Just like an apple, a PDF document is an object. Anything on the page is also an object. I identified the properties of the apple, and they can be written like this:

```
apple.color
apple.size
apple.scent
apple.firmness
apple.stem
```

Note

Many objects have common properties. To view a list of these properties, see the Acrobat JavaScript Object Specification, available by selecting Help ➤ Acrobat JavaScript Guide. Common properties for form fields, for example, are discussed starting on page 158.

Now, this doesn't give any values to the properties, just identifies them. I can assign a value to each property as follows:

```
apple.color = "yellow";
apple.size = "medium";
apple.scent = "strong";
apple.firmness = "hard";
apple.stem = false;
```

You will notice that the last property is given a false value. That is because this property description has only two options: true and false. The same could also be used for scent and firmness, but I chose a more descriptive route.

Same thing works with a page. Suppose you have added a table to a page. The page is an object and has properties. The table is an object and has properties. Likewise for each cell. Look at this description for a field color, for example:

```
this.getField("Name").fillColor = color.ltGray;
```

This means the table field will be light gray.

What about what you can't see? For example, consider a textbox. Say that this textbox is supposed to contain the user's last name. Because you have learned to name objects in other chapters using a standard method, and have put this method into regular practice, you are in a good position to move from naming objects to using them in Acrobat JavaScript. Let's say the textbox is named "Name.Last". The contents of the textbox (or its value) is written as

```
this.getField("Name.Last").value
```

And when we assign a property to that, it becomes

```
this.getField("Name.Last").value="Smith";
```

Which means that the content, or property, of this field must be the word "Smith".

One other thing to note before I go on to methods is the structure of the properties. You can see in the example here that it is arranged in a hierarchical fashion.

Methods

Now let's talk about the eggs. Objects, like eggs, have a certain number of things that can be done to them. Different objects do different things. If I wanted to write methods for cooking eggs, I would write `egg.fry()` and could enter different options such as `egg.fry("scrambled")` or `egg.fry("overEasy")`.

In this example, the object is the egg, the method is fry, and the description is the type of frying method used. How is this used? Like this:

```
var breakfast = new Object();
```

Now we have a new object, which is generic and has no properties. We can assign both methods and properties to the object, depending on whether the reference is data or requires calculation, like this:

```
breakfast.favorite = "omelet";
breakfast.quick = "scrambled";
breakfast.calculate = function (a,b) { return a - b; }
```

In these examples, the first two statements create properties and assign values to them. In the third example, I have created a new method for the object by assigning a function to it. This statement means that the breakfast calculation is a function with a value of a minus b. In the next section, I will show you what to do with this function.

This is all well and good. We have seen how objects have properties and how methods are employed against these objects. But the real question is, what makes it all go? Answer: events.

Why I Went Shopping in the First Place

An event had to trigger my fictional trip to the grocery store. In all likelihood, it was the sound of a knife scraping the inside of the peanut butter jar over and over, accompanied by heavy sighs, and then a thunk as the jar hit the recycling bin. This is an *event*, which triggered a range of activity—find the car keys, drive to the store, and so on. And this was also the last installment of the shopping trip story. From here on in, it is just the facts, ma'am.

JavaScript Events and Functions

JavaScript uses an event model. This means an event is defined to trigger functions to run. The most common events are those involving mouse functions and buttons. Others are used for page and form functions. We will look at these in more detail further on in the chapter as I discuss specific activities in Acrobat. We have also seen this in action in projects in other chapters (for example, Chapters 10, 12, and 15).

Speaking of functions, a function can be named at will, because you are defining it yourself, and is written as follows:

```
function DoIt (variable(s)) {
// what needs to be done
}
```

So what does this mean? Allow me to disassemble this:

- function: Add this word to indicate you are going to create a function.

- DoIt: The name I gave to this function.

- variable(s): There can be more than one. They are sent to the function when it is called. Variables sent to a function are known as *parameters*.

- { (The left curly bracket, or *brace*): Written at the end of the function's call line, it starts the enclosure of the script that will be executed when the function is called.

- //what needs to be done: Depends on the function. Here you add statements and declarations.

- } (the closing brace): This indicates that both the statements and the function are ended.

You have to call the function when you want to use it. Enter the name, variables (parameters), and end the line with a semicolon, like this:

```
DoIt (today);
```

Breakfast Revisited

In the last section, I referred to methods, and said the value of a variable can be either a string (the word "omelet") or a calculation. Because this script can accept variables and requires calculation, it is a function. Let's have another look. This is the earlier statement reproduced here for your convenience:

```
breakfast.calculate = function (a,b) { return a - b; }
```

This variable is written to calculate the number of eggs left depending on which variable I chose. For example, I could specify that omelettes take 3 eggs, and scrambled eggs take 2 eggs. If I then said that a carton of eggs contains 12, I can write one more variable that will calculate the eggs remaining in the carton depending on what I cooked, like this:

```
var remainder = breakfast.calculate( 12, 3 );
```

This variable will call the function that I created earlier, and `'remainder'` has a value of `'9'`.

But what if a decision has to be made to do one thing if something happens, and another if something else occurs? Glad I asked. Coming up, our last general topic: making decisions.

Tips on Using Variables

Now a bit on variables. We have used variables to write custom scripts in other chapters, but here are some basic rules for using them:

- Variables have to be declared. They are most often declared with the word "var".

- Variables must start with either a letter or an underscore and are case-sensitive.

- When working on a large project, pick a naming convention and stick to it. This will make your life run more smoothly.

- Variable names should describe what they are. Just because you think you will always remember what something means, don't count on it.

- Establish a pattern of assigning values (or initializing). For the work we are doing in Acrobat, the value of the variables is generally known. So assign the value when the variable is declared. This saves time and frustration later.

- End each variable statement with a semicolon.

- To print characters, enclose them inside quotes. Otherwise, a string of characters is considered a variable. For example, var b = data is a variable, var b = "data" will print the word *data*.

- Add comments to your code to make it more understandable to yourself and others. Any comments should start with // to differentiate them from something that is to be processed as part of your code.

Decision Making

A common occurrence in all types of programming is decision making. This is referred to as a *decision branch*. JavaScript uses a common type of if statement, written as in Listing 16-1.

Listing 16-1. Content of a Simple if Statement

```
if (condition) {
do something
} else {
        do something else
}
```

We will look at this in Acrobat specifics later in the chapter. For now, I want to show you a simple example of how this works.

Suppose you have a form. Go on, just imagine it. On this form, you are collecting information for marketing purposes. You want to tailor responses to the user based on gender. You want all women to receive one response message and all men to receive another response message when the form is submitted. The script will be written as shown in Listing 16-2.

Listing 16-2. Writing an if Statement

```
var gender=this.getField("gender").value;
if (gender == "female") {
app.alert("Thank you. Ask about our Fashion Specials");
} else {
app.alert("Your form has been submitted.");
}
```

Let me explain this on a line-by-line basis:

1. First of all, you will have to declare a variable. The content of the gender box on the form will be transferred to a variable named "gender".

2. The response is questioned in the first line of the if statement. Is the gender equal to female?

3. An alert box will be displayed if the question is true; that is, gender is equal to female.

4. If the answer to the question is false, this alert box will be displayed; that is, if gender is not equal to female.

This concludes our tour of basic JavaScript—very basic JavaScript. I have limited the discussion to those elements we will be dealing with in the rest of this chapter. I would encourage you to consult any of the many JavaScript books and online resources available for further information.

Now, let's finally look at how Acrobat uses JavaScript. Before we get into it, I want to point out that there are differences between JavaScript used in HTML and that used in Acrobat. For example, many common objects and methods are not part of the core JavaScript language. Instead, they are part of either server-side or client-side scripting. With either of these uses of JavaScript, the code is executed either on the page or through the Web server. Similarly, JavaScript for PDF has its own objects and methods, and is executed in either Acrobat itself or Acrobat Reader.

For this reason, I heartily recommend that you spend some time with the Acrobat JavaScript Object Specification, available within Acrobat by selecting Help ➤ Acrobat JavaScript Guide.

Using JavaScript in Acrobat

In other chapters, I have shown you bits and pieces of Acrobat JavaScript used for particular purposes. We have used scripts for some simple calculations and to navigate through a document. That only scratches the surface. Now let's look at some more real-life, practical uses of JavaScript. Along the way, I will offer some description and advice, but no more grocery shopping.

In some of the discussion, I will show you how to use dialog boxes within Acrobat to add scripting. In other cases, we will have to build some scripts. To bring some order to the presentation of how to use JavaScript, I have organized it according to where it is being used—that is, whether you are using it inside a document or outside a document.

Using JavaScript in a Document

You can attach JavaScript to a document in seven different ways:

- With Page Open and Page Close actions

- With Document actions

- With bookmarks

- With links

- With form fields

- At the document level (or top level)

- From the JavaScripts folder on your hard drive

Let's have a look at these JavaScript options. How and where you access them in Acrobat varies. I'll run through the processes, and then we will look at some in detail in upcoming projects.

Opening and Closing Pages

First up, using JavaScript with Page Open or Page Closed actions, the script is executed when the page opens or closes. A logical use of this event would be updating a date on the page. If you would like to try this as
I explain how it works, open an Acrobat file—any file will do, but save the project files from this chapter for use later in the chapter.

To add a page action, follow these steps:

1. Select Document ➤ Set Page Action. The dialog box shown in Figure 16-1 will open.

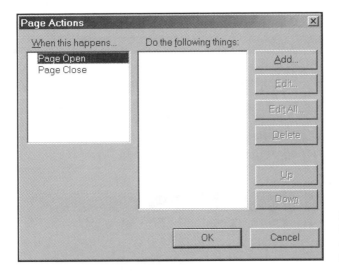

Figure 16-1
Start the process of attaching a script to a page action from this dialog box.

2. There are two options available in the left pane, Page Open or Page Close. (If you are working along, choose Page Open.) Click Add. The generic Add An Action dialog box will open. Select JavaScript from the drop-down menu, as shown in Figure 16-2.

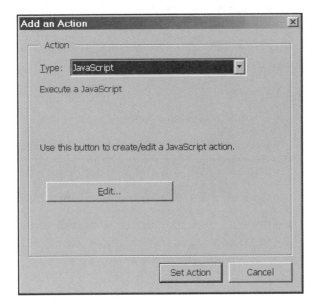

Figure 16-2
Select JavaScript as the action type.

3. Click Edit. When the JavaScript Edit window opens, add a script, such as:

```
app.alert ("Welcome to my document.");
```

4. Click OK to close the dialog box and return to the Add An Action dialog box.

5. Click Set Action. The dialog box will close, and you will return to the initial Page Actions dialog box. A green dot will be displayed to the left of the option originally selected, Page Open.

6. Click OK to close the dialog box. Save the file.

To test the script, reopen the file. When it opens, you should see the alert message that was added, as shown in Figure 16-3.

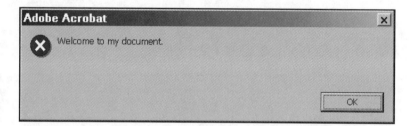

Figure 16-3
The document now displays this alert when it is opened.

Now let's discuss attaching JavaScript to document actions.

Document Actions

Document actions relate to different states of a document, and include the following:

- Document Will Close (when a document closes)

- Document Will Save (before a document is saved)

- Document Did Save (after a document is saved)

- Document Will Print (before a document is printed)

- Document Did Print (after a document is printed)

The states that include "Did" in their names will run the script immediately after the function—either save or print—is completed. Add document actions by following these steps:

1. Select Tools ➤ JavaScript ➤ Set Document Actions. The dialog box shown in Figure 16-4 will open.

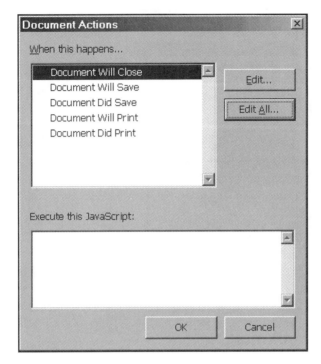

Figure 16-4
Choose a document action from the list in this dialog box.

2. Select the JavaScript action from the list, and click Edit.

3. When the JavaScript Edit window opens, add your script. Click OK to close the dialog box and return to the Document Actions dialog box.

4. The script will appear in the bottom pane, and a green dot will appear to the left of the action's line in the listing, as shown in Figure 16-5. Click OK to close the dialog box.

If a number of scripts are attached to the same document at this level, you can view them all in this dialog box. Simply select the action from the list at the top of the box, and the corresponding script will be displayed in the bottom pane.

If you click Edit All, the JavaScript Edit window will open, displaying all the scripts attached to the document. More on that coming up shortly. Let's first have a look at bookmark scripts.

Note
You may have noticed that there is no Delete button on this dialog box. You can delete an action, of course. Select the action from the list at the top of the dialog box and click Edit to open the JavaScript Editor window. Delete the code and click OK. The code is now removed.

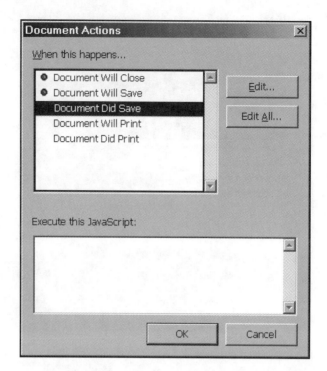

Bookmarks

You can add JavaScript to bookmarks by following these steps:

1. Select a bookmark from a document's listing (or add a bookmark).

2. Open the Properties dialog box by right-clicking the bookmark and selecting Properties from the context menu (or select Bookmark Properties from the Bookmarks drop-down menu).

3. From the Bookmark Properties dialog box, select JavaScript from the Action drop-down menu.

4. Click Edit to open the scripting window.

5. Write or paste in the script, and click OK to close the window.

6. Click Set Action to add the JavaScript and close the Bookmark Properties dialog box.

Attaching JavaScript to links is similar. I will describe the process for linking next.

Links

Links are commonly used elements for attaching JavaScript. To attach JavaScript to a link, follow these steps:

1. Select a link by clicking on it with the Link tool (or add a link).

2. Double-click the link or right-click the link and select Link Properties from the context menu. The Link Properties dialog box shown in Figure 16-6 will open.

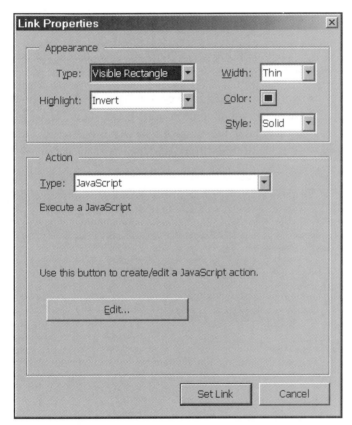

Figure 16-6
Set link properties and add JavaScript from the same dialog box.

3. From the Link Properties dialog box, select JavaScript from the Action drop-down menu.

4. Click Edit to open the scripting window.

5. Write or paste in the script, and click OK to close the window.

6. Click Set Link to add the script to the page and close the Link Properties dialog box.

One of the most common uses of JavaScript is with form fields. I have shown you in other chapters how to add JavaScript to form fields, and we will use them again in a project coming up in this chapter.

Form Fields

I want to give you some general guidelines for using JavaScript with form fields in Acrobat.

1. Using the Form Tool, double-click a field (or add a new field) to open the Field Properties dialog box.

2. From the Actions tab, click Add.

3. Depending on the type of field you have defined, there are a number of options for adding scripts:

   • For Button fields, as shown in Figure 16-7, you can add scripts to any of the six button states listed. Again, as we have seen in other dialog boxes, once a script has been added to an action, it is identified with a dot to the left of the action's listing.

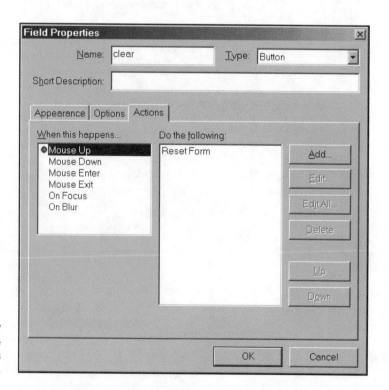

Figure 16-7
Add JavaScript to one of the button states listed in the left pane.

- For Text fields, you can also add scripts for the same set of mouse events.

- In addition, with Text fields, you can add Format, Validate, and Calculation scripts. The Format tab is shown in Figure 16-8. For all three tabs, click Edit to add a custom script.

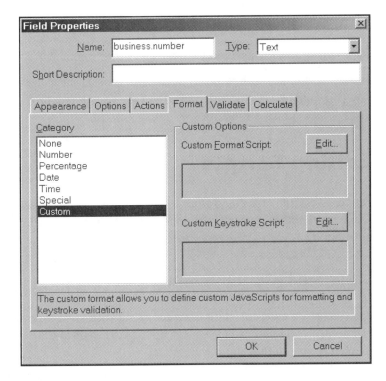

Figure 16-8
Add custom scripts for text fields.

4. More than one script can be added for a single event. Scripts will be executed in the order they are added.

Document-Level Scripts

I mentioned that scripts may be added at the document level. This means that scripts added here can be accessed by any other JavaScript in the document. Hence the alternate name, top-level script.

To add a document-level script, select Tools ➤ JavaScript ➤ Document JavaScripts. I will return to this topic at the end of the chapter when we have a look at batch scripts.

The JavaScripts Folder

Finally, I listed the JavaScripts folder. This folder resides on your hard drive. It contains several scripts, which Acrobat calls when they are required. The three types of scripts are as follows:

- Folder level: Stored in the application and user folders

- Console JavaScripts: Primarily used for debugging

- Batch JavaScripts: Used to create and run custom batch scripts

I have some more information on these scripts later in the chapter. I am sure you would like to try some of these processes in a real project, but first I want to touch on some script editing options.

Editing Scripts

Before we get into a project, I want to touch on two features new to Acrobat 5. These features are designed for the do-it-yourselfer. Both are quite handy.

Using an External Editor

Note

For Mac users, this feature is not available.

You can use an external editor program to edit your JavaScripts. By assigning a preference, whenever a script has to be edited from inside Acrobat, your external editor will launch.

Select Edit ➤ Preferences ➤ General. The Preferences dialog box will be displayed (the top portion is shown in Figure 16-9). Click JavaScript in the left pane to open the preference options. Click External Editor, then click Choose and browse to the location of your external editor, and click OK. Click OK at the bottom of the Preferences dialog box to make the change and close the window.

Figure 16-9
You can choose an external editor in the Preferences dialog box.

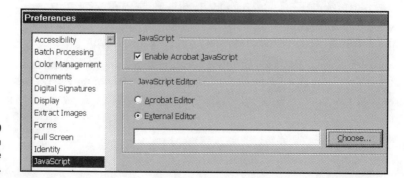

Once this preference has been set, whenever you edit a JavaScript, Acrobat will create a temporary file and open it in your editor. In order for the changes to be integrated into your PDF file, you will have to save the file. Acrobat will be locked when the file is being edited. To return to Acrobat, you must close the external editor first. (Personally, I don't have a problem with using Acrobat's internal editing capabilities, so I haven't felt a need to use an external editor.)

What if you want to see all the scripts you have created in one document? That is possible now as well.

Editing All JavaScripts in a Document

You can have a look at all the JavaScript you have added to one document. Again, this is new to Acrobat 5, and is tied in with the XML capabilities of this version. Select Tools ➤ JavaScript ➤ Edit All JavaScripts. The window shown in Figure 16-10 will open.

Let's have a look at some of the features:

- The scripts are organized by XML tag.

- This page has two calculated fields. Each of them calls the same top-level script, AcroForm.

- Each script is identified separately, and lists the content of the scripts I added to the document at the field level.

The same feature can be accessed via buttons strategically located in some dialog boxes (for example, the Actions tab in the Form Fields Properties dialog box).

Well, I think this has been more than enough discussion. Coming up is a project using JavaScript attached in several different ways.

Workflow Tip
A Warning to Make Your Life Easier

Do not mess with the XML tags! Acrobat uses this tag information to organize the whole works. Although you can freely change anything in the scripts, if you change the tags (anything in < > brackets), Acrobat likely will not accept your changes.

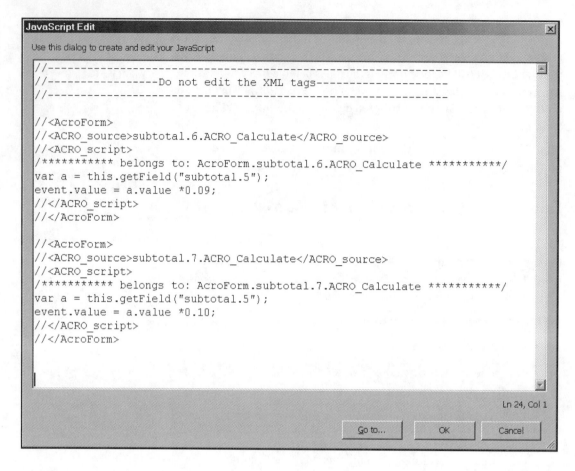

Figure 16-10
The JavaScript Edit window showing all the scripts attached to a file

Project **Project 16-1. Brad's U-Park, Part I: A Lot of Parking for a Lot of Money**

In other chapters that discussed forms, my focus was on their construction, use, optimization, naming of form fields, and the like. In this chapter, the focus instead is on using JavaScript. We will add scripts in a number of different ways.

For this reason, the file you will need for this project is quite simple. It was designed with tongue firmly planted in cheek. Since what we are doing with it is so serious, it seemed like a good idea to make the material amusing.

The form has two pages. The file, survey.pdf, is on the CD-ROM in the Chapter 16 projects folder. There is also another file, scripts.txt, which contains the text you will need for the scripts in this project. You can either enter the scripts manually or copy and paste them from this file.

What's on the Form?

As I said, not too much. However, it has been constructed to allow for a number of activities. Page 1 is shown in Figure 16-11.

We Need Your Help!   *A lot of parking -- for a lot of money*

Brad's U-Park has been proud to offer you convenient parking while shopping or working at HighEnd Overpriced Mall. We value all our customers, especially those who choose our services on a regular or daily basis.
A new city bylaw allows us to enforce rules in our lot, including fines for inappropriate driving behavior. In order to improve our services, and to offer you the best possible parking experience, we would like you to complete this survey. Our courteous attendants have helped us prepare a list of the 5 most common complaints we have heard from our customers.

Here's how to complete this survey:

The 5 common complaints are listed below. Please respond to each complaint in two ways -

- how often you encounter this problem on a scale of 1 (rarely) to 5 (regularly).
- how annoying/irritating the problem is to you on a scale of 1 (not very) to 5 (severe).

It is important that you answer these questions carefully. Your totals will be used to determine the cost of fines for parking lot infractions.

When you are done, click the Print button to print the survey. Hand it to your attendant on your next visit. You may also email us with more comments. Click on the Email button.

Click on the Start button to go to the survey page. Thank you.

Figure 16-11
Page 1 of the survey

Although the page is primarily discussion and instruction, we are going to add some scripts to it. We'll do the following in this project:

- Insert an automatic date field at the top of the page.

- Add a Start button, with an action (go to page) attached.

Page 2 is the heart of the survey, as shown in Figure 16-12.

Here are the questions. **Click the button indicated for a total; click Reset to start over.**

Common Complaints	How Often?	How Annoying?
Drivers who stop in the middle of the lane and block traffic while waiting for a parking spot.		
Drivers who park on the lines, taking up two spots.		
Drivers who park too close to adjacent cars so the other driver must grease up with Vaseline to squeeze into his or her car.		
Drivers who ignore the painted lanes and drive diagonally from one end of the lot to another.		
Drivers who stop in front of a mall exit and wait for passengers to arrive, blocking traffic.		
Your total score is:		

This survey has been sent only to those registered customers who provided us with an email address. Thank you for your participation.

Figure 16-12
Page 2 of the survey form

We will add a number of scripts to Page 2 by performing these tasks:

- Place an automatic date field on this page as well.

- Add custom field entries to the fields for the survey responses.

- Create a hidden field that displays a grand total defining the user's overall level of irritation once all entries are complete.

- Add several buttons (you can see their finished placement in Figure 16-34).

- Attach a print function to the Print button.

- Attach a document-level script that displays a message after printing.

- Attach a custom script to send e-mail.

All this on one little survey! So let's get to it. Open survey.pdf in Acrobat.

Today's Date Is . . .

First up, adding date fields. We are going to add a document-level date field to both pages. We are not going to add two separate fields that each need configuring and programming. Instead, by adding two fields with the same name, they will also share the same value. We will make them look different visually.

Follow these steps:

1. Create a text field above the title on Page 1 as shown in Figure 16-13.

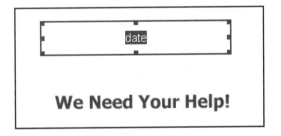

Figure 16-13
Add the automatic date field to Page 1 in this location.

2. The Field Properties dialog box will open once the field has been drawn on the page. Select text from the Type drop-down box, and name the field **date**.

3. Set the appearance of the field:

- Deselect all border options.

- Select Helvetica (or similar) 9pt font, and select the dark teal text color (from the Color palette, this is the fifth color in the third row).

4. Click the Read-only check box to select it. (This is a calculated field, and the user doesn't interact with it.)

5. Select Format ➤ Date and select the format dd-mmm-yy (for example, 01 Jan 02).

6. Click OK to close the dialog box.

Now that the field has been added and named, we will attach a document-level script to it. This means that each time the document is opened, the script will be attached to any applicable field it finds. To attach the script, follow these steps:

1. Select Tools ➤ JavaScript ➤ Document JavaScripts. The Document Script dialog box will open. Name the script **date** and click Add.

2. When the scripting window opens, delete the text from the window.

3. Enter this text (or copy the lines of script named "Date" from the scripts.txt file):

```
var d = this.getField("date");
d.value = util.printd("dd-mmm-yyyy", new Date());
```

4. Click OK to close the JavaScript Edit dialog box. The script will now appear in the JavaScript Functions dialog box as shown in Figure 16-14. Click Close to close this dialog box as well.

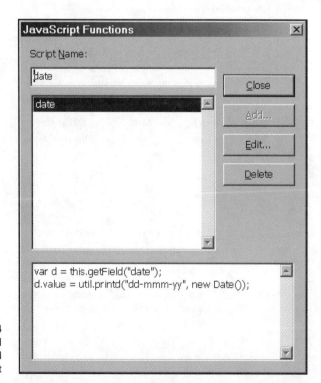

Figure 16-14
The completed document-level JavaScript

The script has now been attached. Let's look at it before carrying on. In the first line, I declared a variable "d" (for "date"). The field "date" is bound to the variable. In the second line, the value is defined. The date format is displayed and a new object is created to hold the date object. The date is formatted with the utility object (that is, util.printd).

While we are at it, we may as well add the date field to Page 2 as well. Because the field has already been created and configured once, and a script has been created, this process is simpler. When the document is loaded into Acrobat, each field will call and execute the same script.

1. Using the Form tool, click the date field to select it. Copy the field (Ctrl-C or Edit ➤ Copy).

2. Move to Page 2 of the survey form. Paste the field (using Ctrl-V or Edit ➤ Paste). Move it into position at the bottom of the page, as shown in Figure 16-15.

Figure 16-15
Add another date field in this location on Page 2.

3. Save the file. Test the file by closing and reopening it. You should have the current system date displayed in both text boxes in the chosen format, as shown in Figures 16-16a and 16-16b.

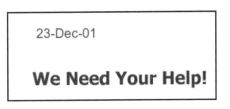

Figures 16-16a and 16-16b
The date displays correctly in the desired location on both pages.

Workflow Tip

Save Time with Time Settings

Before testing your scripts, make sure that the date format in your script and the date format you set in the Field Properties dialog box match. If not, you will receive an error message.

That's it for the date fields. Now back to Page 1 to add a button and an action.

No Lights, No Camera—But We Have Action

This is a very simple form, and realistically doesn't require adding buttons for navigation. I have added navigation to other projects in other chapters (see, for example, Project 12.1, "Adding Destinations to the Makeup Manual," in Chapter 12); but I wanted to briefly include this type of function here to round out the discussion.

Most actions associated with a button should be attached to a MouseUp trigger. Although actions can be attached to other button states, this convention is the most convenient for the user, and also the one most often used professionally.

Follow these steps:

1. Create a form field in the lower-right corner of Page 1. When the Field Properties dialog box opens, name the field **start**. Select Button from the Type drop-down list.

2. Set these options for the button appearance:

   - Border Color: Dark teal (as in the date text)
   - Background Color: A light beige color (I used a custom color with an RGB value of 255/251/234.)
   - Width: Thin; Style: Beveled
   - Text Color: Dark teal; Font: Arial Bold Italic, size 8pt

3. Click Options. Specify these options:

   - Highlight: Push
   - Layout: Text only
   - Button Face When: Up
   - Text For Button: Start

4. Click Actions. Select MouseUp from the left pane. Click Add. From the Type drop-down menu, select JavaScript. Click Edit.

5. Now attach the script to the button state. In the script window, enter this line of script:

   ```
   this.pageNum++;
   ```

6. Click OK to close the JavaScript Edit window and return to the Add An Action dialog box.

7. Click Set Action to return to the Field Properties dialog box. A green circle will now appear to the left of the MouseUp listing, indicating a script has been attached. Click OK to close the Field Properties dialog box.

8. Save the file, and then test the button.

Note

This massive script, which I've named Start, is also included in the script.txt file. I think it would likely take more time to open the file, copy the line, and paste it in the script window, but it is there if you want to use it! There are also scripts in the scripts.txt file for other page actions.

The default settings I created with the original file show each page of the survey at full size, so the button's action should display the second page as designed.

That completes the scripts for Page 1. Now some more for Page 2. We are in button-building mode, and have the default settings in the Field Properties dialog box set for buttons, so let's carry on with the other button actions. Yes, this is out of sequence if you consider the form from top to bottom. From a practical standpoint, however, it makes sense.

Printing the Output

One of the simplest things to do is attach menu functions to buttons. Let's do that now, and have the file printed (for the user to hand in to the friendly attendant on his or her next visit to Brad's U-Park). Follow these steps:

1. Create a form field in the lower-right portion of Page 2. When the Field Properties dialog box opens, name the field **print**. Select Button from the type drop-down list.

2. Use the same appearance options as for the button on Page 1.

3. Click Options. Leave the options as set for the last button, add **Print** as the text for the button face.

4. Click Actions. Select MouseUp from the left pane. Click Add. From the Type drop-down menu, select Execute Menu Item. Click Edit Menu Item.

5. The Menu Item Selection window will open. Select File ➤ Print. As shown in Figure 16-17, the selections will be displayed.

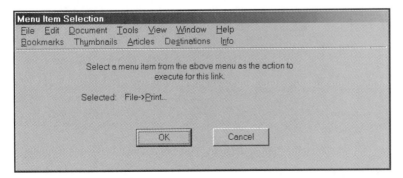

Figure 16-17
Select menu items to attach to buttons through this dialog box.

6. Click OK to close the Menu Item Selection window and return to the Add An Action dialog box.

7. Click Set Action to return to the Field Properties dialog box. A green circle will now appear to the left of the MouseUp listing, indicating a script has been attached. Click OK to close the Field Properties dialog box.

8. Test the button. Clicking the button should launch the Print dialog box.

We need to include one more spiffy action before we add the next button.

Telling the User What to Do Next

Let's now attach a document action script. Earlier in the chapter, I outlined a set of document actions, including DocumentDidPrint. We will attach a script to this action, and display a pop-up message for the user.

1. Select Tools ➤ JavaScript ➤ Set Document Actions.

2. Click DocumentDidPrint from the list at the top of the dialog box. Click Edit to open the script window.

3. Enter this script, then click OK to close the script window.

```
app.alert("Thank you. Please give this form to your attendant on your next
visit to Brad's U-Park.", 3);
```

4. You will now see the script displayed in the Document Actions dialog box, as shown in Figure 16-18.

5. Save the file and test the button. When you click Print, the Print dialog box will open. In order to have the message display, you must click Print.

The new message is shown in Figure 16-19. Now on to more buttons.

Note

The application alert is required to open an alert window. You can see at the end that I have added the number "3"; this defines the type of alert that is displayed. Leaving it as a default will cause an error icon to display. This will result in the display of an information icon instead.

Note

You have to write this script differently than you would write an alert script for JavaScript used in a browser. The object is an application alert, rather than a generic alert. If you do not include the full name, that is, app.alert, you will receive an error message.

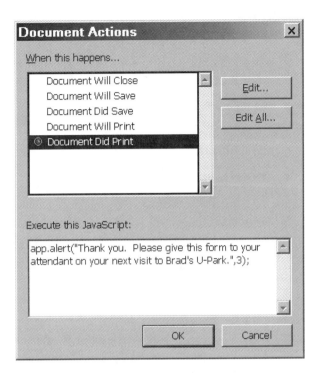

Figure 16-18
The new script
will be displayed in
this dialog box.

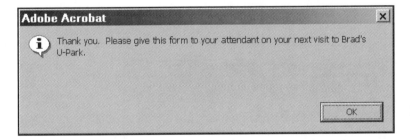

Figure 16-19
An instruction for the user
will be displayed after the
document is printed.

Send Me Mail

There are different methods of sending e-mail from a PDF document. You can send a form, send the form data files (FDF) only, or simply launch an external e-mail editor.

In this part of the project, we will add a button to send the form as an e-mail attachment.

> **Note**
>
> Brad's U-Park is a fictional company (big surprise). The instructions for this project will actually launch your e-mail authoring program, ready to send a message addressed to me. Say hi if you like.

Follow these steps:

1. Create a form field in the lower-right portion of Page 2 to the right of the Print button. When the Field Properties dialog box opens, name the field **email**. Select Button from the Type drop-down list.

2. Use the same appearance options as for the button on Page 1.

3. Click Options. Leave the options as set for the last button, and add **Email Us** as the text for the button face.

4. Click Actions. Select MouseUp from the left pane. Click Add. From the Type drop-down menu, select JavaScript. Click Edit.

5. Now attach the script to the button state. In the script window, enter this line of script:

```
this.mailDoc(true, "dbaker@skyweb.ca", "", "", "Hi");
```

6. Click OK to close the JavaScript Edit window and return to the Add An Action dialog box.

7. Click Set Action. A green circle will now appear to the left of the MouseUp listing, indicating a script has been attached. Click OK to close the Field Properties dialog box.

8. Save the file and test the button. Your e-mail editor should launch, as shown in Figure 16-20.

Figure 16-20
The results of adding
the e-mail button

A Quick Look at the Script

Although not really necessary for completion of the projects, I want to show you how the script is built, and how you can add to it.

Mailing a document requires a document method. `this.mailDoc` refers to the document you are looking at. `true` is a parameter of the method that refers to how the document is handled. `true` means that an e-mail program's interface will be open before mailing; `false` means that the document will be mailed silently, that is, without opening a user interface.

My address follows. The extra sets of quotes can be used to add cc copies to the file. At the end, I have written the word "Hi". This string is the value of a variable that will display the content of the message line in your e-mail editor; in other words, when the e-mail program opens with a new message displayed, the subject will be written as "Hi".

Here's how you would add a second e-mail address:

1. Reopen the script.

2. Add a secondary address between the first set of double quotes, like this:

   ```
   this.mailDoc(true,"dbaker@skyweb.ca","softwareprincess
   @skyweb.ca","","Hi");
   ```

3. Close all dialog boxes.

4. Test the button. As shown in Figure 16-21, the form will now be sent to both me and my alter ego.

At this point, I want to end this project, discuss a few more ideas, and then carry on.

Field Calculations

In other chapters in this book, I have discussed field calculations in some depth. I have added more information, along with the basic process for adding calculations to your document, to make this chapter a more inclusive reference. For more step-by-step instruction and expla-nation, refer to the projects and discussions in Chapters 10, 12, 14, and 15.

Note

This script can also be written as follows:
```
mailDoc({ cTo:
"dbaker@skyweb.ca",
cSubject: "Hi" });.
```

Note

There are also ways to send e-mails using JavaScript. I have included other options in the scripts.txt file.

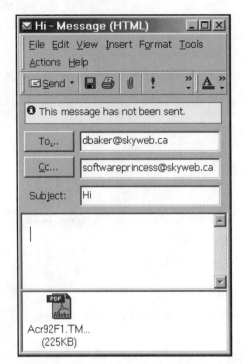

Figure 16-21
Easily send a form to a
secondary recipient by
altering the script.

Arithmetic Operators

Operators are used to operate on values. Consider this snippet of code
from a calculated field:

```
var a = this.getField("amount.0");
event.value = a.value *0.50;
```

What does this mean? In the first line, I have declared a variable, "a".
Then I have assigned a field object to it ("amount.0"), which is returned
by the document getField method.

The use of the event object is dependent on when the script is run. In this
case, the script is run whenever a calculation must occur. The script
needs to put the value for the calculation event into the value property
of the event object. The calculated value is the value of the "amount.0"
field multiplied by 0.5.

There are a number of common arithmetic operators you can use. I have
listed these, along with examples, in Table 16-1.

Table 16-1 Arithmetic Operators

Operator	Description	Example	Result
+	Addition	6 + 2	8
-	Subtraction	6 - 2	4
*	Multiplication	6 * 2	12
/	Division	6 / 2	3
%	Modulus (returns remainder after division)	7 % 2	1
++	Increment	x = 5; x++;	x is set to 6
--	Decrement	x = 6; x--;	x is set to 5

Calculating Values

Follow these steps to create calculated fields:

1. Use the Form tool to create a text field. When the Field Properties dialog box opens, name the field (for example, Field.1).

2. To calculate money amounts, click the Format tab, and select Number. Choose two decimal places, currency symbol, and separator style.

3. Click the Options tab, enter a default value (use 0), and click OK.

4. Create and name the second field (for example, Field.2). Use the same settings in the Format and Options tabs.

5. Create and name the third field that will be used for calculations (for example, Field.3). Use the same settings in the Format tab.

6. Add a custom script. Click the Calculate tab. Select Custom Calculation Script, and click Edit.

7. When the script window opens, add the calculation script. You will need three lines for the script:

   - Declare the first variable, whose value is the first field object.

   - Declare the second variable, whose value is the second field object.

   - Populate the event value (remember the value of the calculation event is stored in the field that is being calculated), and perform the calculation.

An example is shown in Listing 16-3.

Workflow Tip

Make It Easier

Rather than building the second or any of a number of fields from scratch, especially a group that shares common settings, use Ctrl-click and drag from the first field to copy and paste other fields. Alternatively, use Ctrl-C to copy, and Ctrl-V to paste. Rename each field.

Listing 16-3. Creating a Calculation Script

```
var a = this.getField("Field.1");
var b = this.getField("Field.2");
event.value = a.value * b.value;
```

8. Click OK to close the script window. The script will be displayed in the Calculate Tab as shown in Figure 16-22.

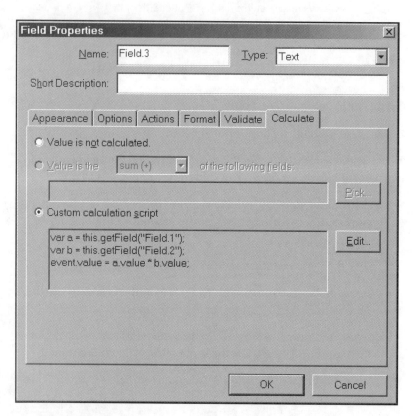

Figure 16-22
Example of a custom
calculation script

9. Click OK to close the Field Properties dialog box.

In this example, when the values are entered in both Field.1 and Field.2, the product will be calculated and entered automatically into Field.3.

Comparison Operators

What if you want to create conditional expressions? That is, you want to create an if statement that compares two options, and executes one action if the comparison is true and another if it is false. For this effect, we use *comparison operators*. There are six common comparison operators, listed in Table 16-2, and most of them will look familiar from introductory algebra.

Note

If I have dredged up any painful math class memories, I apologize!

Table 16-2 Comparison Operators

Operator	Description	Example
==	Is equal to	9 == 9 returns true
!=	Is not equal to	9 != 8 returns true
>	Is greater than	9 > 8 returns true
<	Is less than	5 < 9 returns true
>=	Is greater than or equal to	9 >= 8 returns true
<=	Is less than or equal to	9 <= 8 returns false

Project Tutorial: Using Conditions to Manipulate Fields

There are a number of ways you can "lock" a field until a specific condition is met. Most commonly, a field may be hidden or read only. Regardless of the method used, the user will not be able to interact with the field until the condition is met. Let me show you how this works. It's neat.

To illustrate this process, I have created a simple form in a file called example.pdf, located on the CD-ROM in the Chapter 16 projects folder. You can use the file if you would like to follow along. The file includes an example of each of these methods for manipulating the fields. Regardless of the type of manipulation, a value of 25 or greater must be added to the first field in order to activate the second field.

Custom Validation Scripts

In order to be able to see both effects in the same form using the same comparison, I have made a set of corresponding fields. That is, for each condition, there is both a field to enter a value and the field that is being acted upon. The pairs of fields, names, and custom scripts are displayed in Table 16-3 (the scripts are also included in the scripts.txt file on the CD-ROM in the Chapter 16 projects folder).

Table 16-3   Form Fields and Their Scripts

Field Name	Script	Set Common Properties
hide	`var h = this.getField("see.it");` `h.hidden = (event.value < 25);`	None
see.it	None	Form Field is hidden
read	`var r = this.getField("do.it");` `r.readonly = (event.value < 25);`	None
do.it	None	Read only

Building the Fields

Now to add the fields and scripts to the form:

1. Create a set of four text fields, named according to the listing in Table 16-3.

2. Set the common properties of the target fields as described in the table (the common properties are located at the bottom of the Appearance tab in the Field Properties dialog box).

3. Position the fields as shown in Figure 16-23. As you can see in the image, I have added the fields to correspond with each label.

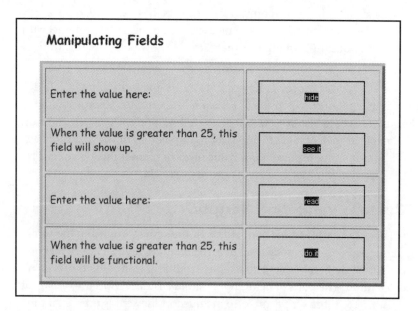

Figure 16-23
Add fields like this.

4. For each field, double-click to open the Field Properties dialog box. Click the Validate tab, select Custom Validation Script, and click Edit.

5. Add the scripts to the value fields (scripts are in the scripts.txt file). Click Validate, then click Custom validate script. Click Edit to open the JavaScript window. Copy and paste the script into the scripting window, then click OK.

6. The custom script will now be displayed in the Validate tab, as shown in Figure 16-24. Click OK to close the Field Properties window.

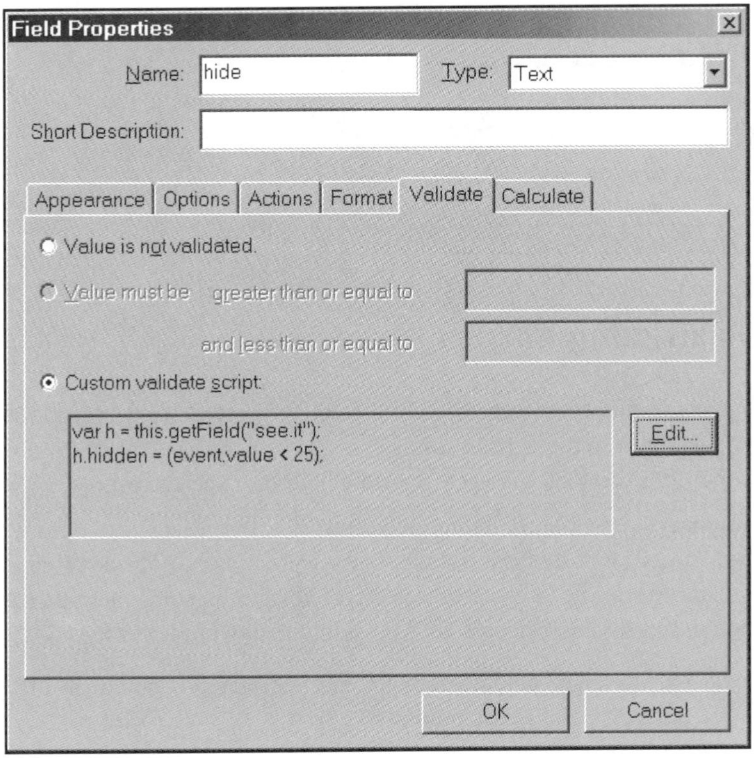

Figure 16-24
Add a custom script to display a hidden field depending on the value entered in another field.

Test the fields. As shown in Figure 16-25, the value entered in the first field is less than 25, so the hidden field stays hidden. On the other hand, the second value field is over 25, so the read-only field can now be manipulated.

One last manipulation topic, and then back to finish up Brad's U-Park, Part Deux. This is a discussion—no file attached.

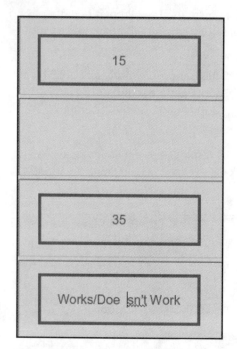

Figure 16-25
Test the function of
the custom scripts.

Note

These validation options
work only with text or
combo box fields and
only in fields using
number or percentage
formats.

Restricting Entries

It is common practice to set conditions on a field to make the data more
usable. That is, if a certain range of values is possible, you can place
conditions that will allow entries only with that specific range.

You may have noticed, in earlier screenshots, that there is an option on
the Validation tab of the Field Properties dialog box that allows for
assigning specific values. However, you have to set some other options
before this becomes active. Let's have a look at what is involved:

1. Create a new field. I created a text field named "demo" in the
   Field Properties dialog box.

2. Click the Format tab. You must use either a number or percentage
   format, as I said. Set the Number Options as shown in Figure 16-26.

3. Click the Validate tab. You will see the range option is now available. Click the Value Must Be option, as shown in Figure 16-27.
   Enter your desired upper and lower range.

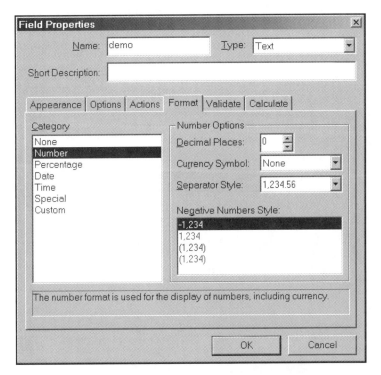

Figure 16-26
Select and format the number options to define the allowed entry values.

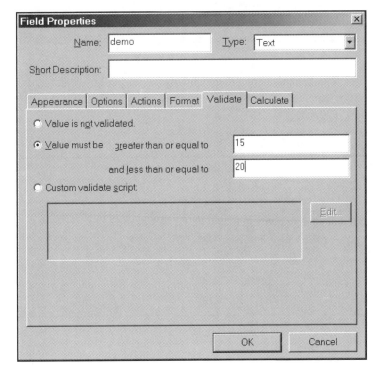

Figure 16-27
Enter the range of entry values allowed for the field.

4. The process is technically complete now, but you can add one further element as well. Click the Options tab to limit the number of characters the user is allowed to enter, as shown in Figure 16-28.

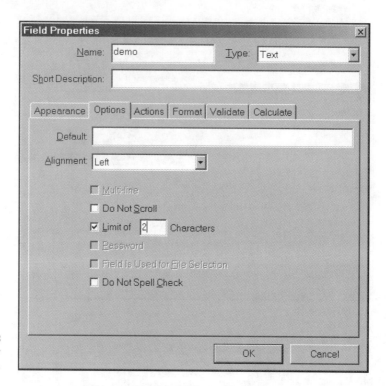

Figure 16-28
Set a character entry
limit in the Options tab.

How does it work? Have a look. In Figure 16-29, I have entered a value outside the defined range. When I move out of the field, the alert message is displayed.

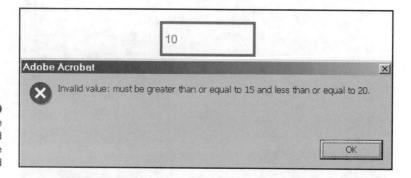

Figure 16-29
Error message
when value entered
is outside the value
bounds of the field

These processes are fairly simple to use, and will result in much more accurate and usable data from your forms (which is the point of creating them, after all). Now, let's get back to that U-Park survey and finish it up.

Project Project 16-2. Brad's U-Park, Part II: How Irritated Are You?

This project picks up where the last one leaves off. If you have worked through the first project, use your project files. If you chose to start with this project, fear not. On the CD-ROM in the Chapter 16 projects folder, you will find a file named survey1.pdf. That file contains the survey project complete to this point. If you would rather simply follow along with what is going on here, a completely finished version is on the CD-ROM as well, named survey2.pdf.

What's Left to Do?

Not that much, actually. The response fields must be built. We will also assign value ranges to them. There are some total fields to create, and we will add a hidden field that displays a grand total when the form is complete. Just for good measure, we will also add a reset button.

Adding the Response Fields

I have shown the basic set of fields in Figure 16-30. As you can see, the fields are numbered in sequence. Below each response column, I have included a subtotal field.

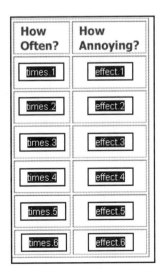

How Often?	How Annoying?
times.1	effect.1
times.2	effect.2
times.3	effect.3
times.4	effect.4
times.5	effect.5
times.6	effect.6

Figure 16-30
Add these fields using this naming convention.

1. Add the response fields. Each has these properties:

   - The fields are numbered in sequence. That is, times.1 to times.5; effect.1 to effect.5.

   - In the Appearance tab, set the text size to 10pt Helvetica, black.

   - In the Options tab, set a character limit of 1 character.

   - In the Format tab, select Number, with 0 decimal places.

   - In the Validate tab, enter a range. Set the lower limit of the range to 1, and the upper limit to 5.

2. Add the subtotal fields. Name them times.6 and effect.6. Each has these properties:

   - In the Appearance tab, set the text size to 10pt Helvetica, black. Set the field as Read Only.

   - In the Format tab, select Number, with 0 decimal places.

   - In the Calculate field, select the middle value option. Select sum from the drop-down list. Click Pick, and select the entry fields that correspond with each total field. (As shown in Figure 16-31, select the five times.*x* entries for the times.6 total; select the five effect.*x* entries for the effect.6 total.)

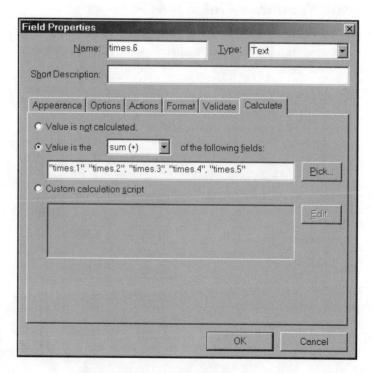

Figure 16-31
Select the fields to be added for the subtotals.

3. Save and test the file. Because the character number is restricted, you can enter only one character. Try entering a number outside the specified range. You will receive a message like that shown in Figure 16-32.

Last item: Let's add a hidden field that is displayed based on the total values.

Note

I haven't discussed the layout processes for the fields. See Chapter 10 for a discussion on how to make the fields "pretty."

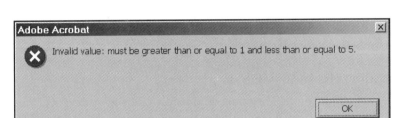

Figure 16-32
Restricting the values to a defined range produces usable results.

Gee, You Sound Upset

It is just sound business. It's one thing to get your customers thinking about your service. It's quite another to ask them how annoyed and irritated they are and then not control the responses. This is a good reason to restrict the possible entry values. If I were severely annoyed about something, even if given a choice of 1 to 5 as possible responses, I would be tempted to enter a value in the millions. This certainly would express my opinion, but wouldn't be helpful from a data collection perspective.

To finish the project, we will add two more button fields and two hidden fields.

Note

If the respondent's grand total is 50, we could display a message asking the respondent to take the bus from now on. (Kidding, but tempting isn't it?)

Adding the Button Fields

We will add two button fields to finish up the function of the page.

1. Ctrl-click and drag the Print field to the left to add two more fields. As shown in Figure 16-33, name the fields **reset** and **finish**.

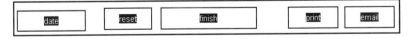

Figure 16-33
Add two more buttons.

2. Label the new buttons in the Options tab:

- Add the label **Reset** to the button field reset.

- Add the label **Click When Finished** to the button field finish.

As shown in Figure 16-34, if you have added the fields as described in Step 1, the default values should be set as the other buttons.

Figure 16-34
The set of four finished
buttons

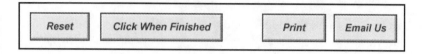

The buttons still need some actions, but we will come back to that once we add the hidden fields.

Adding the Hidden Fields

Add two more fields. They are both hidden, and will be displayed once the user clicks the field to indicate the responses are complete.

1. Add a text field. Again, the simplest method is to Ctrl-click and drag one of the text fields to carry over the default settings. The field, named "total", is a calculated text field. Locate the field as shown in Figure 16-35 (in the last row of the table).

Figure 16-35
Place the final field
in this location.

Your total score is: total

2. Set these properties for the total field:

    *   In the Appearance tab, set visibility to hidden, and select Read only.

    *   In the Format tab, select Number, and set decimal places to 0.

    *   In the Calculate tab, select the Value Is The Sum Of option. Pick the fields "effect.6" and "time.6".

3. Save the file.

Now back to the buttons to finish this up.

Finishing with Flair

We still have a pair of processes to finish. We want to have the totals calculated and displayed. We also want an option to reset the form.

1. Double-click the finish field to open the Field Properties dialog box. Open the Actions tab, and add this MouseUp action:

    *   Show/Hide Field: Show the total field.

2. Close the Field Properties dialog box.

3. Double-click the reset field to open the Field Properties dialog box. Open the Actions tab. Add these MouseUp actions:

   • Reset Form: In the Field Selection dialog box, click All, Except, click Select fields, and exclude the Date field.

   • Show/Hide Field: Hide the total field.

4. Close the Field Properties dialog box. Save the file.

Now let's see what we have. Figure 16-36 shows the form with values entered. When the Reset button is clicked, all the values are reset, except for the date. The total value field is also hidden.

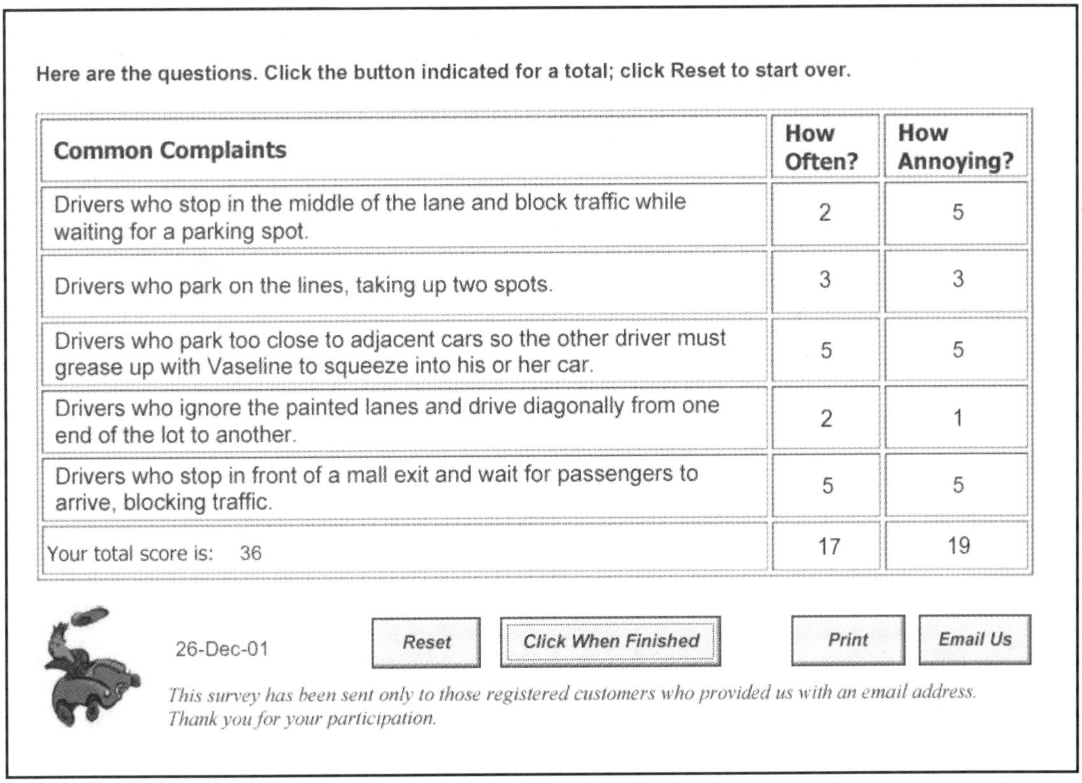

Here are the questions. Click the button indicated for a total; click Reset to start over.

Common Complaints	How Often?	How Annoying?
Drivers who stop in the middle of the lane and block traffic while waiting for a parking spot.	2	5
Drivers who park on the lines, taking up two spots.	3	3
Drivers who park too close to adjacent cars so the other driver must grease up with Vaseline to squeeze into his or her car.	5	5
Drivers who ignore the painted lanes and drive diagonally from one end of the lot to another.	2	1
Drivers who stop in front of a mall exit and wait for passengers to arrive, blocking traffic.	5	5
Your total score is: 36	17	19

 26-Dec-01   [Reset]   [Click When Finished]   [Print]   [Email Us]

This survey has been sent only to those registered customers who provided us with an email address. Thank you for your participation.

Figure 16-36
The final layout of the form, complete with responses

Final Words for Tweakers

There are some other different things you may wish to do in this project, depending on your inclination. For example, rather than using any of the automatic scripting options within the Field Properties dialog boxes, you may wish to enter custom scripts.

You may also want to move some of the scripts from the field to the document level. For example, you may want to use messages that ask users to e-mail Brad's if they scored over a certain amount.

Regardless, it is plain to see that there are many ways to use scripting, both within a document, as well as within elements of a document. Which brings me to my last major topic of this chapter: using scripts externally to any one particular document.

External JavaScripts

We have had a good look at different types of JavaScript that can be used within a document. These types of scripts are saved with the document. You can also create and use scripts externally—that is, within Acrobat, but not restricted to any one document in particular. Once a script has been written, copy the text file into the Acrobat JavaScripts folder, or into the JavaScript folder in your system directory.

There are three types of external JavaScripts:

- Folder-level JavaScripts: These files are stored in the application and user folders. Acrobat 5 uses several folder-level script files, which will be read and executed when you start the program. The folder-level files used to run my copy of the program are shown in Figure 16-37. You can see them on your system through the Explorer following this path: Program Files ➤ Acrobat 5.0 ➤ Acrobat ➤ Javascripts.

- Console JavaScripts: For the hardcore developer, enter JavaScripts into the Acrobat console and execute them. I have shown the scripts listed in the console in Figure 16-38. This feature is primarily used for testing and debugging large scripts in Acrobat.

- Batch JavaScripts: The new batch sequence feature enables you to create scripts that can be run on any files selected.

Speaking of batch sequences . . .

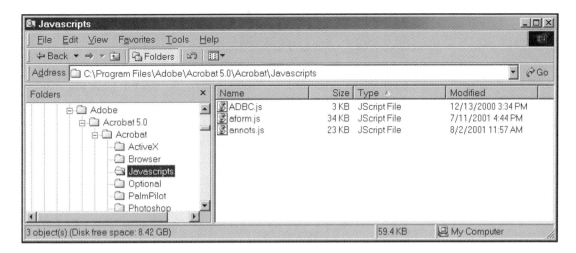

Figure 16-37
Location of folder-
level JavaScripts

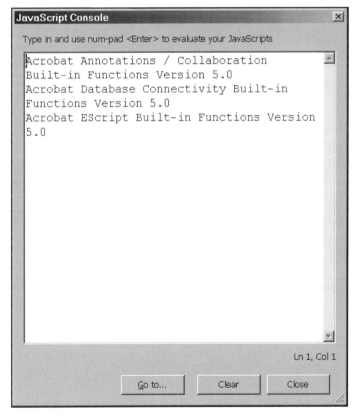

Figure 16-38
The JavaScript Console
displaying external scripts

Creating Batch Sequences Using JavaScript

Note

There is a PDF file, named "Batch Sequences: Tips, Tricks and Examples," on the Acrobat 5.0 installation CD-ROM that describes batch processing. Read this file for more information and instruction.

We looked at using the batch sequencing processes in Chapter 7. Did you think that was all there was to it? Of course not.

You can also write batch sequences for Acrobat using JavaScript. Although it is beyond the scope of this book to discuss this level of programming in detail, I want to show you some of the possibilities. Also, it helps to round out the JavaScript discussion. And it gives you something to work on when you have nothing else to do!

Basics of Batches

This process picks up where simple batch sequencing using menu items leaves off. As before, batching can be performed on files in one of four ways, as you specify through these options:

- Selected Files

- Selected Folders

- Ask When Sequence Is Run

- Files Open in Acrobat

If you recall, selected files are those you manually select from your Explorer window. Selected folders are also manually selected from the Explorer window, and the commands will be run on all files in those folders. Logically, the next option, Ask When Sequence Is Run, prompts you for a file selection when you run the batch. Finally, you can choose to run commands against files you have open.

The drop-down menu for assigning the commands is shown here in Figure 16-39.

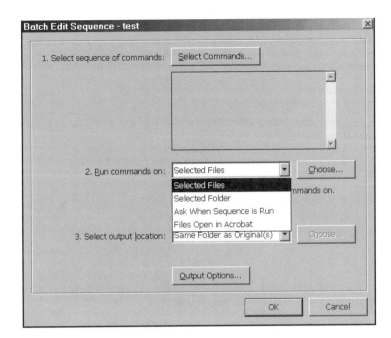

Figure 16-39
The Batch Sequence dialog box showing the command options

Using Batch File Scripts

The batching information file on the installation CD-ROM includes a section listing problems, solutions, and some sample scripts. I have summarized what is presented in the file in Table 16-4.

Table 16-4   Common Batch File Scripts and Their Uses

Category	Problems and Comments
Bookmarks	List All Bookmarks: Creates a PDF document that lists the bookmarks in another PDF document. The new document can be saved and/or printed.
	Count Bookmarks: Counts the number of bookmarks in a specified PDF document.
	Gather Bookmarks To Document: Creates a series of bookmarks in a document open in the viewer that point to selected files (not currently open).
	Copy Bookmarks From Array: Uses the collection of bookmarks as described in the Utilities section, and inserts them into selected files.
	Copy Bookmarks From Document: Takes the bookmarks from the open document, and copies them to each of the selected files.
	Insert Bookmarked Pages: Merges a set of single-page PDF files into one file with bookmarks to each page.
Comments and forms	Insert Stamp: Inserts a stamp on the first page of each file of a group of selected files.
	Insert Barcode: Inserts a barcode on the first page of each file of a group of selected files.
	Cross Doc Comment Summary: Gathers comments contained in selected files, sorts them by author, and creates a combined report.

Table 16-4   Common Batch File Scripts and Their Uses (Continued)

Category	Problems and Comments
Database	Populate and Save: Uses SQL select criteria for a particular database to populate an open PDF form with data satisfying the criteria, and saves the form to a folder.
Icons	Import Named Icons: Imports a series of icons into the document currently open. Insert Navigation Icons: Inserts a set of navigational icons on each page of each file in a selected set of files.
Pages	*Extract Pages to Folders: Extracts each page of each file from a set of selected files, and saves the extracted pages to a folder.
Security	Change Security to None: Removes the password protection from selected files. These must be protected with the same password. Gather DigSig Information: Writes a report on digital signatures in selected files. Signature Sign All: Adds an invisible signature to each file of a group of selected files.
Spell check	Spell Check a Document: Words that are incorrectly spelled or questionable are marked with an underline squiggle annotation. The annotation contains suggested spellings. Can be used on single or selected groups of files.
Utilities	Count PDF Files: Sets the global variable, global.FileCnt, equal to the number of Selected Files. Gather Bookmarks To Array: Creates and saves a global array of bookmark information from selected files.

Now What?

So you have seen what kinds of issues can be resolved using batch scripts, now you want to know what's next. How do you use them? Where do you put them? Ah, such intriguing questions. Read on.

As I mentioned at the beginning of this section, JavaScript can be applied to any of the sequences as you would apply prebuilt batch commands. Basically, what you are doing is substituting a custom script for any of the scripts supplied with Acrobat. I will answer the first question in a short tutorial. As for the second question, they aren't put anywhere, as such. They become part of a stored batch sequence, unlike large external JavaScript files that are stored on the hard drive in the folder Acrobat 5 ➤ Acrobat ➤ Javascripts.

Now back to the first question: how to use a custom batch script.

Project Tutorial: Creating and Running a Custom Batch Script

For this tutorial, I am using a file created as output in Chapter 12, manual1.pdf. You can either use the file you created in that chapter, or use the one on the CD-ROM in the Chapter 12 projects folder. This is a big file, with a lot of bookmarks. Rather than counting the list of bookmarks, we are going to run a cute little script that will do the counting ("cute" being a relative term, of course).

Let's See That Script

The script is shown it in its entirety in Listing 16-4.

Listing 16-4. The Count Bookmarks Script

```
/* Count Bookmarks */
/* Recursively work through bookmark tree */
function CountBookmarks(bm, nLevel)
{
if (nLevel != 0)
counter++; // don't count the root
if (bm.children != null)
for (var i = 0; i < bm.children.length; i++)
CountBookmarks(bm.children[i], nLevel + 1);
}
var counter = 0;
CountBookmarks(this.bookmarkRoot, 0);
console.show();
console.println("\nFile: " + this.path);
console.println("The number of bookmarks: " + counter);
```

This script, from top to bottom,

- Names the script.

- Defines the function.

- Not including the root, assesses each bookmark, and incrementally adds a number to the counter for each bookmark encountered. In a batch event, the *this* object is the current document being processed by the batch engine.

- Displays the script console, and prints two lines: first the path for the file, and then the number of bookmarks.

To complete this process we will have to

1. Create the batch process.

2. Save and run the command.

Creating the Batch Process

You may wish to copy the script from the Batch Script file on the installation CD-ROM and paste it into the sequence as we develop it. For your convenience, I have provided a copy on the CD-ROM in a text file called scripts.txt. The script you need is named "COUNT BOOKMARKS SCRIPT," and is the last script in the file.

Aside from this step, the rest of the process is similar to that used to set up other batch processes. Follow these steps:

1. Open the batch.txt file in a text editor and copy it. Close the file and the application. Open Acrobat.

2. Create a new batch sequence. Select File ➤ Batch Processing ➤ Edit Batch Sequences. When the Batch Sequences dialog box opens, click New Sequence, and enter a name for the custom sequence. I named mine "count bookmarks". Click OK. This will close the Batch Sequences box, and return you to the Batch Sequences dialog box.

3. As shown in Figure 16-40, the new batch sequence should be selected. Click Edit Sequence.

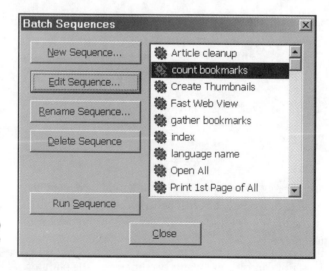

Figure 16-40
The new batch sequence now appears in the listing.

4. The Batch Edit Sequence – Count Bookmarks dialog box will open. There are three steps to complete in order to run our script:

- Select the commands.

- Select the files against which to run the commands.

- Select the output location.

5. Click Select Commands. The Edit Sequence dialog box shown in Figure 16-41 will open. This is where we insert the custom script. Scroll down the list to the Execute JavaScript option. Click Add to move it to the command section.

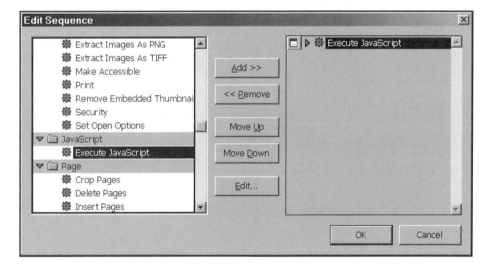

Figure 16-41
Add the Execute
JavaScript command.

6. Click Edit. The JavaScript Edit window shown in Figure 16-42 will open. Paste the copied script into this window. Click OK.

7. Click OK to close the Edit Sequence dialog box and return to the Batch Edit Sequence – Count Bookmarks dialog box.

Now let's set up the files and storage locations.

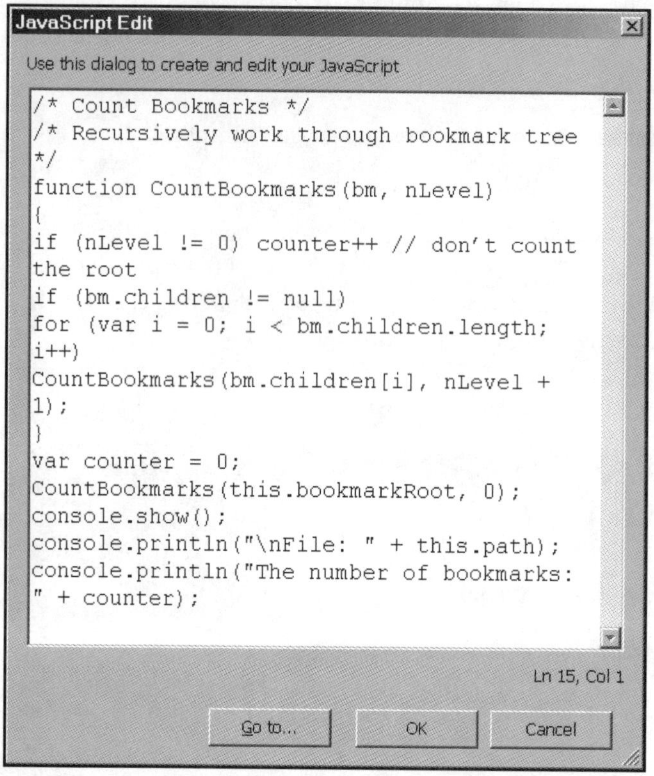

Figure 16-42
Paste the custom script
into this window.

Finishing the Setup

This is an interesting script. Depending on what type of work you are doing, you have several options. Some scripts will only run on selected files. This script, however, is generic enough that it can run on any option.

1. At this point, the Batch Edit Sequence – Count Bookmarks dialog box should be displayed. Open the Run Commands On drop-down menu, and select Ask When Sequence Is Run. This is the most generic option, and will allow you to run this script against anything.

2. Leave the default output location, which is to store output in the same folder as the originals. The final selections for this script are shown in Figure 16-43. As you can see in the image, I have clicked the drop-down arrow to the left of the command line to display the script's name.

3. Click OK to close this dialog box and return to the Batch Sequences window.

Now for some action.

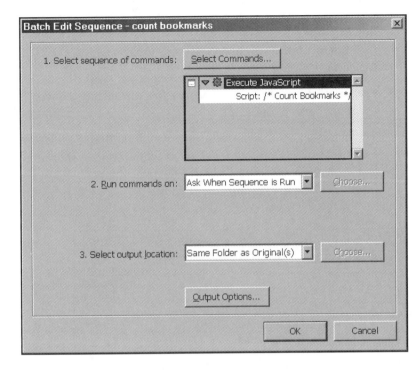

Figure 16-43
The final selections for
this batch sequence

Running the Script

Finally, let's do some counting.

1. The Batch Sequences window should be open. Click Run Sequence.
   The dialog box shown in Figure 16-44 will display to confirm the
   batch you wish to run. Click OK.

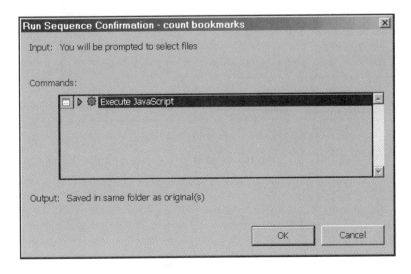

Figure 16-44
Confirm the batch
sequence to execute.

Workflow Tip

Is It Worthwhile to Set Up Batch Scripts for Something So Simple?

Depends. If this is something you will encounter on a regular basis, of course it is worth the 15 or 20 minutes it will take to set up a sequence. On the other hand, there is no point if it is something that will happen once a year on one file.

2. An Explorer window will open for you to select the file to process. Browse to the location of the file you wish to count (I have used the manual1.pdf file from the Chapter 9 projects folder). Click OK to select the file.

3. The script editing window will open before the file is processed. Click OK to accept the script to be run.

4. When the sequence is complete, the JavaScript Console will open and display the information requested by the script, as shown in Figure 16-45. When you have duly noted the number of book-marks, click Close to dismiss the window.

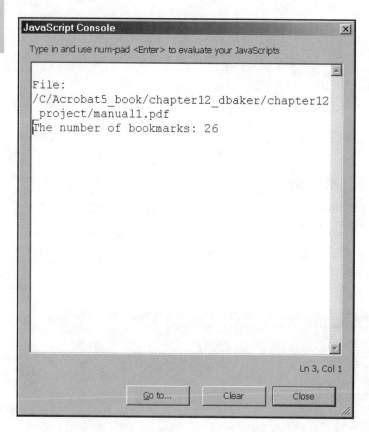

Figure 16-45
The output from our counting script

This brings our discussion of external JavaScript, and this chapter, to an end.

Up Next

From the JavaScript perspective, there are so many things that I merely touched on or didn't even cover. For example, did you know you can add new menu items to the program using JavaScript? You can. As I have mentioned in this chapter, please spend some time in the Acrobat JavaScript Object Specification.

From the overall perspective of the book—this is it. Where you go from here is up to you. I strongly encourage everyone who has read up to this memorable point in the book to use what you have learned in every way you can. I have demonstrated the power of Acrobat, but I have also shown you many ways in which to use the program as a tool for making your work life more efficient and more productive.

I encourage you to read through the appendixes. The first one, which is also on the CD-ROM in PDF format, lists URLs from Adobe, organizations and information sites that I have found helpful. The second one discusses the multitude of plug-ins we have used in this book. The third one, for those who must move on in a big way, is a list of the exam criteria for the Adobe Certified Expert exam for Acrobat.

Thanks. It's been a blast.

Appendix A

References and Further Information

This appendix contains a list of URLs referenced in this book, as well as other sources of information you may find useful in your work.

Here are some sites that will give you more information on specific areas of this book's content. The CD contains a PDF version of this appendix. Use it to link directly from the file to the Web sites.

Adobe Sites

You may access these areas directly, or from the main Adobe Acrobat site:

Note

Forums will require a site login. If you have created a profile at Adobe in the past, you will have a cookie in your system. Otherwise, all these links will take you to the same registration screen. Log in there first.

- Downloads for Windows and Macintosh:
  http://www.adobe.com/support/downloads/main.html

- User to User Forum/Macintosh:
  http://www.adobeforums.com/cgi-bin/webx?14@@.ee6b2ed

- User to User Forum/Windows:
  http://www.adobeforums.com/cgi-bin/webx?14@@.ee6b2f2

- Acrobat Technical Guides:
  http://www.adobe.com/support/techguides/acrobat/main.html

- Adobe Studio (requires login and ID):
  http://studio.adobe.com/expertcenter/acrobat/main.html

- Acrobat Support Knowledgebase:
  http://www.adobe.com/support/products/acrobat.html

- Adobe Acrobat certification exam information (Adobe Certified Expert Program):
  http://partners.adobe.com/asn/training/acehowto.html

Information Sites

Here are some of the sites I frequent:

- Planet PDF: http://www.planetpdf.com. This site has lots of information on PDF issues, uses, and third-party extensions.

- Planet eBook: http://www.planetebook.com. One of the Planet PDF sites. This one concentrates on e-book issues and information.

- Planet Publish: http://www.planetpublish.com. Another Planet PDF site. This site deals with electronic publishing, XML, and information design and development.

- Creativepro.com: http://www.creativepro.com. This site offers articles, issues, and reviews for designers.

- Publish.net: `http://www.publish.net`. A network site to all manner of things graphic: news, information, tips, and third-party extensions.

- PDFzone: `http://www.pdfzone.com`. This is the PDF site of Publish.net.

Organizations

Major organizations offering insight and information exchange include the following:

- ACM SIGGRAPH (computer graphics organization): `http://www.siggraph.org`

- The IEEE Computer Society international professional bodies for IT professionals: `http://www.computer.org`

- Association for Information and Image Management (AIIM): `http://www.aiim.org`

- International Digital Enterprise Alliance (formerly Graphic Communications Association): `http://www.idealliance.org`

- Society for Technical Communication: `http://www.stc.org`

Appendix B

Acrobat Plug-ins

*Acrobat 5 comes with numerous
plug-ins, as well as several third-party
plug-ins. Here's a rundown on
their installation and use.*

Adobe Plug-ins Included with Acrobat

Many plug-ins are available for Acrobat. There are no requirements on your part to have this set of plug-ins installed; they will autoinstall with a typical install setting when you're loading Acrobat from your installation CD.

I have included basic information about the plug-ins in Table B-1.

Table B-1 Installed Plug-ins

Plug-in Name	File Name	Description/Information
Accessibility Checker	AccCheck.api	Checks documents for compliance with Adobe PDF standards.
Catalog	Catalog.api	Creates a full-text index of a document or document collection. Also provides a search function. Contains Verity Collection Building Engine from Verity, Inc.
Comments	Annots.api	Allows users to mark up online and offline documents with Acrobat.
Database Connectivity	ADBC.api	Allows users to interact with databases using JavaScript.
Digital signature	DigSig.api	Provides users with a generic PDF digital-signing process that can integrate with other signing plug-ins (Adobe Self-Sign Security included).
ECMAScript	Escript.api	Allows the use of ECMAScript with PDF documents.
ExecMenu	Execmenu.api	Creates links to access Acrobat menu items.
Export PS	Exportps.api	Converts PDF pages to PostScript or encapsulated PostScript.
External Window Handler	EWH32.api	Allows users to view PDF files in a Web browser.
Forms	AcroForm.api	Enables users to work with electronic forms in Acrobat.
Highlight Server	Hls.api	Allows users to view search highlights from Web searches in PDF files in a Web browser.
HTML2PDF	HTML2PDF.api	Converts HTML to PDF files (known as the Web Capture feature).
Image Conversion	ImageConversion.api	Allows users to open and save image formats as PDF; allows image extraction.
Infusium	Infusium.api	Supports the accessibility functionality—this is the structure toolkit.
Internet Access	IA32.api	Creates Internet access in Acrobat.
MoviePlayer	Movie.api	Allows users to integrate movie and sound clips into Acrobat using QuickTime.

Table B-1   Installed Plug-ins (Continued)

Plug-in Name	File Name	Description/Information
MSAA	MSAA.api	Allows PDF files to be accessed by the Microsoft Active Accessibility Interface.
PDF Consultant	Scrubber.api	Creates a framework for object-level modification. Used to optimize a document: removes undesired elements, evaluates disk space used by document parts, and optimizes bookmarks and links.
Reflow	Reflow.api	Enables users to reflow the content of a page to fit a window's width.
SaveAsRTF	SaveAsRTF.api	Saves PDF file content as Rich Text Format (RTF) for export.
Scan	Scan.api	Imports raster data from TWAIN sources and from Photoshop Acquire plug-ins.
Search	Search.api	Allows users to search full-text indexes created with Acrobat Catalog. Contains the TOPIC Full Text Engine from Verity, Inc.
Self-Sign Signatures	PPKLite.api	Uses a public key–based, self-signed, direct-trust handler for PDF document digital signature and encryption purposes. Includes libraries licensed from RSA Security Inc.
SendMail	SendMail.api	Adds a button to the toolbar to send the current document as an e-mail attachment.
Spelling	Spelling.api	Checks form text fields and comments for spelling errors.
TouchUp	TouchUp.api	Allows users to perform touchup editing of content and document tags.
Web-Hosted Service	WHA.api	Integrates Adobe Web services into Acrobat.
Web2PDF	WebPDF.api	Facilitates the Web Capture feature's functions.
WebBuy	Webbuy.api	Includes libraries licensed from RSA Security Inc. and Iomega Corporation. Used for e-commerce of protected PDF content.
Weblink	Weblink.api	Allows users to link to Web pages from PDF documents.

Third-Party Plug-ins Included with Acrobat

The Acrobat installation CD installs some third-party plug-ins. As with the Adobe plug-ins, their use is seamless, and the plug-ins are integrated with the program's menu options.

Note

All plug-ins installed with a typical Acrobat installation are version 5.

Acrobat Table

The Acrobat Table/Formatted Text plug-in version 4, from Adobe Systems, is used for creating tables and managing information export from tables. It uses technologies developed by BCL Computers, Inc.

This plug-in functions seamlessly within Acrobat. You can set its preferences by selecting Edit ➤ Preferences ➤ Table/Formatted Text Preferences. The dialog box shown in Figure B-1 will open.

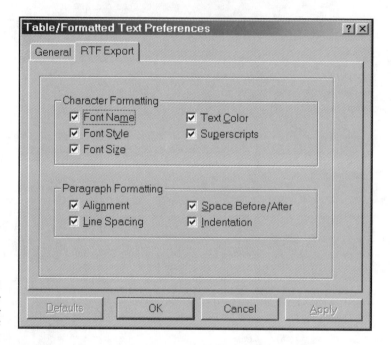

Figure B-1
Preferences for
exporting table or
formatted text as RTF

On the General tab, you will find preference options such as border color. On the RTF Export tab, however, you can specify specific character and paragraph formatting options.

InterTrust docBox

docBox is used for digital rights management (DRM). Included on the Acrobat installation CD is DRM PD version 1.3.0.15 and plug-in version 1.0.0.30. Both are from InterTrust Technologies Corporation.

docBox is used for the sale and secure distribution of PDF content. It is included as part of Acrobat 5 and Acrobat Reader 5, or at both ends of the distribution chain—that is, publisher and user. User rights are determined through a certificate system.

docBox version 1 runs on Windows 98, Windows Me, Windows NT, Windows 2000, and Windows XP.

VeriSign

The VeriSign digital document signer is not preinstalled with the Acrobat typical installation, but it is on the installation CD. The version supplied is VeriSign Document Signer v1.

VeriSign signatures function in a similar fashion to the Adobe Self-Sign Signature process. As with the preinstalled signer, VeriSign creates and manages signatures, and it provides options for viewing signature properties and validating signatures.

In addition, VeriSign allows you to perform other functions. First, validation is done online. VeriSign stores information about a digital ID. Digital IDs expire after a year and may be revoked for improper use. VeriSign maintains a list of signatures that have been revoked on its Web site.

Once you've installed the plug-in, you can update the VeriSign Document Signer by selecting Tools ➤ VeriSign Document Signer ➤ Update Plug-in. Your browser will launch and open the VeriSign Update page. Follow the instructions on the page to update your signer.

Other Plug-ins Used in This Book

In addition to the plug-ins installed with Acrobat, a number of other plug-ins are used in this book. These plug-ins all increase functionality, are readily available, and are free.

Paper Capture Plug-in

For those whose work entails using scanned documents as input sources, optical character recognition (OCR) is invaluable. Without OCR capabilities, a scanned document is simply an image of a document.

OCR translates an image into characters. No OCR capability is included with a typical installation of Acrobat. A plug-in is available for download from Adobe's site, however. The Paper Capture plug-in has a 50-page scanning and translating capacity.

Note

There is a 585KB update for this plug-in available that corrects a potential problem with running Acrobat 5 under certain conditions. It will update your version of the plug-in to Version 1.0.0.35. It will also update the name of the plug-in, which has been changed to Rights|PDF Plug-in. The update is at http://pdf.intertrust.com/support/update.html.

Requirements

These are the OS requirements, as well as some installation information:

- Acrobat 5

- Intel Pentium processor running Windows 98, Windows Me, Windows NT, Windows 2000, or Windows XP

- 32MB of RAM (64MB recommended)

- 115MB of available hard-disk space

The download is 14.3MB. The plug-in is available from Adobe at `http://www.adobe.com/support/downloads/acwin.htm`.

The executable file is papercapture.exe. Once installed, the plug-in, PaperCapture.api, is available under the Tools menu.

Make Accessible Plug-in

The Make Accessible plug-in creates a tagged Adobe PDF file from an untagged PDF file. Tagged PDF files contain logical read orders for the content, and they create a structure tree based on a standard set of tags. Use this plug-in in concert with the Accessibility features of Acrobat to create accessible files.

Requirements

These are the OS requirements, as well as some installation information:

- Acrobat 5

- Intel Pentium processor running Windows 98, Windows Me, Windows NT, Windows 2000, or Windows XP

- 64MB (128MB recommended)

- 200MB of virtual memory

- 115MB of available hard-disk space

- 870KB of disk space

The download is 1.8MB. The plug-in is available from Adobe at `http://www.adobe.com/support/downloads/88de.htm`. The installation file is MakeAccessiblePlugIn.exe. Once you install the plug-in, you can access it by selecting Document ➤ Make Accessible.

Note

At the time of this writing, no Macintosh version of the Paper Capture plug-in was available.

Note

At the time of this writing, no Macintosh version of the Make Accessible plug-in was available.

Save As XML Plug-in for Windows (Beta 2)

The Save As XML plug-in for Acrobat 5 is used for repurposing content. The plug-in saves content from a tagged PDF file as XML, HTML, or plain text. At the time of this writing, only the beta version was available.

The plug-in can generate these formats:

- XML-1.00 without styling

- HTML-4.01 with CSS-1.00

- HTML-3.20 Accessible

- HTML-3.20 without CSS

- Text-only

Note
The Save As XML plug-in does not work with Acrobat Reader.

Requirements

These are the OS requirements, as well as some installation information:

- Acrobat 5

- Intel Pentium processor running Windows 98, Windows Me, Windows NT, Windows 2000, or Windows XP

- 64MB (128MB recommended)

- 200MB of virtual memory

- 5MB of available hard-disk space

The download is 1.7MB. The plug-in is available from Adobe at http://www.adobe.com/support/downloads/detail.jsp?ftpID=1209. The installation file is SaveAsXMLPlugIn_beta2.exe. Once you install the plug-in, you can access those options by selecting File ➤ Save As. As shown in Figure B-2, the options will appear in the Save As dialog box when you're saving a file.

Save As XML Plug-in for Macintosh (Beta 2)

The Save As XML plug-in for Acrobat 5 is used for repurposing content. The plug-in saves content from a tagged PDF file as XML, HTML, or plain text. At the time of this writing, only the beta version was available.

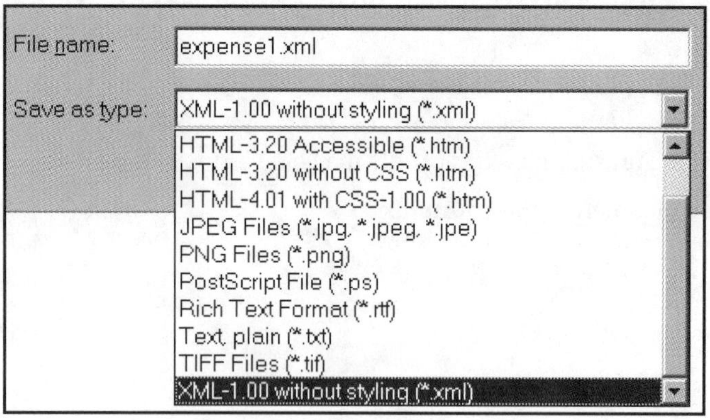

Figure B-2
Increase your output
options using the
Save As XML plug-in.

The plug-in can generate these formats:

- XML-1.00 without styling

- HTML-4.01 with CSS-1.00

- HTML-3.20 Accessible

- HTML-3.20 without CSS

- Text-only

Note

The Save As XML plug-in
does not work with
Acrobat Reader.

Requirements

These are the OS requirements, as well as some installation information:

- Acrobat 5

- Mac OS 8.6, 9.04, or 9.1

- 32MB of RAM (with virtual memory on); 64MB recommended

- 5MB of disk space available

The download is 2.8MB. The plug-in is available from Adobe at
`http://www.adobe.com/support/downloads/detail.jsp?ftpID=1208`. The
installation file is SaveAsXMLPlugIn_beta2.bin. Once you install the
plug-in, you can access those options by selecting File ➤ Save As.

Readers

A number of readers are available for download. Here's a rundown of
the ones required to view outputs from this book: Acrobat Reader,
Acrobat Reader for Palm OS, and eBook Reader.

Acrobat Reader 5.0.5 for Windows

These are the OS requirements as well as some installation information:

- Intel Pentium processor running Windows 95 OSR 2.0, Windows 98, Windows Me, Windows NT, Windows 2000, or Windows XP

- 64MB of RAM

- 24MB of available hard-disk space

The download is 8.6MB. The reader is available from Adobe at http://www.adobe.com/products/acrobat/readstep2.html.

Acrobat Reader 5.0.5 for Macintosh

These are the OS requirements as well as some installation information:

- PowerPC processor

- Mac OS software version 8.6, 9.0.4, 9.1, or OS X (some features on versions 8.6 or OS X may not be available due to OS limitations)

- 64MB of RAM

- 24MB of available hard-disk space

The download is 700KB. The reader is available from Adobe at http://www.adobe.com/products/acrobat/readstep2.html.

Acrobat Reader for Palm OS 1.1

This reader will work on a Palm OS device with English version of Palm OS 3.1 or higher. These are the OS requirements as well as some installation information:

- 200KB of available space on the Palm OS device

- 2MB of RAM on the Palm OS device (8MB recommended)

- Intel Pentium processor running Windows 98, Windows Me, Windows NT, Windows 2000, or Windows XP

- 16MB of RAM

- 20MB of available hard-disk space

The download is 6.3MB. The reader is available from Adobe at http://www.adobe.com/products/acrobat/readstep2.html.

Adobe Acrobat eBook Reader 2.2

Adobe's eBook Reader 2.2 is available in both Windows and Macintosh versions.

Windows eBook Reader

These are the OS requirements as well as some installation information:

- Intel Pentium or AMD Athlon processor

- Microsoft Windows 95, Windows 98, Windows NT 4, Windows 2000, Windows Me, or Windows XP

- Color palette with more than 256 colors (recommended for best display)

- Internet Explorer version 4.0 or 5.0 (but any browser can be used to access material)

The download is 10.3MB. Install from the downloaded eBookReaderInstall.exe file. The reader is available from Adobe after registering at http://www.adobe.com/products/ebookreader/registerNA.html.

Macintosh eBook Reader

These are the OS requirements as well as some installation information:

- PowerPC processor

- Mac OS software version 9.0 or 9.1

- Color palette with more than 256 colors (recommended for best display)

- QuickTime version 4 (recommended)

- Internet Explorer 4.5 or later (recommended), AOL 5 or later, or Netscape Communicator 4.75 or later

Note

Mac OS X is not yet supported in either classic or native mode.

The download is 9.8MB. Install it from the eBookReaderInstaller.bin file. The reader is available from Adobe after registering at http://www.adobe.com/products/ebookreader/registerNA.html.

Microsoft Reader

Microsoft also has an e-book reader available. The version current at the time of this writing was 2.0, which was released on October 4, 2001. The reader has other components and add-ins, including Encarta Pocket Dictionary, an add-in for Word 2002 named Read in Reader to create e-books , a text to speech component, and an extension to create e-books from QuarkXPress.

Requirements

These are the OS requirements:

- Any PC running Windows 95, Windows 98, Windows NT 4, Windows Me, Windows 2000, or Windows XP

- Pentium 75 or higher processor

- 16MB RAM

- 19MB of free hard-drive disk space to complete the installation

- Internet Explorer 4.0 with Service Pack 1 or higher

The download is 3.6MB. The reader is available for download from `http://www.microsoft.com/reader/download.asp`.

Installation

Installation requires activation of Microsoft Passport.

1. Download msreadersetup.exe.

2. Double-click the file to begin installation.

3. During the installation process, you will be prompted to activate the reader. This will require activation of Microsoft Passport.

4. Continue with the installation process. Restart your PC when the installation is complete.

Appendix C

Adobe Certified
Expert Exam Criteria

*Been through the whole book?
Done the projects? Think you have
mastered Acrobat? Prove it.*

Exam Criteria

The information in this appendix is taken from the Adobe Acrobat 5.0 Exam #9A0-023 Exam Bulletin for the Adobe Certified Expert exam. The chapter(s) in the book that corresponds to the information in the Exam Bulletin's contents is shown in parentheses after the topic or after the bulleted item. You can find more information and other references about the exam on Adobe's Web site (http://partners.adobe.com/asn/training/acehowto.html).

General Knowledge (All Chapters)

- Common terms and technologies
- PDF workflows (7, 11)
- Key features and benefits of Adobe Acrobat 5 (1)

Installing Adobe Acrobat (1, 2, Appendix B)

- Installation process
- Managing and using plug-ins within Adobe Acrobat
- Updating Adobe Acrobat by using the Update Preferences option

Creating Adobe PDF Documents (3, 11, 12)

- Object types that can be added to a PDF document
- Using the Acrobat Distiller settings
- Using the Adobe PDFMaker macro
- Managing fonts and images in PDF documents
- Using files with transparency in Acrobat Distiller
- Importing scanned documents into Acrobat
- Customizing compression options in the Job Options dialog box of Acrobat Distiller

Viewing and Navigating (2, 7, 8, 11, 14)

- Using commands from the Document and View menu commands

- Commands or tools required to view a PDF document

- Configuring viewing and navigation options for PDF documents that will be posted to the Web

Modifying and Enhancing PDF Documents (All Chapters)

- Using the PDF Consultant

- Creating a tagged PDF file

- Associating actions with links, buttons, and form fields

- Using Tabs palettes (including bookmarks, thumbnails, annotations, Web links, signatures, tags, and information)

- Adding sound and movies

- Using the Import and Export commands

- Modifying pages in a PDF document (including Insert Pages, Extract Pages, Replace Pages, Delete Pages, Crop Pages, Rotate Pages, Number Pages, and Set Page Action)

Document Review and Distribution (7, 11, 12, 14)

- Spell checking a PDF document

- Using Adobe Acrobat to compile online comments

- Using the Comments and Compare commands

- Using document review tools (including Digital Signature, Notes tool, Highlight tool, Select Text tool, and TouchUp tool)

- Using preview options available in Acrobat

- Managing ICC profiles

- Correcting and editing PDF documents by using tools on the Basic and Editing toolbars

- Preparing PDF documents for distribution to various output devices (including service bureaus, printers, byte-serving, and monitors) and for Web distribution

Working with Forms (10, 12, 14, 15, 16)

- Creating PDF forms
- Creating form fields
- Customizing forms using JavaScript
- Integrating a PDF form with a Web server

Indexing and Searching (9)

- Building and maintaining indexes in a PDF document
- Defining index search options
- Using JavaScript to search in a PDF document

Managing and Processing Large Numbers of Files (7)

- Managing a document collection by creating and executing a batch script

Scripting (11, 12, 15, 16)

- Creating a script using the scripting editor
- Describing the JavaScript event model and JavaScript syntax used in Acrobat
- Creating and using a menu item by using JavaScript
- Creating a JavaScript plug-in to add a menu item

Managing Security (4, 5, 13)

- Using the standard security handler to protect a PDF document
- Protecting a PDF document by using self-signed security
- Using digital signatures to protect a document

Index

A

D

P

Apress Titles

ISBN	PRICE	AUTHOR	TITLE
1-893115-73-9	$34.95	Abbott	Voice Enabling Web Applications: VoiceXML and Beyond
1-893115-01-1	$39.95	Appleman	Dan Appleman's Win32 API Puzzle Book and Tutorial for Visual Basic Programmers
1-893115-23-2	$29.95	Appleman	How Computer Programming Works
1-893115-97-6	$39.95	Appleman	Moving to VB. NET: Strategies, Concepts, and Code
1-59059-023-6	$39.95	Baker	Adobe Acrobat 5: The Professional User's Guide
1-893115-09-7	$29.95	Baum	Dave Baum's Definitive Guide to LEGO MINDSTORMS
1-893115-84-4	$29.95	Baum, Gasperi, Hempel, and Villa	Extreme MINDSTORMS: An Advanced Guide to LEGO MINDSTORMS
1-893115-82-8	$59.95	Ben-Gan/Moreau	Advanced Transact-SQL for SQL Server 2000
1-893115-91-7	$39.95	Birmingham/Perry	Software Development on a Leash
1-893115-48-8	$29.95	Bischof	The .NET Languages: A Quick Translation Guide
1-893115-67-4	$49.95	Borge	Managing Enterprise Systems with the Windows Script Host
1-893115-28-3	$44.95	Challa/Laksberg	Essential Guide to Managed Extensions for C++
1-893115-39-9	$44.95	Chand	A Programmer's Guide to ADO.NET in C#
1-893115-44-5	$29.95	Cook	Robot Building for Beginners
1-893115-99-2	$39.95	Cornell/Morrison	Programming VB .NET: A Guide for Experienced Programmers
1-893115-72-0	$39.95	Curtin	Developing Trust: Online Privacy and Security
1-59059-008-2	$29.95	Duncan	The Career Programmer: Guerilla Tactics for an Imperfect World
1-893115-71-2	$39.95	Ferguson	Mobile .NET
1-893115-90-9	$49.95	Finsel	The Handbook for Reluctant Database Administrators
1-59059-024-4	$49.95	Fraser	Real World ASP.NET: Building a Content Management System
1-893115-42-9	$44.95	Foo/Lee	XML Programming Using the Microsoft XML Parser
1-893115-55-0	$34.95	Frenz	Visual Basic and Visual Basic .NET for Scientists and Engineers
1-893115-85-2	$34.95	Gilmore	A Programmer's Introduction to PHP 4.0
1-893115-36-4	$34.95	Goodwill	Apache Jakarta-Tomcat
1-893115-17-8	$59.95	Gross	A Programmer's Introduction to Windows DNA
1-893115-62-3	$39.95	Gunnerson	A Programmer's Introduction to C#, Second Edition
1-59059-009-0	$39.95	Harris/Macdonald	Moving to ASP.NET: Web Development with VB .NET
1-893115-30-5	$49.95	Harkins/Reid	SQL: Access to SQL Server
1-893115-10-0	$34.95	Holub	Taming Java Threads
1-893115-04-6	$34.95	Hyman/Vaddadi	Mike and Phani's Essential C++ Techniques
1-893115-96-8	$59.95	Jorelid	J2EE FrontEnd Technologies: A Programmer's Guide to Servlets, JavaServer Pages, and Enterprise JavaBeans
1-893115-49-6	$39.95	Kilburn	Palm Programming in Basic
1-893115-50-X	$34.95	Knudsen	Wireless Java: Developing with Java 2, Micro Edition
1-893115-79-8	$49.95	Kofler	Definitive Guide to Excel VBA
1-893115-57-7	$39.95	Kofler	MySQL
1-893115-87-9	$39.95	Kurata	Doing Web Development: Client-Side Techniques
1-893115-75-5	$44.95	Kurniawan	Internet Programming with VB

ISBN	PRICE	AUTHOR	TITLE
1-893115-38-0	$24.95	Lafler	Power AOL: A Survival Guide
1-893115-46-1	$36.95	Lathrop	Linux in Small Business: A Practical User's Guide
1-893115-19-4	$49.95	Macdonald	Serious ADO: Universal Data Access with Visual Basic
1-893115-06-2	$39.95	Marquis/Smith	A Visual Basic 6.0 Programmer's Toolkit
1-893115-22-4	$27.95	McCarter	David McCarter's VB Tips and Techniques
1-893115-76-3	$49.95	Morrison	C++ For VB Programmers
1-893115-80-1	$39.95	Newmarch	A Programmer's Guide to Jini Technology
1-893115-58-5	$49.95	Oellermann	Architecting Web Services
1-893115-81-X	$39.95	Pike	SQL Server: Common Problems, Tested Solutions
1-59059-017-1	$34.95	Rainwater	Herding Cats: A Primer for Programmers Who Lead Programmers
1-59059-025-2	$49.95	Rammer	Advanced .NET Remoting
1-893115-20-8	$34.95	Rischpater	Wireless Web Development
1-893115-93-3	$34.95	Rischpater	Wireless Web Development with PHP and WAP
1-893115-89-5	$59.95	Shemitz	Kylix: The Professional Developer's Guide and Reference
1-893115-40-2	$39.95	Sill	The qmail Handbook
1-893115-24-0	$49.95	Sinclair	From Access to SQL Server
1-893115-94-1	$29.95	Spolsky	User Interface Design for Programmers
1-893115-53-4	$44.95	Sweeney	Visual Basic for Testers
1-59059-002-3	$44.95	Symmonds	Internationalization and Localization Using Microsoft .NET
1-893115-29-1	$44.95	Thomsen	Database Programming with Visual Basic .NET
1-59059-010-4	$54.95	Thomsen	Database Programming with C#
1-893115-65-8	$39.95	Tiffany	Pocket PC Database Development with eMbedded Visual Basic
1-893115-59-3	$59.95	Troelsen	C# and the .NET Platform
1-893115-26-7	$59.95	Troelsen	Visual Basic .NET and the .NET Platform
1-59059-011-2	$39.95	Troelsen	COM and .NET Interoperability
1-893115-54-2	$49.95	Trueblood/Lovett	Data Mining and Statistical Analysis Using SQL
1-893115-16-X	$49.95	Vaughn	ADO Examples and Best Practices
1-893115-68-2	$49.95	Vaughn	ADO.NET and ADO Examples and Best Practices for VB Programmers, Second Edition
1-59059-012-0	$49.95	Vaughn/Blackburn	ADO.NET Examples and Best Practices for C# Programmers
1-893115-83-6	$44.95	Wells	Code Centric: T-SQL Programming with Stored Procedures and Triggers
1-893115-95-X	$49.95	Welschenbach	Cryptography in C and C++
1-893115-05-4	$39.95	Williamson	Writing Cross-Browser Dynamic HTML
1-893115-78-X	$49.95	Zukowski	Definitive Guide to Swing for Java 2, Second Edition
1-893115-92-5	$49.95	Zukowski	Java Collections
1-893115-98-4	$54.95	Zukowski	Learn Java with JBuilder 6

Available at bookstores nationwide or from Springer Verlag New York, Inc. at 1-800-777-4643; fax 1-212-533-3503. Contact us for more information at sales@apress.com.

Apress Titles Publishing SOON!

ISBN	AUTHOR	TITLE
1-59059-022-8	Alapati	Expert Oracle 9i Database Administration
1-59059-015-5	Clark	An Introduction to Object Oriented Programming with Visual Basic .NET
1-59059-000-7	Cornell	Programming C#
1-59059-014-7	Drol	Object-Oriented Flash MX
1-59059-033-3	Fraser	Managed C++ and .NET Development
1-59059-038-4	Gibbons	Java Development to .NET Development
1-59059-030-9	Habibi/Camerlengo/Patterson	Java 1.4 and the Sun Certified Developer Exam
1-59059-006-6	Hetland	Practical Python
1-59059-003-1	Nakhimovsky/Meyers	XML Programming: Web Applications and Web Services with JSP and ASP
1-59059-001-5	McMahon	Serious ASP.NET
1-59059-021-X	Moore	Karl Moore's Visual Basic .NET: The Tutorials
1-893115-27-5	Morrill	Tuning and Customizing a Linux System
1-59059-020-1	Patzer	JSP Examples and Best Practices
1-59059-028-7	Rischpater	Wireless Web Development, 2nd Edition
1-59059-026-0	Smith	Writing Add-Ins for .NET
1-893115-43-7	Stephenson	Standard VB: An Enterprise Developer's Reference for VB 6 and VB .NET
1-59059-032-5	Thomsen	Database Programming with Visual Basic .NET, 2nd Edition
1-59059-007-4	Thomsen	Building Web Services with VB .NET
1-59059-027-9	Torkelson/Petersen/Torkelson	Programming the Web with Visual Basic .NET
1-59059-004-X	Valiaveedu	SQL Server 2000 and Business Intelligence in an XML/.NET World

Available at bookstores nationwide or from Springer Verlag New York, Inc. at 1-800-777-4643; fax 1-212-533-3503. Contact us for more information at sales@apress.com.

books for professionals by professionals™

About Apress

Apress, located in Berkeley, CA, is a fast-growing, innovative publishing company devoted to meeting the needs of existing and potential programming professionals. Simply put, the "A" in Apress stands for *"The Author's Press"*™ and its books have *"The Expert's Voice"*™. Apress' unique approach to publishing grew out of conversations between its founders Gary Cornell and Dan Appleman, authors of numerous best-selling, highly regarded books for programming professionals. In 1998 they set out to create a publishing company that emphasized quality above all else. Gary and Dan's vision has resulted in the publication of over 50 titles by leading software professionals, all of which have *The Expert's Voice*™.

Do You Have What It Takes to Write for Apress?

Apress is rapidly expanding its publishing program. If you can write and refuse to compromise on the quality of your work, if you believe in doing more than rehashing existing documentation, and if you're looking for opportunities and rewards that go far beyond those offered by traditional publishing houses, we want to hear from you!

Consider these innovations that we offer all of our authors:

- **Top royalties with *no* hidden switch statements**
  Authors typically only receive half of their normal royalty rate on foreign sales. In contrast, Apress' royalty rate remains the same for both foreign and domestic sales.

- **A mechanism for authors to obtain equity in Apress**
  Unlike the software industry, where stock options are essential to motivate and retain software professionals, the publishing industry has adhered to an outdated compensation model based on royalties alone. In the spirit of most software companies, Apress reserves a significant portion of its equity for authors.

- **Serious treatment of the technical review process**
  Each Apress book has a technical reviewing team whose remuneration depends in part on the success of the book since they too receive royalties.

Moreover, through a partnership with Springer-Verlag, New York, Inc., one of the world's major publishing houses, Apress has significant venture capital behind it. Thus, we have the resources to produce the highest quality books *and* market them aggressively.

If you fit the model of the Apress author who can write a book that gives the "professional what he or she needs to know"™," then please contact one of our Editorial Directors, Gary Cornell (gary_cornell@apress.com), Dan Appleman (dan_appleman@apress.com), Peter Blackburn (peter_blackburn@apress.com), Jason Gilmore (jason_gilmore@apress.com), Karen Watterson (karen_watterson@apress.com), or John Zukowski (john_zukowski@apress.com) for more information.

Apress™

License Agreement (Single-User Products)